DISCIPLINE AND BEHAVIORAL MANAGEMENT

A Handbook of Tactics, Strategies, and Programs

David A. Sabatino
University of Wisconsin—Stout

Ann C. Sabatino
River Falls School District

Lester Mann
Pennsylvania State University

AN ASPEN PUBLICATION®
Aspen Systems Corporation
Rockville, Maryland
Royal Tunbridge Wells
1983

Library of Congress Cataloging in Publication Data

Sabatino, David A.
Discipline and behavioral management.

Includes bibliographies and index.
1. School discipline—Handbooks, manuals, etc.
2. Classroom management—Handbooks, manuals, etc.
I. Sabatino, Ann C.   II. Mann, Lester.   III. Title.
LB3012.S32 1983   371.5   82-24427
ISBN: 0-89443-933-2

Publisher: John Marozsan
Editorial Director: R. Curtis Whitesel
Executive Managing Editor: Margot Raphael
Editorial Services: Eileen Higgins
Printing and Manufacturing: Debbie Collins

Library of Congress Catalog Card Number 82-24427
ISBN: 0-89443-933-2

Printed in the United States of America

2   3   4   5

Table of Contents

List of Contributors   ix

Foreword   xi

Preface   xiii

Chapter 1—Discipline: A National Issue **1**
    Ann C. Sabatino

    Introduction   1
    Behavior Changes   2
    Traditional Principles of Punishment   4
    Traditional Disciplinary Practices   4
    A Review of Current Disciplinary Problems   5
    Litigational Issues: Corporal Punishment   7
    Protective Rights under the Law   9
    Alternatives to Corporal Punishment   14
    Corporal Punishment: Control and Learning   15
    Preventing Violence and Vandalism   20
    Summary   21

Chapter 2—Prevention: Teachers' Attitude and Adaptive Behavior—
           Suggested Techniques **29**
    Ann C. Sabatino

    Introduction   29
    Perspective on Teaching   30
    The Role of Teacher Self-Concepts   32
    Steps to Good Discipline   33
    Teacher Accountability   34
    Trust and Respect: Power and Authority   42

Class Climate 47
When To Manage 55
Social Reinforcement 59
Classroom Environmental Management 79
Summary 82

Chapter 3—Isolation, Expulsion, Suspension, and Detention   85
    David A. Sabatino

Introduction 85
Squeaking Wheels 86
Detention and Isolation 89
Detention 89
Isolation 99
Summary 106

**Chapter 4—Behavioral Characteristics and Management
       Strategies 111**
    Ann C. Sabatino and Maribeth Montgomery-Kasik

Introduction 111
Behaviors 112
    Attention-Seeking 112
    Chronic Disobedience 113
    Disruption of Class 118
    Distractibility 121
    Encopresis 124
    Enuresis 125
    Fears 126
    Hyperactivity 127
    Hypoactivity 129
    Impulsivity 130
    Impulsiveness (Cognitive) 132
    Inattentiveness 134
    Inflexibility 134
    Instability 135
    Lying 136
    Tattling 137
    Negativism toward Self 137
    Overcompetitiveness 138
    Extreme Social Passivity 139
    Perseveration 140
    Hostile Physical Aggression; Destructiveness 140

Self-Concept 149
Psychosomatic Complaints 150
Antischool Phobia 151
Sexual Deviations; Interpersonal Behavior
    Deficits 152
Shyness, Nonassertiveness 153
Social Immaturity 155
Truancy 156
Verbal Aggression 157
Social Withdrawal 158
Summary 159

Chapter 5—Disciplinary and Classroom Management Programs ...   163
David A. Sabatino

Introduction 163
The LEAST Approach to Discipline 164
The Saturday School 165
The Atlanta Program: Humane Discipline 169
Vineland North Program To Reduce Vandalism 172
Deinstitutionalization and Status Offenders 176
Alternative Discipline and Suspension 177
The Utah Statewide Program 181
Erie's New Direction Center 185
Positive Peer Culture, Group Guided Interaction 186
Contingency Management 188
Off-Campus Learning Center (OCLC) 192
The Philadelphia Story 196
Summary 197

Chapter 6—Social Development: Building Human Relationship
Skills   201
Ann C. Sabatino and David A. Sabatino

Introduction 201
Observing Social Development 201
Personal-Social Objectives 202
Social Goals in Curriculum Development 207
Objectives, Activities, and Materials 209
Supplemental Materials 211
Eliciting Social Discussion and Growth 215
The Group Counseling Process 222

Avoiding Failure and Learned Helplessness   227
Summary   229

Chapter 7—Personal Development and Self-Realization **231**
Ann C. Sabatino, David A. Sabatino, and
Maribeth Montgomery-Kasik

Introduction   231
Self-Realization   232
The Decision-Making Model   235
Personal Decisions and Feelings   236
Self-Concept   238
Assertiveness Training   243
Picturing a New Self   247
Emotionality and Learning Disabilities   249

Chapter 8—Self-Control: Behavioral and Cognitive **259**
David A. Sabatino

Introduction   259
Basic Components of Self-Control   260
Summary: Behavioral Self-Control   271
Cognitive Self-Control   272
Summary: Cognitive Self-Control   277

Chapter 9—Substance Misuse: Drugs, Alcohol, and Tobacco **281**
Sheila Lane Davis and Suzanne Lanning-Ventura

Introduction   281
Historical Significance   282
The Scene in the 1980s   283
Use and Abuse   283
The Users   285
Drugs and Other Abusive Substances   286
Narcotics   286
Opiates   286
Stimulants   289
Depressants   293
Hallucinogens   297
Marijuana   301
Inhalants   303
Alcohol Abuse   305
Tobacco   310

Substance Treatment Programs 312
Alcohol Treatment Programs 316
Tobacco Abuse Treatment Programs 317
Summary 317

Appendix A—Glossary of Terms **321**

Appendix B—Street Use of Drug Terms **323**

Appendix C—Materials on Substance Misuse **325**

Appendix D—What To Do in Case of Overdose **329**

Appendix E—Resource Materials **331**
Pearlie M. Qualls

Index **373**

List of Contributors

SHEILA LANE DAVIS, M.S.
   Graduate Assistant
   Department of Special Education
   Southern Illinois University-Carbondale
   Carbondale, Illinois
SUZANNE LANNING-VENTURA, Ph.D.
   Educational Consultant
   Arrowhead Education Agency
   Fort Dodge, Iowa
MARIBETH MONTGOMERY-KASIK, Ph.D.
   Visiting Assistant Professor
   School of Education and Human Services
   University of Wisconsin-Stout
   Menomonie, Wisconsin
PEARLIE M. QUALLS, M.Ed.
   Supervisor of Learning Disabilities
   Milwaukee Public Schools
   Milwaukee, Wisconsin
ANN C. SABATINO, M.S.
   Behavioral Disorders Teacher
   River Falls School District
   River Falls, Wisconsin
DAVID A. SABATINO, Ph.D.
   Dean
   School of Education and Human Services
   University of Wisconsin-Stout
   Menomonie, Wisconsin

Foreword

Why another book on discipline and behavioral management? We asked that question when we started this project that wrecked one summer, lots of television evenings, and Christmas and spring vacations. We entered this project because:

1. Most of the valued books on discipline are (from a moral development point of view) fairly old.
2. Most of the books on behavioral management exclude all other approaches except conditioning practices.
3. Educators have no ready resource they can consult for first aid when something is about to occur or is happening.
4. Discipline and behavioral management practices reflect the state of the art; that means they change quickly, and so must communication about them.
5. Much misinformation exists about strategies, tactics, and programs that work and that are alternatives to traditional disciplinary practices.

What is attempted here is to provide a reference to student development and behavioral problems that both teachers and pupils face.

This is a book for educators, working in regular and special education settings, written by educators, and presented in an easy-to-use format.

It is comprehensive. It assumes that behavioral principles are mechanical tasks well implanted in the modern educator. Therefore, it goes beyond that point. It is designed to raise the level of consciousness on this issue, to examine teacher attitudes, and to explore good teaching—a synonym for prevention of classroom crisis. It then studies specific management practices for common disruptive behaviors and examines self-control, self-realization, and social relationships. It looks at traditional discipline and modern alternatives in both classroom strategy form and program format for administrators. It concludes with a review of drugs, alcohol, and tobacco and the problems they engender in education.

It is our intent that this be a user's guide, a handbook, a reference system for managing student behavior and teaching social-personal skills, by providing teachers with necessary tools for daily existence. In the words of Burgess Merideth in Rocky II, "You got the heart, but not the tools." Discipline is a necessary component of public school curricula, not an add-on. Here is a curriculum guide for educators in developing student responsibility and self-determination, not for the teachers' sake but as principles to be taught to maintain democratic order.

A point on style: the numerous legal citations are abridged in text to name of case and year but are given in full in the references at the end of each chapter.

A final word of gratitude and appreciation to Alicia A. Cabrera, Sherry Des Jardins, Debra M. Mibb, and Afsaneh Sarikhani for their typing of this manuscript.

David A. Sabatino
Ann C. Sabatino
Lester Mann
August 1983

Preface

Discipline and classroom management remain major concerns for both regular and special educators. Disruptive students, who display aggressive outbreaks and misdirect their hostility, are simply and plainly a threat to school personnel. Withdrawn students impose a different but equally serious burden on teachers' time and energy. There is little doubt that the 10 to 15 percent of any middle, junior, or senior high school student population who demonstrate chronic disruption or norm-violating behaviors, or draw undue attention to themselves, require an inordinate amount of human and financial resources. Yet what the public schools can do and what they are doing contributes to problems seen in society today as:

1. disproportionate increases in prison populations
2. increases in alcohol and drug abuse
3. a growing number of adults undergoing treatment in community mental health centers
4. a constantly rising divorce rate
5. job absenteeism that costs industry billions of dollars in down time
6. vandalism in the schools that exceeds $8 billion annually
7. an annual dropout rate that remains constant in the range of 17 to 23 percent and a suspension rate that runs from 5 to 30 percent.

The race is on between the internalization of self-control and external discipline. No other facet of American life poses such a threat to the quality of life, if not the way of life. As H.G. Wells put it back in 1920, "Human history becomes more and more a race between education and disaster."

Chapter 1

Discipline: A National Issue

Ann C. Sabatino

Marion Youth Faces 4 Charges In Beating of 91-Year-Old Woman

David Phelps, 17, Marion, will be arraigned March 12 on charges of burglary, theft, home invasion and aggravated assault involving the beating of a 91-year-old woman.

Cora B. Cain, 205 W. College St., remains in Marion Memorial Hospital for treatment of injuries, including a broken wrist and head lacerations, suffered about 9 p.m. Monday.

According to police, her assailant forced open the front door, beat her with a heavy object, took money from her purse and fled. Mrs. Cain went to the nearby Wilson Funeral Home, where employees notified police.

Authorities said Phelps turned himself in at the Williamson County Sheriff's office Tuesday night. The charges were filed Wednesday in circuit court in Williamson County in Marion. Phelps remains in the county jail in lieu of $5,000 cash bond.

The home invasion charge is the first filed in the county under a new state law which provides a mandatory six-year sentence upon conviction. (*Southern Illinoisan*, Feb. 21, 1982)

INTRODUCTION

This chapter provides an overview of the problem of discipline in the schools. Its objective is to create an awareness of the data available and of the reality and importance of this ever-changing situation. It identifies current problems and possible solutions.

BEHAVIOR CHANGES

Running in halls, chewing gum, making noise, wearing improper clothes, and getting out of turn in lines were misbehaviors listed frequently by most educators as major disruptive behaviors just prior to World War II. Major offenses in 8,000 schools, according to Zirkel (1980), were rape, robbery, assault, personal theft, burglary, disorderly conduct, drug abuse, arson, bombings, alcohol abuse, and carrying weapons. Discipline, or the lack of it, has been a concern in public education since the beginning. Obviously the problems are becoming more serious as time progresses. Classroom conduct has deteriorated from the level of misconduct to felonies committed by youths under age 18 (Stoops, Rafferty, & Johnson, 1981).

Lack of discipline tops the Gallup Poll of 1980 as the major problem facing the nation's schools (Gallup Poll, 1980). One in four respondents listed classroom discipline as their primary concern in today's schools. Low income and minority groups were particularly affected. Taxpayers, parents, and the public in general view discipline as one of the worst examples of ineffectiveness in America's educational system (Aird, 1981).

Crime among children is increasing and the adult community's responses seem only to exacerbate the problem rather than to reduce it (Cohen, Intili, & Robbins, 1979). If the situation is to be corrected at all, then community attitudes must be changed. Parents, teachers, and the community at large need to be aware of the gravity of offenses that can lead to a broader spectrum of crimes outside the school. The community needs to become involved and work cooperatively to alleviate this deterioration of the educational system.

Statistics show that 73 percent of the nation's schools experience a major crime every five months and 50 percent report more than one major crime in a semester. In any year, 3 percent of all children are referred to juvenile court (Achenbach, 1975). The national average of punishable offenses is a disturbing 6.8 percent per 1,000 enrollments (NCES, 1978). The dropout rate has remained constant since compulsory schooling began in 1906 (Kirk, 1976), ranging between 17 and 23 percent yearly.

Teachers become frustrated as their role as mentor becomes more that of disciplinarian, policeman, prosecutor, and judge. Teachers do not study to be "officers of the court" or "prison wardens;" they do so to educate the nation's youth in the hope that brighter minds and worthy skills will progress to a better tomorrow. Because of high rates of behavioral problems and the increasing frequency of crimes at school, the status of teaching as a career is declining. A third of the nation's teachers would opt for a different career. Only 48 percent of those responding in the 1980 Gallup Poll indicated they would like a son or daughter to become teachers, compared with 75% in 1969 and 60% in 1972.

Stress has become synonymous with teaching and a reason for teachers to leave education. Why? One student death per week from violent assault was reported by the head of security in one large school district; 5 percent (52,000) of the nation's secondary school teachers are physically attacked each year, with 10,000 requiring medical attention; and more than 5,000 teachers are attacked on high school campuses each month (Stoops, Rafferty, & Johnson, 1981). In addition, 60,000 teachers are robbed, and 12 percent (120,000) lose personal property from theft or damage. Boycotting or avoiding particular instructors is the excuse used by 30 to 50 percent of students reporting absenteeism (McQuire, 1979); up to 40 percent of high school students are absent each day without cause; and taxpayers spent some $1 billion to repair school vandalism in 1979. That's why.

The absence of control in society has reached staggering proportions. The prison population in Illinois doubled from 1972 to 1982 and so did the annual cost per inmate. In most states, the prison system is the major competitor with public education for state general revenue funds. Are students graduating from crime in school to those of worse degree? A report in the *Illinois School Board Journal* (Gierach, 1981) reveals more than half of all crime in the state was committed by persons under 21. Juvenile arrests nationally account for 51 percent of all property crimes, 23 percent of all violent crimes, and 43 percent of other serious crimes (Miller, Sabatino, Miller, & Stoneburner, 1979). More crimes are committed by youths under 15 than adults over 23. The description of the typical offender is: male, with a history of misdemeanors, driving offenses, sporadic employment, and a very interesting consistent phenomenon called school dropout.

The *Carnegie Council Policy Studies* (Kerr & Ragland, 1979) estimated that a third of today's youths are ill educated, ill employed, and ill equipped to compete successfully in society. The education system must make amends. If youth crime is to be deterred before it develops into a lifelong pattern, the school must accept responsibility and do its utmost to change juvenile delinquents' course of destiny. The ill educated, ill employed, and ill equipped must be rerouted to provide them with the skills necessary to compete and survive in today's world. The need for change is paramount, but how do educators, as "the system," make an effective change?

For example, junior high school teachers predict youth offenders will be incarcerated. Question: could those teachers prevent or modify the course of the young offenders' future? If a future of incarceration could be predicted, could it have been prevented? Gierach (1981) wrote that early intervention is essential. A shift from expulsion, detention, and suspension to prevention is necessary. Kicking troublemakers out, suspending them from the social group, sitting them in corners, or isolating them from peers is not the answer unless educators desire to build more prisons, not schools.

TRADITIONAL PRINCIPLES OF PUNISHMENT

"Pinch the young where they are most tender" was the philosophy of the elaborate behavior improvement scheme of a London schoolmaster, Joseph Lancaster, a Quaker who in the early 1800s established free education for the industrial class that could not afford to pay fees (Emblem, 1979). His Proclamation of Faults, Confinement After School, and Instruments of Punishments were disciplinary measures tested and proved in his era. The theory upon which they rested was: discipline worked when it was used effectively to hurt and embarrass youngsters. The principles of discipline were:

1. Punishments should be novel and varied.
2. Punishment techniques should create displeasure, be repeatable, and be noninterrupting to the mind or temper.
3. Punishment should not interfere with regular work.
4. Punishment is most effective if self-administered.
5. Hall monitors should include the active, lively tempered boys.
6. School procedures are ineffective in offsetting home environment.
7. Teachers should administer punishment to themselves before employing it with children (Lancaster, 1808).

TRADITIONAL DISCIPLINARY PRACTICES

What were punishable behaviors of the 1800s and how did the teachers of the period apply those disciplinary principles to the management of their classrooms?

The punishable misbehaviors were tardiness, hyperactivity, short attention span, profanity, and immorality.

The all-time favorite punishment for tardiness or truancy in 1808 was after-school detention. The inconvenience of supervision was solved by tying the youngster to a desk or placing the student in a log in such a manner that the pupil "could not loose himself" (Lancaster, 1803). For rowdy students who could not refrain from skipping and running in the halls, a shackle was applied. The shackle was a piece of wood about a foot long, with a loop to tie the legs. Lancaster explained, "when shackled, the violator cannot walk but in a very slow measured pace . . . sometimes the legs must be tied together." There were alternatives: adding extra shackles, tying the left hand behind the back (an attempt to produce dependence on the right hand), or attaching a shackle from elbow to elbow.

For group violations of running the halls, the "Caravan" was developed. Four to six boys could be placed in a portable pillory, a gang-shackle cut from a piece of wood and fastened around the necks of all in the group. Thus confined, they paraded through the school, being obliged to pay attention for fear of running against objects that might cause the yoke to hurt their necks or to keep from falling. A common refinement of the Caravan was to have the group walk backward.

The Log was prescribed for students with short attention spans. Those who fidgeted and squirmed had a cord slipped over their heads and a 6-pound log was balanced on each individual's shoulders. The slightest motion one way or the other and the equilibrium was lost, with the log putting a dead weight on the neck. The log did not hinder the students' freedom of movement nor interrupt attention to business so it was considered efficient and effective in decreasing fidgeting and increasing time on task.

A youngster who was disobedient to parents, profane in language, behaved immorally, or appeared disheveled was treated to a "Parade." Two boys preceding the offender marched around the school chanting the student's deficiency in a sing-song rhythm. The violator often was dressed in a costume with a paper cone on his head, and pinned to his apparel were labels such as "Dirty Mouth," "Sissy," or "Lazy Lad."

The most dreaded instrument of punishment was "The Basket," a simple, dramatic, and profound method. Often, just a mention of The Basket stifled mischievousness. The offending students were put into a sack or a basket and suspended from the roof of the school for all to see. Horace Mann applied this description to a school of his day:

> In one of the schools, to which I ascribe the motto, 'Authority, Force, Fear, and Pain,' there were 328 separate floggings in one week of five days, or an average of 65 and 3/5 each day. In another, eighteen boys were flogged in two hours in the presence of a stranger. In another, twelve or fifteen in one hour. (Mann, 1855, p. 1)

A REVIEW OF CURRENT DISCIPLINARY PROBLEMS

Disciplinary problems in elementary and secondary schools have not changed in the years since. Hyperactivity, short attention spans, and acting-out behaviors still are major issues. To establish order, teachers, past and present, have tried Lancaster's disciplinary rules, with some modification—birch rod to behavior mod, whipping posts to token economies. By the time students receive professional recognition for deviant behavior, the behavior is learned.

Biology, family, or school may precipitate the behavior, i.e., malnutrition, poverty, child abuse, neglect, divorce, and death; yet in today's system of education, the student is punished but with very little attention focused on the causes of behavior—rarely is the distinction between the two made. Have the methods of dealing with problem behaviors been modified or improved? Are the punishable behaviors the same? Are today's methods of dealing with inappropriate behavior more effective than those in the 1800s?

Unfortunately, existing methods of behavior control are not much better than the past, as evidenced by the severity of discipline problems. The motto of "Authority, Force, Fear, and Pain" is a credo still practiced in many schools today. "Shame" probably could be added as a means of suppressing undesirable behavior. In a review to make this point Unks (1980) notes several recent legal cases:

- In Washington, D.C., a private school requires male nonconformists to roll their trousers up to their knees, swatting them with a yardstick on the calves of their legs until they urinate or pop all the buttons off their pants.
- In Greensboro, N.C., a second grade teacher gave motivation as the reason for gathering the children around a classmate and leading them in chanting, "Dummy, Dummy, Dummy."
- In Illinois, a teacher in the presence of the class called an 11-year-old boy "worthless, undependable, and incompetent" (*Wexell v. Scott,* 2 Ill. App. 3d 646, 276 N.E. 2d 735 (1971)). When parents sued for assault, the case was dismissed because the teacher had not acted maliciously.
- A principal in Illinois punished a boy for scuffling with a girl by locking the child in the school safe for an hour.
- In South Carolina, a child who whispered was punished by a severe shaking that broke the pupil's neck, resulting in death.
- In North Little Rock, Ark., an eighth-grade boy was reported hospitalized for two days after a beating by his principal for talking out in class.

Unsafe, inhumane disciplinary actions practiced yesterday and still in existence today highlight the educational system's lack of progress. Educators have learned that public humiliation, compliance by fear, and inhibition of action by pain do not solve the problem; if anything, they enhance it. Yet these measures still are practiced. Modifications have been made, but are they any better?

An Illinois court sanctioned rules requiring a student to sit in the cafeteria at a restriction table with other persons under discipline, denying them the right to mingle with peers, then spending the rest of the day in the same chair in a small classroom (nicknamed "jail") for three days (*Fenton v. Stear,* 1976). The court held that the student's education was not materially infringed and characterized these penalties as trivial disciplinary sanctions.

Refrigerator packing crates have been used in classrooms, not as private cubicles to study or to minimize distractions but as jails. A door and window have bars painted on them and the world "JAIL" at the top, creating an area for hyperactive or misbehaving students to be restrained or paraded. If the crates are large enough and a student's desk will fit, endless days may be spent there. Unks (1980) described a 1972 incident in which a small child had encephalitis and, upon recovery, displayed hyperactivity. His teacher, perceiving him to be disobedient, put him in jail and moved his desk there for most of the school day. The child started sucking his thumb, wetting the bed, and suffering nightmares. Unaware of the events at school, the parents took him to their doctor, who administered an EEG. Because of signs of regression, the child was placed on Dilantin and was described as a nervous wreck during school.

In another example, a wooden structure with a hinged door and sliding bolt on the outside is still used in one school. An article in the local newspaper did not mention a window or air holes but did say students were placed in the box for 5 to 25 minutes, only upon written consent of parents. However, this punishment procedure was to be used only with behaviorally disordered or special education students, not regular pupils. When asked, the building administrator justified the punishment on the ground that the results were constructive and forced individuals to deal with their problems openly. A policy handbook for a school district in North Carolina says carrying a gun rates five demerits while disobeying a teacher gets 10. Accumulation of 15 demerits qualifies the student for a paddling each day of school for the next three days.

Isolation may be a preferable answer to physical pain, but is "jail?" Even though these methods were upheld by the law, court approval does not necessarily equate what is right or best in a given situation. So, where have we come? The terminology and techniques may be different today from those of yesterday, but the underlying principle still is the same. Unfortunately, the results are the same as well. Physical restraints, beatings, humiliation, and public embarrassment do not make students better. Such grave actions may only serve to make a bad problem worse. If a student lacks self-esteem and motivation to achieve, are public degradation and belittling going to increase self-concept?

LITIGATIONAL ISSUES: CORPORAL PUNISHMENT

Corporal punishment has been used for 3,000 years to beat sin out of and goodness into children. The rod still is the implement used to maintain discipline. At a lumber yard displaying a stack of paddles appearing to be fraternity souvenirs, an employee explained that most of the paddles were in fact sold to teachers for discipline. The school system's reply was: "One good paddling produces ten good themes."

What are the case and legislative laws regarding corporal punishment? Forty-seven states allow corporal punishment in schools. The Supreme Court in *Ingraham v. Wright* (1977) upheld its use. Furthermore, the majority of the nation's citizens and teachers favor corporal punishment (Hyman & Wise, 1979).

Data on the use of paddling in schools are incomplete, although what information is available reports frequent use:

- In Houston and Dallas in 1972, a combined average of 6,100 instances of paddling by school staff per month was reported (Hyman & McDowell, 1979).
- In California in 1972-1973, half of the school districts reported 46,000 instances of corporal punishment on the school records, 65 percent of which occurred at the junior high level (Hyman & McDowell, 1979).
- In Georgia in a 1974 survey of high school principals, 60 percent reported the use of corporal punishment (Hyman & Wise, 1979).
- In a 1978 survey by the National Institute of Education, 61 percent of rural junior high schools and 36 percent of all secondary schools reported paddling during a given month (NIE, 1978).
- In one junior high school, of the 1,395 students referred to the office for misconduct, 428 received a paddling (Ainsworth & Stapleton, 1976).
- In a 1968 survey in Pittsburgh, 68 percent of teachers reported they had used corporal punishment (Rothman, 1977).

Why is corporal punishment in school readily accepted? Who is in favor of paddling? Looking at corporal punishment from an international perspective, it is in most common use in English-speaking countries. In England, Highfield and Pinsent's (1952) survey revealed that 89 percent of teachers supported the practice. They also reported that more than a third of difficult children had been caned (hit with a cane) during their public school years. In a New Zealand book on caning, Mercurio (1972) reported an average of five canings per day per high school. In contrast, most of the countries of continental Europe and all of the Communist countries do not allow corporal punishment in schools (Hyman & McDowell, 1979).

In a country that prides itself on democratic policy, why is the United States the "heavy" when it comes to school discipline? It must be realized that there is little or no information on disciplinary actions in schools in Communist countries or on their alternatives and their effectiveness. However, one possible reason for the widespread use of corporal punishment in American schools may be that it is upheld by the courts.

Court cases indicate 10 or 15 moderate blows with a ruler is reasonable but 50 to 60 is clearly excessive. (Rovetta & Rovetta, 1968). Judicial decisions have upheld the use of willow sticks (*Thomas v. State,* Texas, 1898), table tennis paddles (*Suits v. Glover,* Alabama, 1954), blackboard pointers (*Christman v. Hickman,* Missouri, 1931), hand paddling on buttocks (*Watt v. Wynn Parish School Board,* Louisiana, 1953), slight face slap to girls (*In re Neal,* New York, 1957), and, where used, peach tree branches and mesquite switches. Improper instruments include fists (*Cottingham v. Sharples,* Louisiana, 1938), unless in self defense against an assault and battery attack, 18-inch sash cord (*Houeye v. St.*

Helena Parish School Board, Louisiana, 1933), rubber hose, open-handed slap to ear (*Swainback v. Coombs,* Connecticut, 1955), and unnecessary force (Rovetta & Rovetta, New York, 1968).

The laws seem almost immutable. It is not easy to change an established system, be the individual a parent, teacher, or other. In states where corporal punishment is legal, a district hoping to prevent random whipping cannot prevent teachers from doing so. School authorities in a Texas town had been told a 10-year-old boy who was dying of a blood disease had received more than ten whacks for talking in class. The angry father was told there was nothing he could do because it was legal (Hentoff, 1973). The U.S. Supreme Court in an Illinois case upheld corporal punishment as permissible over parental objections (*Baker v. Owen,* 1975). Indeed, paddling has been administered for violations as minor as sloppy appearance or careless handwriting (Merlis, 1975).

PROTECTIVE RIGHTS UNDER THE LAW

Students in public schools are not protected from paddling unless it is excessive or unreasonable. The Supreme Court ruled 5 to 4 that corporal punishment applied by teachers and administrators without prior notice or hearing did not violate the Eighth Amendment prohibiting cruel and unusual punishment since a school was not a place of imprisonment. Justice Lewis F. Powell Jr. stated for the majority: "The prevalent role in this country today privileges such force as a teacher or administrator reasonably believes to be necessary for the child's proper control, training or education" (*Ingraham v. Wright,* 1977).

An assault and battery case was brought against a teacher who had administered corporal punishment to an 11-year-old. The youngster did calisthenics in the opposite direction from the rest of the class and refused to sit down. For this transgression the child was struck nine times by a wooden paddle 3 inches wide, 20 inches long, and ½ inch thick. The doctor who gave medical assistance to the student said he treated the severely paddled areas as a third degree burn (*People v. Ball,* Illinois, 1974).

The Ingraham Case

This case began when James Ingraham and Roosevelt Andrews, eighth- and ninth-grade students in Miami, Fla., were paddled during the 1970-71 school year. The severity of the beating caused Ingraham to miss 11 straight days of school and deprived Andrews of the use of an arm for a week. The students filed suit in U.S. district court, charging that the severe paddling constituted cruel and unusual punishment in violation of the Eighth Amendment as well as a deprivation of liberty without due process of law in violation of the Fourteenth Amendment.

The court ruled that the boys' constitutional rights had not been violated and the court of appeals affirmed this judgment. The punishment therefore is protected by the cruel and unusual punishment clause of the Eighth Amendment.

While the Eighth Amendment guards against cruel and unusual punishment of criminals, children are not protected under this or any other amendment to the Constitution. Bolmeier (1973) cited cases from the 18th and early 19th centuries supporting a school's right to resort to corporal punishment. The court in ruling on teacher liability (*Lander v. Seaver,* Vermont, 1859) said:

> The teacher is not to be held liable . . . unless the punishment is clearly excessive and would be held so in the judgment of reasonable men. . . . But if there is any reasonable doubt whether the punishment was excessive, the master teacher should have the benefit of the doubt.

While the courts decide what is reasonable legally, the teacher who chooses to inflict corporal punishment must be prepared to accept the responsibility of having such action judged by the following factors:

- Was the force used free from malice or anger?
- Was the force moderate?
- Was the punishment appropriate to the offense?
- Did the punishment enforce a reasonable rule of the school?
- Was the force used excessive if judged by adult peers, considering age, sex, size, weight, strength, and overall health? (Rovetta & Rovetta, 1968)

Selected cases in which corporal punishment was not upheld were:

- *Johnson v. Horace Mann Life Insurance Co.* (Louisiana, 1970), excessive whipping causing multiple bruises
- *Nelson v. Heyne* (Pennsylvania, 1974), physical punishment administered in a correctional institution.

Generally, corporal punishment has been found permissible if reasonably applied (*Roy v. Continental Insurance Co.,* Louisiana, 1975).

In determining the reasonableness and degree of punishment a student experiences, the court takes into consideration the following:

- the pupil's offense
- the pupil's history of misconduct
- the pupil's motive and attitude
- the influence of the pupil's inappropriate behavior on other students

- the pupil's age, sex, weight, and health
- the teacher's motive
- the instrument used to punish
- the severity of the punishment compared to the gravity of the offense
- the force applied and the extent of injury to the pupil
- the reasonableness or validity of the educational purpose for which the punishment was applied.

Due Process in Public Schools: The Goss Case

In 1974, the Supreme Court in *Goss v. Lopez* required due process in all student suspension cases. The punishment in this case was based on charges of misconduct that, if placed on their record, could damage the students' standing with their teachers and "interfere with later opportunities for higher education and employment."

The case began in 1971 when many students from the Columbus, Ohio, schools were suspended without first receiving hearings. Some were suspended even though they claimed to be innocent bystanders. No evidence was presented against them and they never were told what they were accused of doing. A group of students, suspended for up to ten days without a hearing, claimed their right to due process of law had been violated. A federal district court agreed and the school administrators appealed to the U.S. Supreme Court.

What process is due? The Court noted that due process was a flexible and practical concept and that, at the very minimum, students facing suspension must be given some kind of notice and afforded some kind of hearing. It explained the kind of notice and hearing required in connection with a suspension of ten days or less: (1) the student must be given oral or written notice of the charges; and (2) if the student denies them, must be presented with an explanation of the evidence the authorities have and an opportunity to present the other side of the story. In cases of school emergencies in which prior notice and hearing would not be required, particularly when there were dangers to persons or property, the Court required only that fair procedures be followed "as soon as practicable" after removal of the danger or disruption.

The Court did not directly address the issue of what procedures would be required in cases of suspensions for more than ten days or for expulsions. Due process is a concept that must be tailored to the severity of the possible punishment. The Court also held that judges should not interfere with the daily operation of schools except to protect important constitutional values.

The decision did not call for elaborate or time-consuming formalities. It said there need be no delay between the time notice was given and the time of the hearing. In short, the minimum procedures required by *Goss* can guard against error without prohibitive cost or interference with the educational process.

Ingraham did not authorize the beating of school children but did deny them the protection of the Eighth Amendment. In *Goss,* however, the Court extended the protection of the Fourteenth Amendment's due process clause to students faced with suspension from school, requiring, under normal circumstances, an explanation of the charges and evidence and an opportunity to reply. It did not demand full-dress hearings, cross-examinations, representation by counsel, or many other elements of due process accorded to the criminally accused.

Can anything be done if school officials violate a student's rights? Yes. In another 5-to-4 decision, *Wood v. Strickland* (1974), the Supreme Court ruled that school officials could be held liable if they knew or (reasonably) should have known that the action they took within their sphere of official responsibility would violate the constitutional rights of the students affected. What if school officials simply are not aware of the student's rights? The Court responded that an act violating a student's constitutional rights cannot be justified "by ignorance." *Goss* and *Ingraham* exemplify the kinds of judicial decisions that can be applied effectively in the classroom.

Reasonable Corporal Punishment

As noted earlier, there are protections under the law for both students and teachers. However, the laws can appear to be flexible enough to allow for differences between schools, making possible varying practices and policies from state to state. The laws need to be more clearly defined. Corporal punishment in school is acceptable under the law, but what is considered acceptable can vary to a great extent between states and between school systems. If corporal punishment is to remain in the schools, whether or not it is the best solution, the specifications of punishment need to be delineated clearly. If punishment is used, it must be uniform.

This author does not advocate corporal punishment as the best alternative to solving behavioral problems in school. However, in lieu of the ineffectiveness of other tried alternatives, punishment may be necessary as a last resort and, in some cases, may be a better solution than others. Unreasonable use of punishment definitely is not advocated. The judicial system has ruled out physical punishment for all other persons under the law. Sadly, school children are the last Americans who may be beaten legally. Punishment is one issue but unreasonable, cruel treatment is another. The courts have yet to define what is reasonable corporal punishment and what is not reasonable. Each case is decided by the facts of each individual case (Rovetta & Rovetta, 1968).

State legislation supports the use of corporal punishment. Vernon (1968) surveyed the states and found that 25 had specific statutes dealing with corporal punishment. Of those, only New Jersey forbade its use at that time. The remaining 25 states had no specific statutes on the subject. A 1972 report by the National Education Association (Merlis, 1975) found only two states had prohibitive laws. In all other states, unless banned by state or local school boards, such as in Maryland, corporal punishment was permissible.

Although the use of corporal punishment in the United States has been slowly declining over the past few decades—particularly in major cities—the process has not been uniform. Los Angeles, with more than half a million pupils, abolished corporal punishment in 1975, only to reinstate it in 1980.

Behavioral Disordered Youth

Corporal punishment is used more commonly on the poor, minorities, handicapped, and males. "The lower the social class, the larger the paddle," is the philosophy of a California principal (Ramella, 1974). Ramella reported on a school in which three different sized paddles were used according to the social class of the student involved. In the *Ingraham v. Wright* (1977) case discussed earlier, the school principal struck the plaintiff 20 times with a wooden paddle while two assistants held the child down. Medical treatment and school absence of one week was the result. The use of corporal punishment across social classes for similar offenses is rare elsewhere. Because of the nature of many inequalities in treatment of children of lower social classes, the likelihood that the handicapped will be exposed to excessive corporal punishment is high (Smith, Polloway, & West, 1979).

The misuse and overuse of corporal punishment with exceptional students is indeed a common practice. Such children are assigned labels: emotionally disturbed, mentally retarded, or learning disabled, according to referrals and judgments by classroom teachers based on classroom behavior. These are students who display behavioral variances. Many of them, once placed in self-contained classes or residences, now are in public schools.

The characteristics that caused educators to label them exceptional often are the same behaviors that result in their being regarded as candidates for corporal punishment. Blanket rules describing the punishment for offenses for all students is the rule, rather than the exception. Allowances seldom are made for individual infractions. While multidisciplinary staffs spend many hours in meetings to identify individual characteristics, to pinpoint the most appropriate exceptional handicap label, and to list the most effective ways to remediate student weaknesses, this author has yet to see an individualized discipline strategy compiled for a learner.

Many texts offer recommendations for class management and lists on what to do once a deviant problem occurs, but most of them make little or no mention of individual characteristics of the students (Leviton, 1976). Educators must not assume all children are alike and respond in the same manner to similar disciplinary techniques.

Punishment does not have a uniform effect across all students. Interrupting Student A's behavior may be punishing for that pupil but may reinforce and encourage Student B because of the immediate attention Student A has received. Discipline needs to be individualized for all students, but especially the handicapped (Leviton, 1976).

In some states, a student may not be expelled or suspended for behaviors related to a handicap but may be removed from school entirely; the suspending school district then is responsible for providing homebound instruction to that individual. Regulations prescribed by Section 504 of the Rehabilitation Act of 1973 (Public Law 93-112) and by the Education for All Handicapped Children Act of 1975 (P.L. 94-142) forbid methods of administration that have the effect of subjecting handicapped persons to discrimination. Section 504 (Sec. 84.34) says only that the educational needs of "disruptive students" whose conduct "significantly" impairs the education of others in a regular classroom cannot be met in such a setting and the regulations would not be required there. Both Section 504 and the act are silent on discipline or punishment.

ALTERNATIVES TO CORPORAL PUNISHMENT

This chapter so far has addressed the problem per se. Knowing a problem exists does not necessarily lead to a solution. The remaining sections provide some viable alternatives. When correcting a behavioral problem, it is crucial to alleviate the observable, disrupting behavior without diminishing or oppressing the individual in the process. The alternatives discussed here are not all-inclusive. Later chapters focus more specifically on problems and selections.

Quay (1969) listed five categories of behavior disordered children: (1) conduct disorder, (2) anxious, withdrawn, (3) inadequate or immature, (4) socialized delinquent, and (5) autistic. Each of these students requires different classroom management procedures. There is no assurance that pupils with these characteristics will be prelabeled, so teachers will have no specific expectancy in regard to behavior. Each of these young people requires different behavioral management procedures based on type of conduct (emotional/disability) and degree of severity.

Example 1

With a restless, attention-seeking, disruptive, uncooperative student, the conduct disorder should be ignored. The individual should be provided with earned attention and rewards for positive behavior, thus learning that good behaviors earn more attention than impertinent ones. To provide attention to such a student's inappropriateness would only increase the attention-getting repertoire to include more exuberant acting out.

Example 2

With an immature student, the objective is to help the individual to mature and grow socially. Group activities, good role models, and activities to develop self-control and self-confidence should be emphasized. When the student acts out, isolation, public punishment, detention, or suspension should be avoided. Ideally, one-to-one discussions and possibly parental involvement should occur.

Example 3

With a socialized delinquent whose peers rewarded misbehaviors, the teacher would be encouraged to disassociate the student from the delinquent group and make serious efforts to keep the individual in school, reduce truancy, and make the misconduct unrewarding. Such individualized discipline strategy acknowledges variances in students' behaviors and in dealing with them.

Among exceptional pupils, corporal punishment may only accelerate the deviant behavior (Bandura, 1973). Many exceptional children learn by incorporating response models into their behavior repertoire (Altman & Talkington, 1971). For example, a student who receives corporal punishment learns that physical aggressions and inflicting of pain are justified and the punisher assumes the roles of power and influence, two characteristics highly valued by youths. The student views the teacher as an authority figure, and when the instructor uses power and physical force to enforce rules, the pupil may interpret that as the right to use brute force on weaker peers.

CORPORAL PUNISHMENT: CONTROL AND LEARNING

The New York Times (1971) reported that youngsters were being taught by example to rule by bullying. Therefore, in their dealings with others, students apply that rule. A member of the National Advisory Committee on Child Abuse, after recommending totally abolishing corporal punishment in schools, stated that society promoted reasoning in middle and secondary schools yet, by example, said it was all right for school officials to beat students (Hentoff, 1973). Unchanged is the fact that many educators justify corporal punishment as the ultimate method of control over their classes as the only penalty device many students understand.

Punishment causes a deterioration in the learning process. If acceptable behavior is an educational goal, and the building of approvable conduct through appropriate instructional techniques is important, these methods must be based on positive orientation. Punishment is best recognized as an immediate behavior suppressor. Reliance on corporal punishment as a technique for behavior management may then lead to inhibitive students' learning rather than their acquisition of adaptive behavior skills. Punishment does not teach.

Erlanger (1974) explored the myth "the only way these kids learn is by spanking, since it's the way they're taught at home" and reported the myth was widely exaggerated. He found that corporal punishment could be correlated significantly with social class, supporting the observation that the majority of lower class parents did not engage in the severe type of punishment often attributed to their child-rearing practices. Physical punishment from parents by itself does not appear to have a uniform effect on youths' behavior. In a fascinating study, Lefkowitz, Eron, Waldu, and Huesmann (1977) found that paternal punishment reduced aggressive behavior in youths who were strongly identified with their fathers, but when such positive identifications were not present, paternal physical punishment was associated strongly and positively with increased aggression. In general, there is a highly positive correlation between parental physical punishment and aggression in youths (Welsh, 1978). The relationship is particularly close for violent youths (Farrington, 1978).

The belief that some students respond to corporal punishment could indeed mean that they have not been exposed to other techniques of external control. Physical punishment is not a tried-and-true method of obtaining long-term responsibility for self (internalization of self-control). Supporters of the myth posit that corporal punishment is good because students develop personal responsibility, self-discipline, and moral character from an occasional paddling. In essence, they believe corporal punishment is the only way for teachers to maintain order and control.

Physical punishment occurs most frequently in the primary grades. What are primary teachers being protected from that requires physical punishment? What are youngsters taught when corporal punishment occurs? The teacher is modeling aggressive behavior as a problem-solving solution (Altman & Talkington, 1971; Fishback & Fishback, 1973). Because some violators are not caught, students learn at an early age that it is not what they do but getting caught that hurts.

To summarize, arguments against corporal punishment are:

1. It may cause the student to develop deep-rooted masochism and an increased desire for revenge.
2. It can affect the mental health of teachers who administer physical punishment frequently.
3. It does not change behavior, it only suppresses it; violent behavior begets violent behavior.
4. It blunts the recipient's feelings concerning justice.
5. It escalates deviant behavior.

6. It may cause deterioration of the learning process.
7. It may lead to modeling of physical aggression.
8. It may expose lower social classes to excessive corporal punishment more often than it does the middle class.
9. It exposes possibly exceptional children to excessive corporal punishment.
10. It may lead the students to withdraw from punishing situations.
11. It may encourage peers to react negatively to the punished student.

Corporal punishment appears to have an immediate, though temporary effect in decreasing certain types of misconduct. However, it does not relate positively to longer term measures of improved student behavior. Corporal punishment has not been shown to decrease the need for suspensions, particularly where it does not have parental support.

Based on testimony and research, a National Education Association task force on corporal punishment (1980) provided 15 conclusions. Among these were findings that physical punishment:

- was an inefficient way to maintain order and usually had to be repeated over and over

- had potentially undesirable effects on the student, i.e., involving underlying feelings, acceptable alternatives, and self-image

According to Dewey (1941), discipline requires training and thus must be experienced if it is to become self-directed. The development toward self-direction and social responsibility is a component of everyone's education. "The fundamental basis of good discipline in a school situation is a curriculum in which appropriate recognition is given to the interests, needs and status of the pupils to be taught" (Jones, 1980). The progressives, Caswell, Foshay, Hanna, Hartung, Leonar, Miel, Shane, Smith, and Tyler, always were optimistic and believed in human intelligence as a key to human behavior. Their objectives for youth were developmental and their approach to discipline *positive*. They viewed physical coercion as undesirable.

They believed that physical coercion would terminate the disruptive behavior but that the individual's basic disposition would not be altered in desirable directions. "I am able, valuable, and responsible and I will act accordingly" is an important self-perception for a student to have developed during school years. Students treated with dignity and respect are less likely to present disciplinary problems; sarcasm and ridicule breed negative attitudes about themselves and others. Students who develop self-discipline and self-responsibility in school enhance their ability to deal with conditions beyond the school or its control.

Behavioral change is a characteristic of education. When schooling is effective, learners develop and apply productive behaviors in all settings. Students do not learn automatically how to choose their actions intelligently in a given set of circumstances but do acquire such knowledge through practice. The process must be taught. Dewey (1941) argued that ''a disciplined person is one who is trained to consider his or her actions and undertakes them deliberately.''

Discipline is a universal problem. It is a part of everyone's education. The teaching of discipline requires discipline. Teachers tend to teach as they themselves were taught. ''Few teachers have the necessary skills to set teaching/learning tasks that stimulate pupils to self-discipline'' (Jones & Tanner, 1981, p. 495). The tendency today is to view discipline as a managerial problem instead of as the learned inner skill of an individual.

For example, vandalism is viewed as a flaw in school design. Schools then are built without windows, ergo, vandalism repairs are reduced but the problem of discipline is not addressed. Self-control and community responsibility/self-responsibility seldom are considered, yet they can be taught.

One very successful program where civic responsibility, self-reliance, and responsibility are stressed is located at Deep Springs College, where the students and faculty form a nearly self-sufficient community in a remote region of California. Their emphasis is on social development of students, the lack of which has drawn criticism for public schools. Six concepts of Deep Springs College are:

1. Equal opportunity is available for all.
2. The whole person is trained.
3. Individual and group discipline are fundamental to all human interaction. Supporting this concept is the belief that deterioration of individual and group discipline has led to problems in the educational system. When a student does not participate in the work program or other aspects of the curriculum, the failure produces an imposition on fellow students. Fair play, interpersonal exchange, and peer pressures are emphasized.
4. Students should take part in all aspects of the educational process. They need to learn that responsibilities accompany privileges. Enthusiasm, motivation, and initiative lead to self-discipline in the whole person. Students cannot assume a passive role, as in the public schools, where passive, emotionally disabled persons often go unidentified. Everyone must be active at Deep Springs.
5. Leadership is emphasized. Undisciplined entering students quickly ''get the message'' and evolve into initiating, self-motivated persons, unable to succumb to passivity in a program demanding personal action.
6. The talented are obliged to serve. Each individual needs and depends on classmates for their input. A student who has a strength that would indeed be beneficial to the group feels obligated to perform and produce.

Although the Deep Springs program is for the gifted, many of its concepts can be considered for a class, a school, or an entire system (Newell, 1980).

Mayer and Butterworth (1981) demonstrated that there were successful educational strategies for reducing vandalism and deviant school behaviors (more than $200 million is spent annually in California alone to repair damage caused by school-age children). The common causes, and therefore preventive measures which must be addressed including school vandalism, are: (1) overreliance on punitive methods of control, (2) a mismatch between student reading levels and course materials, (3) aggressive behavior by teachers, (4) failure to use cathartic activities to release pent-up aggression, and (5) misuse of behavior management procedures. The Mayer and Butterworth work is an example of effective inservice training for educators, as a first step in the prevention (decrease) of disciplinary and vandalistic problems.

In-School Suspension

In-school suspension is steadily gaining acceptance as an effective control on disruptive behavior. However, Mizell (1979) stated that alternatives to suspension, such as having the student sit in a room, were not likely to help the individual. Isolation, by itself, is not the total solution. Alternatives that keep the student in school are: time-out rooms, guidance centers, tutoring, and parental involvement. The goals are not to remove the student as the problem but rather to remediate the situation and teach the pupil self-discipline.

Timeout

A type of in-house suspension, timeout, may be defined as the removal of the opportunity for a student to obtain positive reinforcement following an undesirable behavior, thus reducing its frequency. Timeout does not necessarily mean seclusion. Ignoring a behavior may be sufficiently damaging to reduce and suppress it. Removal of the student from the immediate area of peer reinforcement, while not allowing the youth to participate or enjoy reinforcement, may be ample discipline.

When mild timeout measures are ineffective, removal to another room may be justified. The decision as to the less restrictive environment lies with the teacher, who decides the degree of timeout needed, depending on the particular individual, the specific event, and the behavioral response demonstrated. Although placement in a timeout room may be appropriate for aggressive, acting-out behaviors, it may be very inappropriate for milder conduct that is not threatening to others.

The decision to use a more restrictive form of timeout may depend, first, on the nature of the behavior, and second, on the relative effectiveness of previous interventions. Documentation should include at a minimum the name, time of day when the student went into timeout, release time, behavior causing the isolation, duration and type of timeout, and conduct during the seclusion (Gast & Nelson, 1977). Baseline rates of inappropriate behaviors should be collected before (if possible) and after timeout. If a timeout program is ineffective, modifications should be made.

The implementation of timeout is a complex and valuable tool for classroom teachers. Selection of appropriate procedures, consideration of the problem behavior, facilities available, need to satisfy legal requirements, i.e., gathering of data before and after the event, site preparation, adequate descriptions of the problem conduct, and documentation all are necessary for proper, legal, effective timeout procedures.

Mizell (1979) suggested going beyond punishment by teaching the students self-control. Student, teacher, family, and community all should be involved in the problem-solving process. Indianapolis has in-school suspension centers in ten high schools and some junior high schools. These centers offer support to teachers on how to cope with student misbehavior (Solomon, 1964).

The teacher is only one person who influences a student. If other significant individuals do not attempt change, chances of altering the problem are poor (Blackman & Silberman, 1971). Their case studies demonstrated the importance of coordination—enlisting the aid of parents, counselors, and other teachers. Committees composed of staff, parents, and community members were set up in Cincinnati. These panels establish goals for the school and the students.

PREVENTING VIOLENCE AND VANDALISM

Not only do deviant, disruptive behaviors in the classroom need to be alleviated, so, too, do the violence and vandalism that abound in many middle and secondary schools. Each year the problem becomes worse. Why do students act out their hostilities and frustration through violent actions? For many, violence and physical outbursts have become learned conditioned behaviors executed when they are angry and frustrated. Some youths do not know how to seek alternatives or how to express and vent their problems in ways other than violence.

How can educators provide these students with more acceptable alternatives? A widespread interest has developed in preparing teachers for skills to develop more appropriate behavior by positive, as opposed to negative, means.

In a three-year project (1977-1980) at California State University, Los Angeles (Mayer & Butterworth, 1981), teaching strategies derived from social learning and operant theories were emphasized during two 10-hour workshops involving teams composed of a principal, a counselor, and two model teachers from selected schools. Strategies employed were:

1. high interest academic materials appropriate to the student's reading level
2. positive recognition for progress in working on and completing assigned tasks
3. reduction in the use of punishment
4. appropriate and timely use of various learning principles and behavior management procedures
5. proper training of counselors and school psychologists in behavioral consultation skills.

Dissemination of workshop techniques, monthly team meetings, and efforts to include interested onsite personnel increased during the project. Data on the financial costs of school vandalism and on student and teacher behaviors were collected monthly. Vandalism repair costs declined after the onset of treatment and these savings were maintained in the third year. Inappropriate student behavior (i.e., physical aggression toward staff members and inanimate objects, refusing to do academic tasks) decreased each year.

Mayer and Butterworth reported that the data revealed student behavior change throughout each school year involved in the project, not just in the model classroom. They stressed the importance of training teachers to be aware of the classroom techniques and methods they used that might have contributed to student aggression and vandalism. Once an awareness was developed, elimination of these contributing factors and substituting preventive measures proved effective in decreasing the problem behaviors. The methods were disseminated to other teachers, who welcomed activities that decreased the dreaded discipline problems of student yelling, cursing, striking, and throwing of objects.

SUMMARY

Teachers are hired to teach and cannot do so without order. Therefore, they usually impose punishment after a class disruption. They might comment, "If we can just get rid of that kid, that troublemaker, we can teach the class." Often the disruption itself attracts less student attention or teacher anxiety than the moments that follow when verbal or physical punishment is meted out. Highly skilled teachers often are challenged with spur-of-the-moment disciplinary situations that seem unanswerable.

For hundreds of years teachers have been using or threatening to use punishment either to motivate learning, to thwart misbehavior, or to maintain order. The rod was employed as a teaching tool because it worked. Corporal punishment was successful, seemingly enough, at a time when overt pupil behavior was one of the few criteria for effective teaching and for effective learning.

The concept of teacher has evolved from that of stern taskmasters concerned with strengthening the minds and spirits of their students by providing mental building exercises to that of the professional educators concerned with guiding the learning process as a unique, personological experience.

The role of the teacher has changed, and so too have the disciplinary techniques. A strong authority, unilateral in decision making, cannot guide each student's learning process. If the teacher functions as a facilitator, providing a stimulus to learning, then the pupil must have positive feelings toward that practitioner. A student who has received ruthless, arbitrary corporal punishment may lose interest in learning. Respect and positive feelings of fairness contribute greatly to learning democratic principles.

Considerable time and effort have been spent studying whether corporal punishment is effective. That may not be the most appropriate question. Is it effective in promoting learning, or simply an efficient means of social control? If educators are concerned with classroom management as a form of easily maintained control, then corporal punishment is efficient. If a teacher is interested in creating a positive social and academic environment, then less of a reverent church atmosphere is needed, with more focus on dialogue on rules and on self-direction and its consequences. The following chapters provide acceptable alternatives to corporal punishment, offering a wide array of classroom management techniques and specific teacher behaviors to decrease stress on practitioners. (A review of some of the court cases involving discipline is provided in Zirkel's (1980) Quick-Quiz Update (Exhibit 1-1). Try it, just for fun.)

Schools administer corporal punishment because it is quick, readily available, effective, provides instruction to peers (Killory, 1974; Mercurio, 1972), and has received the full endorsement of the American judicial system. Alternatives to corporal punishment are suspension, expulsion, detention, in-house suspension, timeout, and behavior modification—all of which require preparation, staff involvement, time evaluation, and often extra funding. In the order of the frequency of their occurrence, verbal chastisement, detention, and suspension are the three most common practices. Detention may be served in the halls, in a corner of the classroom, or in the principal's office. In-school and out-of-school suspension quarantine the student from class. Indeed, suspension has several shortcomings that should be considered:

- Students are denied the opportunity of an education, miss classes, and fall farther behind in assigned work.
- Students may intrude into other schools or become a problem in the community.
- Parents must be absent from work to attend school meetings concerning expulsion.

Exhibit 1-1 Zirkel Quick-Quiz Update on the Law Concerning Student Conduct

Answer each item with an "X" in the appropriate box. Rather than guess, use the "Don't Know" box and avoid a one-point penalty for each incorrect answer. Correct answers are keyed at bottom.

	Yes	No	Don't Know
1. Does the Supreme Court's decision in *Ingraham v. Wright* provide unqualified immunity for school officials to administer corporal punishment in states with permissive statutes?	☐	☐	☐
2. Is liability under *Wood v. Strickland* (for violating students' clear constitutional rights) limited to actual damages?	☐	☐	☐
3. Have the due process requirements of *Goss v. Lopez* (for suspensions up to ten days) been applied by federal courts to the disciplinary removal of students from class for the purpose of transferring them to other schools in the same system?	☐	☐	☐
4. Does a student have the right to call the accusing teacher as a witness during an expulsion hearing, according to the Eighth Circuit Court of Appeals?	☐	☐	☐
5. Do expulsions of special education students require significantly more due process procedures than expulsion of other students, according to various courts?	☐	☐	☐
6. Have most of the recent school search decisions required of administrators the relatively strict standard of "probable cause" that generally has been applied to law enforcement officers?	☐	☐	☐
7. Can dogs be legally used in searching students for drugs, according to the federal district court in Indiana?	☐	☐	☐
8. Are strip searches of elementary and secondary school students automatically unconstitutional?	☐	☐	☐
9. Have federal judges in recent decisions consistently rejected administrators' attempted regulation of school-sponsored publications?	☐	☐	☐
10. Have courts generally sided with school authorities in recent cases involving dress and appearance requirements?	☐	☐	☐

Exhibit 1-1 continued

Calculate your score as shown below:

Number Correct		Number Incorrect		Net Score
_____	Minus	_____	Equals	_____

Key: 1, No; 2, Yes; 3, Yes; 4, Yes; 5, Yes; 6, No; 7, Yes; 8, No; 9, No; 10, Yes.

Source: Reprinted from "A Quiz on Recent Court Decisions Concerning Student Conduct" by Paul Zirkel with permission of the *Phi Delta Kappan,* 6(3), 206, © 1980.

- It is a humiliating experience.
- It authorizes "vacation" from school, thus rewarding the very behavior that earned the suspension.
- Schools may lose state funds because of absence.

Still, most school districts use suspension as the method to control unruly students. In-house suspension is better than out-of-school suspension because:

- The offender is in school in a restricted area.
- Individual remediation is available.
- The amount of lesson work is increased while on suspension.
- The student is not a problem to the community.
- In-house suspension does not go on the permanent record.
- No state funds are lost because school days are not lost.
- The student receives remediation in classroom behavior.

REFERENCES

Achenbach, T.M. The historical context of treatment for delinquent and maladjusted children: Past, present, and future. *Behavioral Disorders,* 1975, *1*(1), 3-14.

Ainsworth, L., & Stapleton, J.C. Discipline at the junior high school level. *NASSP Bulletin,* February 1976, *60,* 54-59.

Aird, R.B. Motivation: Key to educational problems. *Phi Delta Kappan,* September 1981, *63*(1), 56-58.

Altman, R., & Talkington, L.W. Modeling: An alternative behavior modification approach for retardates. *Mental Retardation,* 1971, *9*(3), 20-23.

Baker v. Owen, 423 U.S. 907, 46 L. Ed. 2d 137 (1975).

Bandura, A. *Aggression: A social learning analysis.* Englewood Cliffs, N.J.: Prentice-Hall, Inc., 1973.

Blackman, G.J., & Silberman, A. *Modification of child behavior*. Belmont, Calif.: Wadsworth Publishing Co., Inc., 1971.

Bolmeier, E.C. *Legality of student disciplinary practices*. Englewood Cliffs, N.J.: Prentice-Hall, Inc., 1973.

Christman v. Hickman, 225 Mo. App. 828, 37 S.W.2d 672 (1931).

Cohen, E., Intili, J., & Robbins, S. Task and authority: A sociological view of classroom management. In D. Duke (Ed.), *Classroom management: The 78th yearbook of the National Society for the Study of Education*. Chicago: The University of Chicago Press, 1979.

Cottingham v. Sharples, 28 La. App. 2d 551, 83 P.2d 50 (1938).

Dewey, J., & Kallen, H. (Eds.). *The Bertrand Russell Case*. New York: The Viking Press, 1941.

Emblem, D.L. For a disciplinarian's manual. *Phi Delta Kappan*, February 1979, *50*(6), 339-340.

Erlanger, H.S. Social class and corporal punishment in childrearing: A reassessment. *American Sociological Review*, 1974, *39*, 68-85.

Farrington, D.P. The family backgrounds of aggressive students. In L.A. Herson & M. Berger (Eds.), *Aggressive and antisocial behavior in childhood and adolesence*. Elmsford, N.Y.: Pergamon Press, 1978.

Fenton v. Stear, 423 F. Supp. 767 (W.D. Pa. 1976).

Fishback, S., & Fishback, N. Alternatives to corporal punishment. *Journal of Clinical Psychology*, Fall 1973, *2*.

Gallup Poll. School ratings up slightly; discipline still top problem. *Phi Delta Kappan*, 1980, *6*(3), 206.

Gast, D.L., & Nelson, C.M. Legal and ethical considerations for the use of timeout in special education settings. *The Journal of Special Education*, 1977, *11*(4), 457-467.

Gierach, W.E. Working together, schools and courts can stem the flow of young criminals. *Illinois School Board Journal*, May-June 1981, pp. 14-16.

Goss v. Lopez, 14 S. Ct. 1405 (1974).

Hentoff, N. A parent-teacher view of corporal punishment. *Today's Education*, 1973, *62*(5), 18-21.

Highfield, M.E., & Pinsent, A. *A survey of rewards and punishments in schools*. London: National Foundation for Educational Research, 1952.

Houeye v. St. Helena Parish School Bd., 223 La. 966, 67 So. 559 (1933).

Hyman, I.A., & McDowell, E. An overview. In I.A. Hyman & J.H. Wise (Eds.), *Corporal punishment in American education*. Philadelphia: Temple University Press, 1979.

Hyman, I.A., & Wise, J.H. *Corporal punishment in American education*. Philadelphia: Temple University Press, 1979.

In re Neal, 164 N.Y.S. 2d 349 (1957).

Ingraham v. Wright, 430 U.S. 651, 51 L. Ed. 2d 771 (1977).

Jones, R.S. *An inquiry into the classroom discipline legacy from the progressive education movement*. Unpublished doctoral dissertation, Temple University, 1980.

Jones, R.S., & Tanner, L.N. Classroom discipline. *Phi Delta Kappan*, March 1981, *62*(7), 494-498.

Johnson v. Horace Mann Life Ins. Co., 241 So. 2d 588 (La. 1970).

Kerr, M., & Ragland, E. Pow wow: A group procedure for reducing classroom behavior problems. *Pointer*, 1979, 24, 92-96.

Killory, J.F. In defense of corporal punishment. *Psychological Reports*, 1974, *35*, 575-581.

Kirk, W.J. Juvenile justice and delinquency. *Phi Delta Kappan*, February 1976, *57*(6), 395-398.

Lancaster, J. *Improvements in education* (1st ed.). London: 1803-1808.

Lander v. Seaver, 32 Vt. 114, 76 Am. Dec. 156 (1859).

Lefkowitz, M.M., Eron, L.D., Waldu, L.O., & Huesmann, L.R. *Growing up to be violent: A longitudinal study of the development of aggression.* Elmsford, N.Y.: Pergamon Press, 1977.

Leviton, H.S. The individualization of discipline for behavior disordered pupils. *Psychology in the Schools,* October 1976, *13*(4), 445-448.

Mann, H. On school punishment (Lecture 7). *Lectures on Education.* Delivered in 1840. Boston: Ide and Dutton, 1855. (Originally published, 1845.)

Marion youth faces 4 charges in beating of 91-year-old woman. *Southern Illinoisan,* February 21, 1982.

Mayer, R.G., & Butterworth, T.W. Evaluating a preventive approach to reducing school vandalism. *Phi Delta Kappan,* March 1981, *62*(7), 498-499.

Mercurio, R. Corporal punishment in the school: The plight of the first-year teacher. *New Zealand Journal of Educational Studies,* November 1972, *7*(2), 144-152.

Merlis, S. Problems and experiences with drug trials outside the U.S., the time lag in new drug availability. *Diseases of the Nervous System,* July 1974, *35*(7), 5-7.

Miller, T., Sabatino, D., Miller, S., & Stoneburner, R. Adolescent violent behaviors directed at the schools: Problem and prevention. *Counseling and Human Development,* February 1979, *11*(6), 1-8.

Mizell, M.H. Designing and implementing effective in-school alternatives to suspension. In A. Garibaldi (Ed.), *In-school alternatives to suspension.* Washington, D.C.: National Institute of Education, U.S. Government Printing Office, 1979.

National Center for Educational Statistics (NCES). *Digest of education statistics.* Washington, D.C.: U.S. Government Printing Office, 1978.

National Education Association, 1980.

National Institute of Education. *The safe school study.* Washington, D.C.: U.S. Department of Health, Education, and Welfare, 1978.

Nelson v. Heyne, 491 F.2d. 352 (7th Cir. 1974).

Newell, L.J. *Among the few: A study of Deep Springs College alumni, 1917-1980.* Deep Springs, Calif.: Deep Springs College, 1980.

New York Times, March 7, 1971, 1:5.

People v. Ball, 58 Ill. 2d 36, 317 N.E. 2d 54 (1974).

Quay, H.C. Dimensions of problem behavior and educational programming. In P.S. Graubard (Ed.), *Children against schools.* Chicago: Follett Publishing Company, 1969.

Ramella, R. Anatomy of discipline: Should punishment be corporal? *PTA Magazine,* 1974, *67*, 24-27.

Rothman. E.P. *Troubled teachers.* New York: David McKay Company, Inc., 1977.

Rovetta, L., & Rovetta, C. *Teacher spanks Johnny: A handbook for teachers.* Stockton, Calif.: Willow House Publishing, 1968.

Roy v. Continental Ins. Co., 313 So. 2d 349 (La. App. 1975).

Smith, J.D., Polloway, E.A., & West, G.K. Corporal punishment and its implications for exceptional children. *Journal for Exceptional Children,* January 1979, pp. 264-268.

Solomon, R.L. Punishment. *American Psychologist,* 1964, *19*, 239-253.

Stoops, E., Rafferty, M., & Johnson, R.E. *Handbook of education administration* (2nd ed.). Boston: Allyn & Bacon, Inc., 1981.

Suits v. Glover, 260 Ala. 449, 71 S. 2d 465 (1954).

Swainback v. Coombs, 19 Conn. Supp. 291, 115 A. 2d 468 (1955).

Thomas v. State, 43 S.W. 1013 (Tex., 1898).

Unks, G. The front line: Teaching by torment. *High School Journal,* November 1980, *64*(2), 33-35.

Vernon, T.E. *Legality and propriety of disciplinarian practices in the public schools.* Unpublished doctoral dissertation, Duke University, 1968.

Watt v. Wynn Parish School Bd., 66 S. 2d 340 (La. 1953).

Welsh, R.S. Delinquency, corporal punishment and the schools. *Crime and Delinquency,* 1978, *24,* 336-354.

Wexell v. Scott, 2 Ill. App. 3d 646, 276 N.E. 2d 735 (1971).

Wood v. Strickland, 14 S. Ct. 1932 (1974).

Zirkel, P. A quiz on recent court decisions concerning student conduct. *Phi Delta Kappan,* June 6, 1980, *6*(3), 206.

Chapter 2

Prevention: Teachers' Attitude and Adaptive Behavior—Suggested Techniques

Ann C. Sabatino

INTRODUCTION

Facing a class of potentially violent youths or a group seemingly interested in a mischievous plan can be a horrendous experience, one that is both personally and professionally threatening. Teachers are responsible for preventing classroom upheavals. Since there is no proved theory, method, or technique guaranteed to produce appropriate behaviors, teachers must develop their own management program through trial and error, based on their professional preparation, experience, and, most importantly, personal values and philosophy.

This chapter focuses on the teacher. Therefore, it is sensitive and personal. It is intended to provide helpful information and workable solutions. This is not a promise of workable solutions but of suggestions that may make teaching an easier, more rewarding, and a less stressful vocation.

When individual students or entire classrooms become unmanageable, whom do parents, community, and administrator hold responsible? One-word answer: Teachers. Teachers can be poor academically, ineffective in instructional management, display poor personal behaviors, evidence the 9-to-3 o'clock work syndrome, and be loved by all if they maintain classroom order. The opposite also is true. With discipline, success is possible; without discipline, chaos results. As long as discipline is maintained, a teacher's job seldom will be in jeopardy. Let the very finest academic instructors evidence an inability to maintain pupil control and the laws of the land will be invoked against them. The maintenance of discipline is indeed the "law of the land" in public education:

> *Maintenance of discipline.* Teachers and other certified educational employees shall maintain discipline in the schools, including school grounds . . . they stand in the relation of parents and guardians to the pupils. *(Illinois School Code,* 1981, Article 34-84a, p. 229)

Understanding their own self-concept can enable teachers to understand their feelings, behaviors, and attitudes toward certain student conduct. This chapter presents ineffective and effective teaching behaviors and recommends basic rules governing instructors' responses. Many times teachers inadvertently cause disruptive behaviors by verbal statements or physical behaviors. The material here should make them more aware of their personal classroom behaviors that could increase the likelihood a disruptive, aggressive student would act out.

This is not to suggest that teachers should walk on thin ice around such students, merely that they be more aware of classroom variables that are under their control that may be totally acceptable to the majority of students yet could trigger a troubled one into an acting-out behavior, thereby disturbing everyone. Most of the suggestions require minimal change in teachers' behavior yet might prevent class disruptions.

PERSPECTIVE ON TEACHING

Colleges and universities prepare professional educators in classroom management techniques through special courses, workshops, and inservice training. Most educators are exposed to theoretical models on preventive and positive classroom behavioral management.

They generally do not draw upon a single classroom management theory; instead, they choose from among a variety of strategies and mold them into a personal style for handling disciplinary problems. Many teach the way they were taught. The major difficulty with that is that most classroom problems, no matter how difficult, thus get the same treatment.

Educating teachers in only one theory is just as dangerous, for what is right for one student or instructor may be wrong for another (Katz, 1972). Disciplinary practices that tend to be similar for each student in a classroom, regardless of individual differences, result in a situation similar to an assembly line that mass produces like items all cut from the same pattern. If teachers are to be professionals and not technicians, they should: (1) weigh alternative intervention strategies, (2) examine results, (3) decide on long-range and short-range behavioral goals, and (4) modify existing program aims accordingly. A technician in the guise of a teacher always gives the same treatment for the same behavior, regardless of the differences among students or the problems they present.

Teachers can peruse many professional books that promise solutions to managing troublesome students and can attend complex workshops and other inservice processes. Even after all that, they still can be hampered by the limits on what is believed to be the solution to disruptive pupils because it is impossible to apply a social abstraction as if it were something learned concretely in the classroom.

Social rules govern behavior and social rules are relative—as relative, indeed, and as arbitrary as those who enforce them. Schools and teachers have assumed the role of differentiating the good from the bad and marking them for society (Sabatino, 1978).

The 1980s continue the trend of increased stress and of vast new informational frontiers for educators. Traditionally, public school teachers were equipped to manage homogeneous groups. The students usually came from backgrounds similar to those of the instructors, both socioeconomically and in terms of race, religion, and culture. Management techniques that worked with one student tended to have similar effects on others. When a student became troublesome, teachers and principal often were aware of events within the family that could have triggered the change in behavior, i.e., a death, a new baby, illness, relative moved into home, father out of work, family conflict, new neighbors. The teachers could call the parents or stop by on the way home because they knew the family.

Four common stress areas that challenged many pupils then as now (Klein, 1962) were:

1. separation of child from family
2. demands of task-oriented learning
3. adjustment to a large number of peers
4. sharing attention of one adult teacher.

However, these formerly could be dealt with more easily because of familiarity and small class size. Schools now contain heterogeneous mixtures of students and teachers. Family involvement is less as a result of the increased mobility and various multicultural factors in a community. Desegregation and mainstreaming no longer separate races or special groups from regular populations. Such diversity cannot be changed. Homogeneous classrooms are not likely to develop except in rural, sparsely populated regions, and even then, as in rural Wyoming, that tradition can be changed overnight by a boom in coal or oil production.

Effective teaching requires that individual student differences be recognized. Teachers rigid in classroom management practices are hard pressed to acquire the flexibility necessary to see beneath a cloak of masking behaviors. To meet the challenge of these special needs, educators require an expansive knowledge of alternative behavioral management skills. Normally, teachers stress understanding the needs and goals that are important to the students: what makes them happy or sad, what conditions make it easier or more difficult for them to learn, what areas require considerable teacher awareness of both pupils and of self. Teachers are professionals, a result of training; they also are people, with needs for recognition and for power, with fears and anxieties, and with feelings of success or failure.

THE ROLE OF TEACHER SELF-CONCEPTS

There generally are several points of view to any story. Teachers are not alike in personality or disposition any more than are selected people from any walk of life. This helps explain why cookbook approaches for handling misbehavior are nearly impossible. A good first step in analyzing a problem is to look at it from both the students' and the teachers' point of view. Combs (1981) defines the desirable self-concept of the educator as involving an individual who is:

1. opposed to identifying with persons who are withdrawn, removed, or separated from others
2. able to cope with problems and feelings of inadequacy
3. reliable, dependable, and trustworthy
4. capable of coping with events as they happen in all settings
5. wanted, rather than unwanted, likable, and attractive
6. worthy, dignified, and possessing integrity.

It should come as no surprise that how others perceive individuals is highly dependent on how they perceive themselves. If teachers (or anyone else) like, trust, and have confidence in themselves, they are likely to see others in the same light. Can persons who do not like themselves be liked by others? Is growth easier when it is in a relationship with someone who trusts and believes in their capacity?

Expectancy studies (Rosenthal & Jacobson, 1968), although suffering some serious design flaws, suggested that students achieved academically to the degree teachers thought they were capable of and behaved in a manner they were expected to (Reckless, 1967). Teachers rated as good by students generally:

- have more positive views of others—students, colleagues, and administrators
- are not as critical of others and do not attack them with ulterior motives; instead they are friendly, helpful, and worthy
- have a more favorable view of the democratic process in the classroom
- have the ability to see things as they seem to others, i.e., from the others' point of view
- do not see students as persons "you do things to" but rather as individuals capable of doing for themselves once they feel trusted, respected, and valued.

Teachers with positive self-concepts have more positive views of others, expect success, and reward student accomplishments, both academically and behaviorally. It is important that they evaluate how they themselves feel since this enables them to understand why certain actions and reactions with students occur. Sensitivity, empathy, and perceptiveness are important for teachers. These characteristics aid in identifying and predicting accurately how students feel and what they may do (Smith, 1966). Teachers' competencies and interests must be established. What are their limitations? What motivates them? What are some personal teaching interests that could be integrated into the curriculum that both pupils and practitioner would enjoy? Teachers should be aware of their own personal and professional weaknesses and strengths and consider them when planning programs.

Awareness of being hurt easily by vicious student statements may not assuage teachers' feelings but may aid in better managing responses and understanding the possibility of overreacting. Teachers should know if one of their personal characteristics is taking too seriously the statements students may make when they are very angry, frustrated, or striking out, such as: "Get away from me," "I don't like you," "You're ugly," "I hate you." Knowing teachers take statements so seriously may be the reason the students voice them. Students are reinforced by teachers' behavioral reactions or expressions—tears, anger, ignoring. Being aware of sensitive areas can help teachers manage reactions and perhaps overcome the hurt feelings, thus denying the students the pleasure of creating a reinforcing behavior from the instructors.

Teachers should build into the educational program personal interest areas they can look forward to discussing, such as aquariums, music, plants, entomology, fishing, bird watching, crafts, hi-fi equipment, rock collecting, or stamp or coin collections.

STEPS TO GOOD DISCIPLINE

The school should continually strive to be a place where people are courteous, where laughter is heard, and where communication is practiced. It should be a place that has democratically determined rules that everyone agrees on because they are beneficial to each individual and to the group, where administrators support and participate actively in an approach to discipline that teaches self-responsibility. Teachers should:

- Be personal, with statements to students such as, "I care about you."
- Avoid references to the past.
- Emphasize behavior, not feelings.
- Stress value judgments; ask students to evaluate their own.
- Plan, work with students to formulate successful, simple alternatives.
- Be committed.
- Give positive reinforcement.
- Use behavioral contracts.

- Decline to accept excuses.
- Decline to punish since punishment lifts responsibility from students.
- Never give up but hang in there longer than the students expect.

Teachers also should set aside some quiet thinking time for themselves. They should choose students who are continual disciplinary problems to work with. They should analyze the list above, then ask themselves, "Are these techniques working?" If not, they should make a commitment not to use any of those responses the next time a problem develops.

They should plan better tomorrows for their students. One step would be to send them on special errands or do something that says, "You're special. I care about you." Teachers should not expect immediate improvements. The students may reject teachers even more strongly than before, so they must stay calm and be persistent.

"What are you doing?" Such a question often causes students to stop what they are doing and think about it, which sometimes can help them to own the behavior. The answers probably will contain some embellishment or distraction ("I pushed him, but he pushed me first"). When answers contain the behavior, teachers should simply say, "Please stop it."

"What are you doing?" "Is it against the rules?" "What should you be doing?" Explicit in the third question is the idea that the teachers expect the unacceptable behavior to be replaced by the answer. Teachers must try to convey warmth, support, and firmness.

"We should work this out. What kind of plan can you develop to follow our rules?" The plan has to be more than just, "I'll stop." It has to be a plan of positive action that helps the students move toward responsible behavior. The more they consider the plan their own, the better it will work.

TEACHER ACCOUNTABILITY

Teachers often devise special programs for their troublesome students, then fail to evaluate and modify their own strategies according to the data received. Are disruptive outbursts always the students' fault? Do teachers sometimes unknowingly intimidate or create disruptive situations? How frequently do they analyze their personal and professional behaviors? In most cases they call in a specialist in the hope that the expert will know more than they and will provide a solution beyond theirs.

Educators' professional dream is to itemize the students' problems, then devise a special program that will correct the situation quickly and pleasantly. Teachers often fail to modify or even evaluate their own management plans or the skills needed for them. Too often misbehavior is viewed as a student problem, and solved only by home environment, peers, or significant others in the pupils' life.

A study by Lasley (1981) suggested teachers were instrumental in causing and preventing disciplinary problems. Ignoring student backgrounds and learner characteristics frequently led to teachers to react in such a manner as to exacerbate classroom behavioral disorders. It is worthwhile to examine the real issue. Does everyone in the class get the same amount of attention? Is an undue amount of time and attention spent on those displaying inappropriate behaviors? If the answer is yes, the teacher may be inadvertently reinforcing inappropriate behaviors.

Teacher Self-Evaluation

Teachers can check themselves by making a chart and dividing it into sections suitable for their schedule (Exhibit 2-1). Whenever they make a negative comment to a student, they should put a negative sign (−) on the schedule and a plus (+) for positive statements. At the end of the day, are there more pluses or minuses? If the negatives outweigh the positives, the practitioner may inadvertently be reinforcing inappropriate behaviors, teaching students that to get attention they need to misbehave, and probably discouraging appropriate behaviors. There should be a balance between the pluses and minuses.

Rules for Teacher Responses

Following are five suggested rules for teacher responses. They are not meant to be anything more than guidelines to aid teachers in relations with students.

Rule #1: *Don't direct peer (classroom) pressure to a misbehavior publicly when the matter can be handled gently and privately.*

Some responses promote more positive and appropriate behaviors than others. A good example is to respond to the student privately, not publicly (Lasley, 1981). A student who is corrected in public loses face and is humiliated. That response places the individual in a defensive position that correctly forecasts aggressive behavior. When students are reprimanded privately, they have a choice: they can comply, adapt, or repeat the misconduct. Private reprimands are visible to a few students at most and generally do not attract attention so the disrupters are not rewarded by peer recognition. Only the student being disciplined should be aware of the sanction. In summary, a private reprimand places neither the student nor the teacher in a no-win situation.

Example: At the sound of the classroom bell, Jason, who often misbehaves, remains standing at the window instead of taking his seat. He

Exhibit 2-1 Teacher Checklist for Self-Evaluation

When self-evaluating, consider the following questions:

_____ During what type of class activities are most misbehaviors exhibited?

_____ What task—lecture, Ditto and workbook sheets, group discussion—restricts student and teacher movements, thus forcing the teacher to be highly visible when disciplining students?

_____ Is the teacher mobile in the room?

_____ Does the teacher handle nonconforming behavior privately or publicly?

_____ Are nonverbal techniques used effectively?

_____ Does the teacher usually reprimand verbally and publicly?

_____ Do students understand what inappropriate behaviors are?

_____ Does the teacher understand what inappropriate behaviors are?

_____ Is the student redirected to a more appropriate activity after receiving a reprimand?

_____ Are assignments clear? Do the students understand the task?

_____ Are specific students identified when misbehaving?

_____ Is it clear, when a reprimand occurs, which students are misbehaving or is the entire class criticized or penalized?

_____ Can the teacher punish less and offer praise more often?

_____ Does the teacher realize different students have different values?

_____ Do the students believe the teacher is concerned about their personal and social concerns?

_____ Does the teacher limit the students' thinking?

Example: "Were you happy when you did well on your paper?"
              Better: "How did you feel when you were so successful?"

_____ Does the teacher listen when the students talk?

_____ Does the teacher establish eye contact with students?

has an attitude of daring the teacher to address him. When the teacher's request is public, "Jason, sit down at your desk right now," everyone in the class and possibly in the hallway can hear this valid demand. Either the teacher or student can lose face. If the student takes his seat, there is no guarantee he will resume acceptable behaviors. He may sulk, slam his books, or make an underbreath slur that nearby students hear and add to, with increased socially disruptive behavior in a ripple effect. The teacher's next statement probably would be, "You had better sit down right now.'' This would be spoken louder and more harshly than before, and the teacher probably would start moving toward the student. The next statement might be, ''I'll tell you one more time to sit down.''

Rule #2: *Do move toward the student, creating an aura of personal contact.*

Had the teacher decided to reprimand Jason quietly and privately, the threatening situation might have been avoided. The teacher now must move toward the student to initiate a private communication because remaining at the desk would make private sanctions difficult. For private corrections to work, mobility is necessary. The teacher must move up and down the aisles, around the room, and between the seats.

> *Example:* The teacher should approach the student, possibly putting an arm around his shoulder, and firmly and quietly state, ''You need to be in your seat, Jason. Go to your seat now, please.'' At this point the teacher could gently but firmly turn the student's shoulders with the arm just used to get his attention and start him on his way back to his desk. At this point the teacher can choose to return to the desk and proceed with the schedule, or unobtrusively follow the student to his seat and continue proceedings from there, or leisurely walk to another area of the room.

Rule #3: *Do develop nonverbal cues.*

An effective classroom manager is mobile and is skilled in the use of nonverbal messages. Stares, changes of head positions, and gait all can be effective in controlling student behavior. Nonverbal communication will not eliminate the verbal, but it can increase control and decrease confrontations.

> *Example:* Two students in study hall are whispering at a low, slightly audible level that distracts others. The teacher steps forward, nods slightly to one side, grimaces, furrows the forehead, and shakes the head, then points firmly with an index finger. The whispering students understand the teacher is requesting them to please be quiet. They respond and return to work.

Rule #4: *Do identify the misbehavior after the reprimand and direct the student toward the activity.*

The teacher who requires an immediate student response should identify the misbehavior, deal with the reprimand, and refocus on the lesson (Wegmann,

1976). Many times the teacher can say the first name of a student and the latter will change the behavior. The teacher should be sure that, following a correction, it is clear what behavior is expected. The student must know what was done wrong and what needs to be done to change the behavior in order to make it acceptable.

> *Example:* When a teacher states, ''Please sit down and begin reading your government assignment,'' the expectation is clear. An ambiguous request such as, ''Quit wandering around the class and go where you are supposed to be before I lose my patience and make you,'' may cause the student to sit down but not necessarily do the assignment. The student may sit and wonder what would have happened if the decision had not been complied with and might think, ''How could the teacher make me sit down?'' ''Could the teacher make me sit down?'' The student might enjoy manipulating the teacher to the point of a temper explosion. After all, when a student causes a teacher to lose emotional control, who is in control?

Rule #5: *Do direct the sanction to a specific person.*

Knowing when to respond to groups is another teacher behavioral skill that often proves useful. Group demands are easy for misbehaving students to ignore (Lasley, 1981).

> *Example:* ''Jonathan, please stop looking out the window and get back to work. Ted, Seth, you too. Thank you.'' ''Maggie, do your friend a favor and stop whispering so she can work.'' Teacher smiles. ''O.K., you too, Jenny.'' There may be resistance to such suggestions but aggression is less likely.

> *Contrast Example:* ''Susan, don't be so loud. I could hear you all the way down the hall.'' ''Quit being such a loudmouth. You're not a cheerleader, is she, class?'' Such excessive individualized reprimands could cause a student to become aggressive and act out. Humiliating, dissenting, directed individual commands often elicit aggressive reactions (Lasley, 1981). Instead, ''Susan, please turn your volume down about three notches. If you speak softly, people will try harder to hear what you say and they will listen, right, kids?'' ''Thanks Susan, and the class thanks you.'' Teacher smiles. Pat on back.

Following is a list of suggestions when developing a preventive approach to discipline problems in a classroom.

1. Group pressure may be used to enforce rules, but an entire class should not be punished because one student has broken a rule.
   Example: "No one will go to the pep rally until the person who threw the spitball stands up."
2. Embarrassing a student as punishment causes resentment and future problems.
   Example: "You all were supposed to be doing your lab work assignment. However, Jeannie used the time to write Tony a love letter. Would you all like to hear her love letter? 'Dear Tony, I don't love Tom, I love you. . . .' "
3. It is important not to carry grudges against students for any length of time.
   Example: "No, you may not leave for the track meet ten minutes early. I remember how angry you were last week when I wanted you to finish your assignment and the terrible things you said to me. You can stay right here and work. Maybe next time you will think twice about speaking to me in that tone. I don't forget those things, you know."
4. A student's misconduct should not be viewed as a personal confrontation.
5. Students who misbehave should not be put in the hall or in front of the class since either of these experiences may be socially rewarding.
6. The full class should not be neglected while one disciplinary problem is handled. The teacher should try to develop methods to make it possible to deal with problems later, after class or in the hall while others are working. A crisis teacher program could be facilitated.
7. The teacher must learn names and pronounce them correctly.
8. The teacher must become familiar with permanent records.
   Example: The teacher should learn as much as possible about a misbehaving student before that individual arrives in class. This would include talking with previous teachers, mental health personnel, and social workers; inquiring what management techniques seem most effective; getting an idea what has been tried with the student; if possible, observe the pupil in the current setting. The teacher should explain clearly the standard of behavior expected of the student and define the rules of the classroom and the rewards of good behavior. It is important to be clear and concise when giving directions.
9. The teacher must be prepared.
10. It is very helpful to be alert to illnesses or emotional upsets, i.e., deaths, divorces.
11. The teacher must use or develop peripheral vision.
12. The teacher will find it advantageous to be polite.
    Example: "Thank you, class. I appreciate your being quiet while I was in the hall."

13. The teacher must move and not become glued to the desk.
    Example: The teacher can walk alongside the student, sit side by side, kneel by young pupils.
14. The teacher should develop body language and class management cues (Exhibit 2-2) and use them in class so all may read the cues. Many times students do not know how to read body language so they do not anticipate the teacher's attitude or warnings. Poor judgment of moods and attitudes of others is a social perception deficit in some students (Lerner, 1971).
15. The class can play a game in which some students teach others body language, informing the teacher and their peers of social cues.
16. Teachers should be themselves but also watch other teachers, modify what they do, and find what works with different types for different behaviors and with their own personality.
17. It is essential to avoid getting into a willpower struggle.
18. It is wise to consider allowing the student to choose behavioral alternatives before imposing punishment.
19. Alternative ways to work off punishment should be offered.
20. The teacher should send positive news home to parents regarding their students.

Three basic educational distortions that impede freedom of choice and contribute to teacher-student conflicts have been isolated by Fagen, Long, and Stevens (1975):

1. Externally controlled academic tasks are evident when the teacher defines the nature of the task without giving consideration to the learner's needs, interests, and abilities. For example: the teacher decides what is to be done, when, and by whom, without significant input from the student.
2. Restrictive competition for grades and recognition exists when the number of students receiving positive reinforcement is curtailed substantially. Praise, acclaim, encouragement, or affection are offered on a space-available basis (physical proximity of reinforcee!).
3. The focus should be on narrow academic products, tangible signs of productivity, the correct answer, and the material outcome.

Continuous teacher control, with specific expectations regarding both behavior and academic performance, casts the students into a role of dependency, helplessness, and frustration. Unless "beaten" into a role of submission, students inevitably will test the environment—home, school, or community—for limits to their own power and control. For example, a student who defies a teacher may be attempting to exercise a degree of control over a frustrating educational situation.

Exhibit 2-2 Body Cues and Their Meanings

Cue	Meaning
Arms folded across chest	Impatience
Heavy sighs	Tired
Hands on hips	Get to work
Close and open thumb and forefinger rapidly	"I know you have gum"
Motion to wastebasket	"Spit it out"
Point to wristwatch	"Time to go"
Drop head and raise eyebrow	"I am watching you and I'm not happy"
Point pencil	"Get to work"
Shake head slowly	"I wouldn't do that"
Lift eyebrow	"Are you doing what you're supposed to be doing?"
Stare at student	"That's enough"
Stop talking	Teacher's becoming irritated
Special handshake	"You are outstanding"
Wink at student	"Come on and do what I asked," or "I see you and we'll let it go this time"
Clearing of throat	"I'm tired of talking over your whispering," or "You have my attention, and I want you to quit your mischief"
Hug	"Thanks" "I like you"
Tap on desk	"May I have your attention?" "Stop it"
Drop hand at student's desk	"Pay attention"
Friendly pat on back	"Good try" "Now listen" "I like you" "Help me"
Pat shoulder	"I see you working" or "Keep trying"
Hand on student's shoulder	"Nice job," "I'm proud of you" (depends on atmosphere of moment and pressure exerted) or, "You are to behave right now."
Move student close to teacher's desk	"Don't make a scene. You misbehaved so I must put you near me where I have more control—away from your friends"

Teacher behaviors, curriculum experiences, and objectives should be used with a thorough knowledge of the disturbed student's individual affective needs. When an educational program is used with the entire class, some students will fail both academically and affectively and will feel less adequate and less independent.

Bloom's (1976) data, demonstrating a declining concept of self with cumulative years of unsuccessful school experience, are evidence of the relationship between unmet student needs and teaching-learning behaviors. Bloom cites as educational constraints the fact that (1) "school learning . . . is largely group learning," (2) "school learning is subject centered," and (3) "students are expected to learn from a set of materials and a teacher" (pp. 20-21).

Unfortunately, many classroom settings continue to represent external control models in which teachers possess the power to make all decisions for students— what they will learn and how. Indicative of this pattern is one study that revealed that elementary teachers spent more than 90 percent of their time evaluating, monitoring, lecturing, directing, and criticizing and less than 10 percent encouraging students, building on their ideas, and accepting their feelings (Rich, 1973). Under such circumstances, many students will not achieve the prescribed objectives or develop self-control or a positive self-concept.

TRUST AND RESPECT: POWER AND AUTHORITY

In the previous discussion the teacher occupied an authoritarian role:

> *Example:* Sit in your seats, stop talking.
> Turn to page 52.
> When you finish your work, I want you to sit quietly and wait until everyone is finished.
> I will tell you the answers when I see everyone is completed and is sitting quietly.
> You must all get this assignment so you can go to the next one.

In such cases, the students have no choice but to tolerate authority. Indeed, in many classrooms, dialogue would be perfectly acceptable, and most socially and academically achieving students would abide. But what happens to the norm violator, to the inquisitive, to the slow learner, to the rebellious? The norm violator hurries to finish and possibly misses many items in the rush to complete the assignment earlier than the others. The inquisitive student finishes rapidly and becomes restless because of the boring nature of the rigid class structure. The curious youth who needs attention and answers wants to know why they cannot work on something else and why it is necessary to sit while others work when this individual is done and wants to turn to something else. The slow learner is embarrassed for the task seems endless and classroom peers are angry because they must sit while that student completes the work.

If the situation allowed, the teacher could change the statements to:

> *Contrast Example:* We need to complete page 52.
> If you need help, let me know and we will work on it together.
> Anyone who finishes may work on something else at their seat or quietly go to the extra activity area and select an individual project such as tape and headphone, photograph album, science magazine, art and craft, model building, pet hamster, fish watching, and so on. O.K., let's get busy.

This second situation requires mutual trust and respect between teacher and class. It implies recognition of individual learning styles and includes the feelings of the students as people.

Teachers may build students' self-reliance and self-confidence by stressing the control they have over their activities. Teachers are there to lend a hand, respecting the students for what they can do and trusting that they are doing their best. The students, in turn, must respect peers' and teachers' need for order while others receive help. Peer tutoring would be practical in this situation, with those completing work early offering assistance to slower-paced students.

Conflicts between students and teachers often stem from whose needs are more important. There are at least four views of most classroom situations:

1. Many teachers believe they have no time to deal with disruptive students.
2. Students should do what they are told, when they are told to.
3. Teachers and students can work together with mutual concern and reasonableness when conflict can be resolved through satisfaction of mutual needs.
4. Students and teachers feel good about themselves and their relationship, which removes the necessity of constant manipulation and struggle for authority.

Rule #6: *Do make mutual respect the rule, not the exception, for classroom management.*

> *Example:* Beth and Diane are whispering while the teacher is presenting directions. The teacher may say, "Stop talking and get to work!" No response. "I said, stop talking or you'll both stay after school." No result except possibly dirty looks, words spoken under the students'

breath, and snickers from those seated nearby who could hear the insult. "That's it! Both of you stay after school 30 minutes!" Or, "I heard what you said. You apologize immediately or. . . ."

Contrast Example: "Diane, Beth—I cannot explain the assignment to the class because you are talking out loud. I'm frustrated because I will have to explain this all over again." Diane and Beth may respond with, "We had to talk. Beth has to know when I'll pick her up tonight to go to dance class. This is the only chance I'll have." At this point, the teacher has several choices: "Please wait until I finish my instruction to the class, then I will give you a brief time to exchange plans," or "You have three minutes to complete your conversation, then may I have my turn?" Smile, chuckle, or wait till after class and settle the problem in the hall.

The objective is to find a solution that can provide mutual respect. There are times when the teacher must control but proper handling of absolute control can increase mutual understanding between students and teachers. The teacher has the right to acknowledge objectives or intentions, but students also have that right. They are not the majority to be ruled by the minority in a democratic society. When a teacher's needs are always the first satisfied, such a solution surely is a poor one and breeds aggression by placing the students in a defensive position.

Rule #7: *Do give the students opportunities to experience decision making and outcomes.*

Such a give-and-take allows the students to make decisions. If teachers are always authoritarian, there is no room for students to make choices and all their decisions are made for them. Self-discipline and inner control are not easy to learn or teach. Students must be permitted to make decisions and suffer or enjoy the consequences.

Rule #8: *Do consciously plan decision-making opportunities and build them into the curriculum so students can accept responsibility for their own behavior.*

Example: "Beth and Diane, you may go out into the hall and discuss your plans for tonight in getting to dance class, but realize you will miss the assignment and instructions on how to complete the work correctly. If you think you already know, fine. On the other hand, consider . . . it is your choice."

Before making this alternative available, the teacher will need to know whether the girls are concerned about grades and whether failing to know the assignment will be punishing to them so they will wish they had decided to pay attention. If they are not concerned about class accomplishment, then such an alternative would be meaningless. The teacher must know the students' views of the situation. Another example of students', instead of the teacher, being permitted to make the decision is to have them enforce the request.

> *Example:* "David, as editor of the school newspaper, you will be requested to appear before the school board and defend the slanderous column. You'd better be certain what you printed was factual." When the paper was published, the school board was very disturbed by the article. David was called before the student government committee and school board. His peers questioned him and discovered he did not have facts and that slanted statements had been printed. He was told to print an apology and resign as editor.

Teachers are given authority over students and are responsible for rewarding and punishing. Some students respond to authoritarian teachers. These often are self-motivated, self-controlled, excited by the challenge of learning, and are intrinsically rewarded by doing a good job. They have background experiences in making good decisions. Others do not have a successful background in decision making and need planned experiences in the class. Still others respond to authoritarian teachers with defensive, aggressive, and rebellious behaviors. They often will not do what they are told by authoritarian figures. More often than not, the teacher did not offer special consideration or change techniques.

Rule #9: *Do be aware there is a critical difference between classroom control and authoritarian controlling of a student or group of them.*

The development of mutual trust and respect is a cornerstone underlying meaningful learning. It can replace authority with reciprocal concern. The teacher, as an adult, is in position to accept the primary responsibility of exemplifying respect and trust as well as the development of self-control.

> *Authoritarian Example:* "You have three minutes to go to the water fountain. If you are not back, I'll come to check on you."

> *Reciprocal Example:* "Yes, you may get a drink. Please do me a favor and return straight to your room with no confusion."

In the reciprocal request, the teacher will not peek into the hall or follow the students. When they return, the teacher will praise and thank them for their promptness. The teacher may talk to the students about trust and respect, giving examples and explaining that when people can be trusted, they are allowed to do things that others who cannot be trusted are not allowed to do.

> *Example:* ''When you say you are going to the water fountain and you go there, I learn to believe you and respect you for doing what you say you will. I can count on you. The more times you show me you are honest, the more trust I have in you, and you will earn additional privileges. Some people fail to learn self-control or develop willpower; they do not do what they say they will. You do what is proper and respect others. I think highly of you for displaying control of yourself. I respect you. You are good citizens and the school is proud of you.''

The crux of this technique is the teacher's verbal acknowledgment that respect exists. On the other hand, if other students observe that when the teacher trusts a student, that individual is allowed privileges that are rewarding, i.e., a few minutes longer at recess, the chance to referee a ball game, extra chocolate milk at lunch, passing out papers, listening to the radio during free time, going to other rooms to visit, feeding class pets, winning a free pass to a theater, etc., then earning respect, trust, and honesty will take on value.

The following example represents a personal discussion with a class in an effort to develop a meaningful atmosphere of mutual trust and respect.

> *Example:* ''I brought my new 'Foreigner' album to school for all of you to enjoy because I know I can trust you to be careful with it. If we are careful with this one album, I will bring others, and so can each of you. First, you must prove to me that each of you will be responsible through it and care for others' property.''

> *Authoritarian Example:* ''Do not touch this record. I do not want it broken. If I catch anyone playing with my record, that student will be sent straight to the office. Do you understand now? Leave it alone!''

In the latter example, the students are deprived of the opportunity to handle others' property with care and caution. Ideally, the teacher should instruct students how to handle records correctly. In such a case, they would experience a real-life situation: how to take care of records and respect others' property. That could be changed slightly to put the responsibility for the care of the record, or other items—i.e., plants, tape player, Christmas ornament—on one student. The teacher thus demonstrates trust that the student will take good care of an item, establishes a peer model, and creates a reward that many in the class would desire. Such situations require planning and foresight. The teacher must value students' decision-making experiences, their values, and their judgments, even when they are wrong. To correct a wrong, it should be proved to be faulty and should not be overridden in authoritarian fashion.

CLASS CLIMATE

Rule #10: *Do create a climate of meaningfulness.*

The author views mankind and the nature of man as holistic and humanistic. Each individual student possesses goodness and worth, is unique, and has dignity. There are certain needs this person attempts to fulfill (Maslow, 1960):

1. the need for love, acceptance, and belonging
2. the need for competence and interacting effectively and creatively with the environment
3. the need for self-esteem and self-identity
4. the need for a sense of purposefulness and responsibility.

In the process of educating students, teachers must deal with the whole person and must not separate cognition from needs of belonging and identity. The variety of students' affective needs may be reduced to two concerns: (1) their positive feelings about themselves and (2) a degree of control over their environment. If learning is to be meaningful, it must be related to individuals' concerns, meet their social and personal needs, and promote interaction with their environment.

> *Example:* A student instructed to diagram sentences from a workbook might see no pertinence in such a task compared to writing a paragraph or sentence about a personal snapshot, then analyzing the parts of speech used; or, studying the materials used in a hornet's nest that the learner or a classmate brought to school versus reading about the life style of nomads because it is the next chapter in the workbook.

Even adults respond to requests of authorities readily and usually willingly when the task appears to be meaningful to them personally. Certainly, meaningfulness is important to youngsters who may have difficulty understanding long-term reinforcements of successful memory exercises, rote learning, and busywork.

Perhaps the teacher would respond by making gentle requests and meaningful assumptions to students with, "Jason should learn to do the tasks assigned. A teacher should not have to justify assignments, rules, or policy to a class."

Johnson and Bany (1970) provided a list of student behaviors symptomatic of group norms associated with negative or meaningless classroom environments:

A hostile, aggressive classroom group is one that subtly defies the teacher and often disrupts instructional activities:
1. There is murmuring, talking, and lack of attention throughout the group when tasks are assigned.
2. Constant disruptions interfere with carrying out academic tasks.
3. Defiance, united resistance, and group solidarity are evident.
4. Students do not conform to generally accepted school policies.
5. There is solidarity in class resistance to teachers' efforts.

A class may be dissatisfied with conditions in the room and frustrated because of pressure stemming from inappropriate teacher control techniques:
1. The group applauds disruptive behavior.
2. It approves defiant acts.
3. It sometimes reacts with imitative behavior.
4. It promotes fights between individuals.
5. It shows apathetic attitudes toward academic tasks.
6. It is indifferent about completing tasks.
7. It exhibits little problem behavior in the classroom but is aggressive and always in trouble on the playground.
8. Its members are well behaved when the teacher is present but unruly and aggressive when the teacher is away.
9. The students make little attempt to be a group.

An insecure, dependent class has not developed a good functioning group:
1. Students are easily distracted when an outsider enters the room.
2. They cannot adjust to routine.
3. They are easily upset by rumors.
4. They are upset by changes in the weather.
5. They may resent newcomers.

Given this unique nature of group norms and teacher-group relationships, a number of teacher role behaviors seem to be prerequisites to the establishment of a positive climate. Smith, Neisworth, and Greer (1978) identified five teacher characteristics as essential to a positive learning climate:

1. showing a positive attitude
2. presenting a planned instructional approach
3. having the ability to be flexible
4. maintaining consistency
5. showing understanding

Each of these is directly related to the establishment of an appropriate learning climate. A positive attitude is necessary to project an attitude of optimism regarding students' academic accomplishments. A planned instructional approach is required if the teacher is to enable the students to learn academic material. Flexibility in expectations and behavior is needed if students are to be considered individuals and not stereotypes. Consistency is necessary if students are to accurately identify and predict the important rules of the classroom. Understanding between human beings, i.e., empathy, concern, or appreciation, goes a long way in promoting a positive classroom environment.

How a teacher teaches is vital. Teaching behaviors that enhance achievement tend to reduce deviant behaviors, and vice versa. Teaching behaviors that do not promote achievement, positive attitudes, or student involvement are linked with higher rates of deviant behavior (Coker, Medley, & Soar, 1980).

Teachers respond differently toward different students. When such variations exist, teacher response may account for a great deal of the success or failure of individual students. Teachers translate varying expectations into instructional differences (Brophy & Good, 1974). Sadly, the disturbed students most often constitute lows in the following list of teachers' instructional expectations. Teachers tend to:

1. Wait less time for *lows* to answer.
2. Fail to stay with *lows* in failure situations. Teachers give *lows* answers or go to other students.
3. Reward inappropriate behavior of *lows*. Teachers sometimes praise incorrect response.
4. Criticize *lows* more frequently when they give wrong answer.
5. Praise *lows* less frequently. When *lows* give correct response, they are less likely to be praised.
6. Pay less attention to *lows*. Teachers attend more to highs, i.e., more social praise.
7. Call on *lows* less frequently.
8. Allow secondary classroom highs to become more dominant.
9. Seat *lows* away from teacher.
10. Demand less from *lows*, i.e., give easier test or not request student to do work. (Brophy & Good, 1974, pp. 330-333)

Knowledge of Individual Students

Matching the appropriate management technique with individual students requires teachers to be aware of academic, psychological (if available), and physical characteristics.

Example: A student who is impulsive and repeatedly gives incorrect answers requires different management than others with low self-concept. The impulsive student might be encouraged to wait 30 seconds and ponder the answer, while the learner with low self-concept would be reinforced for eagerly participating.

Example: Students who lack verbal skills may be more receptive to physical pats on back and smiles than to verbal reinforcement.

"Learner's Leeway" is the belief that students perform in accordance with individual characteristics.

Example: All students will not complete a math assignment at the same time and with the same accuracy.

The teacher therefore should expect individual differences and provide leeway. Students thus do not reach the developmental milestones at the same time or at the same rate.

Example: Boys are generally more motor-active than girls. Coordination, lying, tattling, and grooming are behaviors that may reflect a developmental stage.

When interfering behaviors are developmental in nature, then maturation is the most effective intervention technique. If a student came to class with a broken arm, evidenced by a cast, the teacher would not say, "He could write if he wanted to."

The Focus on Specific Behavior

Some students may engage in a series of disruptive behaviors on occasion.

Example: A student may arrive late, slam the door, engage a classmate in conversation, stumble over the wastebasket, drop a book, and finally be seated rather loudly and clumsily. The teacher may use a similar series of verbal managements: "You're late . . . don't slam the door . . . no talking . . . watch where you're walking . . . pick up that book . . . sit quietly, please!"

The teacher's attempted management is ineffective for a number of reasons but mainly because of the effort to control every deviant behavior within a few seconds. The teacher's effectiveness might have been increased if a single behavior had been selected. In this case, being on time should have been the focus because the subsequent behaviors would have been unimportant if the class had not started.

Development of a Variety of Techniques

Sending students to the principal, raising the voice, telling learners to sit down or be quiet, and giving them the "evil eye" are techniques used in most classes. Students usually know when, where, how, and with whom teachers will intervene.

Success with a behavior management strategy does not imply that it will continue to produce the same results because changes occur in students, activities and the environment, making it necessary to develop other management techniques.

When the Student Is Being Good

Disruptive behaviors have a distracting quality that creates negative teacher attention and intervention. Such responses provide attention for the deviant, whereas students whose behavior is appropriate—those who are sitting still, completing their work, and remaining quiet—serve a more positive function. Students who are disruptive for attention can learn that deviations are punished and appropriate behavior is rewarded.

> *Example:* Even though out of the seat 40 minutes in an hour, there are 20 minutes an hour in which the student is demonstrating in-seat behavior. For every examination, homework assignment, or project, disruptive students have performed something correctly: completing one problem, writing their names on the paper, or turning a paper in to the teacher.

Such performances should not go unnoticed. The teacher should catch the students being good and reward them.

Positive Removal of Disrupters

There are times when students lose control and become a threat to themselves or others. The removal of a student from class should be made as positive as possible by avoiding the purely punitive aspect of exclusion. The teacher's interpretation of the isolation process can be a positive management technique.

> *Example:* The teacher could verbally interpret the action as a helping action: "I'm sending you to the hall because the way you are acting, you

are going to get into trouble. I don't want you to get into trouble. When you can handle the situation, come back." or, "People are trying to learn in here and you won't let them, so I'm sending you outside. When you think you can help people to learn, I'd like to have you back in the classroom."

The teacher's message conveys the need to help, not punish. Consequently, the student's reentry into the classroom is based on behaviors or expectations that promote a positive relationship.

Maintenance of Communication

Students often retreat into a solitary world, not communicating with either peers or teachers. Attempts to identify the problem or find a solution are negated by the fact that they are nonverbal and nonresponsive.

Even though the teacher may not be able to deal directly with the issue, it is necessary to maintain contact by involving the students in an area or activity that is psychologically safe. At a later time, when communication has been reestablished, the teacher may elect to deal with the original crisis.

> *Example:* A student accused of theft, cheating, or related behaviors may choose this regressive course of action as the least painful, particularly if the individual lacks the skills necessary for adequate self-protection.

Maintaining communication requires that the teacher involve the students in conversation completely unrelated to the situation that motivated the crisis.

> *Example:* The teacher should find a psychologically comfortable area in which the student can relax the defenses and engage in appropriate behavior. If the crisis involves peers, then the teacher may want to provide the student a solitary learning responsibility; if the teacher was the source of the crisis, then peer group activities may be more appropriate; or if stealing or cheating was the accusation, then communication involving baseball, dancing, or hobbies may be areas of renewed communication.

Attention to Feelings

The listening technique requires two basic ingredients: interest and time. On the simplest level, listening to feelings is being physically available to a student at a time when the individual needs to vent emotions that are about to explode.

Example: The teacher, by sitting close, leaning forward, providing eye-to-eye contact, and showing understanding by nodding or smiling, can provide the body language necessary to convey a personal interest in the student.

The passive listening technique does not approve or condemn the circumstances that precipitated the feelings but does indicate teacher interest in the student's problem. Many students are comforted by the fact that a sympathetic ear is available and that they do not have to deal with their feelings all alone.

Response to Feelings

An interpersonal management strategy goes beyond passive listening and adds the dimension of teacher response. The teacher becomes an active listener, accurately interpreting the meaning of the message sent by the student and responding in a way that reflects the latter's feelings.

Example: A student who has failed an exam may feel inadequate unless the teacher projects the failure by saying, "You said this part of the book wouldn't be required on the exam." Similarly, a student who feels threatened by a peer may want protection but says, "I don't feel well today; I don't want to go out to recess."

Teacher responses to feelings should reflect the feelings, not the overt message.

Example: Teacher responses should be: "You're saying that it hurts when you don't do well on a test," "Everyone needs someone to help us when we are afraid," or "It really hurts when we are ignored."

These examples are based on the teacher's knowledge of the student, an empathetic understanding of the problem, and a desire to help.

Contrast Example: "I specifically said that the entire unit would be on the exam," "You weren't ill five minutes ago," and "Then why did you try out for the squad?"

Effective responding techniques can reduce the probability of deviant behavior by demonstrating teacher understanding of the student's personal crisis. Strong feelings and emotions that are not reduced but rather are increased by responses that condemn, question, or emphasize the negative can explode into crises that consume extraordinary amounts of time and energy.

Closeness Control

Many students, both elementary and secondary, need the physical presence of an adult to aid them in controlling impulsive, anxious feelings and emotions. After interfering behaviors are evidenced, movement of the teacher toward the student is associated with reduced deviance. The student must interpret that movement as concern and reassurance, not preparation for punishment. Teacher movement often does little more than remind students that they are off-task, which is sufficient to reduce deviance in many situations. Classroom movement, or closeness control, can be used to reduce the frequency of interfering teacher intervention.

Hurdle Help

The hurdle technique requires individual tutoring to help a student overcome an academic roadblock. This individual help can be a preventive strategy when students need minimal information to get them functioning appropriately.

> *Example:* Instead of asking for help and exposing himself to the teacher's wrath for not paying attention, Jason establishes contact with neighbors, finds some interesting trinket in his pocket, or draws on his desk. Providing directions or explanations gets the student back on task, eliminating the deviant behavior.

Teacher Interest

The lack of motivation is accompanied by nonperformance, followed by boredom or restlessness. In the latter stage, students begin to engage in behaviors that disrupt the classroom.

> *Example:* The teacher should demonstrate interest in the student's assignment or performance. "That's an important assignment you're doing," "You have a difficult assignment, but I'm sure you can do it," can motivate the student.

Dealing with the Present

> *Example:* The teacher makes statements such as, "This is the third time you've been late," "You did the same thing last week," or "How many times have I had to tell you?"

These are direct signals to the student that the teacher will continue to use past behaviors to evaluate current performance. As problems occur, they should be dealt with in the here and now, without bringing past problems into the discussion.

Management for Learning

Teacher intervention into the personal realm is viewed with skepticism by many students.

> *Example:* "Did you wash your hands?" "Did you comb your hair?" "Did you slam the locker?" "Did you lie?"

Strategies that attempt to change personal behaviors only compound the management problems.

Prevention Rather Than Management

Most teachers know in what situations and under what circumstances a student becomes a management problem. It seems pointless to subject a student to a condition that will cause the learner to get into difficulty and require the teacher to manage the behavior. The teacher can prevent the problem by moving to the student, providing an interesting activity, restructuring the environment, or utilizing other techniques suggested in this chapter. Once a deviant behavior has developed, the energy and resources necessary to intervene effectively are much greater than those needed to prevent the conduct.

WHEN TO MANAGE

Where some teachers encourage student movement, verbalization, and exploration, others manage the same behaviors. Management is conducted by human teachers with human feelings and will always reflect a degree of idiosyncratic behavior. Management should not be totally dependent upon teachers' personal or spontaneous whims. To provide some consistency among teachers, Long and Newman (1961) presented a set of criteria to guide them in knowing when to manage behavior:

1. Reality dangers: students playing with matches or throwing dangerous objects
2. Psychological protection: scapegoating or making derogatory racial or ethnic comments
3. Protection against too much excitement: losing control or feeling very unhappy

4. Protection of property: carving on desks or tearing clothing
5. Protection of a continuing program: yelling or being obnoxious
6. Protection against negative contagion: causing tension or spreading gossip
7. Highlighting of an area of school policy: teachers explaining why it is not possible for everyone to be first in line, or how poor communication creates misunderstandings
8. Avoidance of conflict with the outside world: disrupting a school assembly or littering on a class trip
9. Protection of a teacher's inner comfort: cursing or talking back. In many cases the teacher may have to learn to be more comfortable with the behavior rather than to manage it.

Emphasis on Natural Consequences

Failing grades, suspension, and even corporal punishment are common consequences that are administered for students' failure to respond appropriately to classroom rules and teacher expectations. These are not natural consequences but are forms of punishment that may occur only in school-related environments. Many students do not understand the relationship between their behaviors and these consequences.

Greater emphasis on life situations and adjustment, particularly for older students, is more meaningful since they may perceive school as an irrelevant obstacle in the path to adulthood. The motivation to perform more effectively will be increased for those students who understand that adult success is based at best in part on correct behavior but is not necessarily related to teacher expectations.

Undesirable natural consequences are negative experiences that occur logically and functionally as a result of behavior.

> *Example:* A failing grade is not a natural consequence if a student does not study. The natural consequence is that the student will not learn the information necessary for a vocation. Physical fights can hurt, the inability to get along with peers can cause loneliness, and resentment of authority can lead to limited job opportunities.

Planned Ignoring of Behavior

Teachers must be careful in the use of planned ignoring. Before employing this technique, they must be certain that (1) the behavior is one that can be ignored, (2) that the teacher (not the peer group) is the reinforcer, and (3) that nonreinforcement will produce the desired change. This technique does have the advantages of being unobtrusive, limiting contagion, and permitting the teacher to remain with the instructional activities.

Intervention Signals

A variety of body postures, hand movements, and facial expressions are used routinely to convey approval and disapproval of student behavior.

> *Example:* Smiles, winks, and a pat on the back convey approval; frowns, throat clearing, and finger snapping are used to deter behavior.

Signals can be effective during the initial stage of deviance; their usefulness is limited after deviance has moved into advanced stages of behavior and emotions.

If signal intervention is to remain a relevant technique, creative uses must be developed. Special, individualized signals can be designed to communicate with selected students.

> *Example:* Tugging the ear, touching the nose, or pulling out a handkerchief contain clues.

Entire classrooms also can participate in the development of signals whereby students become managers of deviant behaviors.

> *Example:* The class may decide to use the ''peace sign'' if the noise in the classroom becomes so loud that it is distracting. Any student or the teacher could raise the peace sign, which, when observed, every individual in the class would imitate until the room was quiet.

Removal of Temptations

Most students can handle the variety of stimuli that bombards the classroom. Some students who are hyperactive, brain-damaged, or impulsive have difficulty separating relevant from irrelevant stimuli.

> *Example:* The globe may be more attractive than the math assignment, the baseball on the teacher's desk may be more enticing than the reading assignment, or the student's new lunchbox may be more visually alluring than the spelling words.

The teacher should remove the temptation, placing the globe, the ball, or the lunchbox out of sight. Observation may reveal that some students are more inclined to be distracted by specific objects. In such situations, the removal of temptation would help the students focus attention on the lesson and reduce task avoidance behavior.

Alteration of Instructional Methods

Students often are satiated with a repetitive task or a routine instructional method.

> *Example:* Answering every question box in a textbook, completing a specified number of math problems each day, and the teacher's limiting the instructional method to lecturing or reading can make the day boring.

Intervention is the teacher's willingness to alter the instructional methods and/or requirements.

> *Example:* Using a blend of verbal and written responses, devising a math program that emphasizes utilization rather than paper-and-pencil practice, organizing exploratory discussion sessions as a substitute for lecturing are types of differing teacher interventions.

Routine Structure

Structure, at least initially, is a preferable management strategy when students need the security of predictability. A stringent schedule of sequential activities accompanied by teacher consistency and punctuality, as well as permanent resources, may reduce student apprehension and thus reduce deviant behavior.

Students who have failed to develop basic trust in themselves, others, or their environment are psychologically threatened by confusion, spontaneity, and unstructured situations. When the classroom setting is unpredictable, these students express their fear and anxiety through withdrawal, hyperactivity, crying, and other behaviors that interfere with their learning.

> *Example:* Students can be affected adversely when teachers change their minds or make exceptions to selected rules or behaviors, when free-time activities or active games are introduced, or when the class schedule is interrupted by announcements, special events, or even a substitute teacher.

Rule Reminders

A rule reminder is a minimal management technique designed to prevent deviance or a need for more dramatic intervention. A teacher should be aware that escalation of confusion may eventually erupt into behaviors that will require direct management. Before that point, the teacher should remind the group or individual students of the rules lest they be violated.

> *Example:* "Remember, you must remain in your seat," or "The rule is 'keep your hands to yourself,' " should be announced as reminders before such violations can occur.

Signal interference or closeness control may serve the same function as a verbal reminder.

Teachers should routinely remind students of important classroom rules even when they are on-task and such violations are not anticipated. These reminders reinforce classroom behavior, provide predictable structure, and convey the message that rules are important.

SOCIAL REINFORCEMENT

Interpersonal interactions can be used to increase the strength of a behavior. Social reinforcement is one of the easiest and most convenient procedures for influencing a youth's behavior.

> *Example:* Pats, praise, attention, and smiles are social reinforcers when they result in an increase in acceptable behavior.

Social reinforcements can be administered immediately following a desirable response without costly commodities or equipment. Social reinforcers can be delivered by a number of individuals in a range of settings. Their influence on behavior is not likely to be specific to one situation. The social reinforcement of one youth's behavior is likely to have a positive influence on other individuals (modeling) who are observing the reinforcing interaction.

Social reinforcement is limited in that some behaviorally disordered students may not be motivated by social interactions.

> *Example:* Those whose learning histories are characterized by frequent punitive interactions with others may not react to social reinforcement.

Less natural reinforcing events (e.g., tokens, money, food items, free time, movie passes, etc.) may be paired with social approbation until the reinforcement value of praise is developed. The social reinforcement may occur inadvertently as a consequence of disruptive behavior (e.g., attending to aggressive outbursts). To avoid this, practitioners should be aware of the impact of their interpersonal interactions on the occurrence of adaptive and disruptive behaviors.

Example: Jan, a 12-year-old withdrawn student, seldom combed her hair, brushed her teeth, or completed other personal hygiene activities. Reports indicated that she was highly motivated by praise from adults. Therefore, teachers agreed to initiate social reinforcement for her independent completion of personal care responsibilitities. Each time staff members passed her, they were encouraged to identify one aspect of her personal hygiene that was appropriate. They then would identify the skill (process behavior) and refer to the effect of utilizing the skill on her appearance. For example: "You brushed your teeth this morning, Jan. Your teeth sparkle when you smile."

Social reinforcement can be used easily with other procedures. Approximations of a desired terminal behavior (shaping) can be socially reinforced, as can the structured practice of a desired behavior (behavior rehearsal). Finally, successively low rates of a disruptive behavior or incompatible behaviors can be socially reinforced. The teacher should:

1. define target behaviors
2. follow every occurrence of a developing new behavior with social reinforcement; as the behavior becomes consistent, reduce social reinforcement.
3. state the behavior likely to result in social reinforcement, using the youth's name when possible
4. label process and product behaviors verbally; for example: "John, I like the way you wrote your name (process). It is easy to read (product)."
5. deliver social reinforcers enthusiastically
6. pair any use of unnatural incentives with social praise, thus developing their reinforcement value
7. avoid socially reinforcing maladaptive responses
8. encourage significant others to socially reinforce the desired behavior(s) in a range of settings.

Shaping

Shaping is the reinforcement of successive approximations of a desired behavior. The primary advantage of the shaping procedure is that positive behaviors are developed gradually. The shaping procedure involves:

1. reinforcing any response that resembles or approximates the desired response
2. reinforcing a slightly closer approximation of the expected behavior, once the initial response occurs consistently, while withdrawing reinforcement from the more primitive response

3. reinforcing a third, more appropriate approximation when the second behavior occurs consistently while withdrawing reinforcement from the previous response, and so on until the terminal behavior is achieved consistently; the teacher can decide size of the interval between approximations.

Modeling

Modeling involves arranging conditions in the environment so that an individual learns new behaviors or strengthens existing ones through observing another person. The environment should be arranged so that the maximum benefit of observational learning occurs. Modeling can be used in three distinct ways:

1. to teach new responses not in the youth's repertoire (e.g., a pupil learns to stand in line patiently by observing a friend waiting patiently)
2. to inhibit or reduce a response already learned (e.g., after observing another person lose television privileges for hitting, an individual's own hitting decreases)
3. to increase the strength of a previously learned response (e.g., a student begins dieting after observing a friend lose weight through diet).

Example: Jason was a 15-year-old adolescent new to the school. While he was seldom physically aggressive, his first response to any frustrating event was a verbally aggressive statement to peers. Observations of Jason at school indicated that he frequently behaved in a manner consistent with significant peers on the unit. The teaching staff described him as being a follower of the older students. Jason's file revealed that he frequently had been exposed to verbal abuse at home. His records indicated that his parents and siblings were verbally aggressive in their interactions with school and community mental health personnel.

A modeling program was chosen because it seemed that Jason's aggressive verbalizations had been developed and maintained through his observations of others (e.g., siblings, parents, and peers). It was speculated that if Jason had an opportunity to observe more appropriate verbal models, his aggressive verbal behavior might decrease and a socially appropriate one would be substituted.

The school staff members agreed that when another youth made a socially appropriate statement in Jason's presence, they would socially reinforce the individual and restate the appropriate phrase. When Jason made a similar statement, they would socially reinforce him for restating the appropriate verbal statement. Disruptive verbalizations were to be ignored. For example, an individual bumped into a staff member standing next to Jason. The youngster said, "Excuse me, Mr. Miller." Mr. Miller said, "I like the way you said excuse me. That was polite." Thereafter, Jason said "Morning" to Mr. Miller. Mr. Miller responded by saying, "Morning. That sure is a pleasant greeting, Jason."

A youth learns to be aggressive by observing others as they are reinforced for aggressive behavior. Conversely, a student acquires assertive skills by observing others as they gain satisfaction from socially skillful interactions. Both prosocial and disruptive behaviors can be learned through modeling. Regardless of whether or not highly structured modeling programs are initiated, staff members must be concerned with structuring school environments so that problem students watch others obtain satisfaction through socially acceptable behavior while they see disruptive behavior produce unsatisfying consequences. Teachers should:

1. specify the behaviors to be imitated through modeling
2. arrange situations so that the student is likely to observe peers engage in the specified behaviors
3. label target behaviors verbally, using the person's name, when another peer engages in the desired conduct: "You're on time today, Mary!"
4. label the behavior verbally, using the youth's name, when the student engages in an approximation of the conduct: "You were on time, too, Randy."
5. expose the youth to a variety of models and settings to increase the likelihood that the behavior change will carry over to other situations
6. use high status models, older, same sex, when possible, because they will have a stronger influence on the student's behavior
7. avoid situations in which the student sees maladaptive behavior produce satisfying consequences
8. be aware that youths who are easily influenced are more likely to learn through observation.

Counterconditioning

The teacher should encourage a behavior that is in contrast with the acting-out conduct.

Example: The student who is busy working a crossword puzzle cannot fight with a neighbor. A member of the drama team has less time to act-out.

These students are receiving appropriate attention at such times, so the need for inappropriate attention is unnecessary.

Positive Reinforcement

B.F. Skinner (1953) proposed a theory of operant conditioning, stating that behavior is learned through reinforcement. A person who does something and then is rewarded immediately probably will act the same way more often.

> *Example:* A student who speaks in class and is praised probably will increase talking. If students are not reinforced for talking, even when their answers are not entirely correct, discussion periods will not be a rewarding experience.

Six basic steps to follow when applying positive reinforcement provide that the teacher:

1. determine specifically the behavior to be changed
2. obtain a baseline as to how often a student displays adaptive or undesirable behavior so that improvement or decline can be measured
3. arrange the situation so desirable behavior will occur
4. identify reinforcers and determine what is rewarding for a child; most teachers give praise as reinforcement but not all students respond appropriately; teachers may use more concrete reinforcers such as listening to music, working on a project, operating audiovisual equipment, or receiving a privilege; token reinforcement programs can be used where students earn chips to exchange for rewards such as candy, break periods, and money
5. give rewards immediately after an appropriate behavior and provide reinforcement after every desired action until it is a well-established habit; if a behavior is reinforced too consistently, the reinforcer may lose appeal—for example, a hungry person who buys ice cream and eats it will find it pleasurable but after eating nine cones, a tenth one would not be rewarding because the student would be satisfied and sick of ice cream so it would lose its initial reinforcing power through overuse
6. maintain cumulative records to determine whether response strength or frequency has increased.

Behavior Modification

This alternative is one of the newest, yet oldest, methods used to control students, i.e., the Premack Principle (1959), or "Grandmother's Rule," "After you eat your spinach, you can go to the movies." Getting people to do what is wanted of them is a traditional method of controlling their behavior. For behavior modification to be effective, the implementer must make the desired consequences dependent on acceptable conduct. To know what to do, to increase, maintain, or eliminate behavior, the teacher must be aware of and alert to the student's needs and what constitute that youth's reinforcing activities, materials, or foods.

A teacher must pinpoint target behaviors, note undesirable ones, select reinforcers and consequences, evaluate and generalize new conduct to other settings, and teach a behavior to take the place of the one eliminated. Such a program can be very time consuming, and many teachers lack college training in behavior modification. Teachers must be sure students know they are receiving rewards for appropriate behaviors. Rewards must be chosen carefully and must be more satisfying than peer group pressure to misbehave.

Opponents of behavior modification maintain there is (1) little concern about what caused the deviant behavior and (2) much emphasis on trivial, material rewards and little development of intrinsic reward, i.e., the internal feeling of a job well done, internal pride, and internal control. Internal control is traded for extrinsic rewards. Critics say payoffs are substituted for reasoning, and the outcome is immediate reinforcement instead of long-range effects. They further maintain that a system of rewards produced only by behavior modification methods of control is no better than controlling with punishment alone.

Good teaching practices and various techniques to deal with misconduct should be considered. Teachers can be trained to eliminate variables contributing to acting out in the classroom, as was accomplished in California in the Mayer and Butterworth (1981) experimental program (see Chapter 1).

Parent Involvement

Some school administrators consider parental involvement a most effective means of dealing with disciplinary problems. Fifty percent of the administrators authorized to use corporal punishment do so reluctantly and, instead, search for alternatives (Mayer & Butterworth, 1981). Many schools now insist teachers assume an active role in classroom management, no longer putting the principal in the role of punisher. Yet half of these same administrators responded that they themselves did not provide inservice training in classroom or behavioral management.

Student Ideas

Some schools request ideas from students to curb behavioral problems. Among the more common are: peer counseling, student government, and youth counseling that open doors to a broader representation of the study body, and videotapes on risks of alcohol and drug abuse. Schools also use such varying tactics as changes in student schedules, permitting attendance in another class or school, allowing the youths to work at a job in the community during school hours, or permitting special assignments, i.e., riding with the police, observing court proceedings, or spending a day visiting a hospital. Individualized attention, personalized programs, and counseling in settings other than schools are alternatives created to combat discipline problems.

Conversely, students can help teachers make sure their conduct and presentations are clear and meet class needs by filling out school-prepared questionnaires such as that in Exhibit 2-3.

Positive Discipline

The American school system was founded on an authoritarian model and continues to be supported on that basis (Cremin, 1964). In 1840, the principal of the Chauncey Hall School in Boston required boys to be punctual, scrape their shoes on a scraper, sit erect, stand when speaking, and carry books in a satchel; the school also prohibited borrowing or lending, climbing, carrying a pen over one ear, spitting on the floor, or leaving seats without permission. During the nineteenth century, a girl was forced to wear a necklace of sharp Jamestown weed burrs strung on tape for permitting her head to fall forward. When tasks were not completed, a morocco spider belted to a student's shoulders was used at a girls' school of Mrs. Elizabeth Way. Schools in the United States still take an authoritarian and punitive approach to discipline (see Chapter 1). Synonyms for discipline are: punishment, spanking, pain, and retribution. All are negative and unfortunately are related to education.

There are positive aspects to discipline. Scholars, doctors, athletes, and teachers all practice positive discipline—self-control. Questions such as, ''What do I do when Susan sasses?'' or ''What should I do when Jacob hits?'' reflect the teacher's quandary in dealing with difficult students and management problems. The question, ''What will I do to Jacob when he hits?'' or ''How will I punish him when he punches?'' can be changed to positive approaches to discipline. The question then becomes: ''What alternatives can I teach Jacob to replace his hitting behaviors?'' ''How can I help him express anger, frustration, or hostility, or redirect mischievous play in a more acceptable manner?'' ''What would please him as a reward when he is good?'' ''If I enhance his self-concept, make him feel better about himself, will he behave more appropriately?''

To increase positive discipline in a classroom, the teacher must believe in each student's possessing potential goodness, competence, and responsibility. Self-regulation, problem solving, and individually initiated learning are classroom goals in a positive orientated environment.

John Dewey, as well as other progressives, believed the democratic commitment of schooling was to help the young be self-directed. According to Dewey

Exhibit 2-3 The Clear Teacher Checklist

As your teacher I hope I am clear. In order to improve my ability to be clear I need your help. Below are 28 statements that describe what clear teachers do. Read each statement and place a checkmark in the column that tells how often I perform the behavior that is described. In that way I'll know what I do well and what I need to improve.

(Put a check √ in one box after each statement.)

As our teacher, you:

	All of the time	Most of the time	Some of the time	Never	Doesn't apply to our class
1. Explain things simply.					
2. Give explanations we understand.					
3. Teach at a pace that is not too fast and not too slow.					
4. Stay with a topic until we understand.					
5. Try to find out when we don't understand and then you repeat things.					
6. Teach things step by step.					
7. Describe the work to be done and how to do it.					
8. Ask if we know what to do and how to do it.					
9. Repeat things when we don't understand.					
10. Explain something and then work an example.					
11. Explain something and then stop so we can ask questions.					
12. Prepare us for what we will be doing next.					
13. Give specific details when teaching.					
14. Repeat things that are hard to understand.					
15. Work examples and explain them.					
16. Give us a chance to think about what's being taught.					
17. Explain something and then stop so we can think about it.					
18. Show us how to do the work.					
19. Explain the assignment and the materials we need to do it.					
20. Stress difficult points.					

Exhibit 2-3 continued

	All of the time	Most of the time	Some of the time	Never	Doesn't apply to our class
21. Show examples of how to do classwork and homework.					
22. Give us enough time for practice.					
23. Answer our questions.					
24. Ask questions to find out if we understand.					
25. Go over difficult homework problems.					
26. Show us how to remember things.					
27. Explain how to do assignments by using examples.					
28. Show us the difference between things.					

Source: Adapted from ''Additional Investigation Into the Nature of Teacher Clarity'' by J. Kennedy, D.R. Cruickshank, A. Bush, and B. Myers, *The Journal of Educational Research,* 1978, *72,* with permission of the publisher, © 1978.

(1941), discipline requires training and experiencing if it is to become self-directing. Discipline is an educational problem. He reminded educators, ''It is absurd to suppose that a child gets more intellectual or mental discipline when he goes at a matter unwillingly than when he goes at it out of the fullness of his heart.'' If students are to believe they are valuable and responsible, and if they act in such a way, they must be treated by adults with respect and dignity, not sarcasm, ridicule, and tasteless taunts.

According to Marshall (1972), the basic components for creating and maintaining an atmosphere conducive to meaningful learning and positive discipline can be divided into two categories: (1) constructive and preventive and (2) remedial and ameliorative, which is composed of the essential elements of meeting and solving problems of individual students and groups. When a classroom's focus is to create a milieu for meaningful learning, attention must be focused on three components of discipline and classroom interaction:

1. establishing relationships of mutual trust and respect
2. planning the program with problem-solving orientation
3. setting limits.

These form the foundation for meaningful learning (Marshall, 1972). Setting limits is the discipline component and can be a way of expressing care. The teacher must deal with the misbehavior at the time it occurs. Whether the teacher chooses to permit, tolerate, interfere, or prevent a behavior, the conduct has been reinforced negatively or positively.

Stoops and King-Stoops (1981) offered 15 positive suggestion statements for classroom management:

1. On the first day, cooperatively develop classroom standards.
2. Incorporate school and district policies in the classroom list.
3. Establish consequences for good and poor behavior.
4. Expect good behavior from your students and they will try to live up to your expectations.
5. Plan and motivate interesting, meaningful lessons. Show your own enthusiasm for lesson activities.
6. Prevent negative behavior by continuous emphasis upon positive achievement.
7. Develop student self-discipline as rapidly as possible. Lead each student to make his or her own decisions rather than to rely on yours.
8. If behavior problems cannot be solved in the classroom, seek the help of counselors and administrators.
9. Reinforce good behavior by rewarding students in public. Correct or punish in private.
10. Work closely with parents, encouraging them to send the student to you with positive attitudes toward classroom learning.
11. Avoid useless rules, snap judgments, and loss of composure.
12. Be consistent, fair, and firm.
13. Refrain from threats or promises that you may not be able to carry out.
14. Recognize that children have limited attention spans and assign alternative activities.
15. As teachers, *discipline yourself* in manners, voice, disposition, honesty, punctuality, consistency, fairness, and above all, love for your students, so that your own example inspires behavior at its best. (p. 58)

Extinction

Extinction occurs when reinforcement of a behavior ceases. A behavior that does not receive a reward will disappear eventually.

Example: If a teacher refuses to reinforce undesirable behavior, it probably will diminish.

Refusing to reinforce a behavior means ignoring and not calling attention to the inappropriate action.

Example: A teacher who interrupts a class to correct a student for talking may inadvertently be providing reinforcing attention.

There are several characteristics of extinction that should be noted.

Example: A student is more likely to talk loudly and frequently in hopes that persistence eventually will gain attention. However, if not reinforced, the youth will indeed stop eventually.

Most behavioral changes accomplished through extinction are noted within two weeks. A behavior considered extinct may reappear later, but will disappear again if not reinforced and spontaneous recovery rarely will occur a second time.

Peer attention or approval is a powerful reinforcement. If a teacher does not reinforce a student's undesirable behavior but the classmates do, extinction probably will not take place. The teacher thus needs to devise ways to ensure that a student's behavior is not reinforced by the class. Extinguishing a behavior is most effective when coupled with positive reinforcement.

Contingency Management

Contingency management, founded by Premack (1959), proposes that a highly desirable response can reinforce a less desirable one.

Example: Students who remain at their desks for half an hour are allowed to play a game of their own choice.

The desirable activity follows performance of an undesirable one—failure to stay seated.

Negative Practice

Negative practice is probably one of the quickest ways to eliminate undesirable behavior. Negative practice involves eliciting a student's response over and over until the youth is so fatigued there is no desire to produce it again.

Example: Jason had been whistling during class discussions four to five times a day for three consecutive days. At first, the teacher thought he might not be cognizant of the whistling, but inquiries clearly indicated he was aware. The student was required to remain after class and instructed to whistle for 15 minutes. Toward the end of that period, Jason could barely whistle. The whistling did not occur again.

Negative practice is not always recommended, especially if repetition would be harmful. For instance, a student who slammed a fist on a desk would be harmed if required to do this repeatedly.

Pairing

Pairing consists of placing two students together so that one who demonstrates desirable behavior can influence another whose behavior is undesirable.

Example: A student learns to produce adaptive responses through observing others being reinforced for a particular behavior; when imitation occurs, it should be reinforced immediately.

Teachers must be careful when selecting model students. The model must exhibit strong and consistent patterns of desirable behavior; otherwise the effects of pairing may work in reverse, especially if reinforced by peers.

Punishment

Many teachers use negative punishment procedures that can be effective if proportionate, consistent, and reasonable. The results may be temporary if new and more desirable behaviors are not learned.

Example: A student who is reprimanded for running in the hall may stop temporarily. If not reinforced positively for walking, the running probably will recur. At the same time, the youth may learn not to run only when the teacher who delivered the reprimand is present. Another possibility is avoiding the directing teacher.

Negative punishment can result in many accompanying behaviors that are difficult to predict and control. Punishment should be used as the last resort after other methods have been tried with no results. Punishment is an acceptable disciplinary procedure when a behavior would result in immediate injury. When used, it should be followed by an explanation of the desired behavior. If this proper behavior is produced, immediate reinforcement should follow.

Timeout and Systematic Exclusion

Timeout as a preventive practice is reviewed here briefly; much greater detail is provided in Chapter 5.

Timeout requires removing a student who misbehaves for a specified period of time. The student is then permitted to reenter the classroom. If misbehavior recurs, the youth is removed again. Timeout is built on the following assumptions:

1. The student would rather be in the classroom.
2. Specified behaviors occur that result in removal.
3. An isolated area is available for a restricted student.
4. Performance of the maladaptive behavior results in immediate placement in an isolated area.
5. Exclusion for a specific period is the only consequence and is not accompanied by scolding and disappointment.
6. Removal of all rewarding activities in the secluded area is essential. For instance, the room should not have television, cards, or games. However, some magazines, books, and other neutral activities might be appropriate. Students should not be deprived of regular school break periods, lunch, or assemblies.

Timeout procedures usually are conducted within the building in a ''timeout room'' for five to 30 minutes. Generally, the teacher directs the students; however, in some cases, youths may decide to go there voluntarily if they think they might be on the verge of misbehavior. If a separate room is not available, a screened-off corner of a classroom or area in the hall may be used.

Systematic exclusion involves sending a student home for the day immediately following a prespecified behavior. The student returns to school the following day without being reprimanded at home. Obviously, a cooperative parent must be alerted to ensure proper isolation and the presence of only neutral activities. Systematic exclusion involves a student, parents, teachers, principal, and counselor. A written contract between school and student must be used to indicate exact responsibilities and what will happen if these do not materialize. Exhibit 2-4 offers a suggested suspension contract.

Behavioral Contract

A behavioral contract demands certain expectations of each person and assumes signers desire a specified behavior from each other. Each individual's actions reinforce another's. A contract member who does not fulfill responsibilities does not receive a desired reward. Behavioral contracts can be used between teacher

Exhibit 2-4 Systematic Suspension Contract

PARTICIPANTS

1. _____ (student)		5. _____ (parent)	
2. _____ (principal)		6. _____ (parent)	
3. _____ (counselor)		7. _____ (teacher)	
4. _____ (teacher)		8. _____ (teacher)	

GENERAL RULE

On violation of any stated limit STUDENT will be sent from the classroom to the counseling office. His parents will be called and STUDENT will be sent home for the remainder of the day.

LIMITS

1. Not being in attendance at every class to which STUDENT is assigned is a violation.
2. Kicking, hitting, biting, pinching, poking, shoving, jabbing, or tripping any other person is a violation.
3. For additional limits as needed: _____
_____

RESPONSIBILITIES

1. Student: STUDENT agrees that he is fully responsible for himself and that everything he does or does not do is done or not done by his own choice. He agrees to take credit for his failure, as well as his success, regardless of how people treat him.
2. Teacher: On detection of a violation the teacher will send STUDENT to the counselor.

Source: Reprinted from "Strategies for Working with Troubled Students" by Barbara Colorosa. In *The Handicapped Student in the Regular Classroom* (2nd ed.) by B Gearhart and M. Weishahn with permission of the C.V. Mosby Co., p. 219, © 1980.

and student, teacher and class groups, and student and student. A behavioral contract must:

1. be clearly defined and understood
2. be fair—there should be no feeling that any member is not getting as much as any other; if a student agrees to remain seated during class and the teacher agrees to extend only praise, the terms of the contract may be less fair; the student might consider extra recess a more equitable reinforcement
3. be based on a mutually agreed upon goal: getting through a class period without a confrontation would be the chief aim
4. be reasonable and possible for each party
5. not be terminated until the parties agree it has been fulfilled
6. take care to ensure that breaking a contract does not result in punishment by the teacher

7. involve joint negotiation of terms by student and teacher; the purpose is to require that students be partially responsible for the consequences of their own behavior
8. provide for accurate recording of behavior.

Examples of contracts for different purposes are provided in Exhibits 2-5, 2-6, and 2-7.

Control of School Factors

As Mayer and Butterworth (1981) suggested, educators can and should work with factors controllable at school. Student reading levels, instructional materials, and aggressive teacher behavior are specific variables a practitioner can manage. The curriculum and technique can be adjusted to decrease behavior problems. When a student is having difficulty understanding, why talk louder? Instead, the teacher should:

- change the way the material is presented
- move closer
- give the student time to think about the material
- provide a personal opportunity to draw upon the reservoir of patience or plan a different instructional approach
- use high interest materials appropriate to the student's individual reading level, constituting a precise curriculum adjustment.

Teachers should be expert at manipulating the instructional media. They can make some of these adjustments:

- Design the classroom to decrease problems, i.e., change seat arrangement, circle desks, tables, lines, or random positions, move pencil sharpener, change lighting, relocate teacher's desk, situate oneself to be the first element seen when students enter the room; be in the room when students arrive and in a position to be seen immediately.
- Organize groups, peer tutoring, or solo study carrels according to age, social behaviors, or size; change groups for different subjects; vary the group's size.
- Develop after-class procedures.
- Outline antecedent and behavioral consequences.
- Establish structure as to when and where behaviors occur (time of day, area of room, particular activity or subject).

Exhibit 2-5 Performance Contract

STUDENT _____   TEACHER _____
CLASS _____ PERIOD _____ CREDITS _____

BASIC OBJECTIVES FOR THE COURSE:
1. _____
2. _____
3. _____
4. _____

ASSIGNMENTS TO BE SUCCESSFULLY COMPLETED IN ORDER TO RECEIVE
CREDIT FOR THE COURSE: (OR FOR THE WEEK, MONTH, ETC.)
1. _____
2. _____
3. _____
4. _____
5. _____

BEHAVIORAL OBJECTIVES (LIST SPECIFIC BEHAVIORS NECESSARY FOR SUC-
CESSFUL COMPLETION OF THE COURSE):

1. Attend class _____
2. Bring materials _____
3. Other behaviors unique to a student's situation _____

STUDENT CONTRACT FOR A GRADE (IF APPLICABLE):

I understand the requirements for the course and plan to meet the requirements necessary to
receive a _____ for _____.
       (grade)   (credits)

_____   _____
      Date   Signature of student

Source: Reprinted from ''Strategies for Working with Troubled Students'' by Barbara Colorosa. In *The Handicapped Student in the Regular Classroom* (2nd ed.) by B. Gearhart and M. Weishahn with permission of the C.V. Mosby Co., p. 218, © 1980.

Exhibit 2-6 Behavioral Contract

_____PRIVILEGES AND RESPONSIBILITIES DEAL
                    (name)

Effective from _____ to _____
                    (today's date)   (completion date)

RESPONSIBILITIES   PRIVILEGES

1 _____
   a)   a)
   b)   b)

                              | Bonus |

                              | Penalty |

2 _____
   a)   a)
   b)   b)

                              | Bonus |

                              | Penalty |

This deal is scheduled to be renegotiated on _____ _____

Details of responsibilities and privileges are spelled out on the attached sheet. This deal suits me and I agree to take part in it.

_____   _____

_____, counselor

Source: Reprinted from *Intervention Strategies for Specialized Secondary Education* by David A. Sabatino and August J. Mauser with permission of Allyn & Bacon, Inc., p. 103, ©1978.

Exhibit 2-7 Weekly Academic Contract

CONTRACT

	DATE	ASSIGNMENT	COMMENTS
	MONDAY		
MATH	TUESDAY		
	WEDNESDAY		
	THURSDAY		
	FRIDAY		

CONSEQUENCES: _____

_____

_____

_____

_____

STUDENT: _____

TEACHER: _____

DATES: _____

ADDITIONAL COMMENTS:

Source: Reprinted from "Strategies for Working with Troubled Students" by Barbara Colorosa. In *The Handicapped Student in the Regular Classroom* (2nd ed.) by B. Gearhart and M. Weishahn with permission of the C.V. Mosby Co., p. 212, © 1980.

- Use cues—gestures (head nod), voice (volume increased or softened or tone changed), body posture, finger snaps, a note on the piano.
- Use music to reinforce good total class behavior.
- Plan a surprise recess as class reward.
- Reduce class size if possible.
- Alter behavior outbreaks by anticipating and planning for them.
- Recheck curriculum, data, and student records, perhaps using a different mode of delivery, i.e., discussion, lectures, overhead film projector, art projects, trips, guests; make sure the information is relevant to the student and know the prerequisites for the skills being taught.
- Check to be sure the proper skill sequence is being used, i.e., does the student have the background on which to acquire new skills?
- Know information about students' performance and their strengths and weaknesses.

In summary, the teacher must look beyond the behavior, ascertain the reasons it is occurring, and, if the factors can be controlled by the school environment, attempt to alter them. The practitioner should try to view the acting-out, abrasive behavior in class as a symptom of students' problems.

Lectures: A Causal Factor

Most teachers identify a behavior as disruptive when it disturbs their presentation, such as a lecture—a common form of instruction and a time when instructors are easily upset by misconduct. Most lectures produce so much student anxiety that they are detrimental to learning (Ellis & Jones, 1974), yet they constitute the most widely used mode of instructional delivery in secondary school classrooms (Henson, 1980). However, only 52 percent of ideas aired there ever appear in a student's notes, even of those in college (Maddox & Hood, 1975). The lecture thus usually creates a paradox for the unsuccessful student, the underachiever. Ellis and Jones (1974) found lectures to be more anxiety-producing than other modes of instructional presentation.

Lectures tend to be authoritarian, formal, and overly structured but ego-gratifying for the performer—in this case, the teacher. An underachiever in a class where a lecture is being delivered by what the student may perceive as an authoritarian, overly formal person will generate tension and result in acting-out behaviors. The resulting disruption stifles ego gratification for the teacher who is enthralled by the presentation. It must be remembered that "Ego gratification is a major pitfall for an effective lecture, to evolve into the least desirable of *all* teaching methods" (Henson, 1980, p. 116).

A study by Bielin (1959) revealed that teachers were most concerned with behaviors that interfered with their instruction. Student inattention, aggression, hyperactivity, low frustration, tolerance, and temper tantrums were the deviant behaviors checked by teachers in a study by O'Leary and Schneider (1977) involving 12,000 children. The study found that students exhibiting withdrawn behaviors went unnoticed and were not identified as problems or as severely emotionally disturbed.

There obviously are some teachers who are very good lecturers and make lively presentations that stimulate learning. Unfortunately, many more are drones whose lectures generally do not:

- stimulate interest
- promote creativity
- develop responsibility, imagination, or creativity
- help students develop skills in synthesizing, internalizing, or expressing themselves.

According to Lucas, Poshma, and Thompson (1975), "the lecture is effective for immediate cognitive gain and is less effective than educational games for retention over a period of three weeks or longer" (p. 116). Ten to 20 minutes is the average concentration span for most students (Henson, 1980). A state of physical, program-related fatigue—the Pall level—is reached when pupils lose interest. This occurs when the material presented is too simple, too difficult, too long, or too short.

On the other hand, lectures have been found effective when used to introduce a unit, demonstrate a model, clarify, set the scene or focus activities, or summarize major concepts. Wykoff (1973) found movement through the class, gesturing, and pausing had a positive correlation with student recall at the secondary level. However, at the elementary level, the same stimulation lowered student performance. Histrionics or joke telling can reduce tension and anxiety during a lecture (Ellis & Jones, 1974).

The lecture can initiate interest and motivate students when it:

- is organized
- includes a limited number of concepts
- includes humor and avoids tangents
- watches language and is not loaded with jargon, technical vocabulary, or unfamiliar words
- is presented so the speakers listen to themselves.

If the lecture is used to motivate the student into a unit of study, it should be enthusiastic. Interest and motivation are close allies to discipline (Henson, 1980). It is up to the teacher to maintain interest. As Henson found when studying the effects of lectures—boredom breeds trouble. An effective, well-planned, timed lecture is one more way a teacher can use to decrease behavior problems in the class and motivate students to learn.

CLASSROOM ENVIRONMENTAL MANAGEMENT

Classroom physical characteristics have been an overlooked dimension of behavior management. Teachers are aware that factors such as room size, temperature variations, and general decor do affect learning and behavior so they should be able to justify the arrangement of their class.

Classroom arrangement should not be based on historical precedents but on a knowledge of the needs, behaviors, and characteristics of the particular students and teacher. The intervention strategy that has been designed for the students and the teaching-learning strategy most appropriate for them also should be used to determine the physical layout.

Two different examples of classroom physical arrangements are considered here—traditional and informal. Figure 2-1 illustrates layouts for each. However, these represent only a portion of the widely used instructional-managerial designs.

Traditional Classrooms

This more formal design, often referred to as a teacher-centered environment, has been the basic model of classroom arrangement for centuries. The typical arrangement consists of several rows of student seat desks, one behind the other, facing the front of the room, where the teacher's desk and chalkboard are located. The teacher's primary work station, near the desk, enables the practitioner to control the flow of traffic in and out of the classroom, speak directly to students, and maintain visual supervision of the entire group.

The standardized design psychologically emphasizes expected patterns of behavior on the part of teachers and students alike. These expectations include:

- the exercise of authoritative control
- the lecture method of instruction
- the passive use of space
- the presumed homogeneity of students.

The location of the teacher's desk not only communicates the practitioner's isolated role but also physically places that space off limits for student use.

Figure 2-1 Physical Arrangement of Traditional and Informal
Classrooms

Traditional

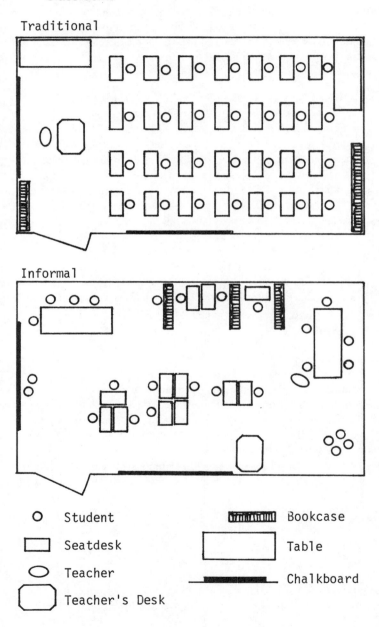

Informal

○	Student
▢	Seatdesk
⬭	Teacher
⬡	Teacher's Desk

▦	Bookcase
▭	Table
▬	Chalkboard

Informal Classrooms

The informal arrangement approximates an open space or student-centered environment and conveys a symbolic meaning different from that of the traditional classroom. The informal classroom reveals a nonuniform arrangement of student work areas, a variety of working surfaces, and both individual and small-group activity settings. The teacher's physical position in the classroom is not well defined and the desk does not constitute a physical or psychological barrier.

The informal arrangement implies the teacher does not occupy a commanding position that is directly visible to all students. Many may be out of the teacher's direct visual range. Noise, movement, and general activity are expected behaviors because the layout is predicated on assumptions of involvement, flexibility, interaction, and individualized programming. Different work surfaces, spatial allowances, and activity settings symbolically suggest that individual differences are accommodated, at least in terms of the physical task requirements and motor needs.

The informal classroom is not a single homogeneous space cube but a network of interconnected and varied microenvironments. It is predicated in part on the assumption that an individualized physical arrangement can reduce environmental constraints that impede student performance.

Figure 2-2 Physical Arrangement of Combined Traditional and Informal Classroom

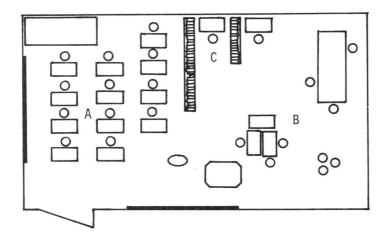

Key: A, traditional classroom area; B, informal classroom area; C, special reduced stimulus area.

The informal arrangement has the advantage of personalizing intervention. It is easier to tolerate selected behaviors when students are not expected to conform to an established pattern of passive behavior. Ignoring behavior, spontaneous closeness control, and individual tutoring similarly are consistent with informal design. Interpersonal management can be conducted within the classroom and does not require waiting for an appropriate time or going out into the hallway as might be expected in the traditional classroom.

No one classroom arrangement can deal adequately with every instructional-managerial concern. Each classroom should be designed with specific objectives, styles, and behaviors in mind. In one combination of both arrangements, a segment of the class is assigned individual seat desks while the other students are working independently or in small groups. Figure 2-2 represents such a classroom, combining traditional and informal arrangements, with a special reduced stimulus area for hyperactive or distractible students.

SUMMARY

This chapter has analyzed antecedents of behavior problems. Teachers, instead of asking "What can we do *to* the student?" after a behavior occurs now can ask, "What can we do *for* the student?" Understanding ways to alter events (antecedents) before a class problem occurs, then changing the events, can decrease teacher stress and the necessity for immediate decision making during and after the disrupting behavior.

The chapter offers many strategies teachers may consider to ease class discipline. While many tactics require minimum changes in teacher behavior, some need preplanning and preparation. These strategies promise the chance of less stress only if teachers are open to the challenge of attempting new strategies. "I've tried everything and nothing works" often means the teachers have tried only tactics in their current repertoire of management techniques. The alternatives presented here expand the teachers' options.

The "sink or swim" philosophy under which many teachers must operate places them in a precarious situation, one that is lonesome and often threatening. This chapter has provided more tools and more skills that, once used, can decrease teachers' stress and allow them the time and opportunity to enjoy students and teach. It challenges teachers to attempt the proffered tactics and decide whether the question, "What can I do *for* the student?" is more desirable than, "What can I do *to* the student?"

Identifying positive reinforcement, extinction, contingency management, negative practice, pairing, timeout and systematic exclusion, and behavior contracts are fruitful disciplinary techniques for middle school, junior, and senior high school teachers and principals. Rewarding adaptive responses that replace deviant behaviors saves using corporal punishment or suspension. Negative punishment is recommended for emergency situations only. Finally, and an important fact often forgotten, behavior modification is effective only if other interactions between students and teachers are positive.

REFERENCES

Bielin, H. Teacher's, clinician's attitudes toward the behavior problems of children: A reappraisal. *Child Development,* 1959, *30,* 9-25.

Bloom, B.S. *Human characteristics and school learning.* New York: McGraw-Hill Book Company, 1976.

Brophy, J.E., & Good, T.L. *Teacher-student relationships: Causes and consequences.* New York: Holt, Rinehart & Winston, Inc., 1974.

Coker, H., Medley, D.M., & Soar, R.S. How valid are expert opinions about effective teaching? *Phi Delta Kappan,* 1980, *62*(2), 131-134.

Combs, A. Humanistic education: Too tender for a tough world? *Phi Delta Kappan,* 1981, *62,* 446-449.

Cremin, L.A. *The transformation of the school.* New York: Random House, Inc., 1964.

Dewey, J., & Kallen, H. (Eds.). *The Bertrand Russell case.* New York: The Viking Press, 1941.

Ellis, H.P., & Jones, A.D. Anxiety about lecturing. *Universities Quarterly,* Spring 1974, pp. 91-95.

Fagen, S., Long, N., & Stevens, D. *Teaching children self-control: Preventing emotional and learning problems in the elementary school.* Columbus, Ohio: The Charles E. Merrill Publishing Co., Inc., 1975.

Henson, K.T. What's the use of lecturing? *High School Journal,* December 1980, *64*(3), 115-119.

Illinois School Code, Article 34-84a, 1980, p. 229.

Johnson, L.V., & Bany, M.A. *Classroom management: Theory and skill training.* New York: Macmillan Publishing Co., Inc., 1970.

Katz, L. Condition with caution. *Young Children,* 1972, *27,* 272-280.

Klein, D.C. Problems in adjustment to school. In H.C. Stuart & D.G. Prugh (Eds.), *The healthy child.* Cambridge, Mass.: Harvard University Press, 1962.

Lasley, T.J. Classroom misbehavior: Some field observations. *High School Journal,* January 1981, *64*(4), 142-149.

Lerner, J.W. *Children with learning disabilities: Theories, diagnoses and teaching strategy.* Boston: Houghton Mifflin Company, 1971.

Maddox, H., & Hood, E. Performance decrement in the lecture. *Educational Review,* November 1975, *28*(1), 17-30.

Marshall, H.H. *Positive discipline and classroom instruction.* Springfield, Ill.: Charles C Thomas, Publisher, 1972.

Maslow, A. Some basic propositions of a growth and self-actualization psychology: Perceiving, behaving, becoming. *ASCD Yearbook,* 1960.

Mayer, R.G., & Butterworth, T.W. Evaluating a preventive approach to reducing school vandalism. *Phi Delta Kappan,* March 1981, *62*(7), 498-499.

O'Leary, S.G., & Schneider, M.R. Special class placement for conduct problem children. *Exceptional Children,* September 1977, *44*(1), 24-30.

Reckless, W.C. *The crime problem.* New York: Appleton-Century-Crofts, Inc., 1967.

Rich, H.L. *The effect of teaching styles on student behavior as related to social-emotional development*. Final report to the U.S. Department of Health, Education, and Welfare, Office of Education. Memphis State University, 1973.

Rosenthal, R., & Jacobson, L. *Pygmalion in the classroom*. New York: Holt, Rinehart & Winston, Inc., 1968.

Sabatino, D.A. Prevention, punishment, education and rehabilitation. In D.A. Sabatino & A.J. Mauser (Eds.), *Specialized education in today's secondary schools*. Boston: Allyn & Bacon, Inc., 1978.

Skinner, B.F. *About behaviorism*. New York: Alfred A. Knopf, Inc., 1974.

Smith, H.C. *Sensitivity to people*. New York: McGraw-Hill Book Company, 1966.

Smith, R.M., Neisworth, J.T., & Greer, J.G. *Evaluating educational environments*. Columbus, Ohio: The Charles E. Merrill Publishing Co., Inc., 1978.

Stoops, E., & King-Stoops, J. Discipline suggestions for classroom teachers. *Phi Delta Kappan*, September 1981, *63*(1), 58.

Wegmann, R.G. Classroom discipline: An exercise in the maintenance of social reality. *Sociology of Education*, January 1976, pp. 71-79.

Wyckoff, B. The effect of stimulus variation on learning from the lecture. *Journal of Experimental Education*, Spring 1973, *41*(3), 85-90.

Chapter 3

Isolation, Expulsion, Suspension, and Detention

David A. Sabatino

INTRODUCTION

As briefly mentioned in Chapter 1, a time-honored alternative to corporal punishment is, and remains, isolation or removal of students for norm-violating behaviors. This author distinctly remembers being told by his high school principal that he was too big to paddle and therefore would be suspended. Ten years later, this author, as a principal, told three 200-pound boys caught smoking in the restroom that they were too large for a paddling, and if they were old enough to smoke they were old enough to obey the rules. Then they were sent home and given one hour to return with both parents, which they did. Thereupon they were given two weeks of school/home work detail that was closely supervised.

Problems involving corporal punishment, and the dismal results that appear to emerge from its usage, have driven educators to search for a reasonable alternative. In the natural order of things, one solution simply is to remove the problem. The logic of such an approach is not one of punishing as much as it is of denying the person a privilege. In the case of detention, youths are denied doing what they wish on time that is normally theirs—free time.

Suspension, and the more permanent expulsion, are legally regulated acts by school officials to bring the school as an organization under manageable control by eliminating a problem. Therein lies the fallacy of such an approach. In executing such a response, school officials have declared a philosophy that, in its kindest form, declares the student to be a problem and to be untreatable (or unmanageable) by the school. Administrators clearly announce that the school has little therapeutic interest when they administer suspension as a final act, thus placing the responsibility for behavior change squarely on the youth with a problem.

Viewed in its rawest form, such a practice (suspension or expulsion) clearly dictates that the strict juvenile justice system, or some other agency if there is one, has the responsibility for assisting individuals with their problems.

That is not the view taken here. However, it is one that exists where the attitudes of the secondary educators have established that attending school is a privilege and not an inalienable right. As a practice, it is an extension of the attitude of many secondary educators that clearly defines the classroom as a center for academic or vocational learning and the role of the students as independent (of the system) responsible learners. If the students fail to achieve academically or socially and offend the system and its officials in the process, the act or privilege of attendance is removed permanently.

On the other hand, the persons with the problems now are in the larger society, frequently without either academic or social skills to cope adequately. Their range of productive alternatives therefore is quite limited. In all, the strength of educators' convictions—the operational aspects, if indeed not the ideology of expulsion—is removed from the societal mainstream. (This was a practice used in Nazi Germany for nearly ten years to remove handicapped and racially different people from its society.)

Philosophically, an attitude that regards the person as the problem, and is willing to remove such a problem individual, should not in any way see itself as tolerant of human rights or a wise utilizer of human service resources with a goal of improving the quality of life.

This chapter reviews, and on occasion describes, usable and innovative behavioral management techniques related to the use of isolation and detention. The last section provides justifications for stopping schoolwide suspension and expulsion. Students need alternative educational approaches, and some of those are reviewed. Youths who are in trouble do not need another well-reinforced experience in feeling social rejection.

The view here is that corporal punishment for youths of any age or weight is an improvement over expulsion. What is needed, then, is not necessarily 200 alternatives for programming poor academic achieving and chronically disruptive youths; instead, what is sought is a change in attitude among many secondary, and some elementary, educators.

SQUEAKING WHEELS

One of the most pronounced difficulties, if not absolute shortcomings, of isolation and detention as student control measures is that they serve the aggressive, acting-out youths but provide no countermeasures for the passive but anxious ones. Since 1928 (Wickman) the primary concern of most educators has been with the visibly aggressive, disruptive students, not those who have given up the struggle and resigned themselves to depression, melancholy, and, yes, juvenile suicide. A study by Cowen, Gesten, and DeStefano (1977) contrasted mental health workers' and teachers' judgment on treatability and prognosis of students with different types of school adjustment problems. Both groups of professionals believed that shy-anxious youths, compared to those who were aggressive, acting-out, and learning disabled, (1) were more appropriate intervention targets, (2) were easier to treat (or correct), and (3) demonstrated better (or more rapid) rates of response to treatment. Both groups also felt acting-out children were the most difficult to work with and, when a concomitant disorder such as learning disability was present, the situation was practically hopeless.

The problem with these data is that passive youths in reality receive very little therapeutic assistance in the public schools. While they may be viewed as being more enjoyable to work with, they rarely are happy or pleased personally with either the human relationship or the schoolwork. Acting-out students are the squeaking wheels who receive the grease; as such, they rarely are reasoned with but more generally are punished for infractions of school rules.

In fact, aggressive and manipulative youths generate feelings of helplessness among many educators that few, if any, therapeutic interventions will work, so maintaining some semblance of order is the most important factor in controlling disruptive behavior. Hartocolis (1972), in a discussion on fear of violence, summarized practices in most secondary schools as those in which teachers afraid of student reprisals had turned discipline over to either an administrator in charge of correction or, in large metropolitan areas, to school security officers.

There also is the prescribed role of the principal when brought into teacher-student disputes. In that role, the principal rarely hears the students' side or (emotionally) even hears the youths at all. The building administrator in most cases unilaterally supports the teacher. The result is that the students now are guilty as charged and rarely are offered even a quasi-judicial review.

School rules are made by members of the adult minority to control the student majority as they see fit. Democracy is no more alive and well in the public schools than it is as practiced by many governments. Schools are in the business of teaching social obedience, and neither the courts nor law officials have any real difficulty upholding authoritarian practices in preparing students to respond to the laws of the land.

Disruptive youths generally are sent to the office because of (in order of occurrence):

- tardiness
- verbal aggression
- vulgarity
- physical aggression with peers.

The principal (vice or assistant, as a rule) usually has these options (in order of occurrence):

- to threaten or order suspension
- to order after-school detention
- to notify the parents and have them inflict punishment
- to call the parents, obtain a witness, and administer corporal punishment.

In junior high schools, it is quite common for teachers to send students to the office. The average frequency for a school with 1,000 to 1,500 students is 1,200 to 2,400 visits per school year, or an average of 7 to 13 per day (NIE, 1978). In Maryland, 39 percent to 46 percent of the total student population was referred to the office for misconduct during a school year. As would be expected, a few youths make frequent trips to the office—6 percent of the student body generally is responsible for 57 percent of the disciplinary visits.

Secondary school administrators have tried to reduce that high rate by requesting that teachers apply active classroom intervention first. This is highly unpopular with teachers on the firing line who are either short on time or simply frightened by large, disruptive youths. In one study, 28 percent of teachers in a large city high school said that they hesitated to confront students for fear of their own safety (NIE, 1978); in another report, 17 percent feared physical assault (O'Toole, 1978). This tactic also is unpopular with teachers because it requires extra effort, time, and an available telephone for quick backup support when necessary. Furthermore, most secondary educators view this as a sign of administrative weakness; they prefer firm and immediate action by the front office (Pardon Our Solecism, 1977).

In any event, a few secondary school administrators report success in increasing faculty responsibility for discipline and thereby decreasing office referrals. In one school (NASSP, 1977), the teacher is expected to complete one or more of the following steps before an office referral can be made:

- teacher-student conference
- teacher-parent conference
- counselor-student conference
- counselor-parent conference.

Most counselors refuse to deal with serious student misconduct because they firmly believe they will lose their counseling effectiveness if placed in a disciplinary role.

In another school, the teacher must proceed through a series of steps before making an office referral, including:

- checking the student's folder
- holding a conference with the student

- sending a report home
- detaining the student after school
- consulting the counselor
- telephoning the parents
- holding a conference with the parents
- changing the student's seat, section, or classroom.

Many teachers want the student to report to the office now—right now. Many union contracts give teachers the right to exclude disruptive students from the classroom immediately (Chesler, Crowfoot, & Bryant, 1979).

DETENTION AND ISOLATION

Detention and isolation are old and trusted forms of discipline. Detention is the most frequent form in secondary schools (Block, Covill-Servo, & Rosen, 1978). Isolation is a major form of teacher-to-student (transfer) measure to teach self-control for behavioral disordered youths in treatment. The most common detention practices are: after school, seat assignment, extra work assignment, study hall or work rooms, detail (work) assignments, exclusion from extracurricular activities, and disciplinary transfer from one setting (classroom) to another.

Isolation can be the declaration of the class dunce, a time-honored practice of moving disruptive students' desks to a position where they cannot distract others. This has some merit in early elementary school but probably is not effective in secondary schools—in fact, it may draw undue attention to the students by setting them apart in a peer acceptable model.

The most frequent form of isolation is removing the student to the counselor's office, principal's office, or extra work room.

Treatment practices for the behaviorally disordered might include a continuum from having the students place their heads on their desk, to a relaxation couch in the classroom, to a timeout area in the classroom where they are monitored, to, finally, a specially designed and arranged facility out of the classroom where they are maintained until they can control their emotionality. Detention is examined next as a disciplinary practice and isolation as a behavioral controlling intervention.

DETENTION

Suspension

Suspension from school was widely used under ambiguous state board of education policies interpreted at the local level until the *Goss v. Lopez* (1974) decision that required administrators to provide parents with immediate information and offer due process hearings before a student could be suspended.

In Illinois, which is representative of many schools in many states, the legal procedures regulating suspension are:

> **Suspension or expulsion of pupils.** (a) To expel pupils guilty of gross disobedience or misconduct, and no action shall lie against them [school officials or school administrators] for such expulsion. Expulsion shall take place only after the parents have been requested to appear at a meeting of the board, or with a hearing officer appointed by it, to discuss their child's behavior. Such request shall be made by registered or certified mail and shall state the time, place, and purpose of the meeting. The board, or a hearing officer appointed by it, at such meeting shall state the reasons for dismissal and the date on which the expulsion is to become effective. If a hearing officer is appointed by the board, he shall report to the board a written summary of the evidence heard at the meeting and the board may take such action thereon as it finds appropriate.
>
> (b) To suspend or by regulation to authorize the superintendent of the district or the principal or dean of students of any school to suspend pupils guilty of gross disobedience or misconduct and no action shall lie against them for such suspension. The board may by regulation authorize the superintendent of the district or the principal of any school to suspend pupils guilty of such acts for a period not to exceed 10 school days. Any such suspension shall be reported immediately to the parents or guardian of such pupil along with a full statement of the reasons for such suspension and a notice of their right to a review, a copy of which shall be given to the school board. Upon request of the parents or guardian the school board or a hearing officer appointed by it shall review such action of the superintendent or principal. At such review the parents or guardian of the pupil may appear and discuss the suspension with the board or its hearing officer. If a hearing officer is appointed by the board, he shall report to the board a written summary of the evidence heard at the report of its hearing officer; the board may take such action as it finds appropriate.
>
> (c) To suspend or by regulation to authorize the superintendent of the district or the principal of any school to suspend pupils guilty of gross disobedience or misconduct on the school bus from riding the school bus and no action shall lie against them for such suspension. Such suspension shall continue until it has been reviewed by the school board, or a hearing officer appointed by it. At such review the parents or guardian of the child may appear and discuss such suspension with the board or its

hearing officer. If a hearing officer is appointed by the board he shall report to the board a written summary of the evidence heard at the meeting. The board may take such action thereon as it finds appropriate upon the board's hearing or the written report of its hearing officer.

(d) The Department of Mental Health and Developmental Disabilities shall be invited to send a representative to consult with the board at such meeting whenever there is evidence that mental illness may be the cause for expulsion or suspension.

The average length of a suspension is three to four days (Edelman, Beck, & Smith, 1975). Usually, one of the conditions for ending a suspension is to have the students report with their parents for a school reentry conference. Repeated infractions may lead to longer suspensions, culminating in expulsion.

Most states or local boards limit the number of days a student may be suspended at any one time or in a school year.

The reasons for suspension seldom are uniform, which causes concern among students. Two students with the same behaviors may receive entirely different treatments. Variations among school districts in a state are extensive, ranging from those where a specific behavior has a prescribed period of suspension to those in which an administrator (or designee) imposes the penalty, depending on what the student has done and/or the record of past performances.

Oddly enough, most studies on suspension indicated that attendance problems, including tardiness and truancy, were the most frequent reasons. In a national study (NASSP, 1977), 50 percent of all suspensions were related to attendance problems. A study in Maryland *(Children's Mental Health,* 1979) reported 20 percent of the suspensions involved cutting classes, while a statewide Ohio survey put this factor clearly first, affecting 33 percent of the reported cases. Two studies, by Williams (1979) and by Edelman, Beck, and Smith (1975), reported attendance problems to be the second most common factor, with disruptive behavior (including fighting, defiance, and unruly classroom conduct) as the primary cause. The later study reported that disruption occurred in about 35 percent of the suspension cases. The reasons for suspension in a New York statewide survey (Block, Covill-Servo, & Rosen, 1978) included:

- disruption of classroom routine—15 to 30 percent
- noncompliance with assignment—15 to 30 percent
- noncompliance with other forms of discipline—15 to 25 percent
- smoking—10 to 20 percent
- destruction of school property—1 to 5 percent
- drug related—1 to 15 percent.

High school principals who were surveyed (Williams, 1979) reported the probability of suspension in the following situations:

- fighting—100 percent
- possession of a weapon—98 percent
- insubordination—95 percent
- extortion—95 percent
- possession of drugs—80 percent
- smoking—95 percent
- class cutting—55 percent
- truancy—44 percent.

Suspension Rates

In Ohio, suspensions ranged from a low of 2 percent per year to a high of 21 percent. The differences were attributed solely to the type of school reporting the data—large city vs. rural areas. Larkin (1979) reported differences in suspension rates among schools in the same district ranged from 2 percent to 105 percent of the student body.

One of the variables that drives up the overall suspension rate is the number of students who are suspended repeatedly. That also suggests something of the effectiveness of suspension as a practice.

The National Association of Secondary School Principals (1977) noted that 52 percent of students who had been suspended were recidivists. This rate was reported in a review of the literature to range from 16 percent to 40 percent (Bass, 1980). Edelman, Beck, and Smith (1975) found the number of repeated suspensions per year ranged from two to seven, with 24 percent of those having been out at least three times a year. The authors estimate conservatively that the percentage of students suspended at least once annually ranges from 0.9 percent in elementary schools to 8 percent at the secondary level. The most frequent repeat suspensions occurred in Iowa high schools, the rate being estimated at 12 to 15 percent annually.

The suspension rate for blacks averaged approximately double that for Caucasian, Spanish Americans, and American Indians, with the latter three groups of minorities sharing a nearly identical suspension rate.

The U.S. Office of Civil Rights has required suspension data to be reported to it for more than a decade. Generally speaking, while secondary school enrollment declined nearly 30 percent in that period, the suspension rate rose 5 percent a year, with the large cities reporting a 10 percent increase since 1970. Male suspensions exceeded those of females in a 3:1 ratio, with female reentry and repeat rates also lower (Kelly, Bullock, & Dykes, 1977).

Alternative Forms of Daytime Suspension

Historically, suspension has been a common practice for removing disruptive students. Since the early 1970s, court decisions have made suspensions more difficult without due process. *Goss v. Lopez* (1974), as noted earlier, held that public education was a property right and that students could not be deprived of that right without due process of law. In *Wood v. Strickland* (1974), local board of education members were held liable for suspensions that violated a student's constitutional rights.

Research on suspension has been limited to the compilation of statistics. Few studies have analyzed the effectiveness of the penalty. One report on the influence of suspension for smoking was not encouraging if reduction in smoking on school property was the measure of effectiveness (Cottle, 1975). One high school principal observed, "We know for certain that suspension from school has been totally ineffective in disciplining youngsters. . . . It's like sending kids out on a three-day vacation. They come back the same " (NASSP, 1977). Osborne (1977) examined the effects of suspension of 311 students in a junior high school population of 3,492 in Kalamazoo, Mich. This study reported the two factors most common to suspension were academic underachievement and race.

In-School Suspension

In-school suspension was first reported in 1971 as an alternative to loss of control and to enhance school management of students (NIE, 1977). Parents are alerted at the outset (Exhibits 3-1 and 3-2). The program then requires the students:

1. to attend a suspension room for two to five days
2. to be deprived of all school privileges during that time
3. to complete all classroom assignments, plus additional work (about twice as much as usual) during that time
4. to complete all work or face continued suspension
5. to accept remediation if it is needed
6. to abstain from all talking in the suspension room
7. to arrive early and go home late
8. to eat lunch earlier than peers and to be isolated in the cafeteria
9. to participate in no extracurricular activities
10. to learn to accept the consequences for their behavior
11. to write a 500-word essay titled, "Where Am I Going, and How Am I Getting There."

Exhibit 3-1 Detention Referral Notice to Parents

Dear _____:

As of this date, your son/daughter, _____,
has been referred to our detention room for a period of _____ days. This referral was done
because of the following reasons:

While in detention, your child will be given opportunities to experience a change of behavior
by being counseled and participating in creative problem-solving activities. The student will
also be required to complete the assignments that would have been given if she/he had not been
referred.

All work will be assigned and monitored. We want your child to be successful. The detention
room is in existence to help. Days in attendance will be recorded as present at school instead of
absent, as would be the case if he/she had been suspended.

In short, while in detention _____
will be required to complete all work, be cooperative, speak and act respectfully at all times,
and be present at school every day.

You will (_____), will not (_____), have to accompany your child for a conference at
the end of his/her detention.

Sincerely,

_____
Principal, Asst. Principal

Source: Atlanta Teacher Corps.

The effectiveness of this in-school suspension project is that most of its participants completed it successfully, with only 23 of 173 being required to repeat the
ordeal.

One principal, in commenting on in-school suspension, said that in the past
when school regulations required suspension or expulsion,

Exhibit 3-2 Administration Detention Assignment Card

IN-SCHOOL SUSPENSION

NAME _____ GR/SEC. _____ INITIAL DATE _____
PARENT _____ ADDRESS _____
                                       PHONE _____

DATE(s)	OFFENSE	DETENTION ASSIGNMENT TOPICS	REFERRED BY	DETENTION PROGRESS

FOR ADMINISTRATIVE USE ONLY

PARENT CONTRACT: _____

ADDITIONAL REFERRALS/REMEDIATION: _____

DETENTION PERSONNEL COMMENTS: _____

RELEASE APPROVAL(s)

_____   _____   _____

Source: Atlanta Teacher Corps.

I'd get people asking me why I hated their kid, why I didn't want their kid to graduate. We don't get those complaints any more. Of course, we talk to all the parents. We tell them why their kid is in in-school suspension, what it means, and how long he'll be there. We really try to work closely with the parents, and I think they appreciate it. (O'Brien, 1976, p. 36)

Another in-school suspension program was developed by the Franklinton (N.C.) City Schools and reported by the superintendent, Kent Mosley (1977), as an Alternative Learning Center (ALC). The major characteristics of the center are:

1. Students earn their way back into the regular school program by exhibiting appropriate behaviors.
2. A specific room is available where this alternative learning can take place in a controlled environment; this isolation also restricts the students' social life in school.
3. ALC teachers provide alternative education coordinated with the students' regular courses.
4. The skill of how to study is an important part of this curriculum. Students must complete all class work in a manner satisfactory to the supervisory personnel if they are to gain early reentry into their regular school program.
5. Counseling is a vital element in the program.
6. Supervision with teachers from the main subject areas of the school is provided, along with the counselors and special personnel, all with the goal of helping students with academic work and behavior problems.

The procedures for operating the ALC are as follows:

After one or more offenses, which singly or collectively constitute a suspendable case as determined by the school administration, a conference is called at which the ALC idea is presented to the student and the parents. Specific teachers having a vested interest in the case may be asked to be present. The principal thoroughly explains the program's aims and student behavior expectations.

If the ALC program is accepted by both parents and student, this is finalized by the signing of an Entrance Contract. Refusal of either parent or student to sign the contract results in out-of-school suspension.

Students who sign in most cases begin the following morning. This gives the principal time to notify the teachers so they will have time to prepare needed materials and assignments (such as in Exhibit 3-3). Assignments for ALC students are submitted to the principal's office prior to the first hour on the day of entry into the program and on all subsequent days.

The ALC teachers help the students with their work and provide instruction directed at their academic achievement level. All completed work is turned in to the regular teacher for grading.

An early exit from the ALC is offered as an initiative for students who are assigned five days or more of in-school suspension and is based solely on their work and conduct. After completing three days of ALC assignments, students may apply for early exit. This is accomplished by filling out the ALC Early Exit Request Form. The ALC supervisors complete the form and submit it to the

Exhibit 3-3 Example of an In-School Suspension Assignment Sheet

Student _____   Teacher _____

Subject _____   Room # _____

Date _____

Please submit assignments for the student for _____ days. Indicate the name and level of textbook the student is working in. Complete this sheet and send all necessary materials to my office immediately, including textbook.

_____

Day 1 _____
_____
_____

Day 2 _____
_____
_____

Day 3 _____
_____
_____

Day 4 _____
_____
_____

Day 5 _____
_____
_____

NOTE: You will be notified if additional assignments are necessary.

Source: Atlanta Teacher Corps.

principal for approval or rejection. If it is approved, early exit takes place immediately.

If students fail to fulfill their work obligations to the satisfaction of the ALC supervisors, the period of their assignment to the center is extended or they are given out-of-school suspension. The principal must contact the parents again and explain the extension to them.

Just before, or immediately after, completion of the time assigned to the ALC, and before students return to the regular school program, the principal and/or guidance counselor confers with them. The purpose of this exit counseling interview is twofold: (1) to ensure that the students are aware of the behavioral change expected as they reenter the regular school program, and (2) to advise them of the penalties for failure to comply with the rules of the school and instructions of the staff. This also gives the administrator an opportunity to commend students who have reacted positively to the ALC program (Mosley, 1977).

In-school suspension as an alternative has been found to be effective when it becomes less a form of punishment and more an active student management plan. In that respect, concentrated close supervision, realistic expectations under heavy student workloads, immediate counseling, and extensive remediation are offered. In-school suspension programs are no-fun, no-frills efforts and must require the students to work hard. No follow-up data have been reported on their long-term effectiveness. However, it could be hypothesized that in-school suspension is effective when counseling, remediation, and strict rule adherence are a part of the program and continue in the transition and follow-up stages.

Expulsion

Expulsion is but a more prolonged suspension, usually for six weeks, two months, or one semester. The intent is obvious: to rid the school of its troublesome students. The reasons for expulsion parallel those of suspension. Indeed, expulsion frequently follows suspension as the final official act between school and student. Generally, a student is suspended one to three times and then, as a final measure, is expelled.

Many local boards of education have policies that automatically require expulsion after three suspensions. This policy tends to push many truant and tardy students from the school rolls. Because of its more permanent nature, expulsion requires a more formal hearing of the complaints and generally a direct personal contact between parent and school officials. In reality, this may be nothing more than a letter explaining that a student has been expelled. It is not unusual for a school to have a behavioral court, retention committee, or some regularly assembled group of officials to hear expulsion cases and appeals for readmission.

The expulsion rate, like the suspension rate, varies greatly among school districts and between buildings in a district. It is cited as low as 1 percent (NIE, 1978) and as high as 6 percent (Olmstead, 1980). These percentages are highly suspect, however. In actuality, expulsion is an unrecognized process for stopping youths from either wanting to attend or actually attending school. The reasonable question is, what number of dropouts were either expelled or more probably in danger of expulsion? If a suspension or expulsion requires papers and even a formal hearing, would it not be easier to make school uncomfortable for chronic disruptive youths and the door to the dropout option plainly visible? Few states

(Block, Corvill-Servo, & Rosen, 1978) provide alternative schools for expelled students and not one, in its school code, requires an alternative placement.

Elliot and Voss (1974) determined the dropout or stopout (forced expulsion) rate to be 23 percent. It is interesting that the rates of misbehavior and of so-called dropouts are parallel (Osborne, 1977), proving that they influence the same population. The recommendation here is that expulsion should be abandoned as both policy and procedure for managing disruptive students. In its place, it is strongly recommended that if expulsion is warranted, then so is an alternative form of school programming. Regular (basic) high school education is intended to assure self-control and self-reliance. However, the size of the American prison population is evidence that that objective is not being met. Youths respond to disruption of their personal and family situations by requiring more attention in school. Suspension and expulsion are cheap and quick responses to their pleas for help.

Much of what is recommended here is discussed extensively with the changing role of the disciplinary principal in Chapter 5 on alternative programs.

ISOLATION

Timeout

The most popular form of isolation is called timeout. Although it may be applied in almost any setting, the most frequent one is in a timeout room. This may be a specially designated area in a regular classroom, a partitioned-off section, or one specially constructed in another classroom or in a closet.

The principle involved is captured in the term timeout. It implies withdrawal of the person whose behavior is disruptive. It is a form of punishment, drawing on the same theory as that of the prison system: an individual sentenced to jail loses all positive reinforcement. Therefore, it probably is more correct to describe timeout in terms of the time students are unable to win positive reinforcement than in regard to the type of setting in which they are placed.

Timeout, then, can simply result in the elimination of positive reinforcement in a rigidly controlled environment or it can be the restrictive placement of students into an area that prohibits such support.

Throughout the period timeouts have been used, one persistent argument has been on the negative nature of this practice (Leitenberg, 1965). One set of data (Burchard & Barrera, 1972) suggested that the condition upon which timeout was imposed was more awesome (punishing) than the procedure itself. In examining this idea, Burchard and Barrera conducted a study at an Intensive Training Unit for the rehabilitation of mildly retarded adolescent boys. The youths in attendance there displayed a high frequency of antisocial behavior (such as stealing, fighting, swearing, bullying, and refusal to complete their work).

In this residential program, behaviors that resulted in timeout and/or response cost (the consequences for displaying a behavior) were classified into the following four different categories:

1. swearing, which was defined as the verbal emission of specific obscene and vulgar words regardless of the situation or the context in which they were expressed
2. personal assault, defined as any negative physical contact between two or more residents or between a resident and a working, visiting, or residential individual, in which the victim reacted with a specific indication of pain or disapproval
3. property damage, defined as deliberate or reckless behaviors that resulted or could have resulted in unnecessary damage to an object
4. other behaviors, defined as a catchall category for those which did not fit into any of the others.

Recording a behavior in the fourth category consisted of describing briefly and objectively the conduct that had led to punishment such as disobedience, trying to escape, being too noisy, and taking things from others.

Timeout consisted of sitting down on a bench behind a partition (the timeout area) for a predetermined period. The time was controlled by a kitchen timer with a bell. Any youths who refused to go immediately to the timeout area or created a disturbance while in such isolation were fined 15 tokens and taken to a timeout room (a small room devoid of anything that could be pleasurable) where they remained in silence for 30 minutes.

The youths were assigned arbitrarily to four experimental groups, differing only in the order of their exposure to each of the four timeout records. The results were logical: there was a direct correlation between students' behaviors and the duration of their stay in timeout with no positive reinforcement. The question then is: How long should they remain in timeout?

One study found students remaining in isolation for periods ranging from 2 to 30 minutes (Bostow & Bailey, 1969). In some cases, they were required to act appropriately in order to terminate isolation, although most investigators have found a fixed period of isolation was successful when followed by a reconstruction of appropriate behavior. Other procedures, such as the loss of the opportunity to attend favored school activities, loss of adult or peer interaction (Risley & Wolf, 1967), and loss of physical contact with others (Tate & Baroff, 1969), have been considered timeout.

Timeout has been used in hospitals, in outpatient clinics, in special classes, and in residential homes. It rarely is used in the public schools with nonhandicapped youths. Studies reporting successful timeout procedures with nonhandicapped youths are modified as no-talk periods in disciplinary study halls where a certain amount of mandatory work was required.

Drabman and Spitalnik (1973) studied the effects of timeout procedures on the behavior of the emotionally disturbed in a special education classroom. They concluded that it was effective because of its punishing properties that denied positive reinforcement and contingent socialization, placing the students in isolation and withdrawing support for a fixed period. They stated that timeout probably was the most effective method of control and management of aggressive behavior in disruptive children and youths.

In-room and out-of-room procedures were studied for their effectiveness by Scarboro and Forehand (1975) with younger children—the potential adolescent disrupters of tomorrow.

For comparison of the two timeout procedures, a triadic procedure was introduced involving: (1) the issuing of a direct command, (2) the use of a warning that clearly stated the alternatives, and (3) the use of timeout itself. This procedure offered a systematic, standardized means of controlling behavior beginning with the issuing of the initial command.

Using 24 normal subjects for baseline comparisons, Scarboro and Forehand concluded that both types of timeout provided sufficient evidence as to its effectiveness as a management procedure for modifying behaviors. Out-of-room periods were brief, those in-room were longer. To obtain behavioral effects similar to those out-of-room, the within-room procedure required a significant increase in the number of applications of timeout. It also was demonstrated that the procedures used in this program could be taught successfully to parents in a short time.

The results supporting the use of out-of-class timeout as the choice of treatments were well justified in the theory of the procedure itself. Timeout involves removal of things that are fun or interesting and situations where peer and teacher recognition and approval could be won—all pleasurable and therefore positive reinforcers.

The most effective method has been to use a warning system that begins by removing reinforcers in the class. With adolescents, the No. 1 reinforcer is peer approval so it obviously is difficult to remove that while keeping a student in the class. Therefore, out-of-classroom isolation in a barren, drab, ugly room, with poor lighting, ventilation, no or few windows, and reduced access to audible school noises is the most appropriate procedure. Most middle and junior high school students should be isolated in timeout for 30 minutes, then should reconstruct a positive set of behaviors to regain admission to class.

Sequencing the Steps to Formal Timeout

Scarboro and Forehand (1975) reviewed eight parameters used in timeout programming. Two of the eight—verbalized reasoning and duration of timeout—were analyzed for their effect on students; the other data were obtained from laboratory studies.

1. Verbalized Reasoning

This should be used before timeout's administration. Most studies in the literature do not indicate whether the student was given the reason for timeout beforehand. Tate and Baroff (1969) said they offered no explanations when instituting timeout from physical contact for a psychotic child who engaged in self-injurious behavior. Obviously, verbal reasoning sometimes is impossible because of the severity of the problem.

The effect of the verbalization of a reason for timeout was investigated with the mildly retarded by Alevizos and Alevizos (1972). They compared timeout plus a reason (e.g., "you are going to timeout because you are out of your chair") with timeout with no explanation. The results indicated that the addition of a reason did not facilitate the effectiveness of timeout for this tiny and highly specialized sample.

2. Warning

Most studies do not indicate whether or not a warning is given. In those that do mention it, the warnings were either quite brief or entirely absent. Zeilberger, Sampsen, and Sloane (1968) used a brief explanation ("you cannot stay here if you continue that"). A threat of isolation was used by Sibley, Abbott, and Cooper (1969) as an advance alert on timeout following intolerable behavior. If the behavior did not stop within five to ten seconds after the warning, timeout was administered. The omission of a warning was reported by Tyler and Brown (1967): when students misbehaved, timeout was instituted immediately. However, they did not report the results of the warning.

3. Removal and Placement

The method used to place the students in timeout typically is a function of their resistance. When they display antisocial behaviors, physical force may be necessary to implement timeout procedures. When possible, it would seem theoretically preferable to use verbal instructions rather than physical force. With instructions, aggression is not modeled, more reasonable interaction occurs between teacher and student, and the youth is given (can be given) the responsibility for self-administering the part of the timeout that teaches self-control and self-reliance.

Ideally, the timeout rules should be such a part of the classroom structure that upon an infraction, the degree of violation determines the duration of the isolation period. That can be written into a code, agreed upon by the students, and hung on the wall for all to live by throughout the day.

4. Location

The removal of the student vs. isolation in a separate area of the classroom in which the norm-violating behavioral act took place is an alternative. Isolation in a separate area such as an empty adjoining room has been reported frequently in the literature. Same-area isolation, which includes standing in a corner or sitting in a timeout chair, has been used less often.

The primary advantage of the separate-area technique is that it increases the probability that positive reinforcement will be removed during the period. With same-area timeout, the supervisory adult may unintentionally provide intermittent reinforcement. There also may be sources of reinforcement that are not under the adult's control. However, a separate room may not be available; in that case, isolation would be restricted to the area in which the behavior occurred. The same-area process puts more responsibility on the teacher to enforce the timeout.

5. Duration

The duration of timeout is important from both ethical and practical viewpoints. Timeout durations that are too long:

- remove the individual from the opportunity to learn desirable behavior
- may actually increase the rate of deviant behavior
- are questionable ethically since they subject the student to unnecessary unpleasant experiences.

Some researchers have used timeout durations of 5 to 20 minutes but ranges of 2 minutes to 3 hours have been reported (Burchard & Tyler, 1965). However, the comparison of timeout durations for various offenses has received little attention.

Burchard and Barrera (1972), using institutionalized mildly retarded individuals, contrasted timeout durations of 5 and 30 minutes based on the amount of antisocial behavior displayed. The results indicated that the 30-minute span was more suppressive of deviant behavior than the 5-minute period. With each successive disruption, the 30-minute timeout resulted in even greater suppression of unwanted behaviors.

The effect of the one-minute timeout depended on the sequence in which it was presented. When it preceded a longer duration, it was highly effective, but if it followed either the 15- or 30-minute treatment, it did not reduce disruptive behavior. Very short timeouts can be used where longer ones have not been tried previously. In addition, longer durations can be implemented if short intervals prove ineffective. Burchard and Barrera (1972) argued that if the duration contrast effect was real, it would suggest that timeout consistency was more critical than the particular span used. Sufficient suppression may be obtained with a brief timeout as long as longer periods are not introduced.

6. Timeout Stimulus

The presence or absence of a signal can be used to indicate the onset and offset of timeout. Adams and Popelka (1971) report that with older students nonverbal signals may be used to indicate the onset or offset of timeout. Adams and Popelka used a tone to signal the duration. The tone was not threatening in nature but merely served a signalling function during an entire 10-second timeout period. Typically, signal systems have not been used to initiate timeout as teachers usually place the students in the timeout area or tell them to go there. Yet signal systems have been frequently used for generations by educators as effective warning devices and as final notification of the penalty. It is assumed (since it is not usually reported) that the adult verbally notifies the student as to when timeout is terminated. Again, there are no statistical data on the effects of a signal system, but users report satisfactory clinical results when they are made part of the structure. Signals may be much better than complaints.

7. Schedule

Since timeout has always been administered on a continuous schedule in clinical studies with students, the relative effects of intermittent and continuous use cannot be compared. However, when numerous timeouts are used, the effects of various schedules on outcome data may be investigated systematically. Continuous electric shock at moderate to high intensities leads to more suppression (greater reduction in responding) but faster recovery (a more rapid increase of undesirable behaviors in responding once electric shock is terminated), while intermittent punishment leads to less suppression but slower recovery of undesirable behaviors. By varying the schedule of administration of timeouts, it may be possible to obtain an optimal balance between suppression and recovery in obtaining socially acceptable behaviors in children and youths.

8. Release from Timeout: Contingent vs. Noncontingent

A constant duration of timeout has been used most frequently with school-age children and youths. These durations have not been contingent on the type of behavior displayed during the timeout period. The disadvantages of such an approach is that undesirable behavior occurring during timeout may be reinforced by release from the punishment. Therefore, it is recommended that a contingency release for appropriate behavior be built into a timeout structure. In short, after a short standard duration, a student may be released from isolation by reconstructing socially approved behavior in comparison to the disruption displayed earlier. Three types of contingent release have been reported:

1. to make release contingent on a specified period of desirable behavior; short periods of "quiet" (two to three minutes) prior to release have been suggested by Patterson and White (1970)
2. to prescribe a minimum duration with an extension of the period until any undesirable behavior occurring during timeout is terminated
3. to extend the period for a fixed duration following undesirable behaviors in timeout.

The relative effect of these variations in procedures is difficult to assess at this time. Comparative research on contingent release clearly is needed.

Timeout: Public School Settings

Thus far the discussion has centered primarily on timeout in special education settings. Webster (1976) described a procedure for using it in the public school.

A 13-year-old acting-out aggressive student threw objects and fought constantly. His teachers felt he was obtaining a high degree of peer and teacher acknowledgment from his acting-out behaviors. Three junior high school teachers met with him and explained that because of the seriousness of his behavior they would be forced to impose specific consequences for certain types of behavior that endangered the other students. The list of specified behaviors was read and explained to him and he was notified as to the consequences each time one of them occurred: He would be sent to a room, 8 feet by 12 feet, containing only a desk and chair and no windows, and would remain there alone for the duration of the class period in which he acted out, upon which he would then go to his next class (where the same rules were in effect). He was free to take only his school books and work with him to the room.

He was given a five-day training period during which, each time one of the specified behaviors occurred, he was reminded verbally of the consequences but they were not enforced. He then was notified as to when he would begin to incur isolation for his unacceptable behaviors. Because of the practical urgency of treatment intervention, the verbal training period lasted only one week.

Each time he was accompanied to the timeout room by one of the teachers, they reiterated the criteria for isolation as well as his responsibility for his behavior. He was told that when he stopped attacking others without provocation, the isolation periods would be terminated.

Throughout the entire procedure, teacher conferences with the school psychologist were held on a biweekly basis to ascertain the rate of aggressive behavior and to provide teachers with support, reassurance, and feedback on progress. A daily record of both the number of times the youth was sent to the timeout room and the amount of time he remained there were maintained by each junior high teacher during the entire process.

No significant decrement in behavior was observed between baseline and verbal training data. The obvious decreases in acting-out in the first two weeks of timeout may plausibly be attributable to a decrease in the amount of time in which he had to act out. The third week, though, revealed a large decrement in deviant behavior, which suggests treatment effects attributable directly to timeout. By the fourth week, he was spending a daily average of only 1.2 minutes in isolation while acting-out only three times during that week. Actual assaultive behaviors were reduced significantly. During the fourth week, teacher reports reflected self-initiated interest in schoolwork with homework assignments turned in without coercion by either parents or teachers.

SUMMARY

The use of timeout with aggressive students can be an effective treatment procedure and can be incorporated into a school routine with relative ease. Its effectiveness lies in the fact that it reduces most deviant behavior and maintains that lower level. Therefore, it remains for middle and high schools to find novel ways to implement these effective procedures, especially in dealing with aggressive behaviors. A study by Wilson, Robertson, Herlong, and Haynes (1979) analyzed the vicarious effects of timeout applied to a student's aggressive in-classroom behaviors. An aggressive conduct was followed by a five-minute period of social isolation. The aggressive behaviors of untreated classmates also were monitored.

Timeout procedures proved effective in modifying the personal and social consequences of aggression and establishing a base for instituting social learning of appropriate behaviors. Aggression, in this case, was defined as when a student made an intense movement directed at another person, or came into contact directly, or used other objects to hit, block, kick, trip, or throw. Teachers administered the timeouts by identifying aggressive acts and immediately removing the student for five minutes of social isolation out of the classroom.

The results of this intervention strongly support its utilization as a regular school, classroom-based intervention. Why?

1. It restores order immediately in the classroom by removing the disrupter.
2. The majority of disruptions are caused by preadolescents or early adolescents attempting to receive peer approval, and isolation cuts down peer approval.
3. Most youths in pursuit of aggressive behavior are manipulating the system; isolation most certainly eliminates such manipulation as it brings students into contact with self.

4. It provides for self-control and, unlike most forms of punishment, reduces the verbal and physical interaction that accelerates outbreaks of the entire class.
5. It teaches self-reliance and self-control; the student has time to examine consequences and think through behaviors that may be more appropriate; indeed, a student's acting through appropriate behaviors to a given situation is highly desirable in deciding on release from isolation.

Isolation, in the final analysis, does not work for all students nor is it effective for all teachers. It is, however, one approach—a positive one, indeed—designed to isolate and remove inadvertent reinforcers for displays of disruptive behaviors.

The drawbacks to isolation are that the student is still in the school, that a management plan for a class with well-explained rules is required, and that it takes more than one teacher's time. It requires building a level of support—a principal who attempts to salvage youths from the eventual erosion of disruptive behaviors that lead to suspension, expulsion, and corporal punishment. Isolation planned through timeout procedures is an in-school alternative worthy of consideration.

REFERENCES

Adams, M.R., & Popelka, G. The influence of "timeout" on stutterers and their dysfluency. *Behavior Therapy*, 1971, *2*, 334-339.

Alevizos, K.J., & Alevizos, P.N. *The role of verbalizing and not verbalizing timeout contingencies in a therapy classroom*. Paper presented at the meeting of the Eastern Psychological Association, Portland, Ore., 1972.

Bass, A. Another approach to suspension. *NASSP Bulletin*, May 1980, *64*(436), 109-110.

Block, E.E., Covill-Servo, J., & Rosen, M.F. *Failing students—failing schools: A study of dropouts and discipline in New York State*. New York City: New York Civil Liberties Union, 1978.

Bostow, D., & Bailey, J. Modification of severe disruptive and aggressive behavior using brief timeout and reinforcement procedures. *Journal of Applied Behavior Analysis*, 1969, *2*, 31-37.

Burchard, J.D., & Barrera, F. An analysis of timeout and response cost in a programmed environment. *Journal of Applied Behavior Analysis*, 1972, *5*, 271-282.

Burchard, J., & Tyler, V., Jr. The modification of delinquent behavior through operant conditioning. *Behavior Research and Therapy*, 1965, *2*, 245-250.

Chesler, M., Crowfoot, J., & Bryant, B.I. Organizational context of school discipline. *Education and Urban Society*, 1979, *11*, 496-510.

Children's mental health (2nd draft). Central Maryland Health Systems Agency Report on Mental Health, Alcoholism and Alcohol Abuse, 1979.

Cottle, T.J. A case of suspension. *The National Elementary Principal*, 1975, *55*, 362-366.

Cowen, E.L., Gesten, E.L., & DeStefano, M.A. Nonprofessional and professional help agents' views of interventions with young maladapting school children. *American Journal of Community Psychology*, 1977.

Drabman, R.S., & Spitalnik, R. Social isolation as a punishment procedure: A controlled study. *Journal of Experimental Child Psychology*, 1973, *16*, 236-249.

Edelman, M., Beck, R., & Smith, P. *School suspensions: Are they helping children?* Cambridge, Mass.: Children's Defense Fund, 1975.

Elliott, D.S., & Voss, H.L. *Delinquency and dropout.* Lexington, Mass.: Lexington Books, D.C. Heath and Company, 1974.

Goss v. Lopez, 14 S. Ct. 1405 (1974).

Hartocolis, P. Aggressive behavior and the fear of violence. *Adolescence,* 1972, *7,* 479-490.

Kelly, T., Bullock, M., & Dykes, M.K. Behavioral disorders: Teachers' perceptions. *Exceptional Children,* February 1977, *43,* 316-318.

Larkin, J. School desegregation and student suspensions. *Education and Urban Society,* 1979, *11,* 485-495.

Leitenberg, H. Is timeout from positive reinforcement an aversive event? A review of the experimental evidence. *Psychology Bulletin,* 1965, *64,* 428-441.

Mosley, K.S. Disciplinarian alternative. *North Carolina Education,* 1977, *7,* 18-19.

National Association of Secondary School Principals. *Disruptive youth: Causes and solutions.* Reston, Va.: Author, 1977.

National Institute of Education. *Conference on corporal punishment in the schools: A national debate.* Washington, D.C.: Author, 1977.

National Institute of Education. *Violent schools—safe schools. The safe school study report to Congress.* Executive Summary. Washington, D.C.: Author, 1978.

O'Brien, D.M. In-school suspension. *American School Board Journal,* Sept. 1976, *169,* 35-37.

Olmstead, L. Expelled youth lose on funds. *The Baltimore Evening Sun,* February 29, 1980, p. D-3.

Osborne, D.L. Race, sex, achievement, and suspension. *Urban Education,* October 1977, *11,* 334-347.

O'Toole, P. Casualties in the classroom. *The New York Times Magazine,* December 10, 1978, pp. 59, 78-90.

Pardon our solecism. *Creative Discipline,* November 1977, *1,* 2.

Patterson, G.R., & White, G.D. It's a small world: The application of "timeout from reinforcement." In F.H. Kanfer & J.S. Phillips (Eds.), *Learning Foundations of Behavior Therapy.* New York: John Wiley & Sons, Inc., 1970.

Risley, T., & Wolf, M. Establishing functional speech in echolalic children. *Behavior Research and Therapy,* 1967, *5,* 73-88.

Scarboro, M.E., & Forehand, R. Effects of two types of response contingent timeout on compliance and oppositional behavior of children. *Journal of Experimental Child Psychology,* 1975, *19,* 252-264.

Sibley, S., Abbott, M., & Cooper, B. Modification of the classroom behavior of a "disadvantaged" kindergarten boy by social reinforcement and isolation. *Journal of Experimental Child Psychology,* 1969, *7,* 203-219.

Tate, B., & Baroff, G. Aversive control of self-injurious behavior in a psychotic boy. *Behavior Research and Therapy,* 1969, *4,* 281-287.

Tyler, V., & Brown, G. The use of swift, brief isolation as a group control device for institutionalized delinquents. *Behavior Research and Therapy,* 1967, *5,* 1-9.

Webster, R.E. A timeout procedure in a public school setting. *Journal of Experimental Analysis of Behavior,* 1976, *19,* 407-412.

Wickman, E.K. *Children's behavior and teachers' attitudes.* New York: Commonwealth Fund, 1928.

Williams, J. In-school alternatives: Why bother? In A.M. Garibaldi (Ed.), *In-school alternatives and suspensions: Conference report.* Washington, D.C.: National Institute of Education, April 1979.

Wilson, C., Robertson, S., Herlong, D., Haynes, S. Vicarious effect of timeout in the modification of aggression in the classroom. *Behavior Modification,* January 1979, *3*(1), 97-109.

Wood v. Strickland 14 S. Ct. 1932 (1974).

Zeilberger, J., Sampsen, S., & Sloane, H. Modification of a child's problem behaviors in the home with the mother as the therapist. *Journal of Applied Behavior Analysis,* 1968, *1*, 47-53.

Chapter 4

Behavioral Characteristics and Management Strategies

Ann C. Sabatino and Maribeth Montgomery-Kasik

INTRODUCTION

This chapter offers a quick reference system for managing or controlling a wide array of behaviors. It is intended to provide busy practitioners with as much fingertip information in as few words as possible. The procedure: the characteristics associated with a fairly specific behavioral disorder classification are described briefly, then one or more treatment procedures are offered. If one doesn't work, another can be tried. The procedure that works with a given student may or may not be tested here but alternatives are provided from which to choose.

Most textbooks on behavioral disorders are long on theory and short on practical suggestions. They frequently focus on a particular theoretical framework or report an eclectic smattering of techniques under a general treatment rubric. The opinion here is that that process is not practical for busy teachers who do not dare or care to unravel a theoretical position that describes why a behavior occurs in order to manage it. Teachers have just enough time to try a treatment procedure if they are given a suggestion. This chapter contains specific suggestions grouped under particular characteristics. It is a ready reference system in that respect.

What it is not is a user's guide to best practice or more appropriate treatment form. Although in reference format it is intended that this be used not as a cookbook but as a helpful guide and starting point for busy educators. The behavioral disorder art has not advanced to the state where comparative data on practices have generated one that is the most appropriate. Given teacher personality, the restraint in a given situation, the classroom, school, and community environment, and the student who is presenting problems, there simply is no scientific basis for saying approach A is better than approach B.

Until that day arrives, there will be no answers, only logical estimates of what can be done. What are presented here are calculated procedures that sound as though they should make sense. That, then, reflects the state of the art and this chapter offers much of that information in a digested, easy-to-use format. At the end of the chapter is a list of ideas for reinforcing activities (Exhibit 4-1).

BEHAVIOR

- Attention-seeking

Definition and Example

- Behavior includes any action the student uses to gain attention from others, generally inappropriately. The attention seeker's level of activity usually decreases after the attention is received. The behaviors include being boisterous, showing off, running away, arguing, finger snapping, tattling, handwriting, whining, shyness, foot tapping, etc.
- The student attempts to manipulate others; also is unable to complete work without involving direct control by an adult.
- The student cannot tolerate control by others and tests their limits.

Remediation and Management

- Count *frequency of* behaviors—they may not occur as often as is believed. Record each incident.
- Provide opportunities for the student legitimately to obtain favorable attention from peers and adults for appropriate behaviors. Each appropriate behavioral response should be rewarded by immediate attention to the youth (boy or girl). Immediate feedback for appropriate behaviors may soon convince students that rulekeeping conduct earns satisfying, positive attention from teachers and peers. If possible, the teacher should ignore inappropriate behavior and perhaps encourage classmates to do so. The student can be put on a regular positive attention schedule.

    Example: The teacher initiates the conversation with the student at times when misbehavior is *not* present.

- Create special projects the students can complete to gain recognition by all their classmates. Refuse to fall for the bait of manipulation struggle.

    Example: When the student shows defiance by failing to complete an assignment, the teacher can say, "I cannot force you to do your assignment. If your choice is not to complete the assignment, what could happen to you?"

- Provide recognition to appropriate, attention-seeking behaviors by permitting the student to collect homework, copy grades, take attendance, monitor the room or hall, etc. Recognize and deal openly with attention-seeking behaviors.
- Provide structural learning environments.
- Establish clear expectations for student behavior and follow through consistently.
- Ignore inappropriate behaviors that facilitate learning.
- Offer praise such as "Good job!" "You're doing fine!" "I like the way you're working quietly," to accentuate good behavior.
- Use in-class timeout.

   Example: After Sam is rude to the teacher, the teacher turns away and ignores him for three minutes.

- View attention-seeking behavior on videotape or hear students' language on tape recorder.
- Have students monitor and record their own behavior.

   Example: Prepare a chart for their desk and provide them a system of recording each time a behavior occurs: talking out—1; out of seat—111. Or have a peer monitor and record a specific behavior.

BEHAVIOR

- Chronic disobedience

Definition and Example

- Behavior includes action contrary to directions of authority figure. The student must be reminded of rules constantly. The youth aggressively challenges authority and will not follow the simplest rule.
- The student is rude, out of seat, argumentative, acting-out.

Remediation and Management

- Include the entire class when setting rules.

   Example: At the beginning of the year, draft class rules, then include all members in finalizing them. Ask students their opinion, discuss why certain rules are necessary, vote on the rules, involve the class in putting them in writing. Try to help the students to personalize the rules. Since they voted their approval, they are referred to a class-run behavioral court when they break rules.

- Reward appropriate behavior.

    Example: Students who are out of their seats a lot should receive reinforcements, specifically when they are in the chair.

- Avoid "You will" statements.

    Example: "You will" statements often arouse challenges in chronic disobedient students: "You will stay in your seat for reading," "You will not talk without permission."

- Consider referral for counseling or use counseling in class.
- Avoid threats.

    Example: "You will erase your name from your desk by the time I count to 30 . . . 1, 2, 3, . . ."
    "You will" statements and "time limits" tend to box disruptive students into behaviors that seldom comply with teachers' demands. The situation becomes a struggle for power. Someone will lose face and the acting-out youth often will challenge the authority figure with aggressive behaviors.

- Be prepared to enforce the rules. When a rule is made, it is to be applied in all situations under most circumstances. Inconsistent enforcement leads to student manipulation of the system.

    Example: Students who break rules should be deprived of privileges, put in isolation or timeout, their parents telephoned, etc.

- Refrain from having one student compete against others and do not compare that one to peers.
- Avoid contests the student has little chance of winning. Eliminate "I" and emphasize "You."

    Example: "You are trying harder." "You should be happy with your work." "You did a very nice job." "You should feel good knowing you did a good job." "You should be proud."

- Negotiate behavior by helping the students evaluate their conduct. Express concern for them as individuals; get involved. Deal with the present behavior. Have students verbalize their behavior, ask them how they propose to correct the acting-out, and help them develop a plan. Have students commit themselves in writing or a handshake. Do not punish students for broken plans; just go back and start over. Direct conversations to them.

Example: "You are a smart person and very likable. Why did you behave like that? Can you tell me what you did? How do you feel when you act that way? How do you think your class feels about you when you behave like that? Do you suppose you could stop? What could I do to help? What should we do? Let's make a plan. Do you have an idea?" etc.

Specific Examples of Chronic Disobedience

Definition and Example

- Unwillingness to accept assignments

Remediation and Management

- Look for attachments between student and peers. Remember the youth's past behavior and start a fresh approach.

  Example: Avoid such statements as: "Put that down and get back to work, or else!" "Don't you dare do that again!" "You are acting like a moron." "Are you retarded? Why do you act like that?" "Don't be such a loudmouth!"

Definition and Example

- Refusal to listen

Remediation and Management

- Design statements such as "What are you doing?" and encourage the student to try to verbally state the misbehavior, then ask, "How does kicking your classmate help you?" "Why do you cheat?" etc. Then, "What do you suggest we do about your behavior?" "What can we do for you or with you so you will not do that again?" Such statements reverse the situation and put the problem on the student instead of the youth's placing the responsibility on the teacher: What are you, the student, going to do about it?

Definition and Example

- Temper tantrums

Remediation and Management

- Conduct a class court.

Example: The last 20 minutes of the day, once a week, representatives of the class meet to discuss problems. At that time, the disruptive student can be involved and the class can decide what to do with that individual. Class courts have voted to exclude the student when there are group activities, asked that the class not be interrupted, taken away the chair since the youth seldom is in it, etc. The class court can set a probation period of good behavior before the student can rejoin projects.

- Attempt not to punish but allow natural consequences to teach the student. Punishment gives attention, enhances power struggle, stimulates revenge, and keeps the student helpless.
- Set clear expectations for student behavior.

    Example: "John, I expect you at your desk, in your seat, when the bell rings."

- Require finished products.
- Reinforce (reward) students for engaging less frequently in undesired behavior.

Definition and Example

- Interruptions

Remediation and Management

- Establish personal monitoring.

    Example: Every time Jake needs to be given a pass to the bathroom he is required to mark a chart. At the end of the week, he may be shocked at the excessive number of times his peers witness his asking for a bathroom pass.

- Establish isolation, a place for the student to sit away from the group to sit quietly and think about a plan for reentering the classroom.

    Example: The first isolation may be away from the group. However, there are many stages of isolation that continue to suspension and expulsion.

- Continue to ask the student, "What are you doing?" "What rules are you breaking?" "Why are you in isolation?" "What are you going to do about it?" "You will not return to your classmates until you have a plan to present to them for your readmission, so what is your plan?" "How will you behave differently?"

- Exercise control by closeness. Movement of teacher toward a student can be associated with reduced deviance. The movement must be positive and interpreted by the youth as concern and reassurance, not an antecedent to punishment.
- Ignore the interruptions.
- Enlist the assistance of other students in cooperating to remove social reinforcements.

     Example: Both teacher and class totally ignore Susan when she talks out or is out of seat without permission.

- Realize a temporary increase of the behavior is expectable before extinction.
- Ignore the increase or the behavior will be strengthened and very difficult to eliminate. However, be certain the behavior is one appropriate to ignore before intervention.

Definition and Example

- Crying, whining

Remediation and Management

- Attend to the student when an appropriate response to frustration is exhibited.
- Ignore obvious attempts to obtain undeserved attention.

Definition and Example

- Swearing

Remediation and Management

- Satiate the student by encouraging repetition of the bothersome behavior until tired of it, thus calling attention to the undesirable features of such conduct.

     Example: A secondary boy constantly uses a vulgar word to gain attention from peers. The teacher might try having him say the word over and over again until he is tired.

- Use a frequency count. When the student realizes the behavior is being observed, it often will decrease. This is an example of self-concept improvement (see Chapter 8).

Definition and Example

- Putting objects in mouth: paper clips, rubber bands, pieces of metal, sticks, etc.

Remediation and Management

- Require immediate countermeasure (such as oral prophylaxis).

  Example: Each time a foreign object is placed in the mouth, the student should brush teeth for five minutes with toothpaste, wipe the mouth, and use an oral antiseptic to kill harmful organisms.

- Use a Good Behavior Clock. Time accumulated on it for appropriate classroom behavior earns tokens that the student may use to purchase privileges or reinforcers that can be shared with peers.
- Put emphasis on choice—let the student make the decision between reinforcement and punishment.

  Example: The class rule is that students do not leave the gymnasium at halftime or they are not allowed to reenter. "I see you decided to leave the gym at halftime. The rule is that you cannot return. It was your decision."

- View behavior on videotape. Have peers record specific conduct as it occurs or let the students record their own behavior. Many times recording a behavior, or the fact that the student knows this is being done, will decrease the behavior.

BEHAVIOR

- Disruption of class

Definitions and Examples

- Interfering with the activity of an individual or group; inappropriate talking, laughing, clapping, stamping, shouting, singing, whistling, vulgarity, sarcasm; slamming a desk top or a book, pushing a chair over.
- Being tardy.
- Using an impermissible hand sign—raised fist with middle finger extended.
- Expressing defiance.
- Jumping out of seat frequently.
- Giving unreasonable answers.
- Cheating.
- Perpetrating practical jokes.

- Wasting time with pencil and ruler.
- Playing with objects.
- Losing homework, clothing, papers, money.
- Taking possessions from peers.
- Leaving the lunch table without permission.
- Screaming, running, throwing tantrums.

Remediation and Management

- Reward appropriate or nondisruptive behaviors. Consistently reward acceptable conduct, indicating to students that to get attention, they must be good and follow the class rules.
- Institute modeling. Direct students to model peers, fictitious or idealized characters, or an important adult.
- Have students monitor themselves or have peers record behaviors.
- Analyze videotaped conduct.
- Behave in same way the students should act.

     Example: A student who screams and is answered by a screaming teacher will continue to scream. A physically aggressive student disciplined by a physically aggressive teacher will continue to be physically aggressive.

- Conduct frequency counts. The behavior may not be a problem, merely one that the teacher notices.
- Offer or cancel an extra recess.

     Example: A ten-minute recess is scheduled for 2:30. If any member of the class signals improper gestures or refers to them, one minute of the recess is taken away from the group.

- Consider the problem of auditory memory deficit. Some students cannot remember what they hear. This is especially noticeable in secondary students. The teacher can: (1) give instructions in a specific order and ask the student to follow one by one; (2) reinforce with written directions; (3) use a tape recorder to play back the initial directions.
- Use saturation to deal with behaviors such as spitting, kicking, giggling, clapping, shouting, singing, etc.

     Example: The student is required to repeat the disruptive action until tired and feels, ''I don't ever want to do that again.''

- Focus on a specific behavior. Select one with the greatest threat, disruption, or interfering effect, instead of several. Plan for one behavior, not many.
- Vary management techniques. Students, activities, and environment change so the teacher must keep changing.
- Deal with the present. Change is more likely when emphasis is put on the present.

  Example: "This is the fifth time you have been out of your seat."

- Conduct individual tutoring.

  Example: Instead of asking for help on a task, the student may whisper, find a toy, or draw. The teacher moves close and provides minimal assistance to start the student functioning appropriately.

- Use closeness control. Movement of the teacher toward the student can be associated with reduced deviance. Movement must be interpreted as positive—concern and reassurance—not as an antecedent to punishment.
- Show interest before disruption can occur.

  Example: "I'm sure you can do the assignment." "That is a tough job. You are doing very well."

- Provide structure in class.
- Provide counseling.
- Resort to overcorrection of a behavior as necessary: have the disruptive student (1) recite the class rule governing such conduct, (2) practice, (3) repeat several times, (4) engage in positive practice during recess.

  Example: The student is aggravated and slams the desk top. "What is the rule about slamming desks?" "Can you state the rule?" "Good, now shut the desk properly. That was better. Do it again and again. Much better. Instead of the normal five-minute break, perhaps you should stay here and practice shutting the desk quietly, then maybe you will learn to do it correctly."

- Use puppet plays, animated stories, cartoons, and role-playing to demonstrate certain behaviors. Allow the student to make the decision as to punishment or reinforcement, then experience the consequences.

  Example: The rule is that a student who goes outside to recess cannot go back into the building. Or a teenager who leaves the high school for lunch is not allowed to return until scheduled. The student who goes back into the building during recess—stays. The one who returns to the school early goes to a study or solitaire carrel until scheduled reentry time. Supervisors should not show anger. "I see you decided to return to the building. Go to your room (go to the study)."

- Use timeout and reinforcement. Hold the student in a chair during a tantrum, reinforce peers to ignore the incident, and reinforce the youth for conduct other than tantrums, i.e., appropriate social skills and academic behaviors.
- Develop student self-regulation.

    Example: "Talk yourself into going to class on time, convince yourself to work longer in class, remind yourself to smile more. Remember to think 'slow down' before hurrying to answer a teacher's question."

- Teach student to self-observe, self-reinforce, or self-punish personal behaviors.

    Example: "I must not get angry." "I must be controlled by myself." "I can control my temper. If I do, I will be proud of myself and that feels good."

- Utilize counterconditioning (reinforcing a behavior that is incompatible to the behavior one wishes to weaken).

    Example: Linda has a tendency to steal, lie, or tattle on peers. When she demonstrates a good behavior, reward her. Keep her on task and make the work meaningful. The more she performs appropriately, the less the likelihood she will revert to her impermissible conduct.

BEHAVIOR

- Distractibility

Definition and Example

- Behavior includes difficulty in attending to or focusing attention on appropriate stimuli in an efficient way; short attention spans and frequent shifts; equal responses to relevant and irrelevant things the individual sees, hears, or touches; makes frequent trips to the water fountain (or watching the clock, or going to the window).

Remediation and Management

- Reward appropriate behavior first.
- Structure the environment. Limit the space and stimuli—visual, tactile, auditory, etc. Reduce environmental stimuli.

  Example: The teacher should sound-treat walls, carpet floors, cover windows, cover bookshelves and cupboards, limit bulletin boards, provide cubicles; establish predictable routines, firm expectations, consistent consequences.

- Modify instructional materials.

  Example: Cleaner materials should be used, i.e., those free of extraneous stimuli such as colorful pictures on a reading page, or math materials; use varying color and form on various stimuli, assign fewer problems to complete.

- Reduce space for each student by creating cubicles.
- Structure the class program with a predictable, stable routine without deviations.
- Enhance the stimulus value of teaching materials.

  Example: The teacher permits only one assignment on the desk at a time.

- Modify instructional strategies. The teacher makes most decisions as to when a student should begin an activity and gives explicit instructions.
- Have students verbalize labels for stimuli and rehearse the instructions. The latter is most beneficial for those who have underselective rather than overselective attention.

  Example: A student working on an arithmetic problem will talk through each step in performing the operations; one who writes spelling will say the letters aloud as they are written.

- Develop behavior modification. Students will attend more to their work if favorable consequences follow promptly after such good behavior. Sometimes reinforcers stronger than the teacher's attention are necessary, i.e., peer approval, grades, awards, principal's praise, or any recognition appropriate for the students' stage of development. The rewards must be meaningful to the teenagers or they will have very little value. For those with short attention spans, being reinforced for paying attention is valid. Paying attention and looking at the teacher can increase the likelihood that correct responses will occur in the future. Students who do not know how to pay attention, what to look for, or how to find information must receive direct instruction in attentional strategies such as looking, performing, writing, listening, hearing. Reinforcement of correct responses to academic assignments will increase the attention span only if the tasks are within the student's potential. It is not reasonable to offer reinforcement for a task a child cannot do.

- Reduce academic demands, then gradually emphasize basic skills.

- Provide rapid feedback, including immediate scoring on all work. Be certain students are aware of their achievements and their continual progress.

- Announce clear performance expectations so the students know what the targets are.

- Try not to punish; instead increase motivation and task completion.

- Show students what to do; reduce verbalization.

- Evaluate students' readiness levels, making certain they are able to perform assignments.

- Avoid abstractions.

- Accept and reward on-task responses.

- Schedule introduction and removal of cues.

    Example: The water fountain is turned off during math and reading. Students who complete their desk work will have free access to the fountain during remaining activities.

- Establish environmental programming: after youths study one hour without roaming around the room, a ten-minute break is granted as free time to fully explore classroom space at their discretion.

SUGGESTED READINGS

Hallahan, D.P., & Kauffman, J.M. Research on the education of distractible and hyperactive children. In W.M. Cruickshank & D.P. Hallahan (Eds.), *Perceptual and learning disabilities in children* (Vol. 2: Research and theory). Syracuse, N.Y.: Syracuse University Press, 1975.

Hewett, F.M. Educational engineering with emotionally disturbed children. *Exceptional Children,* 1967, *33*(2), 459-471.

Lovitt, T.C., & Smith, J.O. Effects of instructions on an individual's verbal behavior. *Exceptional Children,* 1972, *38*(2), 685-693.

Pick, A.D., Christy, M.D., & Frankel, G.W. A developmental study of visual selective attention. *Journal of Experimental Child Psychology,* 1972, *14*, 165-175.

Stevenson, H.W. *Children's learning.* New York: Appleton-Century-Crofts, Inc., 1972.

BEHAVIOR

- Encopresis

Definition and Example

- Behavior is a chronic problem in retaining feces until they can be released in the toilet. This can involve retention of feces that cause constipation, or chronically dilated anal sphincter that allows constant fecal discharge.

Remediation and Management

- Insist on teacher intervention.
- Require a physical examination of the student.
- Ignore the situation.

    Example: When the teacher refuses to show attention when the student soils clothing and refuses to change to clean garments, the problem may correct itself.

- Provide motivation or isolation.

    Example: A student who soils clothing is required to spend 30 minutes in isolation, but when garments are kept clean, the youth is released from an undesirable activity such as completing a workbook sheet, physical education, math, etc.

- Use overcorrection.

    Example: The student brings a change of clothes to school. When the student soils the original garments, the teacher requests that the individual wash up, wash out the soiled clothes with a strong disinfectant, then stay after school to make up for the time lost in cleaning the clothes.

SUGGESTED READINGS

Conger, J.C. The treatment of encopresis by the management of social consequences. *Behavior Therapy,* 1974, *1,* 386, 390.

Edelman, R.I. Operant conditioning treatment of encopresis. *Journal of Behavior Therapy and Experimental Psychiatry,* 1971, *2,* 71-73.

Ferinden, W., & Handel, D.V. Elimination of soiling behavior in elementary school child. *Journal of School Psychology,* 1970, *8,* 207-269.

O'Leary, K.D., & Wilson, G.T. *Behavior therapy: Application and outcome.* Englewood Cliffs, N.J.: Prentice-Hall, Inc., 1975.

BEHAVIOR

- Enuresis

Definition and Example

- Behavior is a chronic problem in retaining urine until it can be released in the toilet. The student wets pants to avoid a class activity.

Remediation and Management

- Require a physical examination. There may be a physical cause for enuresis that can be corrected medically. Until a physical examination has been completed, it is not safe to assume there is not an anatomical defect and that medication is not particularly helpful.
- Use a conditioning device. Two metal foil sheets separated by an insulating pad are connected electrically to a buzzer alarm. When the youth begins to urinate, the moisture completes the electrical contact and sets off the buzzer, awakening the person. The youth then gets out of bed, finishes urination, washes up, changes the sheets, resets the alarm, and goes back to bed.
- Train the student in urine retention by repeatedly practicing voluntary interruption of the stream, then starting the flow again. This exercise should be repeated often.
- Reinforce appropriate urination.
- Have the student increase fluid intake. This provides more opportunity for learning trials and practice in toileting.
- Require student self-correction of accidents.

    Example: The student must get out of bed, bathe, put on dry night clothes, launder stained sheets, change bed linen, and turn out the lights before going back to bed.

- Be truthful.

    Example: "You wet your pants thinking you would be excused to go home so you would miss the field trip. You are going on the field trip."

SUGGESTED READINGS

Baller, W.R. *Bed-wetting: Origins and treatment.* Elmsford, N.Y.: Pergamon Press, 1973.

Nordquist, V.M. The modification of a child's enuresis: Some response-relationships. *Journal of Applied Behavior Analysis,* 1971, *4,* 241-247.

O'Leary, K.D., & Wilson, G.T. *Behavior therapy: Application and outcome.* Englewood Cliffs, N.J.: Prentice-Hall, Inc., 1975.

- Try to ensure success by providing many positive experiences in school-related activities.
- Implement planned ignoring of incidents.

BEHAVIOR

- Fears

Definition and Example

- Behavior is debilitating when it becomes excessive, or interferes with normal activities such as sleep, school attendance, exploration; it also involves fear of high buildings, dogs, the dark, buses, teachers, stage fright, school, etc.

Remediation and Management

- Require intervention when fear interferes with the student's activity.
- Adopt a gradual approach, repeated exposure to feared situation or object, and maintenance of a nonanxious state during exposure.
- Introduce modeling as an effective tactic.

   Example: The student watches peers have fun, play games, work together in groups, cross the street, etc., in a nonanxious attitude.

- Desensitize the situation.

   Example: If the student is afraid of a particular animal, show a film involving others playing with the animal without tensions or anxiety.

- Provide positive reinforcement of the student's nearness to the feared object as this sometimes aids in fear reduction. When the student sees a picture and does not exhibit unnecessary fear, the teacher should reward the behavior; desensitization progress is continued until the youth can be near the object without fear, when a further reward is made. When desired absence of fear is achieved, the teacher maintains intermittent rewarding and verbally reinforcing the student to maintain the individual's comfort with the previously feared object.
- Establish a climate of safety and predictability.
- Provide simple tasks involving the feared item at which the student can be successful 90 percent of the time.
- Maintain meaningful positive reinforcement with social experiences in a structured environment.

BEHAVIOR

- Hyperactivity

Definition and Example

- Behavior involves sustained physical action: persistent, disorganized, disruptive, unpredictable, nongoal directed, overreaction to stimuli in the environment, restless, jittery, impulsive, in constant motion.

Remediation and Management

- Readjust the curriculum and schedule, using brief instruction periods and frequent changes of instructional activities. Divide assignments gradually, increasing or decreasing them as seems appropriate.

  Example: The teacher establishes a schedule of numerous activities of short duration—ten minutes on math, ten minutes to wash the slateboard, five minutes to do a phonic worksheet; then feed the fish, water one plant; then 15 minutes on reading before fifteen minutes of recess.

- Assign physical education more often.

  Example: The student takes physical education four times a day instead of once. The extra physical education classes can be used as rewards: before the student can go to a physical education class, the science worksheet must be completed neatly.

- Develop daily progress charts.

  Example: The teacher sets a goal for the number of minutes the student remains on task, in the seat, without talking. When the behavioral data for a particular period are computed, the student marks them on a progress chart.

- Use a kitchen timer.

  Example: The student is told that the teacher will set a timer but not how many minutes it will run (the setting should be changed constantly). If the student is working when the bell rings, an extra break is awarded or the teacher marks off ten math problems or grants an extra room privilege. The teacher should use verbal praise and constant feedback. It is productive to increase the time, yet intermittently shorten it, so the student will not know what to expect.

- Involve the student in group study to instill the concept of working together rather than going off on solo hyperactive gambits.

    Example: The teacher reads the group a story and asks questions. It is useful to repeat numbers games, add on sentences, memorize poems. The teacher makes assignments, then walks around the room. Tokens are awarded to those on task when the teacher visits their desks. At end of the period, or week, the teacher auctions off a reward or rewards. The more tokens or points a student has, the higher the bid is possible and the more breaks or privileges the individual can buy for next week, a soft drink for today, a movie pass, cookie, comb, etc.

- Set the student in an area of the classroom having minimal auditory and visual distractions.
- Praise the student for completing tasks.
- Make specific rules for class and always enforce them: structure and consistency are important.
- Allow the student to tutor a child in lower grades.
- Center activities primarily on behaviors necessary to learn; learning to learn most important.

    Example: Activities should be child centered, not subject centered. Time on task, controlled talk-out, in-seat behavior, and distractibility take precedence. When the student can improve on these characteristics, learning will be more efficient and easier.

- Introduce modeling as a guidance technique.

    Example: The teacher could direct the hyperactive student to observe normal peers as they demonstrate correct behaviors. The teacher should give reinforcers to the performers who have value to the hyperactive student.

- Use biofeedback to train the hyperactive individual to reduce the muscular activity and tension by monitoring muscle tension.

SUGGESTED READINGS

Braud, L., Lupin, M.N., & Braud, W.G. The use of electromyographic biofeedback in the control of hyperactivity. The *Journal of Learning Disabilities,* 1975, *8*(5), 420, 425.

Csapo, M. Peer models reverse the ''one bad apple spoils the barrel'' theory. *Teaching Exceptional Children,* 1972, *5*(1), 20-24.

- Remove temptations that stimulate hyperactivity.

  Example: The teacher should remove the basketball, pull a curtain, shut the door, etc., getting all distracting articles out of the student's sight.

- Remind the hyperactive student of the class rules on conduct. Reward the entire class, contingent on appropriate behavior by this single student. This also introduces the element of peer pressure on the overactive student to conform.

  Example: When Scott remains at his desk and refrains from bothering classmates for one period, the entire class will receive a privilege, i.e., be excused five minutes early on Friday, receive free popcorn at a ball game, new pencils, sit in a seat of their choice the next day.

- Prompt desired behaviors.

  Example: The teacher requests Peter to pass out game cards, toys, treats, at a time he usually takes such items away from other classmates.

BEHAVIOR

- Hypoactivity

Definition and Example

- Behavior is slow, lethargic/insufficient, unconcerned, related to inability to perceive environment accurately and react to demands appropriately; sense of fear immobilizes the student, who also displays reticence, daydreams, lack of interest, sluggishness, failure to complete assignments, refusal to play at recess; is preoccupied, drowsy; shows little initiative; goes along with group opinion.

Remediation and Management

- Plan a diverse activity program that requires more energy than normal. The more desirable activities should follow less desirable ones. To participate in enjoyable activities, the student first must complete undesirable ones; usually those requiring increased energy output. The teacher should reward the pupil for participation and slowly increase demands for more activity and energy expenditures.

- Use a timer on the student's work response, in effect forcing such individuals to learn to compete against themselves.
- Do not force or punish the student as such tactics tend to increase anxiety.
- Provide the student with a secure environment and personal and emotional support and encouragement.
- Study the individual's eating habits at home and at school—the student may not be receiving a nutritional diet.
- Request that the student have a medical examination. There may be a physical reason why the youth does not have energy to participate in activities or tasks.
- Visit the parents to discover whether the teenager behaves at home the same as at school. Try to ascertain whether the home has illness, conflicts, or traumas that depress the student.
- Provide a wide range of learning activities and methods, cultivate strengths and interests, encourage self-evaluation and decision making.
- Request students to pass out toys, games, treats, etc., run errands to other rooms, act as hall monitors with peers, go on extra field trips with other classes.
- Help students be aware they are making choices.
- Protect them against experiences that produce shame, embarrassment, and doubt.

BEHAVIOR

- Impulsivity

Definition and Example

- Behavior involves instantaneous responses to stimulation, responses that lack thoughtfulness and planning, are rapid and inappropriate, and often result in errors.

Remediation and Management

- Limit instruction periods.

   Example: The student works five minutes on reading assignments ten times a day, gradually increasing minutes on task as the quality of work increases.

- Change instructional activities frequently. As the student's impulsivity decreases and quality of work increases, brief instructional periods and frequent changes of instructional activities can be modified and shortened.

    Example: After reading, the student is directed into an art project, then science and geography, followed by physical activity, then math, and back to reading.

- Reduce extraneous stimuli. By limiting and controlling the distractions to which the student is subjected, time on task increases, with greater focus on learning.

    Example: The teacher erects a carrel around the student's desk, turning the youth in a more private direction.

- Provide immediate feedback. The teacher should respond to completed work quickly and reward/correct effort and assignment at once. The student should not be allowed to go on to the next assignment until the current one is checked. The work also should be checked intermittently to be sure it is being done correctly so the student does not waste valuable time learning an activity incorrectly. Unlearning the incorrect material and acquiring the right version takes too long and further threatens the student's attention. The teacher should help students develop effective use of their attention by directing and timing it. Attention spans that are short must not be shared with too many competing stimuli.

- Make discipline firm but kind.

    Example: "Mary, please don't do that. What should you be doing? Do you need help? No? Then put your head down and try to concentrate on your work. Thank you."

- Involve peer tutoring.

    Example: The teacher assigns a class peer or "buddy" to remind the impulsive student to "slow down, get back to work, quit talking, sit down."

SUGGESTED READINGS

Bolstad, O.D., & Johnson, S.M. Self-regulation in the modification of disruptive classroom behavior. *Journal of Applied Behavior Analysis,* 1972, *5,* 443-454.

Meichenbaum, R., & Goodman, J. Training impulsive children to talk to themselves: A means of developing self-control. *Journal of Abnormal Psychology,* 1971, *77,* 115-125.

Monohan, J., & O'Leary, K.D. Effects of self-instruction on rule-breaking behavior. *Psychological Reports,* 1971, *29,* 1059-1066.

- Introduce self-instruction. The teacher uses modeling, behavioral rehearsal, and verbal instruction to guide the student through correct self-regulating patterns. Slower response style, scanning, and attending are emphasized.
- Induce students to more self-reinforcing self-statements.

    Example: "I can do it. I can stay on task. I will complete my assignment. I am strong. I am doing it . . . I did it, I did it. *WOW!*" (See Chapter 8 on verbal and operant self-control techniques.)

BEHAVIOR

- Impulsiveness (cognitive)

Definition and Example

- Behavior is associated with aggression, deficient moral development (low or no principles), hyperactivity, and inattention; impulsive students respond erratically and produce many errors.

Remediation and Management

- Require the student to delay responding. Teach the individual to scan the alternatives and compare to a standard before choosing. Combining modeling instruction and extra motivation sometimes is effective in decreasing impulsiveness.

    Example: A classmate demonstrates a reflective, slower tempo, directing attention to exactly how to scan, strategize, or make self-statements.

- Introduce self-instruction, showing the student how to use self-statements to regulate speech and behavior.

    Example: The teacher instructs the students to instruct themselves to go slower, think, take their time, and tell themselves to stop and think before answering.

- Instruct students how to make self-management statements directed at themselves: "Jean, . . ."
- Use behavior modification, withdrawing rewards contingent on errors.

Example: Each error "costs" the student a minute of recess or some other reinforcing activity. Each error increases the number of problems to complete; i.e., for each math problem mistake the pupil must do one more problem of the same type correctly.

- Utilize timeout procedures.
- Provide positive reinforcement because many times it will help the student to improve reflective characteristics.
- Practice the correct way of performing.

    Example: The teacher tells Harry, "Before shouting out the answer and shaking your arm in the air, interrupting me and other students only to give the wrong answer, practice saying the correct answer to yourself, then put your arm in the air, and wait to be called on." Such a routine can be practiced and should be rewarding when performed in a real situation.

- Utilize a self-control curriculum that includes units of instruction designed to teach students, among other things, to focus attention, avoid distractions, develop memory skills and sequences, anticipate consequences, appreciate feelings, tolerate and recognize frustration, inhibit overquick reactions, delay responding, and provide relaxation. This should emphasize the importance of feelings, self-understanding, introspection, and attempts to integrate affective and cognitive domains. It should include specific social learning exercises and activities to use with academic tasks.
- Attempt to build ego in the learner. The teacher should discuss the behavior to help the student gain insight into the problems. The student should understand the results and consequences of compulsive actions. Teacher and student should work out solutions at the latter's suggestion. The more input the student has into the behavior and what to do about it, the better the results.

SUGGESTED READINGS

Azrin, N.H., & Powers, M.A. Eliminating classroom disturbances of emotionally disturbed children by positive practice procedures. *Behavior Therapy,* 1975, *6,* 525-534.

Lovitt, T.C., & Curtiss, K.A. Effects of manipulating an antecedent event on mathematics response rate. *Journal of Applied Behavior Analysis,* 1968, *1,* 329-333.

Lovitt, T.C., & Smith, J.O. Effects of instructions on an individual's verbal behavior. *Exceptional Children,* 1972, *38*(2), 685-693.

Meichenbaum, D.H., & Goodman, J. Reflection-impulsivity and verbal control of motor behavior. *Child Development,* 1969, *40,* 585-597.

Meichenbaum, D.H., & Goodman, J. Training impulsive children to talk to themselves. *Journal of Abnormal Psychology,* 1971, *77,* 115-126.

BEHAVIOR

- Inattentiveness

Definition and Example

- Behavior involves an inability to focus on perceived stimuli for a sufficient time to purposely engage in the task. The student cannot complete a task in the allotted amount of time because of preoccupation and daydreaming.

Remediation and Management

- Provide the inattentive student with limited quantities of highly stimulating tasks, including game formats.
- Limit extraneous verbal and nonverbal stimuli.
- Provide direct, precise, structured teaching, using brief periods of instruction and physical activity between in-seat activity. Unstructured time should be limited.
- Reward the student for in-seat behavior.

    Example: Daily progress charts, behavioral contracts, and a kitchen timer should be used. When the timer goes off, the student earns points, tokens, or extra privileges if in the seat.

- Provide a one-to-one relationship.
- Determine whether daydreaming is an escape; if the need for escape is real, that may be the root cause of daydreaming.
- Establish a climate of safety and predictability.
- Accept and reward limited responses.

BEHAVIOR

- Inflexibility

Definition and Example

- Behavior involves a limitation in the quantity and quality of individual adjustment mechanisms. The student repeatedly uses particular responses even though they may be inappropriate for the task. The individual is compulsive, aloof, and inhibited, has restricted interests, is overcritical of self and personal productions, and lives in an overcontrolled fashion, free from joy, excitement, interest, and variety.

Remediation and Management

- Avoid strict discipline.
- Develop a failure-proof plan that encourages risk and a variety of activities in a logical sequence with immediate success.

    Example: The student shoots a bow and arrow standing only ten feet from the target, plays basketball with the free throws that can be self-scored, plays catch at close range with large ball. The teacher provides activities of new interest that are individual and cannot be right or wrong such as an art project or writing assignment.

- Encourage tolerance by others of the individual's errors.
- Provide reinforcement for new and different activities the student attempts.
- Keep competition minimal to enhance self-confidence.
- Help student to feel safe and secure by designing new activities that will be successful, enhancing, and nonthreatening.

BEHAVIOR

- Instability

Definition and Example

- Behavior involves unstable moods, rapid and frequent change in observable behavior without cause, general unpredictability: happy to sad, withdrawn to acting-out, aggressive to submissive, cooperative to noncompliant; irritable, emotionally explosive, or moody.

Remediation and Management

- Stabilize and structure the school environment.
- Establish a climate of safety and predictability.

    Example: The teacher can develop a schedule for the student to place on the desk outlining time, subjects, activities, lunch, and recess.

- Ignore undesirable moods and try to reward desirable behaviors consistently. A student who is unstable often responds best when scheduling, discipline, and rewards are constant and predictable.

- Provide the student with opportunities.

    Example: The teacher makes available physical activities, dancing, skits, games, drawing, and painting.

- Allow verbal expression within predetermined limits and time allotments.

    Example: The teacher sets a time each day, usually for older students, in which they can express themselves verbally. Rules are established as to language, length of time, volume (as needed).

- Confer with pupils.
- Limit competition.
- Reward good behavior.
- Do not dismiss from class.
- Do not punish.
- Do not force apologies.
- Provide one-to-one relationships.
- Exhibit awareness of the student's problems.

    Example: Voice quality and tone are important. A teacher with a sarcastic, biting demeanor may make remarks highly embarrassing to a seemingly unstable teenager who is required to find the place and carry over assignments from day to day. These negative experiences can result in intense antagonistic emotions toward class, teacher, school, and peers.

BEHAVIOR

- Lying

Definition and Example

- Behavior involves telling lies and/or mistruths.

Remediation and Management

- Do not punish the learner for telling the truth in a difficult situation.

    Example: "Mr. Smith, I was running in the hall. I accidently tripped and fell into the trophy case and broke this trophy. I am sorry." The student should not be punished for telling the truth. Perhaps the pupil should pay for the repair of the broken trophy but should be praised for being honest.

- Reward students when they find objects and turn them in to the teacher.

  Example: The school presents awards for reporting objects found; rewards honesty by giving certificates, monetary reward, or a plaque; announcing the student's name on the intercom.

- Give special responsibilities.
- Notice student's efforts.
- Indicate there are many ways to get attention from adults and peers other than lying and tattling.

BEHAVIOR

- Tattling

Definition and Example

- Behavior involves constantly reporting on the conduct of others.

Remediation and Management

- Do not respond when students tattle.
- Refuse to listen to tattling on other pupils.

BEHAVIOR

- Negativism toward self.

Definition and Example

- Behavior includes extreme and consistent verbal opposition or resistance to suggestions, advice, directions from others. The individual dislikes everything, likes nothing, is always saying no, presents much meaningless negativism. Negativism may be a prominent characteristic in aggressive persons.

Remediation and Management

- Ignore the behavior and insist on student participation in all activities.
- Carry out firm and consistent management.

- Provide simple tasks.
- Establish a structured learning environment.
- Set clear expectations for student behavior and follow through consistently.
- Require finished products.
- Establish a firm one-to-one relationship.
- Set up group projects.

BEHAVIOR

- Overcompetitiveness

Definition and Example

- Behavior involves effort to be the first through actions to overcome competition. This behavior can deeply scar the self-concept, especially when competition is unrealistic. The individual exhibits adverse reaction to not being No. 1 and inordinate excitement and frustration in unfamiliar activity; is overconcerned with rules, insisting on changes for personal reasons and advantage; aloof, unwilling to participate in new or modified activity.

Remediation and Management

- Minimize or eliminate competition from all activities. The teacher can encourage the students to enjoy events for the fun of participation or can plan activities in which all are winners.
- Allow the overcompetitive student to demonstrate a special skill or not compete against the more skilled. The teacher should control conditions so that the student competes only where there will be success.
- Discuss the meaning of winning and losing.
- Role-play and ask open-ended questions.

  Example: After a basketball game is over and the student has the lowest score, ask "What should you do?" Or, "When the game is over all players should meet in the middle of the floor and _____."

- Set up group projects and stress sharing.
- Discuss the individual's values and attitudes.
- Provide communication exercises and behavioral rehearsals.
- Practice conversation after losing or winning.

- Provide a wide range of learning activities.
- Encourage self-evaluation.
- Cultivate the student's interests.

BEHAVIOR

- Extreme social passivity

Definition and Example

- Behavior involves suggestible actions by an individual at the request of others to please them without apparent forethought. Such persons tend to be irresponsible, easily led, overcompliant, followers, and insecure in the environment. They will follow a leader, then excuse themselves for behaviors on the ground that they did what the leader requested. They use other persons as excuses for personal actions.

Remediation and Management

- Make discipline firm but not punitive.
- Include opportunities to practice decision making, problem solving, and selection of appropriate courses of action.
- Encourage independent functioning. Many opportunities should be offered for the passive student to participate in group decisions.
- Give special responsibilities to passive students. These sometimes enhance their self-concept enough that they will take pride in the growth of a personal project, i.e., a class pet, a flower, tidiness, neatness.
- Set up group projects.

    Example: The passive student can help classmates build a model volcano, plant a garden, or collect leaves or stamps.

- Provide multisensory experiences.

    Example: The passive student joins classmates in scientific experiments with air, light, heat, gas, or raising an animal or growing plants. The teacher should encourage discovery.

- Encourage pets in the classroom, i.e., rabbits, hamsters, fish. This produces the experiences and the responsibility of having an animal relying on the student for food, love, and shelter.
- Encourage parallel play; do not force interaction.

BEHAVIOR

- Perseveration

Definition and Example

- Behavior involves the tendency to continue an action after it no longer is appropriate for the task at hand. The student has difficulty changing from one task to another, is not goal directed (verbal or physical), and lacks internal control; laughs long after a joke is over, responds to questions when no longer appropriate, writes off the edge of the paper; continues to repeat words, letters, or stories until stopped; continues an act after directions to stop.

Remediation and Management

- Teach external signals.

    Example: When the teacher plays a note on the piano, turns out the light, or taps on the desk, the student focuses on the teacher and ceases whatever activity was going on. Social cues such as a pat on the back, a wink, a pleasant smile should be modeled when more obvious signals are not available. Games can be constructed to practice changing activities at home and at school.

BEHAVIOR

- Hostile physical aggression; destructiveness

Definition and Example

- Behavior involves hostile physical action against self or others that frequently creates fear; hitting, biting, scratching, throwing objects; inflicting personal damage, fighting, bullying, pinching, tripping, roughness; negative physical attack by gestures and words directed to others; destroying, damaging, or trying to destroy or damage any object, upsetting desks, destroying order on the teacher's desk; attacking or attempting to attack with intensity to possibly inflict pain; beating, stabbing, kicking, slapping, hitting, spanking, throwing, grabbing; or damaging or trying to destroy objects, peers, or teachers; learning disabled teenagers become anxious, emotional, and aggressive.

Remediation and Management

- Do not ignore aggressive or destructive behavior.
- Avoid physical punishment.
- Impose deprivation, timeout, isolation, sitting-out an activity but observing others as they participate.
- Withdraw tangible items such as dolls, snacks, toys, driving privileges, lounge pass, off-campus trips.
- Insist on counseling.
- Reinforce acceptable behaviors consistently. When the student does not physically aggress others, the teacher should express praise and verbally discuss that behavior, calling favorable attention to it. It should be explained why the decision not to fight was the better choice; this should be made rewarding to the student. The teacher should make the individual aware of situations in which peers are involved when there is no aggression so the student can see the alternatives to fights.
- Do not merely state a punishment—explain why you must punish.

    Example: Instead of "You will not go out to recess," the teacher should rephrase the punishment to, "You will not go out for three recesses because you hit your friend." Or, instead of, "Because you were fighting, you cannot drive to school," "You will not drive to school for one week."

- Provide communication exercises.
- Avoid physical restraint if it is at all possible; if not, it may become necessary to hold the student to curb harmful or dangerous behavior.
- Offer change-of-pace suggestions: "If the problem is frustrating you, get a drink of water."
- Develop a planned sequence response to violations. The teacher should anticipate possible aggressive behaviors and prepare to intervene.

    Example: The teacher should take respectful, firm deescalation measures; call attention to the anxious behavior of the student, make the individual aware of increasing anger; channel tension to constructive activity—punching a bag, immediate counseling (crisis intervention).

- Establish logical, realistic, and natural consequences. These should be such that the student will choose the more responsible activity. The decision will be the student's.

Example: The teacher says, "What would be the consequence?" "What would you gain?" "Tell me what I did to make you want to hit me?" Be passive. Unclench fists. Listen—encourage student to talk. Ask "What can we do to solve the problem?": swim, shoot baskets?

- Don't be reluctant to be angry. Anger, sadness, or fear can be discussed with the student, explaining how and why the teacher also can be angry, sad, etc. The discussion should cover appropriate ways to deal with these natural emotions.

  Example: George, alone in his room at home, could pound clay or nails, beat on junk, throw bean bags; outside the home, he could throw rocks in an area where no one or property would be harmed.

- Take all threats seriously. The teacher never should walk away from imposing discipline but should stay with and spend time with the student.
- Do not demean the student or put the individual in a corner or in an embarrassing situation in front of the class.
- Watch for a change in personality. If the student becomes sullen, the teacher should be cautious.
- Be aware of sudden grade changes or a decrease in scholastic performance.
- Watch for brooding students who carry grudges.
- Question friends of the student to discover problems.
- Spend time with the student. Fright invites aggression; passivity and fear activate violence.
- Remember that there usually is time to react before the aggressor strikes. The teacher should show a positive reaction of concern for the student.
- Try not to aggravate the confrontation; be humble, but not passive.
- Be prepared: think how to act if confronted. The teacher's potential inappropriate behavior and personal feelings should be identified.
- Provide a supportive structure, using the participation of other students in that structure.
- Help the student to experience needed joy, happiness, or success in the teacher's company.
- Believe in the student. One who experiences a hostile emotion will be more likely to believe in self if the teacher shows that same belief.
- Search for the cause, analyze the behavior. The teacher should consider the surface problem and determine whether it is the real issue or just an underlying cause. The contributing factors and the setting in which the disturbance occurred should be studied, along with the basic questions: who, when, where, why, how?

Example: What did the teacher (or peer) say before the aggression? Exactly how did the adolescent act-out? Was the cause a carry-over from home or playground? Or did the teacher, classroom, or other teenager engender the aggression? If the triggering variable can be identified, it should be eliminated or the student should practice alternative behaviors—behavior rehearsal (see Chapter 3).

- Study the chain of events leading to the aggression. Could the teacher have interfered sooner to have prevented the situation from proceeding to physical aggression? Could the outcome have been predicted? Would early intervention have decreased the event's duration, frequency, intensity?

- Determine behavioral changes that need to be made. What resources are available to make the changes being considered? These can include other teachers, class members, administrators, facilities, and equipment, as well as persons in the community. The teacher should decide what changes are needed and when, consider potential new side effects after the changes, and weigh alternatives.

- Act to make behavioral changes. The teacher should try to involve the class in the problem and the changes in conduct. The class may be satisfied with the changes, help develop new procedures and attitudes, and be supportive of the new mode.

- Take measures to ensure that the student is not rewarded by fighting. Is fighting occurring because of the thrill of breaking rules or for the thrill of committing a dangerous act?

- Channel aggression into constructive pursuits.

    Example: The teacher should explain to the student that anger is all right and can be constructive and ask about other ways to get what is wanted when angry. What are other teacher behaviors when the student is angry besides hitting? Could the same results be achieved using other behaviors? Are there times when a student may need to be angry and respond verbally or physically? How do other people feel when they are struck? What do classmates think of a student who strikes, pinches, bites, or throws objects at them? The teacher can practice more acceptable behaviors in role-playing situations. The student can be challenged to demonstrate a desired behavior in a simulated situation similar to those in real life, with the teacher feeding the results back to the student. If possible, the teacher could arrange a situation to provide reinforcement and support to the student in advancing through the new behavioral learning experience.

- Teach self-control.

  Example: The teacher should explain to the students that when anger or aggression occurs, they often are out of control and teacher aggression is required to control them. Students should be challenged not to lose control so that others will not need to control them (see Chapter 8).

- Find a model.

  Example: If the student respects an athlete or famous person, the teacher can discuss how that person behaves when angry or find similar characteristics in famous people who have demonstrated more appropriate behavior. The teacher must not compare behaviors or find common behavior analogies among peers.

- Attempt to change student perception of aggression. Perhaps that perception is inaccurate. Peer leaders or classmates can explain to aggressive students what they look like when angry and hostile. Do they look strong, silly, wild, or crazy? If adolescents' perceptions of aggression can be modified, many will modify their attitude as to how they view their victims, resulting in fewer hostile acts. The Golden Rule is always applicable.

- Request parent conferencing.

- Teach the student problem-solving techniques.

  Example: The teacher can ask the students for methods of getting revenge other than displaying anger. ''Is revenge necessary? How can you get even without becoming mad? Use the expression attributed to Joseph P. Kennedy—'don't get mad, just get even'—and demonstrate how he outthought and outperformed other people. Why do you need to get even? How will getting even benefit you? What is in it for you?''

- Try to change cognitive and affective patterns. This frequently also alters aggressive behaviors.

- Conduct relaxation exercises. Describe sand, waves, warm sun, soft music, blue sky.

- Do not allow the student to watch aggressive behaviors and model on them. A major determinant of anger is what it accomplishes. The answer: very little except aggression.

- Modulate the social environment.

  Example: Poverty, repression, and lack of opportunity contribute to aggression. The teacher should attempt to teach a skill to students, demonstrating how social stress can be lessened without aggression.

- Model nonaggressive responses in aggression-provoking situations.

  Example: Films, role playing, or animal watching can be used. The student's attention can be called to situations that could arouse aggression in participants but do not.

- Reduce auditory and visual stimulation.
- Reinforce nonaggressive behaviors.

  Example: "Susan, I watched you on the playground and noticed that when Dave pushed you, you controlled yourself and did not get angry. That is difficult to do. To show you how much the class appreciates your self-control, we are going to excuse you from doing ten minutes of reading."

- Offer rewards for nonaggression.

  Example: During recess many students have been reporting students who were playing too rough. The teacher may say, "After recess I have a surprise for the person who receives the most votes by the class as being a fair but active teammate. I wonder who will receive the surprise."

- Devise a program so a student can earn points for appropriate behaviors: talking in a normal voice, refraining from arguments, not hitting, remaining in the seat, talking at proper times, etc. The more points or tokens earned, the better the privileges or awards the student can trade them in for.
- Use timeout as appropriate (see Chapters 1, 2, and 3).

  Example: When Marty bites or hits, he will be placed on a chair outside and away from the class for five minutes. "You hit a classmate, you must sit in the chair." Prompt praise for appropriate behaviors is necessary during class time but timeout must not be rewarded.

- Reconstruct the environment. When a student becomes angry and destroys books or supplies, the teacher can instruct the individual to put things back the way they were.

  Example: When a student steals, the classroom rule is that the individual must return the stolen object, apologize, and attempt to refrain from further thefts.

- State requests, not demands.

  Example: When the teacher demands, instead of requests, the aggressive student often is rewarded just by the challenge of the demand.

Sometimes the student will endure a punishment that could have been avoided but for the reward of "not being controlled." Not complying with a request is not as self-enhancing as refusing a demand. Following a request is easier than following an order. An order invites challenge whereas requests ask for cooperation. The individual is doing as he wants, not as someone *else* wants.

- Insist the student make restitution.

  Example: The student must apologize to peer or teacher and restore the environment as it was before the aggression occurred, then work back through it. What would have been a more appropriate behavior? What else might I have done?

- Remove privileges. The teacher eliminates the ten-minute break between classes, prohibits a lunch hour, bars driving to school, refuses a lounge pass, etc.
- Order detention (see Chapter 3).
- Dismiss the aggressive student from class.
- Assign extra school tasks.
- Request that the school suspend the student.
- Role-play and play-act.
- Hold small group meetings. Problems are discussed voluntarily, with the focus on the individual as part of a group; clarification of values and that person's problems should follow.
- Hold behavior rehearsals. Play acting and role playing can provide aggressive student with new behavioral skills. As these new skills increase, aggressive behaviors can decrease gradually. Under highly structured settings, students can rehearse appropriate patterns and be provided cues and reinforcers, with the hope of increasing the possibility that those new behaviors will occur in the future. An aggressive student is taught to play and work cooperatively. These cooperative behaviors should be reinforced and rehearsed in situations where aggression occurs.

  Example: An adolescent in sophomore physical education has a low skill level in basketball so he fouls—trips, pushes, shoves, and instigates fights. Special time should be spent to improve youth's skills along with one-on-one practice on how to respond to elbows and shoves during a game.

- Have the class develop lists of acceptable and unacceptable behaviors and write them on the board in view of all students, putting the consequence next to each behavior.

Example:
BEHAVIOR:

UNACCEPTABLE	CONSEQUENCE
Student chooses to hit student.	Aggressor misses lunch period.
Student uses verbal harassment.	Peers ignore culprit for one hour.
Student continues talking after bell rings.	Talker is dismissed late according to the length of time it took to become quiet.

ACCEPTABLE	CONSEQUENCE
Student helps a classmate.	Teacher gives verbal acknowledgment at end of day.
Student cooperates with teachers and peers during week.	Student is excused early on Friday.

- Be sure to be consistent—this is a must. The teacher must make the school less a factory and more a family.

   Example: CAO—"care about others." Students are released from one class a week to go into the community and help veterinarians, librarians, housewives, dentists, etc. The teacher should design similar projects for senior citizens and elementary children.

- Provide peer counseling. The teacher should allow students to experience helping in contrast to hurting.
- Conduct relaxation training.
- Provide a crisis teacher and life-space interview. After working through aggressiveness or conflict, a student's defenses may decrease and the individual may be more accepting of change. An important component of crisis intervention is capitalizing on the event itself at the peak of the problem, before the student resumes normal behaviors. During crisis intervention, a life-space interview may be used. It has two components: (1) emotional and (2) clinical exploitation of life's events. When a student misbehaves, the interviewer reconstructs the event, studying what occurred, proceeding immediately to the environment where the problem occurred (called emotional first aid). Other situations could be studied with the student where similar problem behaviors occurred, gaining insight into how they began and developing a sequence of remedial activities. When faced with crisis, many troubled juveniles revert to a common behavior problem—aggression, verbal

abuse, lying, crying, temper tantrums. A life-space interview and crisis intervention together can emphasize the inappropriate behaviors and develop alternative, more acceptable conduct (Morse, 1976; Real, 1959).

• Incorporate useful programs, i.e., career and vocational education, guided group interaction, job coaching.

• Provide an alternative to a large group setting.

> *Example:* The student should be allowed to select an activity within a smaller group.

• Utilize the new "three Rs":

> REALIZE: An adolescent has academic deficits arising from learning difficulties and the emotionality is directed at interrelated instructional problems. Positive, pleasant, happy events associated with academic tasks should be increased.
>
> REMEMBER: Successful experience results in positive emotional learning.
>
> REMEMBER: A dominative teacher style incites dominative behaviors by students—an integrative teacher incites integrative student behavior. (Anderson, Brewer, & Reed, 1976)
>
> REWARD: A behavior to be repeated must be rewarded!

• Conduct self-examination. The teacher should be fair, consistent, punctual, honest, flexible, not rigid and sarcastic, and enforce rules consistently.

• Change instructional materials.

SUGGESTED READINGS

Anderson, H.H., Brewer, J.E., & Reed, M.F. Studies of teachers' classroom personalities, III: Follow-up studies of dominative and integrative contacts on children's behavior. *Applied Psychology Monographs,* 1976, *11.*

Axline, V. *Play therapy.* Boston: Houghton Mifflin Company, 1947.

Baumgartner, B., & Schultz, J. *Reaching children through art.* Johnstown, Pa.: Mafex Associates, Inc., 1969.

Gaston, E. *Music in therapy.* New York: The Macmillan Company, 1968.

Gorman, A.H. *Teachers and learners: The interactive process in education.* Boston: Allyn & Bacon, Inc., 1974.

Morse, W.C. The helping teacher/crisis teacher concept. *Focus on Exceptional Children,* 1976, *8*(4), 1-11.

Real, F. The concept of life-space interview. *American Journal of Orthopsychiatry,* 1959, *29*(1), 1-18.

Underwood, E.W. Ways of vandalism. *Today's Education,* 1968, *57*(9), 69-79.

Wilde, J., & Sommers, P. Teaching disruptive adolescents: A game worth winning. *Phi Delta Kappan,* January 1978, *59*(5), 342-347.

BEHAVIOR

- Self-concept

Definition and Example

- Behavior involves the perception of oneself as a person who is unacceptable in comparison with an idealized self. "I can't do it. He's better than me. I'm no good." There is a lack of self-confidence and a hypersensitivity to criticism. "I'm dumb." "I can't do that, I'm too slow."

   Example: The student balks at an academic task because of a feeling of personal inadequacy. The learning disabled teenager, in particular, becomes anxious and emotional.

Remediation and Management

- Provide failure-proof tasks during initial remediation and use consistent positive reinforcement with social praise. When giving a student who has poor self-concept an academic or social task, the teacher must be certain the success level can be reached easily and the individual already possesses the social skills. Self-confidence is built by enhancing skills in which the student already feels secure.
- Avoid negative reinforcement, punishment, and value statements.
- Provide the student with frequent physical contact and closeness during the first stages of remediation in an effort to create an atmosphere of security and warmth.
- Do not ignore the person, even when avoiding the behavior.
- Assign special jobs that are meaningful, visible, and rewardable.
- Look at the student and move near.
- Limit competition.
- Confer with the student and involve the parents.
- Reward good behaviors but also remove privileges when necessary.
- Do not force apologies; limit punishment.
- Establish a secure environment.
- Accept and reward the student's limited responses.
- Provide one-to-one relationships.
- Act to ensure that the student experiences success.
- Do not assume the juvenile is being stubborn or negative on purpose.
- Improve teaching and academic skills and be compassionate.

- Realize the adolescent can have academic deficits arising from learning difficulties and that the emotionality then will be directed to interrelated instructional problems.
- Increase the number, type, and strength of internal and external events surrounding academic experiences—positive experiences. It must be remembered that successful experiences result in positive, pleasant emotional learning.

   Example: "Lisa, explain to the class how you worked the math problem." She verbally goes through the problem step by step while the class listens. She is exhibiting a newly acquired skill—success. The teacher says, "You did an excellent job in explaining that problem. I like the way you explained the steps. If anyone has a question or needs help, Lisa can assist you. Thanks again, Lisa."

- Remediate reading problems. Poor self-concept often accompanies poor reading. The teacher should maximize and reinforce student success. Life experience reading is rewarding to these students.

   Example: The student explains a real-life experience. The teacher writes the story. That copy becomes part of a book the student studies.

BEHAVIOR

- Psychosomatic complaints

Definition and Example

- Behavior involves interdependence on the physical and psychic human system; psychic conflicts are manifested in physical symptoms such as headaches, upset stomach, nausea, stomach cramps, becoming ill at specific times of the day.

Remediation and Management

- Insist that the student undergo a complete physical examination. If a physician determines that physical disturbances do not exist, proceed with interventions.
- Provide interesting and physically challenging activities, reward the student for participating, brag about the performance and be happy that the person is feeling well.
- Use firm, nonpunitive discipline.

- Ignore complaints. Such a student should not be protected and sheltered or allowed to escape work or activities by complaining. The teacher should reinforce participation.
- Be honest.

  Example: "Paul, each day at this time you say you're ill. I know you do not want to read. You are not sick, you are making excuses."

- Ensure success by giving the student a choice of activities or something to look forward to.

BEHAVIOR

- Antischool phobia

Definition and Example

- Behavior involves the student's desire not to attend school; the individual may become physically ill or cling to a parent, pet, friend, or toy.

Remediation and Management

- Insist that the learners come to school at all costs, even if they have to be carried.
- Involve the parents. Many times parents encourage and reward the phobia when it is they who cannot be separated from the student.
- Introduce the student to the school environment gradually. The method of desensitizing the youth will vary according to the severity.

  Example: The student rides past the school with parents, they sit outside, walk around the building, walk through the school, meet the teacher in the hall and say "hello," visit the classroom. The student helps the teacher, stays longer in the class, helps with a pupil, etc.

- Praise good behaviors by the student and reinforce.
- Avoid assignments until the student feels good about school.
- Emphasize to parents that the student, when not in class during school hours—cutting class by staying home—should not be allowed to watch television, read books, listen to stereo, or color. The stay in the home should be a timeout. When the student remains in school, privileges should be restored at home.

- Use peer tutoring.

    Example: The student should be paired with a popular classmate for tutoring and recess.

BEHAVIOR

- Sexual deviations; interpersonal behavior deficits

Definition and Example

- Behavior involves acts with sexual connotations at variance with accepted practice, voyeurism, fondling young children or animals, verbalization and gestures with sexual implications, excitement about particular topic or activity that excludes all others, castration anxiety, extreme dependence on teachers, lack of zest, sexual attacks, rape, excessively effeminate characteristics in males and excessive masculinity in females.

Remediation and Management

- Provide an acceptable identification figure.

    Example: Behaviors of someone the teacher admires are explained to the pupil without criticizing that behavior. The teacher demonstrates good behaviors for the pupil to model from or provides a model such as another teacher, an older student, or the big brother or sister program.

- Visit the home. If the student comes from an environment that is permissive of sexual profanity, be wary of punishments because if the behavior is allowed at home, the teacher should give careful consideration before punishing.
- Emphasize proper behavior.
- Ignore the behaviors; do not respond physically or verbally.
- Establish an environment of safety and predictability.
- Accept and reward the student's limited proper responses.
- Offer a one-to-one relationship.
- Provide a wide range of multisensory tasks and experiences.

    Example: See the herbs, taste herbs, smell herbs. Spell the names of the herbs. Write how they taste; describe how they look.

- Emphasize reality and predictable outcomes, train the student's mind to expect and predict outcomes.

- Present academic experiences with senses.

  Example: The teacher leads air, heat, light, or sound experiments from science; growing plants and animals, using art materials.

- Educate the student about values and attitudes—values clarification, attitude statements.
- Experiment with cross-age teaching—12-year-old teaching 8-year-old.
- Stress structure and orderly exploration.
- Encourage the student to explore.

  Example: The teacher explains discovery learning (guided exploring), peer projects, self-evaluation.

- Supervise carefully.

BEHAVIOR

- Shyness, nonassertiveness

Definition and Example

- Behavior is evident in a student who seldom initiates conversation, maintains poor eye contact, stays out of games and peer groups, is taken advantage of during group activities, shows helplessness; is too guarded and overly inhibited.

Remediation and Management

- Encourage and reward.

  Example: The teacher provides rewards or praise when the student talks to others, participates in games, stands up for rights, smiles, has eye contact, answers in class.

- Role-play assertiveness.

  Example: "Jack hits you with a spitball. What could you do? At recess, Natalie took your swing away. What are some things you could say to Natalie? Susan pushes you out of line in the cafeteria. What are some things you could say to Susan?"

- Reward assertiveness.

  Example: "You told Natalie to get her own swing, that you had this one first. I am very proud of you. You should stand up for yourself. And you were very nice about the way you told her. You should do that more often."

- Encourage peers to help the shy student.

  Example: The teacher initiates a Friend of the Day Game. At the end of each day, the shy, withdrawn student selects the student who was the friendliest all day long. The Friend gets a button or banner; at the end of the week or month, a trophy or certificate is given the person who was chosen most often as Friend of the Day.

- Do not label the student as shy.

  Example: The teacher must refrain from saying, "Why are you so shy?" Students tend to live up to labels.

- Encourage more outgoing behavior, emphasizing improvement rather than perfection.
- Criticize the student's shy actions, not the individual.
- Keep the student in a group that is willing to help.
- Establish a secure climate of safety and predictability.
- Accept and reward any limited responses.
- Provide one-to-one relationship.
- Limit competition.
- Encourage the shy person to help peers in that student's strong academic areas.

  Example: "Mark, you are good in figuring averages. Can you help Dee? I can't seem to explain to her so she can understand."

- Use broom characters. The teacher saws off a broom handle at the student's height, decorates a brown bag, slips it over the straw, and ties it securely. The student holds the broom character in front of the face and talks to it. The broom character exercise is effective in helping the shy student to appear in front of a group. This is part of the language arts.
- Help students design their own personalized notepaper and run off copies. The students may use the personalized paper to send notes, jot down feelings, ask questions, send thank-you notes, etc.
- Allow the student to bring projects from home to work on at school, such as coin or stamp collections, model cars, embroidery, painting, etc.

- Arrange activities to ensure the students' success, do not let them fail.
- Encourage the students when they become frustrated.

  Example: "I know you are discouraged because learning to read can be difficult. Learning to read is a hard job. Let's pick up the book you threw down, rearrange your desk, and keep trying. I know you are going to improve and be a better reader."

- Place glad notes in a student's book. The notes can encourage, "The assignment is tough, but you can do it!"; can thank, "Thank you for doing your work yesterday!" The teacher can mail glad notes to parents or make glad phone calls when a difficult student has had a good day, suggesting the parents might reward the young person by going out to dinner, excusing the youth from doing the dishes, awarding the keys to the car for half an hour, etc.

BEHAVIOR

- Social immaturity

Definition and Example

- Behavior involves age-inappropriate conduct based on a subjective comparison between the student and a peer group. This frequently is observed when the individual is in an unfamiliar or stressful situation, lacks skill in age-appropriate behaviors, has a social learning deficiency, is called "sissy" and/or "baby" by peers, prefers younger or older children and games below age level, and has a tendency to cry.

Remediation and Management

- Provide enriching experiences at an age-appropriate level. During age-appropriate activities, the teacher should provide a socially immature student with direct instruction and, if possible, peer support. New places, situations, new skills, and unfamiliar acts will require support from staff and peers to help improve self-concept and build self-confidence. The teacher should provide frequent opportunities for the student to practice the appropriate behaviors in the age-appropriate activities and discuss alternative ways of reacting properly in stressful situations.

  Example: The teacher should role-play appropriate behaviors to demonstrate how the student should act.

- Attempt to increase peer contact in secure, structured settings.
- Ensure success.
- Be truthful with the student.
- Carry out segments of planned ignoring.
- Use nonverbal responses such as a slight frown.

BEHAVIOR

- Truancy

Definition and Example

- Behavior is evidenced by unapproved absence from school.

Remediation and Management

- Telephone home when the student first misses.
- Photograph and post pictures of 100 percent attendees for six weeks. An attendance banner can be awarded the class that has perfect attendance each day; hold a contest to see which class can keep the banner the longest.
- Present certificates for perfect attendance.
- Establish behavioral contracts.
- Hold individual conferences with the student and parent to try to ascertain the reasons for the truancy and to discuss remedies.
- Try to make school more meaningful to the truant.

    Example: The student is appointed as patrol monitor, office helper, pet keeper, coach's assistant.

- Arrange a buddy system.

    Example: The buddy walks to school with the truant, tutors, calls on the phone, works on projects.

- Praise attendance verbally.
- Establish environmental planning.

    Example: An adolescent requests peers to refuse to provide rides to school if the student cuts class.

- Provide behavioral programming. The teacher awards students who improve attendance, gives them an event at school to look forward to, presents certificates for perfect attendance, grants extra privileges.

    Example: The teacher offers free admission to athletic games, free food coupons, movie passes, etc., for improved attendance.

- Have the student sign a behavioral contract.

BEHAVIOR

- Verbal aggression

Definition and Example

- Behavior involves hostile action against self or others to demean and create fear; self-destructive statements such as, ''I'm stupid. I'm dumb. I'm bad;'' inflicting psychological hurt is goal; includes swearing, name calling, put-downs, tattling, jealousy, gossip, derogatory complaints.

Remediation and Management

- Do not ignore such conduct. The student using verbal aggression often incites others to physical aggression. The teacher should prepare the others to ignore such verbal aggression since responding to it provides inadvertent reinforcement.
- Avoid subtle verbal aggression.

    Example: The teacher remarks, ''Why don't you pick on someone your own size?'' Or, ''If you keep talking like that, someone will choose not to ignore you and mash you right in the mouth.''

- Create a structured learning environment.
- Set clear expectations for student behavior and follow through consistently.
- Educate students about their values and attitudes.
- Provide communication exercises—rehearsal, role play.
- Cultivate the student's interests.
- Reduce auditory and visual stimulation.
- Record verbal aggression on tape.
- Be cautious that hearing the aggression is not reinforcing.

BEHAVIOR

- Social withdrawal

Definition and Example

- Behavior involves emotionally leaving or escaping from a life situation that the person perceives as causing personal conflict or discomfort; includes isolation, daydreaming, drowsiness, shyness, fear, depression, anxiety; the student is flat, unresponsive, lacks social interactions; is a nonentity, a wallflower; sleeps during class, runs away from school; says, "Water is too cold for swimming" to avoid swim lesson.

Remediation and Management

- Develop trust.
- Devise a failure-proof program, assign tasks and activities where the student achieves immediate success.
- Avoid harsh discipline and physical punishment. The teacher must help the student develop a positive interpersonal relationship with staff and peers so as to feel secure; discourage withdrawal by planning an active behavior modification program and/or a behavior contract.
- Suggest alternative response patterns.

    Example: The student, instead of totally ignoring teacher requests, should be induced to respond by nodding or head shaking, then encouraged to make eye contact and gradually progress. The teacher always provides rewards that are valuable to the student and that constitute positive reinforcement.

- Use art therapy.
- Institute play therapy. Certain types of toys, games, etc., can encourage social play. The student can be instructed in social play skills or prompted with directions for social interactions with toys. Outdoor play equipment is useful.
- Have the socially withdrawn student view films showing pleasant, appropriate social interactions among others—in effect, peer modeling.
- Arrange the environment by surrounding the student with enjoyable activities requiring social interaction and give the individual the opportunity to observe social interaction. The student should be reinforced for participation and social responses.

- Accept and reward limited responses.
- Provide one-to-one relationship.
- Limit competition.
- Establish and maintain a consistent schedule of activities and a predictable routine.
- Ignore the behavior.
- Be truthful with the student.
- Permit pets in classroom.
- Hold informal conversations with the socially withdrawn student on interests, hobbies, etc., to help draw the person "out of the cocoon."
- Encourage parallel play, then gradually stimulate interaction with peers.

SUMMARY

This chapter has stressed a variety of management and prevention techniques to provide teachers with useful strategies for maintaining an effective learning environment. Teachers are given choices to control, reduce, eliminate, tolerate, prevent, interfere, or interrupt disruptive student behaviors. The success of any management strategy in a given situation is determined by the use of a technique appropriate to the academic, psychological, and physical characteristics of the student(s).

Management techniques mentioned include behavioral, humanistic, psycho-educational, medical, and psychodynamic models. Many suggestions can be effective for multiple disorders. As noted in the introduction, there is no intention here to recommend "the" best procedure, only a number that are suitable. The best procedure is the one that is effective—that works—with a particular student and particular teacher in a particular setting. No two students or teachers react or behave the same. This material can better equip the teacher with varied class management choices/alternatives so that the chance of finding the right student/management strategy/teacher combination is increased.

As an example, Exhibit 4-1, beginning on page 160, presents a substantial list of activities that teachers can use to reinforce students and help put them on the path to becoming good citizens.

Exhibit 4-1 Ideas for Reinforcing Activities

The student can be helped in reducing or eliminating impermissible behavior through reinforcement of correct conduct by:

- Getting access to a quiet play area.
- Getting access to the art area.
- Helping clean the teacher's desk.
- Helping grade papers.
- Dispensing treats to classmates.
- Erasing the chalkboard, cleaning erasers.
- Sweeping the floor, washing desks.
- Cutting paper.
- Answering the door.
- Answering the telephone.
- Collecting papers.
- Taking attendance.
- Leading songs.
- Pronouncing spelling words.
- Choosing a new seat.
- Helping in the office.
- Visiting another class.
- Going home for lunch.
- Helping in the cafeteria.
- Using colored chalk.
- Using a typewriter.
- Running a copying machine.
- Stapling papers.
- Giving messages over the intercom.
- Holding a door during fire drill.
- Playing checkers or chess.
- Working with clay.
- Receiving attention from the teacher.
- Receiving teacher attention that makes the student feel competent and appreciated.
- Making positive physical contacts.
- Being granted an extra long recess.
- Hearing the teacher read a story.
- Winning permission to go home or to recess early.
- Serving as captain of a team at recess.
- Carrying out an independent project in science or art.
- Being given a free choice activity.

Exhibit 4-1 continued

- Smiling.
- Receiving time for independent play.
- Running errands for the teacher.
- Listening to the record or tape player.
- Being taken by an older student to the gym to shoot basketballs, lead cheers, etc.
- Reading the newspaper.
- Engaging in arm wrestling.
- Flying a kite.
- Popping corn.
- Making a puppet.
- Carrying the ball or bat at recess.
- Visiting the principal.
- Sharpening pencils.
- Opening mail.

Chapter 5

Disciplinary and Classroom Management Programs

David A. Sabatino

INTRODUCTION

This chapter offers a brief synopsis of current disciplinary and classroom management programs. The focus earlier was on intervention techniques; here, it is on entire programs that should be transportable and applicable to some degree to other schools. Enough descriptive information is provided to offer an orientation to a specific programmatic effort. Needless to say, not every facet of every question is answered because the variance among school systems imposes a very real set of limitations. What is possible in a rural district in South Central Tennessee may not be regarded with much enthusiasm in Philadelphia or New York, or vice versa.

Then, too, significant policy and staff differences exist between buildings. An ivy-colored suburban building with progressive ideas may find corporal punishment, suspension, and expulsion nonacceptable. Its inner city counterpart may have a 20 percent expulsion rate and a vice principal for discipline who brags publicly about how fierce he can be with a one-inch solid oak paddle with eight half-inch holes drilled in it. In one school, a student who was administered the stern end of the rod was then permitted to autograph it, a traditional practice of great tribal importance.

Local or district board of education policies on discipline range from those in a detailed student handbook with every rule and every punishment for each offense well explained, to those that are left completely up to the principal, who considers each case a teacher's professional prerogative. The selected programs reported here do not exhaust the literature—that is almost an impossibility.

These programs are not being recommended as totally effective for all students, but they either report worthwhile statistical data or claim validity based on case studies. Validation of program content is rare. Indeed, the best of all programs can be sabotaged by a doubting staff; the worst can be made to work by teachers who believe.

In sum, what are presented here are some interesting attempts by educators to control unruly behaviors.

THE LEAST APPROACH TO DISCIPLINE

LEAST is an inservice teacher education program contained in a 78-page booklet titled *The LEAST Approach to Classroom Discipline*. It espouses a philosophy of minimum action to attain and maintain effective classroom discipline—a survival strategy for teachers. The title is an acronym for the five steps or options outlined for achieving classroom discipline:

1. *L*eave things alone because no problems are likely to occur (*L*eave Things Alone)
2. *E*nd the action indirectly because the behavior is disrupting the classroom (*E*nd the Action Indirectly)
3. *A*ttend more fully because more information or communication is needed (*A*ttend More Fully)
4. *S*pell out directions because otherwise disruption or harm will occur (*S*pell Out Directions)
5. *T*rack student progress to evaluate and reinforce the behavior (*T*rack Student Progress).

Also included is a ten-page *Facilitator's Guide* that contains a preteaching assessment.

LEAST was developed by the National Education Association (1978). Its editors were Dr. Robert R. Corkhuff, Dr. Andrew H. Griffin, and Richard Mallory. The inservice material produced was field tested in selected sites in eight states, including Georgia, South Carolina, Tennessee, Arizona, Florida, Kentucky, Missouri, and North Carolina. The response was overwhelmingly positive, according to teacher reports. As a result of teacher and learner feedback, the material was refined and modified.

As classroom management is of concern to all teachers at all levels, this program is appropriate for any group of practitioners. It is adaptable to a variety of settings and may be structured according to the time constraints and general purposes of its users.

Two appealing aspects of this program are its quickness of use and its simplicity. In relatively few pages, it offers a proved, effective, common-sense method of classroom management using the least amount of guidance and control necessary to achieve the results desired. The booklet also contains the NEA perspective of classroom management, the implications for negotiations and teacher contracts, and an annotated bibliography on school discipline.

THE SATURDAY SCHOOL

Gooding and Fitsko (1978) described another workable option, a disciplinary Saturday School, to supervise out-of-school suspension. This is an attempt to fill an instructional void in existing high school discipline procedures. The program gives to students who otherwise would be suspended the opportunity to attend Saturday morning sessions and to remain in school. The goal is to assist them in their academic performance, reduce their frustrations about school, and promote positive behaviors and attitudes toward classes.

A student who commits a suspendable offense, along with the parents, is informed of the administration's intention to suspend. The student and parents are given an opportunity to select the Saturday School option as an alternative to out-of-school suspension. A suspension option form (Exhibit 5-1) is then completed by both the student and the family, in effect serving as a contract. The student attends a four-hour Saturday morning study session for the same number of days that the suspension would have carried. There are a number of advantages:

- Saturday School gives students and parents an alternative to suspension and encourages more cooperation between school and parents, who may be more supportive because of the choice as to how their child is to be punished.
- Students are compelled to do schoolwork on Saturday mornings and are likely to maintain or improve their grades and success in the classroom upon return.
- Concentrated activities can be built into the Saturday program, i.e., counseling, tutoring, etc., on an individual basis in an effort to modify academic and social behaviors.
- Teacher/student relationships are encouraged since Saturday School participants are required to bring extra course work from their classrooms.
- The Saturday School may be a strong deterrent to truancy and skipping class.
- Attendance at Saturday School is the best punishment for truancy and skipping class since it requires a student to attend more school rather than less.
- Students who have rarely misbehaved previously may be spared the stigma of being suspended.
- The legal risk entailed in out-of-school suspension is minimized.
- Tutors, volunteer students, or resource persons are available at the Saturday School to help students with their class work.

Exhibit 5-1 Suspension Option Form

Name of Student   Date

_____

Grade/Unit

I understand that I am to be suspended for the following reason(s):

I also understand that, in this case, the following options are being made available to me.

OPTION A: A _____ day out-of-school suspension to begin on _____.
             During this time, I will be under my parents' supervision and will not be
             permitted to attend any Worthington High School activities. All school work
             missed shall be unexcused.

OPTION B: A _____ day "Saturday School" to begin on _____.
             (See attached Saturday School Guidelines.)

After discussing these options with my parents, I have decided to accept OPTION _____.

Student Signature _____

Parent Signature _____

Questions, concerns or clarifications regarding these options should be forwarded to the appropriate Unit Dean.

This form is to be returned to the Dean's office at _____ on _____.
                                                     (time)   (date)

Source: Reprinted from *A Proposal for an Alternative to Out-of-School Suspension for Worthington (Ohio) High School Students: The Saturday School,* © 1978, p. 11.

Physical Facilities

The Saturday School can be located in a large classroom that has direct access to the outside and to a lavoratory so that students need not enter any other portion of the school building. There should be access to a telephone in case of an emergency or so the supervisor can call parents of absent or disruptive students.

Staffing

The supervisor of the Saturday School must have experience in controlling students and skills in human relations while maintaining classroom discipline. Teachers, honor students, or resource persons in the community, i.e., retired persons, professionals, former teachers, are contacted for volunteer work with students in specific academic areas.

Attendance Regulations

The Saturday School attendance rules must be consistent with those in the high school's Student Conduct Code. In addition, students are expected to observe the following regulations:

1. Saturday School will meet from 8 a.m. until noon. Tardy students admitted after 8:15 A.M. will be required to attend an additional Saturday.
2. Students will not be allowed to use the telephone except in cases of emergency or to go to their lockers.
3. Students will not be allowed to put their heads down or to sleep.
4. Radios, cards, magazines, or other recreational articles will not be allowed in the room.
5. Food or beverages will not be consumed during the Saturday School.
6. There will be a 10-minute break at 9:30 A.M. when students may go to the restroom, throw away paper, or sharpen pencils.
7. Students are required to have class assignments with them when they attend the Saturday School.
8. Students who arrive on time, work diligently, and follow the rules may be dismissed half an hour early or may have the number of suspension days reduced; this action is considered to reinforce good behavior.

Feedback and Cost Evaluation

Evaluation is an important aspect of the Saturday School program. Obviously, the ultimate evaluation is a demonstrated change in behavior and attitude and greater academic success for each student.

The supervisor gathers information about student progress and perceptions of the program on a weekly basis using a Student Evaluation Form (Exhibit 5-2). The supervisor also seeks a final evaluation from parents (Exhibit 5-3), students (Exhibit 5-4), and teachers (Exhibit 5-5), this last including an assessment of classroom performance.

Exhibit 5-2 Saturday School: Weekly Student Evaluation

NAME _____   DATE _____

1. In what ways is the Saturday School helping you?

2. What didn't you like about the Saturday School this week?

3. In what specific ways are the Saturday School staff members or volunteers helping you?

4. What specific help would you like with your course work next week?

Source: Reprinted from *A Proposal for an Alternative to Out-of-School Suspension for Worthington (Ohio) High School Students: The Saturday School,* © 1978, p. 12.

Exhibit 5-3 Saturday School: Parent Evaluation

---

1. What is your feeling about our Saturday School program compared to out-of-school suspension?

2. Do you feel your child benefited from attendance in the Saturday School?

3. Were you pleased with the tutoring your child received in the Saturday School?

4. Do you feel Saturday School is a reasonable form of punishment for violation of school rules?

5. Please make any general comments regarding our Saturday School program in order to help us evaluate its effectiveness.

NAME _____
(optional)

Source: Reprinted from *A Proposal for an Alternative to Out-of-School Suspension for Worthington (Ohio) High School Students: The Saturday School,* © 1978, p. 13.

Exhibit 5-4 Saturday School: Final Student Evaluation

Name _____   Date _____

1. What do you think are the advantages in being suspended to the Saturday School instead of being suspended at home?

2. What would you have done if you were suspended at home instead of in Saturday School?

3. In what ways can the Saturday School be improved?

4. If you were faced with these options again, would you choose Saturday School or out-of-school suspension? Why?

Source: Reprinted from *A Proposal for an Alternative to Out-of-School Suspension for Worthington (Ohio) High School Students: The Saturday School,* © 1978, p. 14.

The major cost of the program is for the supervision and instruction of students. Operational costs for the physical plant should be minimal since only one classroom is used, and that for a limited number of hours. The cost of personnel is as follows: Two supervisory teachers, 5 hours per Saturday + 1 hour follow-up = 12 hours @ $10.00/hour × 25 sessions = $3,000.

THE ATLANTA PROGRAM: HUMANE DISCIPLINE

Christian (1979) described the approach toward discipline developed by the Atlanta public schools and the Atlanta Teacher Corps, a program that considers staff and students as people first. The program is data based, and Exhibit 5-6 is the excellent questionnaire that provided the information upon which it was developed.

Following the retrieval of the data from teachers, several manuals were developed and distributed to staff:

- *Atlanta Public School Operations Manual,* containing all major procedures, requirements, rules, and regulations for administering discipline in Atlanta's schools

Exhibit 5-5 Saturday School: Teacher Evaluation

(CONFIDENTIAL)

_____
Name of Teacher

Recently _____ was suspended and spent some time in the Saturday School. In order to evaluate, determine its effectiveness, and improve the program we need your assistance. Please complete the following questions and return it to your Unit Dean. Thanks!

1. After the student returned from suspension, was there any change in behavior?

2. Were the assignments completed satisfactorily by the suspended student?

3. Has the student talked to you about being in Saturday School?

4. What is your feeling about the Saturday School?

5. How do you think the Saturday School can be improved?

Source: Reprinted from _A Proposal for an Alternative to Out-of-School Suspension for Worthington (Ohio) High School Students: The Saturday School,_ © 1978, p. 15.

- _Three Rs of Discipline,_ outlining disciplinary actions, due process, suspension, expulsions, and appeal procedures
- _Guidelines for Effective Learning,_ a student guide to guidelines, rules, and regulations affecting student conduct
- _Parents Must Be Partners,_ a guide to parents, explaining program resources and ensuring them of the school's willingness to help.

The result was the adoption of in-school, as an alternative to out-of-school, suspension. Exhibit 5-7 presents the operational procedures guiding Atlanta's in-school suspension (detention).

Exhibit 5-6 School Climate Survey

(A) To what extent are you familiar with your school's discipline action plan?

    2% ☐ Never heard of it   4% ☐ Saw a copy
   90% ☐ Informed about it in faculty meetings
    4% ☐ Heard about it from other faculty members

(B) Your school's efforts to improve student discipline have been:

    5% ☐ Very effective
   82% ☐ Effective
   13% ☐ Noneffective
       ☐ Nonexistent

(C) How would you describe student discipline in your school this year as compared to last year:

   12% ☐ No change
   12% ☐ Worse
   76% ☐ Better

(D) Student-to-student relationships are:

   31% ☐ Positive
   11% ☐ Negative
   57% ☐ Improving
    1% ☐ Becoming worse

(E) How would you characterize the climate of your school?

       ☐ Fearful   13% ☐ Tense
   40% ☐ Positive   4% ☐ Refreshing
   10% ☐ Negative   34% ☐ Encouraging

(F) Student-to-teacher relationships are:

   46% ☐ Positive
    6% ☐ Negative
   40% ☐ Improving
    8% ☐ Becoming worse

(G) Your overall attitude toward the school system's Discipline Guidelines and policy is:

   48% ☐ Positive
   16% ☐ Negative
   36% ☐ No opinion

Exhibit 5-6 continued

(H) As a teacher, which of the following do you regularly practice?

  50% ☐ Planned "Rap Sessions" with students about the needs for self-discipline, respect for themselves and others; discipline in our schools.

  22% ☐ Student-led discussions about student discipline problems.

  28% ☐ Questions/answers seminars related to concerns about discipline.

(I) In which of the following would you become an *active, committed* participant?

  32% ☐ A "hotline" for calling to a central location that will provide immediate responses and help to you with *private and personal* discipline-related concerns.

  14% ☐ A bimonthly seminar devoted specifically to discipline concerns.

  54% ☐ Helping to organize and be an *active* member of a group to plan an *action movement* for "back to our roots in discipline and respect for authority."

      ☐ Other _____
         _____
         _____

Source: Reprinted from *The Anatomy of a Program of Humane Discipline in the Atlanta Public School System* by M.A. Christian, © 1979. p. 19.

An analysis of the method (Exhibit 5-8) says it does, indeed, work and identifies a number of factors essential to creating and continuing that success. Two of the most important factors are selection of proper teachers and full cooperation of the entire faculty. Others are: isolating the troublesome students in a room apart from other classrooms, offering reduced suspensions if progress is demonstrated by the students' attitudes and amount of work completed, a total ban on all privileges and extracurricular activities, an adequate on-hand supply of materials and equipment, and full explanation of the program to both parents and students.

VINELAND NORTH PROGRAM TO REDUCE VANDALISM

In its first operational year, 1976, the Vineland, N.J., North High School suffered severe vandalism. To offset this, a program was implemented in the second year to cut down the vandalism, slash the costly damage loss ($26,000), and greatly reduce periodic police intervention. This program reduced vandalism costs to less than $5,501 the following school year (Valentine, 1978) through 11 strategies:

1. A student handbook containing the school rules and regulations was produced and a copy presented to each student on the opening day of school in September 1977.

Exhibit 5-7 Procedures for In-School Suspensions

DETENTION PROPOSAL

Purpose: In-School detention is a method designed to isolate students who are rule-breakers—cutting class, disruptive, etc.—from the mainstream of school activities for a period of time. However, this system of detention is to be as meaningful as possible to the student. He/she should carry out some activity that will improve his/her skills in some area of weakness or some other purposeful activities (discussions, watching films, etc.).

Detention is also designed as an additional facet to reduce the number of out-of-school suspensions and to try to discipline the students within the confines of the school setting.

Structure: Room 300 has been designated as an administrative room. Near this room is a water fountain and student restrooms, thus making it a tightly confined area. Students in detention can be escorted directly down the stairs to the lunch room and back.

Teachers will be assigned each period to supervise the students. The on-duty teachers will assist the students with their immediate assignments.

Procedure: As an alternative to out-of-school suspension, the administrative staff will place students in detention. The length of time in detention will be determined jointly by the administrator and the teachers in charge. When a student shows improvement or indicates that he/she can adjust to regular school activities, *then and only then* will he/she be released from detention.

The parents of these students *will* be notified of the school's actions in the same manner as the out-of-school suspensions or other disciplinary actions. Conferences with parents should be carried out after a student is released from detention. These conferences should include at least one of the teachers who supervises detention and one administrator.

A personal record form should be kept on each student placed in detention indicating the reason(s) for detention, length of time, progress (if any), and recommendations.

Duties of Teachers in Charge: Detention teachers are to:

1. Aid students through some meaningful activities. These activities should include learning new skills along with improving their present skills; watching or listening to appropriate audiovisual aid; and performing some jobs around the school or campus.
2. Escorting the students to and from the lunch room.

Remember these particular students are being ''DISCIPLINED.'' We are trying to keep them from the mainstream of school activities for a period of time until he/she can show some improvement.

2. A series of eight orientation meetings for parents was conducted before school opened in September, two of these with an interpreter to accommodate the Spanish speaking.

3. Questions asked by the parents at these meetings were recorded to provide a basis for the new community information program inaugurated by the school.

4. The cooperation of the staff was enlisted in the campaign to improve student behavior and to reduce vandalism. Many departments volunteered to conduct a departmental "Open House for Parents" at which the students were to serve as tour guides and explain the operation of the department to their families.

5. Definite steps were pursued to organize a Parent-Teacher Association.

6. The teachers received information about affective development and their response to human relations techniques and were afforded opportunities to attend workshops that promoted such techniques.

7. The discipline procedures were described and advertised at the opening of school to afford staff members and students an immediate opportunity to know and to understand the consequences of student offenses.

8. A new publicity program was implemented that was aimed at publicizing student accomplishments in each department, as well as the major aspects of the total school program. This program was also designed to respond accurately to all questions about the school.

9. More opportunities for student involvement were included such as the "Open House for Parents," and student good turn projects and exhibits.

10. Four paraprofessionals were employed to facilitate communication between home and school and to improve student promptness and attendance.

11. A peer leadership program was instituted.

As is evident, this was a multifaceted approach to coping with the pervasive problem of vandalism and to improving student behavior—vexing problems that were gnawing at educators and citizens alike.

While the cost of vandalism was reduced by 61 percent, two nondesirable behaviors increased: (1) there was a 174 percent upsurge in class cutting, and (2) a 16 percent advance in general disturbances.

The increases in detentions for those two behavior problems, while alarming, were tempered by the fact that the project strategies made possible the identification of every student offense—many of which would have remained undetected in the previous year. Thus, these increases probably reflected a strict adherence to the rules and regulations rather than a significant increase in those two behaviors. In the preproject year, so much time and effort had been required "just to keep the lid on" that some disturbances and many class cuts simply were not listed and/or resolved.

Exhibit 5-8 Analysis of the In-School Suspension (Detention) System

TOPIC: IN/SCHOOL SUSPENSION—DOES IT WORK?

FROM: Alan C. Harwell, Assistant Principal
Pike County High School, P.O. Box 574,
Zebulon, Georgia 30295

In-school suspension is a program designed as an alternative plan to suspend a student from school. It was found, through experience, that far too often students considered suspension a holiday, during which time they could roam the streets and fall hopelessly behind in their school work, to the point of failing courses and losing credits. In-school suspension is designed to keep students in school and attentive to their course work.

IN-SCHOOL SUSPENSION DOES WORK. Included in the following list are factors which are essential for a successful in-school suspension program:

1. *The choice of the instructor is important because he/she is the person who must see to the work aspect of the program.* An individual who lacks self-assurance and/or values his popularity could quickly allow the work aspect of the program to disappear. Secondly, many of the students who reach the point where suspension is necessary are already severe disciplinary problems. They are rude, rebellious and disorderly at times. The instructor who is emotionally unstable could quickly lose control of the order and discipline in the suspension classroom.

2. *Another important factor of the satisfactory operation of the in-school suspension program is the full cooperation of the total faculty.* The work assigned the student while he is suspended serves a twofold purpose. It is intended to keep the student working, but it is also designed to keep him from falling behind in his work while he is out of the classroom. If teachers fail to supply the proper assignments to the suspension instructor, they make it doubly hard for him/her to keep the student working and deny that student the opportunity to keep up with his studies while suspended. The classroom teachers must, on a scheduled basis, assist the suspension instructor.

3. *The location of the center should be removed from the principal location of the regular classrooms.* A functional communication system is necessary between the suspension area and the administrative offices, and between the administrative offices and the regular classrooms.

4. *An effective tool in dealing with students who have been suspended is to reduce the length of their suspension in accordance with their attitude while suspended and amount of work they complete.*

5. *The operational aspects of in-school suspension must remain consistent.* All privileges are revoked. For instance, the suspended student will be unable to participate in extracurricular activities such as football, band, etc.

6. *It is very important that sufficient materials and supplies be furnished to the in-school suspension area.* Materials such as textbooks, dictionaries, desks, typewriters, pencils, paper, etc., are essential.

7. *The program must be explained to both parents and students.* It will then serve as a deterrent as well as a disciplinary action.

Overall, there was a 76 percent increase in the number of suspensions during the project year. Therefore, based purely on that number, the objective was achieved in only one instance—having more students report for administrative detention. It also is fair to say that the targeted reduction of 25 percent in drug abuse was nearly achieved (it reached 23 percent).

The inference that suspension did deter vandalism elsewhere was somewhat supported by *Violent Schools—Safe Schools, The Safe School Study Report to the Congress* (NIE, 1978), which found that principals, students, and teachers ranked discipline first as a successful strategy in reducing vandalism and improving behavior. Among all the common discipline procedures, suspension and paddling are listed as the most widely used methods in the nation. Thus, while the reduction in suspensions at Vineland's North High School was not achieved, that fact itself may be prophetic, bearing two major implications.

1. The principal, as the educational leader of the school, wields great influence and must accept the greatest responsibility for instituting programs to effectively reduce vandalism and to improve student behavior in the building.
2. Students, parents, and teachers are most willing to contribute extraordinary effort to the improvement of behavior and the reduction of vandalism when they have meaningful direction.

Thus, it would appear that the effectiveness of a school's discipline program weighs heavily on the principal. That may be as it should be because the disciplinary tone and the expectations for student and teacher behavior alike radiate from that office.

DEINSTITUTIONALIZATION AND STATUS OFFENDERS

Another in-school suspension program (ISSP) was attempted in the Northeast High School Complex in Macon, Ga. The students served in this program were delinquents who were on suspension from school. Haussman (1979) noted that all referrals in this program had to be made by the school principal. The average number of days spent in in-school suspension was three. The heart of the program was remedial work on academic subject materials, which was continued after the suspension. A treatment plan was developed for use during the suspensions, involving all school and county resources in a custom-tailored academic and counseling program.

Another remedial tactic was individualized instruction for each of the students. They were required to finish all work assignments to the satisfaction of the ISSP instructors. All work was returned to the regular teacher, who checked and graded it. Because of the structured and quiet atmosphere in these classrooms, students received more help with their assignments than their regular teacher might have been able to provide.

Students taking the program a second time were given an educational or psychological evaluation as well, with parental permission. The confidential results were reported to the parents and to appropriate school officials on a need-to-know basis. The results were used to pinpoint academic strengths and weaknesses, suggest remediation, and identify specific problems that also might require attention.

Telephoned parent contacts were made for first-time students; repeaters whose family had no telephone or could not be contacted received a home visit by the staff. During this call or visit, the parents were informed of the nature of the disciplinary action, the resources of the center were explained, and assistance was offered.

The staff was composed of a project director, two instructors (one certified in language arts/social science and the other in math/science), and an aide/typist. Students reported at regular school times. A morning attendance report was phoned to all schools from which students had been assigned.

Three main advantages were reported from the use of in-school suspension for this population:

1. Students were counted present in school while assigned to in-school suspension.
2. Students were required to complete all assignments before release, which kept them current on their regular class work and often enabled them to move ahead of their classmates.
3. Students were not on the streets associating with other youths, so the likelihood of their contact with juvenile officials was decreased.

Corporal punishment was not used in the program. Students, upon arrival at the suspension center, were informed of the rules, and their signature acknowledged that they had read (or had read to them) the regulations and conditions of the program. A violation of the rules could add extra days to their stay. Violent and disruptive behavior was isolated and restrained. Students were held responsible for their conduct and the consequences for inappropriate behavior were enforced consistently.

ALTERNATIVE DISCIPLINE AND SUSPENSION

Campbell County Junior High School in Gillette, Wyo. (Larsen, 1979) developed an Alternative Discipline and Suspension Program (ADSP), a manual detailing school policy for those entering junior high school. Essentially, ADSP established strict rules, informed all students about them and the consequences for infractions, and offered a behavioral improvement program to those who failed to comply. (Criteria referral to the ADSP are presented in Exhibit 5-9.) The purpose was to teach rule-observing behavior; once admitted to ADSP, students had to earn their way out of one of a four-step phase process by accumulating points:

Points	Items
1	Attends Class
1	Is On Time for Class
1	Uses Acceptable Language
1	Cooperates in Classroom Activities
1	Leaves Work Area Clean
1	Handles Break and Study Time Acceptably
2	Turns In Acceptable Academic Work
2	Treats Others Respectfully

The student was expected to earn a minimum number of points each day as well as an accumulative total of points. Additional points could be awarded at the teacher's discretion for extra work, cleanup, etc. This action was to be kept at a minimum so that students would not expect points for all good behavior.

A student who did not earn the minimum points each day had to repeat that phase or be referred to another phase. Once a prescribed point total was earned, the student was promoted either to a new phase or out of the program.

Phase I

All students referred to ADSP must begin and progress through Phase I. Some referred for minor school rule infractions were required to complete only Phase I; all others had to finish Phase I before being promoted to Phase II, and to complete that before being advanced to Phase III.

Phase I was a two-day assignment in which a student could earn as many as 20 points (10 each day) for satisfactory behavior, with a minimum of eight per day. If they did not reach the minimum, they had to begin again. Students assigned only to Phase I were not required to complete a transition phase back to the regular program (see below).

Since Phase I was basically a detention experience, counseling activities were limited to the basic intake discussions with the student in which the counselor described the program.

Exhibit 5-9 ADSP Referral Criteria

Suspension Infractions

Behavior	*Action Taken for First Offense*
Use of Tobacco Products	Immediate removal from classes. Assignment to ADSP for two days. Suspension from extracurricular activities.
Assault: Unprovoked physical attack on one student by another.	Immediate removal from classes. Assignment to ADSP for ten days. Parents notified.
Verbal Assault: Flagrant inappropriate or profane language directed at school personnel or other student(s).	Immediate removal from classes. Assignment to ADSP for six days.
Theft: Taking property without permission of the owner.	Immediate removal from classes. Assignment to ADSP for six days. Return of stolen item. Suspension from extracurricular activities.
Insubordination: Documented willful and persistent defiance of school personnel.	Immediate removal from classes. Assignment to ADSP for six days.
Use of Alcohol: In possession, under influence of, or transferring an alcoholic beverage.	Immediate removal from classes. Assignment to ADSP for ten days. Suspension from extracurricular activities.
Use of Drugs: In possession, under the influence of, or transferring any substance prohibited by the Controlled Substance Act or drug not prescribed for the student by a doctor.	Immediate suspension out of school for ten days. Must appear before Campbell County Board of Trustees at next regular meeting when the board will consider expulsion for remainder of the school year.
Truancy: Absent from school for any period of time without the consent of parents and/or school officials.	Assignment to ADSP for six days.
Vandalism: Purposeful destruction of personal or public property (property of school personnel or school).	Immediate removal from classes. Assignment to ADSP for six days. Payment for damage and/or face legal action.
Fighting: Two or more involved students in exchange of blows and assault is not determined.	Immediate removal from classes. Assignment to ADSP for six days.
Disruptive Behavior: Conduct that is flagrantly disruptive to normal school activity.	Immediate removal from classes. Assignment to ADSP for six days.

Phase II

Students completing Phase I were promoted to Phase II, a four-day assignment in which up to 42 points could be earned, 10 points per day for acceptable behavior and a mandatory 2 points for satisfactory progress on a commitment contract containing students' performance objectives. The minimums were 8 points a day, or a total minimum of 34, to complete this phase. Fifty accumulative points had to be earned for promotion from Phases I and II. A student who failed to earn the minimum for any one day or total accumulative points had to begin Phase I again. It was possible for a student who diligently pursued the curriculum and demonstrated satisfactory progress to reenter either the regular school program or Phase III early.

Counseling activities in this phase consisted of individualized and group sessions. The objective was to establish students' responsibility for their behavior and their recognition of the consequences (punishment) for rule infractions.

Phase III

The only students who entered Phase III were those who were referred for certain more serious infractions (status offenses) or were recidivists. This phase covered four days. Students earned up to 45 points a day for acceptable behavior, two points for satisfactory progress on the commitment contract, and three points for completion of an academic project of their own choosing during this phase.

The behavioral contract containing the students' performance objectives and academic project were mandatory. The minimum was seven points a day, a total of at least 33 points for this phase, and a cumulative total of 83 for promotion back to the regular school program.

Transition Phase

Students promoted from ADSP back to the regular program had to undergo a three-week probationary period. The first five days of this phase involved intensive observation during which they had to carry evaluation sheets to class and present a checklist to the teacher at the beginning of each session. During class, the teacher observed the student behavior and made appropriate annotations on the evaluation sheet. At the end of class, the students retrieved the sheet. At the end of the day they met with ADSP counselors to assess their activities and determine how many points they had earned.

The point scales were based on the same checklist as that used in regular ADSP programming. For each class in which a student earned at least eight points on the behavior assessment checklist, the teenager received one point. Failure to earn a minimum of six points each day required the student to return to Phase II.

After satisfactorily completing the intensive observation period, the student then moved to the nonintensive portion of the transition. During that phase, the student remained on a probationary status, with ADSP personnel making spot checks; the point system was not utilized. The purpose was to determine whether members of the ADSP administrative and teaching staff felt the behavior displayed was appropriate and that the student was ready for the regular school program. At any time the individual could be referred back to a particular phase of the ADSP program.

THE UTAH STATEWIDE PROGRAM

Nationwide, there are far more inconsistencies than consistencies at the state level on school discipline. Few states have tackled the problem of developing a philosophy, goals, and procedures on this. Indeed, one of the basic issues in most local disciplinary programs is that they function as an add-on to the school curriculum. As long as discipline is viewed apart from the curriculum, it cannot be considered a major issue or as a preventive or constructive program. To that end, Utah has shown much foresight in developing a state philosophy on discipline. In fact, such a philosophy is necessary to the principles of a democratic society.

It is impossible to do full justice to this philosophy here, but a brief review follows. However, it is recommended as necessary reading in its entirety, perhaps because it fits so well with this author's beliefs. What it assumes is that basic teaching of any skill or subject requires that the state philosophy be compatible with that of the teachers (and principals) who are delivering that instruction.

The basic assumptions underlying Utah's position were:

1. There is no discipline problem that cannot be affected.
2. Only individuals can regulate their own behavior—no one can do it for them.
3. Students are guaranteed the same rights as adults under the United States Constitution.
4. Students are much more capable of accepting responsibility for their own behavior than schools generally acknowledge.
5. Students are moral agents, free to choose their behavior and be influenced by others in those choices.
6. Education is a parental responsibility, only part of which is delegated to the schools.

The major tenets of this point of view for educators were:

1. I (teacher) respect students as equals and I view them as they can become.
2. Students don't learn from people they don't like.

3. The major influence on all students is personal relationships.
4. Self-control cannot be learned in the absence of freedom. There can be no true accountability in the absence of choice.
5. I own my own existence, God gave it to me.
6. I must understand the difference between firmness, control, and structure and learn to operate on all three principles.
7. Peer influence is directly proportional to the degree of alienation felt at home and/or school.
8. With all truth comes responsibility, and behavior cannot be influenced in the absence of meaningful truths.

These eight tenets generate, in turn, ten operational principles.

1. We are a government of laws and not of people. The main purpose of laws is to promote peace and understanding; therefore, they must be agreed upon ahead of time (before a behavior can be punished).
2. Powers should be at the lowest possible level. The people are to be self-reliant, not government-reliant.
3. A system of checks and balances is essential. The most common complaints about local districts received at the state level relate to abusive use of powers. For example, a parent and school cannot agree on what course of action should be taken with their child in solving a problem. For the school to be right in every case makes it a dictatorship; for the parent to be right all of the time creates anarchy. Most schools and classrooms lack an adequate system of checks and balances.
4. All is done in the interest of the individual, not the organization. The role of leader is to facilitate the individual. In this context, a superintendent's chief responsibility is the success of the school principal, the principal's the success of individual teachers, and the teachers' in turn the success of individual students. The tendency, if not guarded, is for schools to develop rules in the interest of their employees and their job function rather than in the interest of the students and the parents being served.
5. Those who govern must do so only by the consent of the governed. However, decisions can be presented to those affected, seeking their understanding of the action, their acceptance, concurrence, or at a minimum, support in the form of ''while I don't like it, I can at least live with it.''
6. It is vital to operate by truth and the influence of reason. Influence on the behavior of others comes through truths and persuasion, and the use of coercion, intimidation, or compulsion are inhibiting to personal influence. Even preaching and moralizing are relatively ineffective because subtle intimidation usually is present.

7. Punishment should not be out of retribution but to facilitate growth. Punishment is probably the most misunderstood element of both democracy and discipline. Punishment under democracy is not to be in retribution. It is to be directly related to the crime, is not to be cruel or unusual, and is to consist chiefly of the withdrawal of freedoms related with the offenses that infringed upon the rights of others. Teachers have three appropriate principles of discipline relating to punishment: (a) If they are to maintain their relationship with their students, the punishments they order must never be in retribution. (b) The ideal penalty is the withdrawal of freedoms that were used to infringe on the rights of others. (c) They must use the calmest correction that proves effective in eliciting the desired behavior.

8. Problems are to be solved by a reasonable and orderly process. Problems are not solved until those concerned and directly affected agree that they are solved. The hasty tendency is to make a new rule, and many rules are for power purposes to expand one-sided control. There are many ways other than rules to solve problems. It is better to operate on principles than on rules. Counseling together is a basic ingredient of problem solving in a democracy.

9. In a democracy the people are to act—not be acted upon. Obedience to law should be by choice—not force. "Do it or else" is not a choice. Self-control cannot be learned in the absence of freedom. Many teachers and many parents cannot tolerate mistakes of any kind on the part of their students or children. To deny students the freedom required to succeed is no different from the freedom that permits failure. Students should be permitted to learn from their little mistakes so they don't have to learn from big ones.

10. Rules don't tell what one can do—only what one cannot do. Americans' basic rights allow them to do everything except infringe on the rights of others. The only constraints they are under are those they have given to government to protect those rights. It is disheartening to hear so frequently in schools and classrooms requests for permission to do things when no related prohibitions exist.

Utah proposed an eight-stage curriculum for teaching responsibility for self. It recommended that teachers:

Stage 1: Develop a Positive Relationship

Students don't learn from people they don't like. Discipline case studies in Utah point out a high degree of relationship between the grades achieved and student respect for the teacher. The 1978 Gallup Poll on Education listed the following as the five personal qualities the general public most wanted in teachers:

1. the ability to communicate, to understand, to relate
2. the ability to discipline, be firm, and fair
3. the ability to inspire and motivate the child
4. high moral character
5. a love of children, a concern for them.

Students must perceive teachers as being interested in them and their needs. In the Utah study on discipline, students at all grade levels voted "getting students and teachers to listen to one another" as the No. 1 strategy for solving discipline problems. Just a few minutes of teacher brainstorming in small groups produces a blackboard full of ways that teachers can communicate concern and caring to students.

Stage 2: Present and Receive Information

Information must be delivered in bite-sized chunks that students can swallow. It is as important for them to receive information as it is for teachers to present it. All information is judged as to worth prior to being absorbed. Human beings do not do anything, including learning, without purpose.

Stage 3: Acquire Meaning

Emotion is a critical component of learning. Learning takes place only when there are feelings or emotions associated with acquisition of a skill or information. The difference is clear: "I enjoyed that (subject) a lot, and really got something out of it," or "I hated it; enough said."

Stage 4: Determine Individual Responsibility

Responsibility is a key factor in learning. Students must make a decision as to whether or not they want information and skills. Decision making must be taught; it cannot be assumed. It does not grow automatically but, indeed, is closely related to emotional growth and the opportunity to practice making responsible decisions.

Stage 5: Confirm Meaning and Responsibility

To assume that a student is profiting from the information presented and is incorporating it through mature decision making, is poor teaching at its worst. Teachers must not assume anything. They should confirm learning through four avenues: (1) expert testimony from credible sources, (2) rational thought, (3) reflective thinking, pondering, or meditation, and (4) action designed to test the worth of something.

Stage 6: Make Commitments

Commitments are primarily to self for they have purpose as well as expectation.

Stage 7: Act Purposefully

Based on self-commitment, students determine a plan and carry out the action necessary to meet responsibility. In this stage, the teacher acts as a resource, operating under the students' direction, providing advice and consultation. That is a new role for most teachers. Monitoring becomes an important function. Teachers should not wait to be asked but should provide reassurance and assistance in short encounters they initiate. They also become more readily available to the students.

Stage 8: Assess the Results

Students should be able to review the results of their learning, recognizing the level of their performance. Three techniques are: (1) a sense of personal satisfaction from increased skill or information is the most valuable feedback; (2) new products, increased status, social acceptance, recognition through grades, promotion, parental acceptance all are critical; and (3) a new goal replaces the one accomplished first.

ERIE'S NEW DIRECTION CENTER

In April 1971, Erie's 1,000 teachers struck, many because of the absence of support by principals on disciplinary matters. Erie teachers desired a positive program, which they got. It begins when a teacher feels a particular student cannot function in the classroom. The first step is for the principal to place the student in another class, but only if the teacher of that class accepts the individual, following a briefing by the previous teacher. If the student does not succeed in the second placement, arrangements are made to continue the youth's education for the next six weeks in the New Direction Center.

The Center was established on a private college campus and was staffed by five full-time teachers, all of whom were volunteers, and all of whom either had, or were earning, master's degrees. Their previous training experience ranged from elementary education to counseling. A school psychologist also was assigned to the Center.

Teacher-pupil ratio is kept as low as possible to allow for truly individualized instruction, the basis of which is a 30-day behavior modification program. Students are held accountable for their actions on a day-to-day basis and those who fail to maintain the expected level of performance must begin the 30-school-day cycle again. So, while it is possible for a student to complete the entire program in six weeks, it actually could take much longer.

The center teachers evaluate the students' attitude after completion of the six weeks. In a few cases, if there is no improvement after repeating the program, the students may be referred to an agency outside the school district. Usually, however, the recommendation has been to return them to the school from which they came. A committee of teachers in that building has the right to refuse to readmit such students, although in practice this seldom has occurred.

POSITIVE PEER CULTURE, GROUP GUIDED INTERACTION

The public schools in Omaha began a Positive Peer Culture (PPC) or Group Guided Interaction (GGI) program in one junior high school in 1973. The Lansing Public Schools in Michigan have placed a program in four secondary schools. Additional public schools, such as those in Rock Island, Ill., have adopted PPC. The basic concepts of PPC are:

- Adolescents are commonly more responsive to the values of peers than to those of adults.
- Most negative behaviors emerge from individuals (and groups) who feel badly about themselves and who feel weak and unsuccessful.
- Adolescents are strong resources of idealism and caring and can be assisted to take charge of their own lives responsibly.
- The most powerful experience that can change a person's self-concept and life is helping and being of service to another.

Positive peer culture uses the peer group as the behavioral changing agent. The dynamics that allow negative student learners to influence their peers adversely can be reversed to modify the school environment, promoting social and academic growth. The process of reversing a negative peer culture and developing a positive one is not easy. A counselor trained in PPC techniques is required. Unsuccessful PPC efforts have involved the use of poorly trained professionals attempting to develop a program.

The steps in developing a program include the following:

- Student leaders throughout the school are identified by asking their peers whom they see as the most influential.

- Each trained PPC staff counselor then makes up two groups of nine student leaders.
- The groups are carefully structured to contain a balance of both positive and negative leaders, assertive and quiet personalities, and represent a full range of problems.
- The groups meet once a day, during a regular school period, and the students receive social studies credit for attendance.
- The focus of these group meetings is not on personalities or school policies; instead, it is on solving the problems presented by its members. A structured agenda is required at each meeting; students are required to report all of the problems they have had since the last meeting.
- A standard list of 12 problem areas is identified and related to the individual student problems. They include: low self-image, being inconsiderate of others, being inconsiderate of self, problems with authority, misleading others, being easily misled, aggravating others, being easily angered, stealing, alcohol or drug problems, lying, and fronting (putting up a false front).

The report serves several purposes for a PPC group: (1) it establishes the point that sharing problems is the first step in solving them; (2) it builds trust in the group process as a viable means of exchange and help; (3) it develops in students the realization that they must face their own problems—it teaches responsibility; and (4) it demonstrates that telling their stories redirects the old and unproductive attitude that hiding feelings and denying decision making is an adolescent characteristic.

The second major focus is building group decision making and teaching the panel responsibility for its members. The members initially state whether or not they would like their individual problems to be the focus of the meeting. This process continues until all group members agree to focus squarely on one person's concerns. The group decision-making process is important as it teaches values to each member by providing experience in democratic principles of compromise, mutual understanding, and respect.

The physical arrangement of the group is designed to communicate the leader's role as a facilitator. The leader is not an active decision maker in the group process but rather attempts to enhance the effort to concentrate on one problem and remain task-oriented until a solution is found.

The final event of each leadership class consists of a short summary by the leader. This allows the leader to emphasize the important issues that may have emerged during the meeting, to praise the group for its efforts in helping, and to challenge it to higher levels of functioning. The summary may include participation by the students as the leader involves them in understanding their own motivation.

CONTINGENCY MANAGEMENT

In 1977, Safer, Heaton, and Allen described a contingency management program giving points to reward constructive behavior for disruptive junior high students. The program divided the morning into four academic class periods, concentrating remedial work on four major subject areas. (In the afternoon, the students rejoined the regular school program.) The aim of the contingency management system was to motivate task-appropriate behaviors and decrease disruptive conduct. A checklist (Exhibit 5-10) attached to a work folder was given to each student at the beginning of each week. The sheet had spaces for eight points during each of the four periods so that a student could earn a maximum of 32 points each morning, with two to four additional points awarded for each required afternoon activity. Teachers or the aide gave points as they were earned, confirming them by placing their initials in the appropriate spaces. Points were given contingently for starting, maintaining, and completing assigned work as well as for social behavior appropriate to the classroom. At least initially, it was essential to reward even basic behaviors such as having pencils and work papers and being in the seat at the time the bell rang.

Students earning all but seven of 34 to 38 points on a given day could be awarded a Good Day Slip; if they earned all but two points, they received an Excellent Day Slip. When a student earned four or more Excellent Day Slips, and no less than one Good Day Slip, an Excellent Week Letter was awarded on Friday. A slightly less stringent standard was used for the awarding of Good Week Letters.

Students were responsible for their own Behavior Checklist (BCL); if it was lost or stolen, they lost the points they had accumulated. A teacher could reward a student performing a sought-after behavior such as holding up a hand when wanting to speak. The teacher simply would say, ''I like you to raise your hand (or whatever) when you want to speak, so I am going to give you an extra point.'' This use of extra points also could support a student who was having a bad day and where an emotional explosion was possible.

The weekly individual curriculum expectations for each student were established through a contract negotiated by the subject area teachers and the students. Grades were contingent upon the amount of the contract fulfilled at an acceptable level of accuracy that week.

In cases of misconduct, the offending student was presented immediately with a Disturbing and Disruptive Behavior Slip (D/D). These D/D slips were preprinted with typical infractions encountered in the classroom, such as disruptive talking, wandering around, etc. (Exhibit 5-11). There also was space to write in a behavior that had not been listed. It was stressed that the D/D slips be delivered to the student with as little emotion as possible, very factually. The message was: here is a feedback on your behavior, you know the consequences.

Exhibit 5-10 Student Behavior Checklist

TODAY'S DATE_____   NAME_____   NO._____

BEHAVIORS THAT EARN POINTS:

1. Being in the assigned seat on time.
2. Having a pencil.
3. Having appropriate folder opened and on desk.
4. On-task behavior.
5. Worked successfully on-task.
6. Extra individual behavior: _____

Preparation behaviors

	MONDAY						TUESDAY						WEDNESDAY						THURSDAY						FRIDAY					
	1	2	3	4	5	6	1	2	3	4	5	6	1	2	3	4	5	6	1	2	3	4	5	6	1	2	3	4	5	6
Period 1																														
Period 2																														
Period 3																														
Period 4																														

Prev. Cum. Tot.
Today's Tot. +
Present Tot. =
Today's Expenditure =
Reinfor. Rm.
New Cum. Tot. =

Exhibit 5-11 Example of a D/D Slip

PLEASE CORRECT THE FOLLOWING SERIOUS DISTURBING OR DISRUPTIVE
BEHAVIOR:

        1. Disruptive talking   _____

        2. Throwing objects   _____

        3. Hitting or pushing   _____

        4. Wandering around   _____

        5. Noise making   _____

        6. Being in an unauthorized area_____

IF YOU RECEIVE A SECOND SLIP, YOU MUST REPORT TO THE OFFICE OF THE
ASSISTANT PRINCIPAL.

_____

DATE _____ STUDENT _____ TEACHER _____

A student receiving two D/D slips during the same school period was dismissed from class immediately and sent to the office or to a holding room, if one was available. With serious infractions, the student then could be temporarily dismissed from the program until a parent conference could be held. On less serious matters, the student was held in a timeout situation. During this timeout while away from the classroom, the student lost all points and, hence, the reinforcers that normally would be the objectives.

Afternoon Program

Following the four consecutive morning periods of academic instruction, the program students were sent to the cafeteria to be integrated with the school at large.

The most effective way of handling problems in the integrated aspect of the program was to continue group privileges contingent upon the members' performance. Examples of such privileges included extra auction items and/or the continuation of the early release reward (see below) if they had earned enough points. In order to be released for the last two periods of the school day, the students had to trade a considerable proportion of their points. The release followed lunch or the completion of one of the integrated subjects (art, music, physical education).

A reinforcement room also was used. It was located away from the regular classrooms since program activities tended to be louder than normally would be tolerated in classrooms. The reinforcement room was staffed with one aide (the morning classroom aide), although having more than one aide proved to be a definite advantage when more than five students were using the room.

The primary duty for the reinforcement room aide was to provide activities and maintain some form of order. The students could choose from a variety of games set up in the room, such as pool, table tennis, hockey and soccer games, cards, board games, or slot car racing, and were permitted to listen to music as they pleased.

The student had to earn a number of points on that day in order to go to the reinforcement room for the afternoon. A weekly auction was held for these students every Friday. They bid their accumulated (unused) points on a variety of items held up for auction: records, tickets for dances, movies, and roller skating, food items (e.g., potato chips, ice cream, gum, and mints), coupons redeemable at fast-food restaurants, and plastic models.

Parents' participation in the program was strongly encouraged, and contacts between school and home were developed wherever possible. Unfortunately, the analysis reported that no amount of positive outreach could encourage parents to participate.

The Seven-Step Transition

The transition to the regular classroom was designed to be achieved through seven steps.

Step 1: Self-Evaluation

During the first week or two, the teacher or aide continued to independently assign points for each student's performance. At the end of each day, student and teacher compared points. The smaller the discrepancy, the quicker the student moved to self-evaluation. Only students who were accurately assigning their own points were allowed to attend the auction.

Step 2: Daily Progress Report

Following self-evaluation, a daily progress report became a standard method used to provide feedback to student and parent. Students were given acceptable or unacceptable marks in ''conduct'' and ''academic performance'' for each class period.

Step 3: Teacher Integration

A third method used to prepare the students for the regular school routine was to bring nonprogram teachers into contact with them.

Step 4: Individual to Group Instruction

To approximate conditions of the regular classroom, individual assignments gradually were replaced with group instruction.

Step 5: Regular Class Attendance

At about the seventh week of the fading program, the students began to attend one or two regular classes for a week or two. Then, as they showed progress, they began taking all of their courses in the regular classes.

Step 6: Weekly Progress Report

At six weeks, a weekly progress card was substituted for the daily one.

Step 7: Reinforcers Withdrawn

In the final fading stage, the early dismissal, weekly auction, and home reinforcers were withdrawn.

As noted, the transition lasted about a year and a half and was extremely effective. Most of the students continued to make academic progress and demonstrated social growth. What were the weaknesses of the program? The major one was the requirement that the school staff cooperate fully with the alternative approach.

OFF-CAMPUS LEARNING CENTER (OCLC)

Dembinski (1978) reported on an Off-Campus Learning Center (OCLC) (Schack, 1975) that was established as an alternate school for students unable to make constructive use of a standard school program. This suburban Chicago program, designed for approximately 75 adolescents with behavior problems, was housed in a storefront. The staff consisted of a full-time director, seven full-time instructors, two full-time social workers, a psychiatric consultant, and a secretary/aide.

This was a team effort uniting students, home, and high school staff. The overall goal was total reintegration of the students into the standard high school setting. Several goals were established to help students:

- improve their self-concept and self-respect
- proceed more smoothly in the passage from youth to adult
- deal with frustrations so as to lessen anxiety, depression, hostility, and rejection
- modify specific antisocial performances in the high school and the community
- improve their academic achievements so that they approximated their potentials and measured their abilities
- develop academic skills in order to cope in a standard high school
- develop ethical attitudes about learning
- make decisions regarding academic and vocational goals
- form and maintain meaningful relationships with adults and peers
- be able to improve communication and rapport with members of their families, peers, school, community, and society in general.

The referral and placement process began in the standard high school with identification of the students as troubled by counselor, teacher, social worker, or other professionals who sent the youngsters to a division referral review board to determine whether or not it would be appropriate to develop a case study. Once eligibility was determined, an educational prescriptive plan was designed for each student. Thereafter, student and family met for two interviews with the Learning Center staff to solidify the placement plan with all parties.

The Off-Campus Learning Center provided small classes (not more than eight pupils) where students were directed toward individual academic and social skill-building activities as determined by their individual performance objectives. Students had one teacher instructing them in three academic areas. Subjects include mathematics (both basic and algebra), English, social studies (including United States history), and communication skills, plus a daily physical education class, including team and individual sports as well as crafts and adaptive games.

All students participated in regularly scheduled group counseling with the social worker, teacher, and fellow classmates on a weekly basis. Psychiatric social workers also were available for individual counseling. Regular weekly parent group meetings were available for all who had students in the program.

Teachers worked individually with students to establish performance objectives. The initial planning stage began with a weekly evaluation sheet, formulated by teacher and student, that listed specific behavior and academic objectives. In almost all cases when students entered the program, their school day was self-contained for the first semester. The second semester and thereafter, students gradually were fed back into regularly scheduled classes for specifically recommended courses. Schedules usually were established in a combined effort of the student, OCLC teacher, and division counselor. It is possible to choose division teachers who are best able to deal effectively with the learning center student. Total reintegration of the student back into the standard high school, the ultimate goal, was accomplished within two academic years.

The following represent the program's general course objectives for English, social studies, mathematics, communication skills, and physical education.

English

English Skills 1, 2, 3, and 4: reading, writing, language, and vocabulary skills in four areas of English study

- Skills 1: Man as Individual (to increase awareness of self)
- Skills 2: Man in the Family (to increase awareness of roles in the family)
- Skills 3: Man in Society (to increase awareness of roles in society)
- Skills 4: Man in the Future (to increase awareness of the future).

These courses were designed to help students in both cognitive and affective areas:

- Cognitive
  1. improve reading skills
  2. gain a knowledge of literary techniques
  3. gain a knowledge of specific authors and techniques.
- Affective
  1. acquire insight into the multiple varieties and pleasures of reading
  2. acquire insight into the relationship of literature to their lives.

Mathematics

Math Skills 1 and 2 (Basic and Consumer-Related Math)

- Students will demonstrate the ability to use math concepts to achieve economic success.

Math Skills 3 and 4 (Algebra)

- Students will demonstrate an ability to advance in self-fulfillment by increasing their knowledge and in their ability to communicate.

Social Studies

Social Studies Skills 1, 2, 3, and 4

- Skills 1: Anthropology. Students will be provided with an understanding of the unique nature of man and his culture.
- Skills 2: Geography. Students will be provided with an understanding of how the area in which man lives on this earth is known as the spatial environment, with physical, cultural, political, and economic characteristics.
- Skills 3: Sociology. Students will be shown how man lives and interacts in societies, which determine the norms and values that organize man's behavior.
- Skills 4: Government. Students will be provided with an analysis of the decision-making process in any society or group, defined as involving those political activities from which choices are made between alternate courses of action within a political system.

History

History Skills 1 and 2

- Skills 1: This course will demonstrate to students how history is the selection, recording, and interpretation of man's total experience.
- Skills 2: This course is designed to develop student understanding of United States foreign policy today and analyze the historical intricacies that played a role in shaping it.

Communication Skills

Communication Skills 1 and 2

- Students will be provided with the skills to fulfill their needs to know who and what they are and to relate and contribute to their environment.

Physical Education

Physical Education Skills 1, 2, 3, and 4

- Students will be provided with physical activities that correlate fair play, group cooperation, physical and mental well-being, and others that assist the academic pursuits by providing an outlet into which to channel frustration.

Consequences for inappropriate behavior include extra assignments, cleanup chores, loss of privileges, and suspensions. Continuous and blatant failure to adhere to rules is interpreted as the students' inability to adjust to the structure of the program, thereby indicating that they are not benefiting from the services provided. Termination (expulsion) is then the probable recommendation and procedure.

THE PHILADELPHIA STORY

On the junior and senior high school level, the School District of Philadelphia conducts more than 60 alternative programs (Staples, 1977). One is the Parkway Program, which consists of four different schools or "communities," each of which separately explores the city's educational, cultural, and scientific institutions as part of its extended campus. A core faculty provides instruction in basic skills, offers courses in fields of expertise, and supervises tutors. The tutors constitute advisory groups that provide counseling and supportive interaction. Community volunteers with special skills offer onsite programs, classes, and internships in academic, commercial, and vocational subjects.

PEP (Penn Treaty Junior High School-Edison High School Program) is a dropout prevention program offering ninth- and tenth-grade boys a smaller, more personalized atmosphere in which the teacher can work closely with the group. All PEP students participate in a career education program at the A. Philip Randolph Skills Center. Ninth graders are involved in the trade exploration program; tenth-graders are assigned to specific skill clusters. Some PEP students are placed in paid after-school jobs.

The Penn Treaty Junior High School also sponsors BEST (Better Education through Service and Training), a motivation and career preparation program for girls who are not doing well in regular school. The students at BEST receive special attention in a family-like learning unit. One teacher works with the same class for the entire day in order to establish a closer working relationship. A traditional teaching approach is used, with strong emphasis on developing reading skills.

BEST has a career component that provides girls with work experiences in elementary school tutoring and hospital training. Students in the tutoring program spend two days a week onsite at BEST and three days a week in an elementary school helping pupils improve basic skills. The hospital training program introduces girls to the various careers in such an institution, with similar two days at their hospital jobs and three days at the BEST center.

Edison High School has developed alternatives designed to reach disaffected students and reduce their dropout rate. One of these is the Academy of Applied

Electrical Science, a three-year program where academic subjects are related to electrical training.

The same school operates the Edison Project Dropout Prevention Center, where the major focus is on career education. Half of each student's day is spent in a self-contained classroom improving basic skills in both individual and small group situations, with additional attention available in mathematics or in a reading laboratory. The Career Education Component covers three areas:

1. a work-stipend program that provides students with up to ten hours of work a week at minimum wages
2. in-school work exploration
3. out-of-school experiences that introduce students to the working world through lessons on available careers, application procedures, and visits to job sites.

The program also provides learning stations that offer a week's intensive exploration at business and industrial locations.

In another alternative model, several junior high schools are feeders for the Bishop Learning Center, which is designed to work with students displaying chronic disciplinary problems. The staff attempts to deal with these through counseling, not in academic or other special offerings. Every member of the staff has to be skilled in listening, be patient, have a high degree of empathy and self-awareness, be expert in fostering educational relationships, and be willing to assume responsibility for hostile and impatient students.

Some of the Philadelphia programs concentrate on the students of a single grade. An example is SALE (Southern Alternate Learning Experience) conducted by South Philadelphia High School at an offsite location. This program provides special help to tenth-grade students who are potential dropouts, have low reading and mathematics profiles, have failed to be promoted, or are dissatisfied with school. The traditional curriculum, which includes mathematics, social studies, English (concentrating on reading skills), and science, is followed. Reduced class size, shorter instructional periods, and flexible scheduling are the chief vehicles used to reach students.

SUMMARY

This chapter has reviewed a selected few of any number of excellent programs designed to normalize disruptive youths who are dropouts, truants, and norm-violating in their behavior. There are several program options worthy of consideration:

- Self-Contained Classroom (full-time): Students spend the entire day in the classroom receiving the prescribed instruction.
- Resource Room (part-time): Students spend a minimal amount of time in the resource room, receiving assistance and support at a level that enables them to function successfully in the regular classroom.
- Peer Tutoring and Support: Peers provide assistance to students in areas of skill development, socialization, and career direction.
- Academic/Vocational Preparation: Students spend half of their time in academic areas and half in shop and industrial arts training.
- Work Study: Students attend regular classes for a short period in the morning, then work during the afternoon at a monitored site for a regulated amount of time.
- Vocational Study: Students receive instruction in academic areas while also attending a vocational training center that emphasizes specific career preparation.

These options, in varying ways, provide:

- programmed instruction for low achievers
- programs for students who have high interest in particular careers but low vocabulary needs in those jobs
- career-oriented materials for adolescents interested in vocational craftsmanship
- reading material emphasizing retention of basic information
- material requiring only short-term memory
- material geared to conceptual understanding and response.

The effort is then to go beyond traditional schooling, by providing:

- Appraising (actual observation of student by teachers and other professionals): This gives educators experiential awareness of academic needs and career availability in the community through films, field trips, reading material, recordings, and slide presentations.
- Witnessing: This enables students to spend time as observers at specified commercial establishments, improving their awareness of the skills and competencies required in career paths.
- Work Experience: This provides experience at a learning center in actual or simulated work situations. Similar experiences can be made available in the community at retail stores, industries, or special workshops. Academics

involved generally are related directly to the work experiences but, when appropriate, may have a global direction.

- Work/Study: This presents a general vocational curriculum related to the employment or career planning program the students are developing outside the educational setting. They learn skills on the job and relate their academic and vocational work in the community to their classes.
- Career Cooperative Education: This provides a sequence of academic and experiential opportunities in school that prepare students for a specific career or type of work that they pursue upon completing school. While working in the community, the youths are supervised on the job by their employer and by a job coach assigned as a coordinator.
- Community Work: This is the terminal stage in the students' career/vocational program. Upon completing formal schooling, they will work independently in the community.

Therefore, the community, not the school ultimately, becomes the vocational centerpiece. Several community options for students are highly desirable:

- diagnostic services
- counseling
- programs
- academic instruction
- career/vocation awareness, exploration, and preparation
- off-campus experience
- program evaluation and reprogramming.

In essence, school should not be viewed as an either/or proposition. It can involve:

- full-time school
- part-time school, part-time work
- part-time school, part-time vocational training
- full-time vocational training
- part-time vocational training, part-time work
- full-time work.

200   DISCIPLINE AND BEHAVIORAL MANAGEMENT

REFERENCES

Christian, M.A. *The anatomy of a program of humane discipline in the Atlanta Public School System.* Atlanta: Atlanta Teacher Corps, 1979. (ERIC Document Reproduction Service No. ED 182 015)

Dembinski, R.J. Psychoeducational management of disruptive youths. In D.A. Sabatino & A.J. Mauser (Eds.), *Intervention strategies for specialized secondary education.* Boston: Allyn & Bacon, Inc., 1978.

Gallup Poll. School ratings up slightly; discipline still top problem. *Phi Delta Kappan,* 1980, *6*(3), 206.

Gooding, J., & Fitsko, M. *A proposal for an alternative to out-of-school suspension for Worthington High School students: The Saturday school.* 1978. (ERIC Document Reproduction Service No. ED 169 663)

Haussman, S.E. *Deinstitutionalization of status offenders: An in-school suspension project.* Macon, Ga.: Bibb County Public Schools, 1979. (ERIC Document Reproduction Service No. ED 171 013)

Larsen, L. *Alternatives: Alternative discipline and suspension, program handbook.* Gillette, Wyo.: Campbell County School District, 1979. (ERIC Document Reproduction Service No. ED 172 460)

National Education Association. *The LEAST approach to classroom discipline.* Washington, D.C.: Author, 1978. (ERIC Document Reproduction Service No. ED 166 143)

National Institute of Education. *Violent schools—safe schools: The safe school study report to the Congress.* Executive summary. Washington, D.C.: Author, 1978.

Safer, D., Heaton, R., & Allen, R.P. Socioeconomic factors influencing the rate of nonpromotion in elementary schools. *Peabody Journal of Education,* 1977, *54,* 275-281.

Schack, M. *Off-campus learning center.* Paper presented at the Illinois Conference on Behavior Disorders, Northern Illinois University, DeKalb, Ill., June 30, 1975.

Staples, I.E. Affecting disaffected students: The Philadelphia story. *Educational Leadership,* 1977, *13,* 422-424.

Valentine, C.F. *A program to reduce vandalism and to improve student behavior at Vineland High School North.* Vineland, N.J.: Vineland Public Schools, 1978. (ERIC Document Reproduction Service No. ED 173 899)

Chapter 6

Social Development: Building Human Relationship Skills

Ann C. Sabatino and David A. Sabatino

INTRODUCTION

This chapter provides a framework for improving social relationship skills, a development that cannot be separated from any other academic or vocational learning experience. Social and personal development are merely the two ends of the same continuum. Social development generally refers to social or human relationships (interpersonal), personal development to intrapersonal (self) development. Both require human adjustment: social development, the person to the group; personal development, within the individual.

The initial question in social development is: do students know how to display an appropriate social behavior? The importance of social development is the powerful impact it has on personal development. Youths who do not adjust to the group rarely evidence personal adjustment or feel good about themselves. On the other hand, those who do display appropriate personal development rarely demonstrate appropriate social development. Their feelings of self and self-worth and their ability to care for others and to recognize appropriate social cues all are socially relative, relating the perceptions of the person to the cultural norms of society. Therefore, it is necessary to measure social development through observations of the person, at a particular time and place, in response to a specific task.

OBSERVING SOCIAL DEVELOPMENT

Do the students:

- maintain eye contact?
- address the person speaking to them by recognizing that individual fully?
- speak with the intent of communicating?

- evidence social graces, i.e., manners, please, thank you?
- introduce themselves properly to a wide range of people?
- excuse themselves in any situation, including awkward ones?
- read appropriate social cues, both verbal and nonverbal, from others and in the environment?
- desire to display appropriate social behaviors?
- respond positively to feedback, accepting criticism, and attempting to improve behaviors?
- respect others, respect authority, provide criticism to others in a polite and acceptable fashion?

Most social development materials constitute informal assessment instruments, designed to determine a youth's relationship in response to a particular social setting. Social skills themselves involve a wide range of human functions, principally those that generally improve or decrease a youth's social standing. Therefore, the subjectivity used in making these evaluations serves a definitive purpose since social skills are relative to a given situation and the perception of the viewer (observer). A social development scale may simply be a general judgment of the person in any setting. Exhibit 6-1 is an example of a general, not specific, device to measure sensitivities. The scale also may be an observation related to a specific setting or environment, i.e., work experience (Exhibit 6-2). In short, the two variables being considered are: (1) setting, and (2) specificity or generality of social skill being ascertained or described.

Various scaling devices can be used to develop a profile of social skills. The more specific the scaling procedure, the more usable. Instructionally, Exhibit 6-3 presents a social development instrument that provides a specific vocational program entry.

Social rating scales may combine several subcompetencies, as illustrated in Exhibits 6-4 and 6-5, including (1) care of self, and (2) care of grooming and clothing.

These simple, social development scaling devices provide a means for determining, planning, and evaluating the progress resulting from social skill development programming.

PERSONAL-SOCIAL OBJECTIVES

The personal-social objectives are presented as potential miniunits of instruction. However, close coordination is expected among educators, counselors,

Continues on page 206

Exhibit 6-1 General Sensitivity to Setting

	Poor	Fair	Good
Shows self-confidence			
Is cheerful			
Cooperates with teachers			
Cooperates with others			
Respects teachers			
Minds own business			
Accepts criticism			
Mixes socially with other students			
Is neat and clean			
Other			

Exhibit 6-2 Social Skill Development Related to Work

	Poor	Fair	Good
Is safety conscious			
Is careful of materials			
Completes work on time			
Is conscious of quality of work			
Understands work			
Shows initiative			
Other			

Exhibit 6-3 Socially Related Vocational Development Ratings for
Instructional Placement

	Educational Awareness	Career Awareness	Self-Awareness	Economic Awareness	Appreciation Awareness	Decision-Making	Beginning Competencies	Employability Skills
Living Skills								
Leisure Time								
Mental Requirements								
Career Information								
Career Selection								
Career Orientation								
Vocational Skill								
Physical Requirements								
Social Relationships								
Economic Considerations								
Work Motivated								
Work Interests								
Work Prepared								
Work Behaviors								
Work Reliable								
Work Satisfaction								

Exhibit 6-4 Care of Self

	Never	Sometimes	Usually	Always
1. Daily bath or shower				
2. Teeth brushed				
3. Healthy teeth and gums				
4. Breath properly				
5. Clean and healthy complexion				
6. Hair cut and clean				
7. Eat good food				
8. Nose and ears are clean and cared for				
9. Posture is good				
10. Exercise daily				

Exhibit 6-5 Clothes and Grooming

	Never	Sometimes	Usually	Always
1. Clothes look good				
2. Hair groomed				
3. Hair clean				
4. Clothes look neat and clean				
5. Proper clothes for the occasion				
6. Finger nails are clean and short				
7. Pride in dress				
8. Shoes shined				
9. Socks and underwear are clean				
10. Deodorant and foot powders				

psychologists, and vocational coordinators. The objectives are that the students will:

1. Attain a sufficient understanding of themselves. The students will be able to:

   - Identify a sense of body awareness
   - Identify interests
   - Identify abilities
   - Identify emotions
   - Identify personal needs
   - Understand physical self: physiological development, human sexuality.

2. Obtain positive self-confidence and self-concept. The students will be able to:

   - Express feelings of self-worth
   - Understand how others see them
   - Accept criticism
   - Develop confidence in self.

3. Desire and achieve socially responsible behavior. The students will be able to:

   - Understand character traits needed for acceptance by others
   - Exhibit acceptable behavior in public
   - Develop and understand respect for the rights and properties of others
   - Recognize and follow instructions and rules
   - Identify personal roles in many situations
   - Understand cultural and multicultural values.

4. Choose, develop, and maintain appropriate interpersonal relationships. The students will be able to:

   - Know how to listen and respond to others
   - Understand how to make and maintain friendships
   - Understand appropriate heterosexual relationships
   - Understand how to establish close relationships (friendship).

5. Achieve independence. The students will be able to:

   - Understand the impact of their behavior on others
   - Understand the need for self-organization

- Develop goal-seeking behavior
- Strive toward self-actualization.

6. Make good decisions and solve problems. The students will be able to:

- Differentiate socially relative concepts
- Understand the need for goals
- Consider alternatives
- Anticipate consequences
- Know where to find advice.

7. Communicate appropriately with others. The students will be able to:

- Recognize emergency situations
- Understand the need, and be able, to read effectively
- Understand and be able to communicate effectively in writing and speech
- Understand subtleties of mass and/or personal communication.

SOCIAL GOALS IN CURRICULUM DEVELOPMENT

The secondary school curriculum can be structured to include program goals in support of social development. Classroom instruction, guidance seminars, group counseling, and the resource room all may serve as settings to promote peer, adult, or social group intervention, where a number of situational needs and pressures can be observed, studied, and learned under controlled practice situations. The old idea that all social learning must be under real conditions with real people is simply too expensive. The cost to students who do not have reliable social learning skills may be social exclusion, social ridicule, and loss of self-esteem.

Goals to be achieved by building social development objectives into the regular curriculum are:

1. Social learning with peers. The students will understand a variety of social situational circumstances, including:

- pressures to conform
- emotional involvements
- social rules that are within or outside of laws, customs, and proprieties
- humiliating social factors
- social situations that test the persons before they accept or reject them

- discrimination or exclusion for social reasons, i.e., religion, race, origin, socioeconomic status
- differences in cultural background and environment
- settings in which they are unable to join because of the behaviors of the group or students' interests, training, and background.

2. Reaction to the rules of the group. The students will learn to relate to others in various situations, including:

- acceptance of conformity without sacrificing their own individuality
- participation in friendly give-and-take conversation
- standing up for their own rights when humiliated or insulted
- refusal to try to force their way into situations where they are not wanted
- willingness to give up a part of themselves to participate in a group
- cooperation and performance of their share of the work when needed.
- acceptance of and ability to work with diverse viewpoints.

3. Relationship to adults. The students will learn:

- respect for the maturity of adults
- understanding that adults have had more experience
- adults' advice must be heeded
- the codes of conduct for adults are different from those for adolescents
- the underlying factors behind adults' divergent viewpoints and attitudes
- adjustment to a variety of social situations with different adults, with different interests, in different circumstances.

4. Social group adaption. The students will understand such adjustment if they are capable of participation in groups with different:

- socioeconomic backgrounds
- philosophies
- attitudes
- cultural environments
- customs.

5. Role relationships. The students will be able to quickly and easily change their associations with:

- superiors
- peers
- subordinates.

6. Social interests. The students will be able to adapt their social interests to those of the group through:

- affiliation with a new group rather than remaining an outsider when thrust into it
- recognition of the differences among people in the group, i.e., group membership does not exclude individual needs
- adjustment of personal communication in order to understand others fully while being equally understood fully as persons themselves.

OBJECTIVES, ACTIVITIES, AND MATERIALS

A program for increasing social development can be based on the following elements:

Strategy 1

- The students will be aware of the necessity for (a) dressing, grooming, and courtesy, (b) relationships with others, and (c) good work habits.

Activities

- The teacher discusses what is meant by good grooming and dressing.

1. Have the students examine their appearance at home in the morning before coming to school.
2. Use films and supplemental materials listed under the next heading.
   a. Brief students on what to look for before showing films or distributing books.
   b. Hold a class discussion after showing each film.
3. Develop a bulletin board displaying character traits that they can develop to become successful jobholders.
   a. Emphasize throughout the year how improvement of each trait will help assure them of becoming successful jobholders.
   b. Read to the class the story of the hare and the tortoise, ''A Story About a Winner.''

Strategy 2

• The students will demonstrate the importance of personal appearance through self-evaluation.

Activities

• The teacher will discuss job interview activities and provide checklists for student self-evaluation.

	Yes	No
1. *My Appearance*		
Well groomed	_____	_____
Hair properly cut and combed	_____	_____
Clean shaven	_____	_____
Teeth brushed, mouth clean	_____	_____
Proper bath, deodorant used	_____	_____
Shoes neat and clean	_____	_____
Properly dressed, clothes clean and pressed	_____	_____
Have I forgotten anything?	_____	_____
2. *My Personality & Appearance*		
Good appearance	_____	_____
Easy and confident walk	_____	_____
Good posture	_____	_____
Pleasant while being introduced	_____	_____
Handshake firm but not viselike	_____	_____
Interest shown in potential employer, looks at the person while talking	_____	_____
Questions answered directly with proper address: "Yes, sir" and "No, ma'am."	_____	_____
Interviewer not interrupted, questions answered in simple, honest, brief manner	_____	_____
Response if answer is unknown, "I do not know, sir (or ma'am)."	_____	_____
Sincerity shown at all times	_____	_____
Interview completed with a smile and statement, "Thank you sir (or ma'am), for your time and interest."	_____	_____

- The teacher encourages the class members to make constructive criticism of a simulated job interview. The teacher points out good qualities of the student applicant, then lists improvements to be made.

Strategy 3

- The students will be able to evaluate themselves from the standpoint of social development.

Activities

- The teacher discusses self-evaluation and shares examples of social self-evaluation forms.
  1. Have each pupil complete a self-rating scale.
  2. Discuss the importance of a balanced criticism for self (and others) that is constructive.
  3. Role-play improvements derived from these self-evaluations.

Strategy 4

- The students will role-play personal and lifelike practices in developing relationships with other students, with teachers, and with counselors, involving parents if possible.

Activities

- The teacher should hold a preliminary counseling session with each student to ensure favorable results.
  1. Set specific dates for self-evaluation sessions.
  2. Have students redo self-evaluative instrument if necessary.
  3. Help students further refine their checksheets on appearance and social skills.
  4. Coach students in their responses to the group during role playing.
  5. Encourage parents to sit in on role playing if possible.

SUPPLEMENTAL MATERIALS

You Decide: Opposing Viewpoints (Greenhaven)

For secondary learners, this set consists of 35 booklets presenting pros and cons on crime issues. Each booklet contains articles and essays by leading criminologists, psychologists, lawyers, judges, religious leaders, and sociologists.

Confrontation in Urbia: A Legal Simulation (Classroom Dynamics)

Secondary students simulate a jury trial to decide a case and gain realistic understanding of constitutional rights, due process of law, and the problems faced by the police in urban crises.

Innocent Until . . . A Criminal Justice Simulation (ABT Associates)

This kit helps students understand how the law works by having them simulate a courtroom trial to determine innocence or guilt, assuming roles of judge, jury, lawyers, defendant, defendant's wife, witness, law officers, and courtroom personnel.

About Your Community (Steck-Vaughn Company Publishers)

Two paper booklets in the Family Development Series specifically related to two topics:
    "Being an Informed Citizen,"
    "Where to go, Who to see, What to do."

Math for Living Skillbooks, Reading Level 4.5-5.5 (Mafex Associates, Inc.)

These ten skillbooks provide lessons and activities that give students the math-related skills needed for successful daily living. Single sets may be purchased. The titles of the skillbooks are: *Math for Family Living, Math for the Worker, Math for Citizenship, Math for Banking, Math for Employment I and II, Math for Adult Living, Math for Everyday Living, Your Daily Math I and II.*

Today's Consumer Math Problems, Reading Level 5.0-6.0 (Homemaking Research)

Word problems teach students how to use credit, shop wisely, and budget.

Budget Ideas for Teenagers, Reading Level 3.5-4.5

This captioned filmstrip provides humorous illustrations and easy-to-read captions on budgeting techniques geared to the income and expenses of teenagers.

The Big Buy, Reading Level 4.0-5.0

This captioned filmstrip dramatizes a teenage girl's shopping for a stereo set. It deals with comparison shopping for quality, price, guarantees, and financing.

Payday Game, Reading Level 4.5-5.5 (Parker Brothers)

A game simulating the adult world of budgets, wages, and bills. It includes a gameboard, tokens, dice, expense cards, opportunity cards, payday money, savings-and-loan interest chart, and directions.

Shopping Bag Game, Reading Level 4.0-5.0 (Creative Teachers Associates)

Four high-interest games challenge students to strengthen basic math and reading skills while learning how to shop. It includes four gameboards, 100 problem-solving cards, and a teacher's guide.

Becoming Yourself (Scholastic Book Services)

For elementary learners, the three units—"Exploring My Identity," "Expressing Myself," "Understanding Myself and Others"—stress the concepts of self-respect and respect for others. Each unit has four filmstrips with records or cassettes and a teacher's guide.

Going Places with Your Personality: A Guide to Successful Living, Reading Level 2.7 (Fearon, Education Division, 6 Davis Drive, Belmont, CA 94002)

This booklet uses information, observation, and discussion to help students develop desirable attitudes and habits; it has a strong emphasis on interpersonal skills.

ACCENT/Personality, Reading Level 3-4 (Follett)

Four booklets are designed to teach social skills and encourage the social attitudes needed in society. The four titles are: "You and They," "You Are Heredity and Environment," "Taking Stock," and "You and Your Needs."

Focus on Self-Development, Stage One: Awareness, K-2, Stage Two: Responding, Reading Level 2-4 (Science Research Associates, Inc.)

This development program leads children to an understanding of self, others, and the environment and its effects on them. It contains activities for whole group, small group, or individuals. The program contains a set of five 36-frame color filmstrips and records, four activity records, 20 photoboards, pupil activity book, and teacher's guide.

The Social Learning Curriculum (The Charles E. Merrill Publishing Co., Inc.)

> A very comprehensive kit designed to give special students knowledge, skills, and behaviors that will enhance their opportunities for success in their environment. Physical, social, and psychological elements of the environment are taken into account so that the students receive a balance of stimuli to develop and reinforce important social learning concepts. The kit contains ten phases and has the following components: 10 phase books, 72 stimulus pictures, 10 spirit duplicating books, an assessment and record for each phase, transparencies, supplementary books in physical education, mathematics, and science, a 32-page teacher's guide, and a scope and sequence chart.

Got To Be Me! A Self-Awareness Program for Elementary Students (Argus Communications)

> The program helps develop positive self-images by providing opportunities for students to talk and write about themselves. It includes workbooks, 48 cards, and a teacher's guide.

Lifeline—Education in Human Relations for Grades 7-12 (Argus Communications)

> The kit has three major areas subdivided to deal with situations that involve a variety of value decisions that are part of the growing-up years. The three content areas are: ''In Other People's Shoes,'' ''Proving the Rule,'' and ''What Would You Have Done?'' Situational cards/or booklets are provided for each area.

Making Sense of Our Lives (Argus Communications)

> A program for self-expression includes six units with six exercises in each. The goal is to help students become more aware of their strengths and more respectful of those of others. Each unit has six posters, six spirit masters, and six teacher guides. Unit titles are: ''Learning About Myself,'' ''Expressing Feelings and Emotion,'' ''Self-Concept,'' ''Sensitivity to Others,'' ''Goals and Decision-Making,'' and ''Social Issues.''

Am I O.K.? (Argus Communications)

> This higher level reading book with spirit masters offers helpful, practical exercises in transactional analysis.

If You Don't Know Where You're Going, You'll Probably End Up Somewhere Else (Argus Communications)

> A paperback book and spirit masters for secondary learners outlining major factors such as skills, education, friends, motivation, family, experience, and health, that influence choices.

All About Manners (Interpretive Education)

> These filmstrips and cassettes show, via situations, the options an individual has in displaying acceptable behaviors.

What It Takes—Developing Skills for Contemporary Living, Reading Level 2.4 (Fearon, Education Division)

> This is a paperback book about an urban family's day-to-day problems. It is designed for grades 7-12.

ELICITING SOCIAL DISCUSSION AND GROWTH

Strategy 1

- Role-play a party at one of the student's homes.

Activities

- Designate roles for each student on the basis of previous party experience.
- Discuss appropriate party behavior.
- Review appropriate responses to several party situations.
- Prepare a script on learning and demonstrating appropriate party behavior.
- Act out appropriate and contrasting inappropriate behaviors, using simulated drama.
- Use supplemental materials listed in the previous section to identify an even wider range of appropriate behavior.

Strategy 2

- Develop guided group criticism: establish the purpose to the group—to review each student with critical kindness in terms of manners, grooming, clothing, and social communication.

Activities

- Discuss social communication, practice kind criticism, have each student lodge a genuine criticism toward another person.
- Demonstrate the inadequacy of direct engagement or encounters.

Strategy 3

- Mirror play, with each person providing a critical self-evaluation before a group concerning that individual's appearance. The group then reviews the self-evaluation and produces its own critical comments. Does the mirror lie?

Activities

- Find a full-length mirror, have all students evaluate their own appearance, then have the group provide its opinion of each person's appearance.
- Discuss first impressions: how students look and act, i.e., chewing gum, talking loudly; emphasize grooming.
- Practice walking, standing, sitting, and bending.

Strategy 4

- Review relative social values in dress (appearance): fashionable dress, appropriate dress, inappropriate dress.

Activity

- Develop fashion awareness/clothes coordination according to an identified standard.

Strategy 5

- Prepare audio tape recordings on topics of persistent life situations from materials found in newspapers, magazines, on television, on radio, in brochures.

Activities

- Cover these topics with students:
    1. learning to communicate ideas
    2. understanding themselves

3. learning to travel
4. adjusting to the social and physical environment
5. keeping healthy
6. living safely
7. earning a living
8. homemaking
9. managing money
10. using leisure time.

Strategy 6

- Conduct behavior modeling.

Activity

- Have students demonstrate role relationship with significant others by openly discussing perceived teacher attitude toward them, requesting teachers to provide them with both the personal and professional views of each student.

Strategy 7

- Develop class ability to accurately perceive teacher-student relationships.

Activity

- Have students attempt to summarize the teacher's perceived view of themself, readjusting it to their own view until they obtain a more accurate picture.

Strategy 8

- Have the teacher model teaching behavior (record on videotape).

Activity

- Ask students to demonstrate behaviors appropriate to student-peer and teacher-parent relationships.

Strategy 9

- Put forward a philosophy of encouragement.

Activities

- Ask students to identify the areas of social skill development in which they wish to grow.
- Have students identify factors that will encourage social skill development.

Strategy 10

- Define critical social context terms.

Activity

- Define from a social context standpoint the following terms: values, tolerate, interfere, control, regulate, privilege, a right, frustration, rules; most importantly, discuss the relative nature of social judgment.

Strategy 11

- Show students how to develop self-understanding by writing or tape-recording (audio) an autobiographical story of themselves.

Activities

- Discuss the importance of understanding self.
- Read or listen to taped stories on the lives of others.
- Prepare an outline of significant events, on the attitudes they have shaped, in the lives of the person involved.

Strategy 12

- Evaluate students' stories of themselves in respect to "what kind of person am I;" suggest they may wish to review videotapes and compare observable behaviors to those in their autobiography.

Activities

- Use the autobiographical sketch to answer the question, "What kind of person am I?"
- Discuss the concept of real self, ideal self, predicted self, perceptions, and interaction of person and environment.

Strategy 13

- Enter into a decision-making mode to develop social self-reliance.

Activity

- Help students develop a social situation of current interest, identifying the decision-making points along the pathway to the desired goal.

Strategy 14

- Encourage self-study of socially relevant consequences; define and clarify desirable social traits by putting them into a relevant social context.

Activities

- Identify each decision, the possible choices, and the consequences.
- List desirable personal traits: ability, dependability, initiative, reliability, good attendance, efficiency, loyalty, cheerfulness, helpfulness, unselfishness, and perseverance.

Strategy 15

- Define and clarify undesirable social behaviors, putting them into the same social context.

Activity

- Analyze carelessness, rule breaking, laziness, tardiness, troublemaking, disloyalty, irresponsibility, misrepresentation, dishonesty, lack of self-control, lack of initiative, and intolerance.

Strategy 16

- Study social traits needed to get and hold a job, place each of them into job context.

Activity

- Define and discuss self-control, dependability, punctuality, perseverance, willingness to accept criticism, desire to improve appearance and neatness, courtesy, and ability to relate to others.

Strategy 17

- Have the students make personal inventories of themselves in order to determine their social strengths and weaknesses from the self-descriptive terms previously listed.

Activities

- Develop a list of social strengths and weaknesses.
- Determine which of those strengths should be developed further.
- Determine which of those weaknesses should be developed further.

Strategy 18

- Have students develop a realistic list of social skills, strengths, and weaknesses, then examine themselves against job possibilities, leisure time activities, friends, and personal needs.

Activity

- Make it clear to students that knowledge of their strengths does not automatically provide for "knowing themselves;" knowledge of self must be learned through critical self-examination.

Strategy 19

- Have students learn how to apply knowledge to themselves and how to cope with stress created from social conflict.

Activities

- Develop situations that are capable of producing stress challenge.
- Have students analyze their response to stress, substituting social strengths for weaknesses.

Strategy 20

- Have students understand how to communicate feelings.

Activity

- Have the students, within the context of stress, verbalize their feelings about disappointment, rejection, acceptance, shame, self-pity, anger, hostility, sympathy, and sadness.

Strategy 21

- Ask students to act out their feelings in simulated situations, search for alternatives to directing aggressiveness or withdrawing from pressures generated by stressful situations.

Activity

- Have students address such problems in various types of settings, such as those involving failing a class subject, failing an examination, being rejected at a party, being turned down for a job (unfairly), having purse or billfold stolen, failing driver's license examination, being dropped by girl/boy friend, being grounded by parents for being one minute late, being considered a poor student.

Strategy 22

- Show students how to accept feelings, explain that even bad feelings are OK—everybody has them.

Activity

- Have students develop ability to verbalize their feelings without directing negative feelings toward themselves and others even when confronted by crisis.

Strategy 23

- Explain to students how to develop communication without rationalization.

Activity

- Develop students' ability to accept rejection or feelings of failure and to achieve homostasis (balance) in their adjustment to life.

Strategy 24

- Explore the concept of overreacting and underreacting.

Activity

- Have students understand they should be careful not to overreact or underreact.

Strategy 25

- Develop students to the point at which they should be able to plot the degree of negativeness or positiveness they feel toward a task, a person, or a situation; the degree of feeling may establish the extent of involvement.

Activities

- Explore a continuum of feeling-involvement, beginning with:
  1. negative feelings: anger, displeasure, disgust
  2. neutrality: ignoring or watching
  3. verbal expression of feelings
  4. nonverbal cues: approval and appreciation
  5. physical activity
  6. verbal initiation of new activities
  7. physical initiation of new activities.

THE GROUP COUNSELING PROCESS

Discussion of the implementation of social development would not be complete without providing at least a brief overview of group counseling. Many excellent and complete sources on group counseling are available, so this review highlights only a few critical points.

Group work with adolescents is a time-consuming, difficult, frustrating, and emotionally draining experience for the teacher/counselor. A group can make demands that individual students would not. However, students must be kept on task and the work of the group pointed toward group-derived objectives. The counselor/teacher should realize that social interaction within the group, particularly when peer pressure can be used positively, is most effective. Realistically, group counseling is most beneficial for the student (within the group) who can learn from group norms. That alone makes this intervention process one of the most successful social interaction teaching techniques available.

Benefits from Group Counseling

The benefits derived from group counseling may be summarized as follows:

- It clarifies social relationships not possible with individual students.
- It provides maximum peer interaction.
- It fosters new concepts of self and a place to try them out.
- It provides a stage to teach social coping.
- It assists in exploring problem-solving/decision-making techniques.
- It overcomes feelings of isolation.
- It offers a powerful definition of reality.
- It defines group-determined rules for behavior in many different settings (with that group and in society at large).
- It permits those in the group to discuss their feelings or attitudes toward someone not a member.

Purposes the Group May Serve

There are several different types of groups, depending on their purpose:

- supportive discussion, problem-solving
- theme-centered
- crisis
- family therapy
- self-help
- special populations: students failing academically
- intrapersonal skill development, e.g., coping with drugs, diabetes, stress
- assertiveness training
- tutorial therapy (mixing remediation and counseling)
- decision making.

There are three general types of groups, based on the interaction between leader and members (Exhibit 6-6). The principal type is defined by the role the leader plays. The leader may remain totally directive, or be more passive in the amount of directiveness, or merely clarify the group's work.

The Leader's Role

The leader's role in a group is to direct its force toward a common purpose. Leading a group of disruptive adolescents is a very difficult role because the leader

Exhibit 6-6 Types of Groups in Counseling

Directive Process	Passive-Decision Process	Analytic Process
1. Teacher or counselor led and controlled, structured expectancies/contingencies, structured tasks/forced process approach—group seeks solution to identified problems.	2. Teacher or counselor attempts to reinforce group process, offering clarification of content. Procedure is to allow group members to determine content within established process—leader becomes directive only when group is off task.	3. No formal leader identified. Leader lets process/content emerge from group members. Leader provides clarification or reflective feedback on content/process after intervals of free, nondirected transaction.

must be a teacher, reflector, explorer, clarifier, and supporter. A leader must communicate on the level of the group and be aware and sensitive to its population. The most effective leader keeps the group on target, clarifies and resolves differences, yet guides it through decision-making processes.

Professionals do not have to have special talent or training to work effectively with groups. Most successful leaders begin by establishing interpersonal relationships on nonthreatening topics, unique to each group. Establishing trust is a necessary technique for effective behavior change. Provided the leader is a sensitive, perceptive, and concerned person, any individual—whether professional, aide, or student—can be effective in leading groups.

Some staff members are simply not as effective as others in leading groups. Some may not feel comfortable in group counseling sessions and prefer to be coleaders. However, in a group, every member has something to offer. Group process skills can be learned and improved through direct work experience, observations, inservice training, and working as coleader with some of the better leaders.

The principal leader behaviors that create problems that may interfere with group process are:

- insincerity
- emotional coolness
- bias against a member or members
- differential treatment of members
- preoccupation with matters other than group concerns
- ignoring group desires or goals

- refusing to keep the group targeted
- vagueness
- impulsivity
- lack of self-awareness
- leading the group too aggressively, too quickly
- membership conflict that is not resolved.

The Process of Managing the Group

The leader must operate under a number of basic principles, strategies, and/or tactics. The leader must:

- have a task in mind at all times
- begin the first meeting by clarifying what the group can learn
- clarify how the group can learn techniques or processes for solving problems
- structure initial meetings tightly, reducing structure as progress is made
- differentiate feelings from logic and have members clarify which is being addressed
- attempt to reduce emotionally loaded language
- use academic and group guidance materials as ice breakers.

Know the Students (Group Members)

Leaders must ask themselves the following questions of each student being considered for the group.

- Does the student normally socialize with the other members?
- Does the student reject the group or is the person rejected by it?
- Do the members have common problems?
- Are the group members comparable intellectually, socially, motivationally, with somewhat similar interests?
- Are the students seeking similar social development status?
- Does group process offer the student a more effective avenue for learning and interacting than other forms of intervention?

Group membership is not for every student or for every one in every conceivable group. Groups, to be productive, must be selected and constructed with care.

Goals of Group Process

As in any business enterprise, leaders must establish goals for the group. To implement these, the leader must:

- Teach the students to explore their own views and feelings and those of others in the group. Group process is an excellent intervention mechanism for exploring self-awareness. (Self-awareness is discussed in detail in Chapter 7.)
- Teach the students to be assertive, with and without confrontation. The group leader may use confrontation to encourage responsible, appropriate, and adaptive behavior. Through confrontation, group members are taught to become aware of irresponsible behavior and its self-defeating nature and to understand its consequences. Confrontation may be either direct or indirect. In direct confrontation, the leader helps a group member respond to constructive peer pressure from other students regarding their behaviors. In indirect confrontation, group members themselves confront a student without the leader's assistance. In the face of peer pressure, the individual generally will consider new behavior and attitudes.
- Provide emotional support, which is one of the major advantages of group process. The goal is to have students support others by encouraging them and providing them techniques for solving troublesome problems. It also is supportive to teach students to overcome threatening problems.
- Teach the students to learn by doing, which can give the group practice in sensitivity to the feelings of others; it also can teach some students to follow a directed search for solving a problem.

Just as the teacher/counselor must be able to induce students to express themselves and allow others in the group to confront an issue aggressively, each member must be sensitive to being too aggressive. Most adolescents, especially those who lack a wide repertoire of appropriate social behaviors, are quite sensitive to what their peers think. The teacher/counselor must be equally sensitive to the dynamics of the group, i.e., who is displaying what "agenda" and how the group is handling it. The teacher/counselor also should be sensitive to constructing a view of self-understanding for those who have been seriously confronted in the process of learning to express themselves verbally or emotionally. It may be necessary to support them with individual counseling after it is over. Giving them support afterward will not undo the consequences of confrontation but will help them gather emotional strength to reenter the social learning process. A student will think about what peers have said for a long time but at that point needs emotional support to be able to face those peers, to come back to the group, or to go to school the next day.

Group interaction is important in teaching students to read social cues correctly and to respond with appropriate social behavior. In the beginning the use of structure to direct social learning is important. However, the goal is to eliminate the emotional support and individual directiveness needed.

AVOIDING FAILURE AND LEARNED HELPLESSNESS

This final section discusses social learning from a cognitive standpoint. The goal is to reduce a poor social self-concept by avoiding a "failure" view of self, constructing in its place the students' ability to display appropriate social responses based on properly interpreted social cues while internalizing feelings of success, thus increasing the need to achieve in other situations while avoiding learned helplessness.

Students experiencing failure in school are afflicted by a disruption in normal social learning. Their goals become foggy or difficult to set, reinforcement is not easy because of the absence of success, and that in turn generates greater dependence on external factors for explanation of the failure. Students' dependence on luck and their blaming task difficulty instead of looking to their own abilities and energies show they no longer are self-reliant academically.

The importance of looking to external sources (others) for feedback on their own performance is further exaggerated until a self-fulfilling prophecy takes shape. The nature of that self-fulfilling prophecy is that the absence of success and the fear of failure force the students to view themselves as incapable of any success. Therefore, they become unable to try. Their reaction is that they are unwilling to recognize success even when it occurs. They simply do not feel they have the ability or energy (drive) to achieve and succeed. Those with histories long in failure attribute their record to task difficulties and bad luck.

There also is a loss of relation to significant others as the capability of correctly interpreting environmental (social) cues decreases. What results is a shift in the locus of control from internal to external and a decrease in the ability to sustain achievement motivation. Should such a behavioral response become habitual, the phenomenon is referred to as learned helplessness.

A flow of activities, beginning with a loss of general self-esteem, is exemplified by inappropriate social response based on improperly interpreted social cues, externalization of locus of control, and decreased achievement motivation, resulting finally in learned helplessness.

The critical elements are:

1. The teacher must always provide learners a maximum of information about the task.
2. The teacher also should always provide the learners "realistic" information about themselves.

3. Students are not helped in trying to grow in understanding self by engaging in personal introspection (Fleming, 1971). It does help them when they discover themselves through interaction with others.
4. Self, then, is relative to a given task, person, group, situation, or environment and must be understood in that light.
5. Adolescents need to feel they belong, so any academic task or social situation that reduces those feelings must be understood.
6. The "real reasons" and perceived reasons for failure or success should be examined periodically. One act does not make a concept of self but rather, "The act of becoming produces a sensitivity to others and the environment and embraces a continuous flow of experiences which result from interaction of self with all other forces." (Meyers, 1971, p. 33)
7. Perceptions of task, self, others, and environment may be real or unreal, and treated as such. Perceptions, though, are but one level for understanding self-concept; the other is the feelings associated with the perceptions. The perceptions and the feelings must be understood.
8. Social judgment can be increased by studying pictures of facial expressions and environmental cues.
9. Students can explore alternative approaches to handling situations and tasks.
10. Discussion of "on-task, off-task" behaviors is always good, including explanations of the reasons for the preference of off-task conduct and their consequences for the learner.
11. Group process and role playing provide explorations of skills for responding appropriately to many different situations. They also promote the handling of feelings in extreme situations of learned helplessness.
12. Peer tutoring and student tutoring of others both have been shown to be effective teaching techniques, instilling motivation while raising self-esteem.
13. There is no better way to assist students to feel self-competent than by helping them to recognize their achievement motivation in terms of ideal and actual view of self. Two outstanding references are *100 Ways to Enhance Self-Concept in the Classroom* (Canfield & Wells, 1976), and *Developing Understanding of Self and Others* (Dinkmeyer, 1970).

There are a number of commercially published materials available to strengthen self-concepts, including:

Does the Devil Make Them Do It? (Mafex Associates, Inc., publisher)

A multimedia program to bring students into touch with their feelings. $82. Grades 6-12.

I Like Me. (Mafex Associates, Inc., publisher)

A group of short stories and poems to help students identify interpersonal feelings familiar to all high schoolers. Set of 10 books and guide. $22.50. Grades 6-12.

Me and Others. (Mafex Associates, Inc., publisher)

A multimedia program that enables students to develop self-awareness, awareness of others, and a sense of communication to improve peer group interaction. $109.00. Grades 6-12.

Meeting Yourself Halfway. (Mafex Associates, Inc., publisher)

Easy-to-use, colorful, large format, student text that encourages students to identify values and life styles. $18.50. Grades 6-12.

SUMMARY

A vignette:

"Get out of my sight! Stay out of my room. I *won't* go to resource!" Those were the cries of a 15-year-old boy. Inappropriate social skills; total lack of cooperation, initiative, and leisure skill interests; poor personal grooming; inability to identify emotions or communicate problems—all these defined Seth's behavior repertoire. Certainly behavior was the first item on the "How To Improve Seth" agenda, but where to begin? How and where does an educator start with such a collection of behavior deficits?

A resource teacher (in this case) must have something extra to offer a student such as Seth to induce him to leave his regular setting and move to another where failure is likely to occur. I discovered peanuts. I gave him ten unshelled peanuts to leave his room and go with me to my classroom. No smile, conversation, or eye contact were necessary.

Ten days later he smiled, for it had become a joke between us and he told me, "You don't have to give me peanuts to come with you, I'll work for peanuts, other kids do," and he did. At first, three minutes of on-task behavior learning vocabulary words on application forms earned him ten peanuts. As on-task behavior increased, peanuts were offered intermittently. Today, four months later, I'll offer him an occasional Lifesaver. His on-task behavior and compliance to academic requests reach 40 minutes 90 percent of the time.

Most important to Seth's success story is his change in self-concept. He now brushes his hair and teeth regularly and uses aftershave and deodorant. We examine the papers for sales on hygiene items, make shopping lists, and discuss how the products will be used. Seth wants to look nice and tries to be nice. Other teachers praise him and point to him as a model for other students. He is proud that he can stay on task and is pleased with his academic progress, which we tabulate on charts.

As his resource teacher I make a point to brag about his work, appearance, and behavior. We discuss the "bad old days" and students Seth notices who are doing what he did. Seth enjoys achieving but still is frustrated by difficult work and may push a task off to the side when it becomes too anxiety producing. Now he can say, "I'm upset, I need to rest. I do not want to try any more," or "I need help." Before, he would fold his arms, refuse to talk, and escalate into acting-out behaviors. Now we will go to a task with an immediate success experience for Seth. As we work, Seth in his own time will say, "Help me with this. I can do it, but I need help."

Chapter 7

Personal Development and Self-Realization

Ann C. Sabatino, David A. Sabatino, and Maribeth Montgomery-Kasik

INTRODUCTION

This chapter provides secondary educators, working with interpersonal (adjustment) development, a set of ideas, concrete suggestions, and actual curriculum objectives. By no means should these materials be viewed as exhausting the topic; rather, they represent a wide sampling of behavioral management procedures. Then, too, it is impossible from a practical standpoint to separate objectives distinctly: academic from social, vocational from social, and personal from social. Indeed, the overlap between social and personal objectives is well illustrated in a brief examination of a much overworked topic, self-concept.

Self-concept, as a working construct, may be like the weather: much observed, even reacted to, but difficult to do anything about even when predicted accurately. Maladjustment, emotional disorders, and negative feelings of self all constitute observable stress, distress, anxiety—in short, feelings, which most educators are highly sensitive to and can identify with from their own experiences. Unfortunately, when youths manipulate, act out, and are overly passive or aggressive, they generally threaten significant others, reducing the comfort level in the very educators they may be asking (indirectly, through actions) for help.

Purkey (1970), in his excellent book on self-concept and school achievement, introduces the topic by describing Lowry's (1961) *The Mouse and Henry Carson*. This fictional story describes how a mouse jarred the delicate machinery at the Educational Testing Service that was scoring Henry Carson's College Entrance Examination Boards.

Henry was a very average, at best, high school student. But the mouse changed all that. Henry's scores, which would have been average, emerged from the computer as 800s in both verbal and quantitative.

The impact of the mouse's error was that the word of Henry's "giftedness" spread like wildfire throughout his high school. Teachers, counselors, and college admissions officers did a quick about-face, reevaluating their previous assessments that had underestimated the "true" potential of this budding scholar.

New doors opened for Henry, and as they did, he began to change his view of self. Gaining confidence, he began "to put his mind in the way of great things." Lowry ends the story by noting that Carson became one of the best men of his generation. According to Purkey, the story amply illustrates two phenomena: (1) students are products of how others view them and (2) students react to significant others by attempting to meet the expectations others have for them, especially with academic achievement.

SELF-REALIZATION

Henry Carson's social-personal development was triggered by accident when the mouse got into the act. A major premise is that self-realization must be planned cooperatively between student and significant others. In discussing self-realization and self-concept, it is appropriate to look first at decision making as an objective. Therefore, the first objective should be a study of the decision-making process.

Strategy 1

- The students will discover the process by which rational and satisfying decisions are made.

Activities

- The students select any recent and important decision; for discussion of the factors underlying that decision, the teachers ask the students to:
  1. Describe the basis on which they made choices in that decision.
  2. Read Vicktor Frankl's book, *Man's Search for Meaning,* New York: Washington Square Press, 1963, then list each decision Frankl made and explain the basis for those decisions.
  3. List the key decisions made throughout the day. Classify them according to:
     a. rational decisions
     b. emotional decisions
     c. prejudicial decisions
     d. intuitive decisions
     e. habit decisions
  4. Play group decision-making games, with two questions to be answered: (1) Is every member of the group satisfied with the decision? and (2) What

is the role of chance in decision making? Examples of titles for group decision-making games are:

a. Selecting a Leader
b. Preparing a Dinner
c. Buying a Car
d. Vacationing with the Family
e. Selecting a Job

In general, the process of life can be viewed as growing from experience to decisions. The amount of assistance a teacher can provide depends upon the readiness of the students to handle such information. A guiding rule is to never force either decision making or dependence. The teacher attempts to help the students obtain a full measure of worth from their experiences, providing them as many facts as possible in trying to achieve decision-making capability. Felker (1974) provides a decision-making wheel (Figure 7-1) which graphically depicts the outward spiral of those factors which contribute to personal decision making.

Strategy 2

• The students will analyze the role of personal values in decision making.

Activities

• Read *Values Clarification: A Handbook of Practical Strategies for Teachers and Students* by Sidney B. Simon, New York: Hart Publishing, 1972.
• Study: Maslow's hierarchy of values, with particular emphasis on his theory of universal needs and the components of each need level. *Motivation and Personality* by Abraham Maslow, New York: Harper & Row, 1954.
• Discuss: In think tank groups, identify 20 or so values for each need level and situation and illustrate the need-value relationship for each.
• Other materials:

1. *An Introduction to Value Clarification* by J.C. Perning.
2. "Search for Values: A Tool Kit of Strategies," Pennant Press-Educational Materials.
3. *Self-Perception Inventory* by William T. Martin, Psychologists and Educators, Inc.
4. "Perception of Values Inventory" by Bert K. Simpson and "Analysis of Personality Survey" by Lawrence E. Gardner, both Pennant Press-Educational Materials.

Figure 7-1 Structure of a Decision-Making Wheel

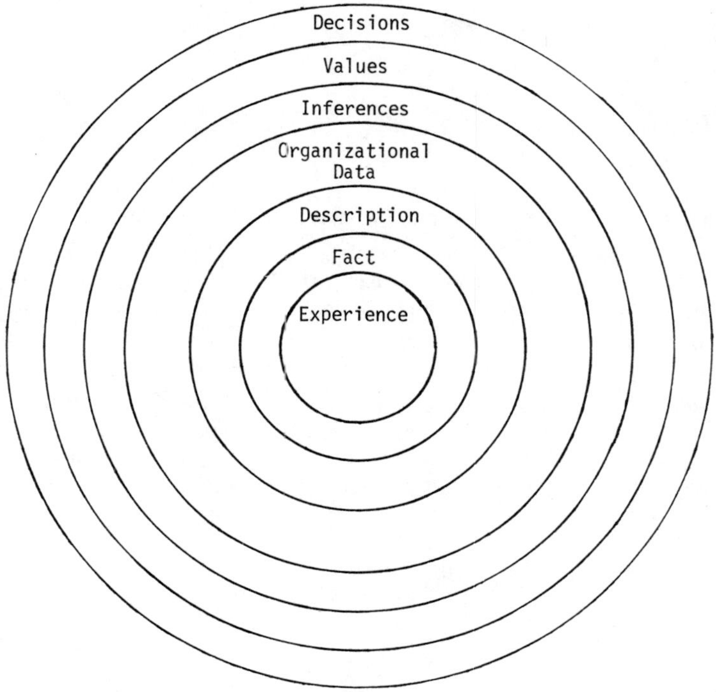

Source: Reprinted from *Building Positive Self-Concepts* by D.W. Felker with permission of Burgess Publishing, Minneapolis, Minn., © 1974, p. 27.

Strategy 3

- The students will construct a portrait of self, based on needs, values, and available resources.

Activity

- The students will attempt to identify their personal needs by prioritizing them, identifying a related value for each need, and determining their satisfaction with each need-value complex as it contributes to their concept of self.

Strategy 4

- The students will examine the relative nature of values and value judgments.

Activities

- The students will:

    1. Read and review the critical value judgments made about great men and women, a study of controversy, and how they persevered.
    2. Review the life of a person or persons in the current news (of interest to the student).
    3. Write or dictate a value struggle in their own life.
    4. Explain how they resolved that problem.
    5. Discuss whether there were better alternatives, had they understood the relative nature of human values.

THE DECISION-MAKING MODEL

An additional aspect of the self-realization curriculum is for the students to learn a consistent technique for resolving decisions. The teacher should develop a decision-making model that, as a process, can be used in many circumstances.

Strategy 5

- The students will be able to use a decision-making model in seeking solutions to simple and complex problems.

Activities

- The students will learn to:

    1. Select a current problem.
    2. Define the problem.
    3. Analyze the problem into the parts that constitute the elements of greater and lesser concern.
    4. Identify possible solutions.
    5. Identify alternative solutions and weigh outcomes.
    6. Give the consequences and identify a best possible solution.
    7. Make a decision because the very fact of reaching no decision is itself a decision.

Strategy 6

- The students will be able to recall the decision-making model and use it with simulated problems.

Strategy 7

- The students will be able to generalize the decision-making model to personal problems.

PERSONAL DECISIONS AND FEELINGS

It is impossible to eliminate feelings from personal decisions. Feelings should not dominate decision-making processes. Students may recognize their feelings, may reject them, and may not even acknowledge having them. Feelings may need to be analyzed as an objective, distinct from decision making. This chapter later discusses feelings as a major area of exploration with youth. The primary role of feelings in self-realization is their influence, in some combination with logic (thought), in arriving at decisions.

External forces occupy the perimeters of most decisions. Conflicting forces require making decisions when under the influence of feelings. Therefore, the feelings must be examined for the role they play in producing conflicting forces. The intensity of the forces can result in turn in producing even stronger feelings. Therefore, identifying the source can result in not only what the decision will be but how it will be made.

Strategy 8

- The students will be able to identify the external pressures and feelings associated with feeling as the individuals enter the decision-making process.

Activities

- The students will:

  1. Analyze the feelings faced by novel or film heroes, considering the external sources of emotionality.
  2. Consider feelings they faced in recent decisions. The greater the weight of the decision, the more intense the resulting feeling usually is.
  3. Identify various aspects of emotionality (feeling) that have entered the decision-making process. (It frequently is necessary for the teacher to draw feelings out in open-ended sentences because the students may be unable to recognize them otherwise.)

     I was angry at _____

     because _____

     about _____.

The thing that bothers me the most is _____.
I am frustrated by _____.
It hurts my feelings when _____.
Other people made me feel _____.
Things (or people) that (who) help me the most are _____.
I am tired of being _____.
I feel _____.

4. Write or dictate a descriptive story about feelings they have experienced in the past few days that have affected a decision.
5. Explain their responses to these feelings in the decision-making process.

Strategy 9

- The students will repeat the activities just listed in response to internal feelings of conflict as a result of a decision.

Strategy 10

- The students will analyze feelings (emotions).
- The students will divide a paper into three columns:

Feelings   *What Caused Them*   *What I Did about Them*

They then will record their feelings in response to daily demands. They will share these records with teacher(s), counselor(s), or groups, talking out the meaning of external and internal sources of feelings.

Other Activities

- The students will participate in other activities that can be used to open up discussions of self:

  1. Write (or dictate) a eulogy for themselves as if they had died quite recently.
  2. Draft a plan of self-improvement.
  3. Respond to these questions:
     a. My greatest dreams for myself are _____.
     b. My greatest decision in life has been _____.
     c. My greatest decision in life may be _____.
  4. Provide statements of strong values (principles) that have influenced a major decision recently.
  5. Identify the person they would most like to be by drawing a lifeline from the present to the future.

6. Identify the roles that decisions play in everyday life and complete the following:

A recent decision I made at home caused my _____
(father, someone)

to become _____.
(feeling, emotion)

A recent decision I made at school caused my _____
(some person)

to become _____.
(feeling, emotion)

A recent decision I made with my (girl/boy) friend caused her/him to become

_____.
(feeling, emotion)

A recent decision I made with friends caused them to become

_____.
(feeling, emotion)

A recent decision I made at work caused my _____
(boss, coworker,
supervisor)

to become _____.
(feeling or observation of self)

Each of these feelings then is discussed with a group. The group plays the game, "If I could choose to be."

SELF-CONCEPT

A premise among educators and psychologists is that self-concept is dependent upon self-realization. If that is true, then a healthy attitude toward oneself is basic to good mental health. The previous section examined self-realization; this one explores self-concept, starting with a look at self-acceptance of emotions (feelings).

Self-concept is the self-perpetuating, learned view of self that influences all human behavior. It is altered and restructured by behavior and unsatisfied needs that may have no relationship to external reality. Self-concept plays a major role in learning, emotion, motivation, perception, intelligence, and self-actualization. Feeling of self may be regarded as the maximum interaction between person (feeling or emotion) and environment. The structure of self is influenced by the past and the present and in turn will influence the future. The concept of self is real and ideal and must confront both worlds.

A number of behaviors are influenced by changes in self-concept:

1. consistency or inconsistency of behavior
2. fluidity of behavior
3. rigidity of behavior
4. morals, ideals, customs
5. aspiration
6. accepted level of success
7. self-confidence
8. realistic expectations for achievement
9. achievement motivation
10. social, family, and cultural development.

The four conditions necessary to change self-concept are:

1. a desire to change
2. the capability of exploring feelings
3. time to organize and reorganize unrelated facts
4. the opportunity to test any newly formed concept of self by practicing it to determine whether it works.

Adolescent youths may not wish to realize success either when it is possible or when in fact it is achieved. The reason is that success may require altering defense mechanisms that can flood them with anxiety resulting from the fear of failure.

An awareness of self is dependent upon the students' capability of making decisions and practicing the self-guiding principles of realization that living is directed by the strength or weaknesses of people in utilizing values to their fullest. It is not easy for teachers to enter into discussions on values because ethnic, racial, and religious issues emerge. However, when students learn or test their values against a perceived reality, a meaningful person concerned with their well-being should provide the model and the instruction; otherwise they may learn about self using a comparison group, values, and view of reality that can compromise their maximum growth.

One factor of great importance in dealing effectively with self-concept is to recognize that it may be a situationally sensitive reaction to a time, place, and task. Far too many educators have viewed and attempted to treat self-concept as a stable personality trait.

The most important simple variable for students in changing self-concept is the teacher. A number of attributes are necessary if teachers are to alter self-concept. They must:

1. provide a positive relationship in which they indicate a willingness to listen, identify, and extend themselves to the students
2. provide realistic information in a constructive manner
3. be warm, considerate, and responsive to the students
4. maintain a socially integrated class
5. maintain a learner-supportive classroom atmosphere
6. resist overreacting to students
7. decline to blame, condemn, or penalize the students
8. find the students' strengths and bolster their self-worth
9. maintain good feelings of their (teachers') own selves since modeling is the single strongest change agent available.

It is essential that teachers realize that the students' current feelings and thinking are important and that the person, not the task, is paramount. Teachers must believe students possess the capacity for growth and change. Any attitude to the contrary is defeating. Teacher expectations most definitely influence the students' level of aspiration.

Teachers provide a great deal of real learning when they mirror or provide corrective feedback to students on the interpretation taking place. The discovery of self is critical to life, using any life discovery mechanism, such as Maslow's (1954) hierarchy of five basic needs:

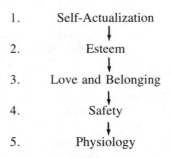

1.   Self-Actualization

2.   Esteem

3.   Love and Belonging

4.   Safety

5.   Physiology

All students, as do all people, search for self in numerous ways, and teachers can be most helpful in that quest. Teachers can play a key role in regulating external forces as they generate internal change. Seeking of self is an important experience that might not proceed past a point of difficulty if help is not there.

There are any number of stages or steps that teachers can recognize. The search for self may begin in the self-perception of differences that may be socioeconomic, racial, religious, ethic, cultural, linguistic, or as simple as height, weight, the part of town one lives in, a career goal, or father's occupation. The self-perception of differences can greatly alter life and the view individuals maintain toward it. Religion, religious values, and the conceived relationship with the Almighty identify one such serious struggle. A lifetime search for emancipation from self-deception clearly depends upon two factors:

1. the development of personal values
2. the development of a clear picture of reality in light of those values.

Distortion of self frequently is associated with confrontation of an overwhelming reality. It is easy to overlook the role of the educator in working with youths to develop a consistent view of self. The principal components for developing such a view are related to study of religion.

Strategy 11

- The students will communicate the concept of self to others, using the results discovered in the last objective.

Activities

- The teacher will:

    1. Have the students synthesize a view of self into a short, concise, written or audiotaped presentation.
    2. Have the group analyze students' views of self in contrast to the way it sees them.
    3. Have the students differentiate their views of self in contrast with the perceptions of others and discuss why such differences exist.
    4. Have the students identify a perfect self, then determine whether it is realistic to expect to achieve it; if not, identify target changes in self that might be worthy of change; also identify values that would promote or deter change.
    5. Invite selected guests into the group or into the relationship (interesting and interested adults, peers, others) and have them identify and communicate their ''selfs.''

6. Have the class communicate its view of the selected guests' selfs; again, discuss the agreement between guests and group and whether there are critical differences in values.
7. Complete the self-concept analysis from "Which Is the Real Me," *Forum,* Spring/Summer, 1969, p. 12.
8. Attempt to communicate the self-concept in the main characters in Virginia Axline's book, *Dibs: In Search of Self.* Boston: Houghton Mifflin Company, 1964.
9. Attempt to have students with verbal difficulty in communicating their self-concept develop dramatic skills around which they can act significant features of self-concept.

Strategy 12

- The students will examine their concept of self against school (environment), the people in it (teachers and peers), and tasks to be performed.

Activity

- The teacher will ask the students to determine both their real and their ideal feelings for school; when they contrast the two, their personal goals should emerge as the difference between those feelings for some aspect of school.

It frequently will be necessary for the students to internalize the necessity of changing their feelings. Typically, they will present a case for the school to alter its views and practices, arguing that it is wrong and they are right.

The matter of right and wrong, good and bad, merits serious discussion. Students must recognize that just as they have values, good and bad (as they perceive them) so does almost every organization of people (social structure) in society. Role playing, group discussion, and individual counseling should address the issue of relative value judgments from every conceivable standpoint. The importance of value judgments cannot be overstressed.

Adolescents view variations in values and the use of labels such as good and bad as the problematic basis for the entire social system. They feel a sharp need for closure, for finality on what is right and what is wrong. This is especially so when they are involved in controversy and are maintaining a view rejected by the adult system, particularly when the decision makers' views support the adults and not the students.

Teachers, counselors, secretaries, and custodians are important in creating an atmosphere that nurtures personal growth. Teachers are critical and do make a difference one way or another.

Thus far, self-realization, decision making, and the values and feelings that contribute to personal growth and, ultimately, maturity have been examined. Independence, psychologically, requires more than the mechanics of self-realization if a self-concept of a mature decision maker is to emerge. Independence from the decisions of others, dependence for the common good, and recognition that most of life's decisions do influence other people may require teaching assertiveness. The next sections discuss some of the considerations in assertiveness training.

ASSERTIVENESS TRAINING

Teachers and counselors may determine assertiveness through observations. Traditionally assertiveness has been associated with an individual's (1) firm voice, (2) looking directly at a person in conversation, (3) using appropriate gestures, (4) being forceful on important points, (5) having a message that reflects self. More recently, assertive training has come to include how well students:

- project themselves into a situation, especially where actual or potential conflict is involved
- analyze the situation (all assertiveness training activities should begin with or include the students' ability to analyze a situation)
- clarify the emotions of others because of circumstances that have developed as they impact on individuals' views of self and the assertive and nonassertive responses the youths propose
- express self clearly, in an affirmative manner
- be able to negotiate a point of view, accepting and learning those of others with feelings of self-control and comfort.

What's Good about Me?

The teachers should concentrate on what is good about the students. The students should develop a list of three to five good personal attributes (in a form such as Exhibit 7-1)—positive beliefs about their appearance, intelligence, range of interests, life's achievements, or whatever. These should be truthful and concrete; for example, "I have a nice smile," "I am a happy person," "I am a good musician," or "I am a good ball player."

The teacher then should assign activities and have students write them on a form such as Exhibit 7-2. These would require students to:

Day 1. Write a positive statement and read it several times a day.
Day 2. Post their positive self-statement on the family bulletin board or refrigerator door or, at school, tape it to their desk.

Exhibit 7-1 Form for Listing Personal Attributes

THINGS THAT ARE GOOD ABOUT ME

1. _____

2. _____

3. _____

4. _____

5. _____

Exhibit 7-2 An Assertive Training Exercise

Day 1. Write a positive self-statement here:

_____

Day 2. Did you post the positive self-statement?   Yes ____   No ____

If so, why? _____

If not, why not? _____

Write positive self-statements about how you answered assertively.

	Comments about your positive self-statement	*Your assertive reply*
1.	_____	_____
	_____	_____
2.	_____	_____
	_____	_____

Day 3. Post a positive statement about a family member or another student. If in a family, pin the note to the person's pillow; if in school, pass it to the classmate.

Reversing Negative Self-Statements

These two exercises concentrated on positive attributes; next is reversing negative self-statements, the self-defeating sentences resulting from threatening situations. To reverse negative self-statements, the students simply repeat and rehearse to themselves the opposites of negative sentences. Instead of thinking, "I am easily discouraged," they should think "I am persistent," "I will be persistent," or "I can be persistent." That is, they should change each negative self-statement into a corresponding positive, self-enhancing one. The following are examples of negative-to-positive shifts in self-statements:

Negative Self-Statements	*Positive Self-Statements*
I am weak.	I can be strong.
I am too passive.	I can be outgoing.
I am frightened.	I can be bold.
I can't speak up.	I can be assertive.
I am helpless.	I can deal with stress.
I am miserable.	I can be happy.

Now, students should review their negative sentences and write an opposite for each, as in Exhibit 7-3. The opposite will be a positive, self-enhancing, or encouraging statement aimed at increasing self-esteem. They also should record how often they worry about negative self-evaluations.

Incompatible alternatives can aid in amelioration of negative self-talk. The process as applied to this concept would be to teach the students to utilize behaviors, thoughts, or talk that are incompatible with the negative talk. One way might be to provide them with a list of positive statements to say when they find themselves engaging in negative self-talk (Exhibit 7-4).

Developing Strong Self-Assertiveness

Teachers can enable the students to improve their positive self-image by seeing themselves as strong and effective in stressful situations. The students can create in their minds a picture the opposite from the one they had before—that is, convert the negative self-image into a positive, self-enhancing one. They then should rehearse it by recalling it several times during each day and rewarding themselves. They also can write a description of themselves as asserters:

Exhibit 7-3 Reversal of Negative Self-Statements

1. _____
2. _____
3. _____
4. _____
5. _____

Record of my negative self-talk:

Date	What I Said to Myself	Chore I Did and Positive Sentence I Said at the End
1/1	"I can never remember items for shopping."	Made out my grocery list and finally said, "I know I'll be able to remember these few items."
1/2	"I can't get myself organized to do anything."	Answered weekly correspondence and said, "Wow, I'm really efficient and well organized."
1/4	"I can't sleep." (Insomnia can be caused by negative thoughts.)	Cleaned silverware for 30 minutes and said, "Now I can sleep like a bear!"

Exhibit 7-4 Elimination of Negative Self-Talk

1. Incompatible alternatives to stop negative self-talk:

Job	Estimated Time To Do Job
_____	_____
_____	_____
_____	_____
_____	_____
_____	_____

2. Record of your negative self-talk:

Your Negative Self-Talk	Chore You Did and Positive Sentence You Said at the End
_____	_____
_____	_____
_____	_____
_____	_____
_____	_____

A POSITIVE SELF-IMAGE

_____
_____
_____
_____
_____

PICTURING A NEW SELF

The next step is for teachers to select an assertive model and picture themselves acting as assertively in a problem situation, then have the students picture themselves acting in new, assertive roles. Teachers can direct the students:

1. Write a few sentences describing a very assertive person you know or have seen behave.
2. Close your eyes and see your assertive model do something you are afraid to do.
3. Now see yourself doing what your assertive model does and feel yourself acting and speaking as though you were that assertive model.

The point of this exercise is for the students to imitate the exemplary model's assertive actions in their imaginations. They should practice assertiveness several times a day for a week or more, copying the actions of an assertive model as they visualize how that person would act in diverse threatening situations. These exercises can enhance the students' self-esteem.

Extending Student Pleasures

The students record how they will picture a forthcoming pleasure as outlined next. The teacher tells the students:

1. Choose an activity you can do by yourself at the end of this week. Make a contract with yourself:
   I will _____
2. Write three sentences that describe the experience before, during, and after the activity:
   I will enjoy _____
   I will enjoy _____
   I will enjoy _____

Exhibit 7-5 Development of an Assertive Record

Where did the situation occur?

_____

What specifically did the other person do or say? (other person's problem behavior)

_____

_____

What specifically did you do or say or fail to do? (your problem behavior)

_____

_____

What specifically do you need to do in this scene? (assertion goal)

_____

_____

Now write a concise description of your problem scene, using the above information:

_____

_____

_____

_____

_____

_____

_____

_____

3. Indicate whether your mental pictures keep you from asserting yourself:
_____ Yes   _____ No   _____ Maybe

4. Evaluate whether it is important to your self-esteem and happiness to improve how you feel about your role in a situation:
_____ Yes   _____ No   _____ Maybe

5. Explain what problems may result if you assert yourself:

_____

_____

_____

6. Explain what negative consequences there are for being yourself:

_____

_____

7. Indicate what positive benefits are likely to arise from asserting yourself in this situation:

_____

_____

The students can use group or real-life situations to determine progress. They then can develop this in a written record (Exhibit 7-5).

Finally, the students may wish to have a means of examining self in a situation to determine the importance of asserting feelings.

1. Do physical feelings keep you from asserting yourself?
_____ Yes   _____ No   _____ Maybe

2. Do negative sentences you tell yourself keep you from asserting yourself?
_____ Yes   _____ No   _____ Maybe

EMOTIONALITY AND LEARNING DISABILITIES

The search to fulfill unmet emotional needs is encountered by practically all learning disabled youths, regardless of the causes or symptoms of their behavior. For example, many learning disabled youths of secondary school age evidence minimal ability to demonstrate sympathy toward others, to stand alone when necessary, to have close friends, or to be aggressively constructive. In short, those who are motivated by unmet emotional needs frequently are characterized as low academic achievers with poor self-concepts.

A study by Shaw, Edson, and Bell (1960) of the self-perceptions of male academic achievers and underachievers indicated that the former felt relatively more positive about themselves than their underachieving counterparts. In a closer look at academic underachievers, Taylor (1964) listed the following characteristics: self-derogatory, depressed attitudes about themselves, and strong feelings of inadequacy and inferiority. General unhappiness with personal circumstances may lead individual youths to seek peer acceptance and high self-esteem through violent acts.

A sex difference also has been noted. The fact that a negative view toward oneself and one's abilities leads to unsuccessful performances in school holds true more strongly for boys than for girls (Shaw, Edson, & Bell, 1960). This is consistent with studies in most Western countries, where the ratio of male to female learning disabled is about six (or more) males to even one female.

LD Behavioral Characteristics

It is difficult to describe the behavioral characteristics of learning disabled children or youths without emphasizing selected symptoms that can result in generalizations. Their range of emotions and behaviors exceeds that of any other age peer group. Therefore, the issue at point becomes their response to peers, authority figures, and the school as a social situation. The school experience to any adolescent can be relevant, or boring, frustrating, and unrealistic.

The common responses of the learning disabled are, generally speaking, a reaction of frustration to the learning environment and those in it, both teachers and other students. That frustration may be displayed by anger (aggression) against or passive withdrawal from learning, teachers, and students who learn. Basic reading, writing, spelling, and arithmetic skills (tool subjects) are so inadequate that they are unusable for purposes of daily living. More importantly, reading vocabulary is so weak that skill deficiencies actually multiply as the youths grow older.

As the learning disabled attempt to learn, and fail, they fail to meet their own expectations for achievement. This lowers their hopes for future success until a generalized fear of failure dominates their attitudes and behaviors. Response generalization to other social, academic, and school-related activities is inevitable and a pattern of learned helplessness results. One of the principal aspects of that syndrome is that motivation to achieve deteriorates, negating self-concept and self-reliance. This produces students who:

1. feel noncompetitive generally and fearful of failure in academic settings
2. feel inadequate in response to the expectations of others and self, having limited feelings of self-worth (self-concept)
3. feel anxious, responding on an aggressive-passive behavioral continuum, in a rigid, nonappropriate manner, evidencing a self-fulfilling prophecy of continued misconduct.

The end products are persons with limited motivation to achieve, and who are practicing learned helplessness. There are at least five partial explanations for some of the symptomatic behaviors that accompany the learning disability syn-drome: (1) limited (poor) relations with significant others, (2) inappropriate re-sponses to social cues, (3) feelings of inadequacy for self, (4) lack of achievement motivation, and (5) learned helplessness resulting in inappropriate expectancies for success and failure. These are discussed next.

Relationships with Significant Others

The nature of learning disabilities is such that these students' comparison of self with others frequently leaves them with a sense of inferiority unless such inade-quacies can be compensated for or offset by success in other areas.

A simple case in point: persons who fail to achieve something expected of self and manifested by others begin to question themselves and develop a greater incidence of off-task academic behaviors. Many of those behaviors are socially unacceptable, resulting in a further separation between those persons and others.

Behaviors that draw (frequently unfavorable) attention to the students that are not readily explainable and tend to be unresponsive to standard teaching practices and reinforcement principles, generally are viewed by teachers as simply off-task conduct. Regardless of the approach used in ascertaining the on-task or off-task social and academic behavior, there is evidence that what teachers expect to happen generally occurs, whether with an individual student or with an entire class.

Inappropriate Responses to Social Cues

People are judged "good" or "bad" in a socially relative sense, based upon their ability to comply with the rules of the social order. Not all rules are written or even spoken. Compliance derives from cues provided a leader, the gang, or a group in any given situation. Learning disabled students are not as perceptive in reading or interpreting social cues as those not so afflicted.

When the learning disabled display inappropriate behavior, it influences their total personality development because personality has been defined as the con-struct describing the aspect of a unified, complex, organized person. Personality is considered to be stable when the characteristic modes of behaving, or interpreting the world in which we live, is consistent. One of the key behavioral characteristics of learning disabled students is that they do not react consistently to similar stimuli in the same environmental situation.

The point is that the social situation shapes and even teaches behaviors, reinforcing or negating them until the students comply with the "rules" of the social order. That assumption is one explanation why learning disabled youths respond inconsistently, fragmentedly, and poorly to social cues. Learning principles are best described as a social learning theory. Rotter (1966) advanced a social learning theory based on seven major postulates:

1. Personality is a byproduct of the interaction between the individual and an environment.
2. Personality is influenced by physiology, biology, and cognitive function, but none of these terms describes it completely.
3. All behavior takes place in space and time, thereby having a framework within which an event may occur.
4. Individuals may display behaviors completely out of keeping with their personality.
5. Behavior reflects experiences, and past experiences influence new environmental interactions.
6. Behavior generally is goal directed and responsive to the reinforcing conditions being provided.
7. Behavior is determined by the nature of the goals, the nature of the reinforcements, and a person's anticipation or expectancy for certain goals.

Locus of Control

As an extension of his social learning theory, Rotter (1966) hypothesized that predictions for a person's need to achieve could be based on what he termed *Locus of Control*. He defined this as a continuum running from internal to external control over an individual's own behavior in a given situation. This situation-sensitive theme suited Rotter's theory of social learning extremely well. The theory explained behavior by observation of its interaction between person and environment. In short, internal control refers to the perception of being in control of the situation and, consequently, one's own actions; external control is the perception of a situation as being beyond the control of the perceiver.

In contrast to self-concept, locus of control attempts to determine why individuals succeed or fail at a task, not how they feel about either self or others in relationship to the task. Researchers using locus of control have hypothesized that people may look inwardly for direction (internalizers) or to others or the task itself (externalizers). Internalizers view their efforts as important to the success and completion of the task.

The relationship between self-concept and locus of control, both of which are constructs to explain behavior, is fairly obvious. Since it generally is assumed that learning disabled adolescents have negative self-concepts, it also may be speculated that they are externalizers. Their view of self in a situation is one of being controlled. The implication for special educators in providing intervention for those who feel "out of control" is that they may persist in failing even when they have mastered basic skills or gained remedially to grade level achievement.

Achievement Motivation in Practice

Motivation, as a construct to explain the desire to learn, has been considered by many educators to be one of the principle factors related to school performance. Motivation is used synonymously with interest in, willingness to, or desire to achieve specific goals. Most educators contrast being motivated to achieve with being lazy, indifferent, or restless, displaying behaviors that are not goal directed for school-related achievement tasks.

Diametrically opposed to on-task behaviors are those called passive or passive-withdrawal from the learning environment or active aggressiveness toward that environment and the tasks and people in it. Most school behavior social-personal adjustment indexes rely on the observer's capability to differentiate between on-task and off-task behaviors, utilizing a passive-aggressive continuum as at least one of the judgmental dimensions to indicate off-task interactions with the environment.

The assumption drawn from these observations and behavioral recordings is that motivation to achieve on a specific task in a particular environment either (a) exists, (b) exists in some gradient, or (c) does not exist. Motivation, then, is a behavioral assumption, a theoretical construct to explain interest, desire, and willingness to learn or to follow directions, or do both.

Learned Helplessness

Self-concept, self-esteem, sensitivity in interpreting social cues, locus of control, and achievement motivation all are constructs that relate perception of self to task in an effort to understand whence the motivation is derived to undertake that activity. These factors are learned and receive reinforcement from social cues in the environment that relate to actual and perceived failure or success for a given task.

The attribution model of achievement motivation postulates that perceived stability of a cause is the critical determinant of the expectancy of success. Failure is believed caused by such factors as low ability levels, task difficulty, or future anticipation of failure because of the task's similarity to one failed earlier. Success is caused by effort and/or luck.

The learned helplessness theory was used originally to describe an interference with escape-avoidance behaviors of dogs prior to an inescapable shock (Seligman & Maier, 1967). Seligman (1973) broadened the concept to include human behaviors such as reactive depression, stomach ulcers, and other phenomena where the person felt unable to respond positively. Seligman hypothesized that learned helplessness consisted of three interrelated factors:

1. the individuals' general disposition toward learning
2. the persons' belief in their capability to achieve success
3. the value placed on achieving success.

It could be concluded that self-concept, academic ability, and social conformity are among the most powerful of predictors of academic achievement. Logically, then, the reasoning that supports learned helplessness should go something like this:

Once failure has occurred, the persons have earned a new title (label) and go through a conditioning process to accept that failure. Acceptance of the failure is confirmed when they see themselves as failures. Usually, the label goes along with the feelings of anxiety sensed in fear of future failure. The learning disabled avoid any situation that appears to be school related, hoping to reduce the anxiety associated with the task, the test, and the situation. Thus, they avoid risking to learn.

Summary of Learning Disabled Problems

It would appear then that:

1. Lowered self-esteem of a more negative self-concept does appear to characterize learning disabled adolescents, in contrast to the nonlearning disabled. Self-concept does seem to be a highly unstable measure.
2. Self-concept seems to be fixed toward school tasks by third grade and remains fairly stable after that.
3. Information on one's condition seems to raise self-concept.
4. There is little relationship between specific academic underachievement factors and specific views of self.
5. Self-concept and academic achievement share a modest relationship with identifiable learning disabled populations. The meaning of that relationship is only speculative. However, initial research would indicate that the variables that impact on self-concept also may affect several other critical factors such as the age at which the problem is recognized, information on the situation, and the amount of control the adolescents feel they have in a given situation. In short, self-concept may reflect social learning for a task in a particular situation and expectations for the person being perceived.

A flow of activities beginning with a loss of general self-esteem is depicted in this sequence:

inappropriate social response
↓
based on improperly interpreted social cues,
↓
externalization of locus of control, and
↓
decreased achievement motivation
↓
result finally in learned helplessness

The critical elements underlying this concept are:

1. Learners always must be provided with a maximum of information about the task.
2. Learners always must be provided with "realistic" information about themselves.
3. Students are not helped in growing in their understanding of self by engaging in personal introspection (Fleming, 1971). It does help them when they discover themselves through interaction with others.
4. Self is relative to some task, person, group, situation, or environment and must be understood in that light.
5. Students need to feel they belong. Any academic task or social situation that reduces those feelings must be understood and remediated.
6. The "real reasons" and perceived reasons for failure or success should be examined periodically. One act does not make a concept of self. Instead: "The act of becoming produces a sensitivity to others and the environment, and embraces a continuous flow of experiences which result from interaction of self with all other forces." (Myers, 1971, p. 33)
7. Perceptions of task, self, others, and situation may be real or unreal and should be treated as such. Perceptions, though, are but one level for understanding self-concept; the other is the feelings associated with the perception. The perception and the feelings must be understood.
8. Social judgment can be increased by studying pictures of facial expressions and environmental cues.
9. Students can explore alternative approaches to handling situations and tasks.
10. Discussion of on-task and off-task behaviors always is worthwhile, with explanations of the reasons for the preference of off-task conduct and their consequences for the learner.

11. Group process and role playing provide explorations of skills to enable learners to respond appropriately to many different situations. They also promote the handling of feelings in extreme situations of learned helplessness.
12. Peer tutoring and student tutoring of others have been shown to be effective teaching techniques, instilling motivation while raising self-esteem.
13. There is no better way to assist students to feel self-competent than by helping them to recognize their achievement motivation in terms of ideal and actual view of self. Two good references are *100 Ways to Enhance Self-Concept in the Classroom* (Canfield & Wells, 1976) and *Developing Understanding of Self and Others* (Dinkmeyer, 1970).

Commercially published materials available include the following:

Strengthening Self-Concepts

Does the Devil Make Them Do It?

Mafex Associates, Inc.
Johnstown, Pennsylvania

A multimedia program that brings students into touch with their feelings. Grades 6-12. $82.

I Like Me

Mafex Associates, Inc.
Johnstown, Pennsylvania

A group of short stories and poems that helps students identify interpersonal feelings familiar to all high schoolers. Set of 10 books and guide. Grades 6-12. $22.50.

Me and Others

Mafex Associates, Inc.
Johnstown, Pennsylvania

A multimedia program that enables students to develop self-awareness, awareness of others, and a sense of communication to improve peer group interaction. Grades 6-12. $109.

Meeting Yourself Halfway

Mafex Associates, Inc.
Johnstown, Pennsylvania

Easy-to-use, colorful, large format text that encourages students to identify values and life styles. Grades 6-12. $18.50.

REFERENCES

Axline, V. *Dibs: In search of self.* Boston: Houghton-Mifflin, 1964.

Canfield, J., & Wells, H.C. *100 ways to enhance self-concept in the classroom: A handbook for teachers and parents.* Englewood Cliffs, N.J.: Prentice-Hall, Inc., 1976.

Dinkmeyer, D. *Developing understanding of self and others (DUSO).* Circle Pines, Minn.: American Guidance Services, Inc., 1970.

Felker, D.W. *Building positive self-concepts.* Minneapolis: Burgess Publications, 1974.

Fleming, R.S. Discovering self. In M.D. Cohen (Ed.), *That all children may learn, we must learn.* Washington, D.C.: Association for Childhood Education International, 1971.

Forum, Which is the real me? Spring/Summer, 1969, p. 12.

Frankl, V. *Man's search for meaning.* New York: Washington Square Press, 1963.

Lowry, *The mouse and Henry Carson,* 1961.

Maslow, A. *Motivation and personality.* New York: Harper & Brothers, 1954.

Myers, K.E. Becoming: For child and teacher an ever changing self image. In M.D. Cohen (Ed.), *That all children may learn, we must learn.* Washington, D.C.: Association for Childhood Education International, 1971.

Purkey, W.W. *Self-concept and school achievement.* Englewood Cliffs, N.J.: Prentice-Hall, Inc., 1970.

Rotter, J.B. Generalized expectancies for internal versus external control of reinforcement. *Psychological Monographs,* 1966, *80*(1, Whole No. 609).

Seligman, M.E. Fall into helplessness. *Psychology Today,* 1973, *7*(1), 43-48.

Seligman, M.E.P., & Maier, S.F. Failure to escape traumatic shock. *Journal of Experimental Psychology,* 1967, *74*, 1-9.

Shaw, M.C., Edson, K., & Bell, H. The self-concept of bright underachieving high school students as revealed by an adjective checklist. *Personnel and Guidance Journal,* 1960, *39*, 193-196.

Simon, S.B., Howe, L.W., & Kirschenbaum, H. *Value clarification: A handbook of practical strategies for teachers and students.* New York: Hart Publishing, 1972.

Taylor, R.G. Personality traits and discrepant achievement: A review. *Journal of Counseling Psychology,* 1964, *11*, 76-81.

Chapter 8

Self-Control: Behavioral and Cognitive

David A. Sabatino

INTRODUCTION

The McGuffey Readers were used to teach reading, but each lesson also presented a story with a moral principle. Historically, one of the purposes of public education was to teach social relationship (interpersonal) skills by requiring students to assume responsibility for directing their own activities in relation to others. In the 1970s, behavioral management stressed the principles of operant and classical conditioning. That emphasis placed the focus on the behavior, the antecedent, the consequence, and the externally driven mechanical principles designed to alleviate the problem. The pendulum of behavioral management principles has since swung back to acknowledge the importance of students' internal thought processes or cognitive reactions, stressing responsibility for their own behavior.

Self-control is not an all-or-nothing process; instead, it appears to be highly situational, with the classroom representing a learning laboratory. The question then is how to teach behavioral self-control effectively in a situation compacted by too many persons who have other instructional goals. The philosophy of this chapter is simple: it suggests that the instructional curriculum is the perfect medium for providing students the opportunity to learn to discipline themselves.

Teaching self-control is not necessarily and never was solely a social learning experience, although that is an extremely important aspect. Nor is it the internalization of cognitive contingencies, until they have far-reaching meaning for behaviors across a wide range of situations and tasks. That, too, is only an aspect. The point of departure is to bring into the teacher-student interaction a discussion on role responsibility. Teachers have an obligation to stay task directed and teach what is to be learned clearly, concisely, and in a style fitting the learners' needs. The students have an obligation to learn, a responsibility that begins by their maintaining on-task behaviors directed at the accomplishment of self-chosen goals at a criteria level acceptable to the student and the teacher (parents or others also may be included).

By definition, then:

Self-control is a primary goal of education, achieved by differentiating for the students their responsibility to direct their behaviors toward the goals they have established independent from control by teachers or an external agent.

Self-control cannot be taught, it must be experienced; therefore it cannot be learned easily unless the teacher places the responsibility for it clearly on the students. The component aspects of teaching self-control thus begin and end in an analysis of students' perceptions of self in response to a task in a given situation.

BASIC COMPONENTS OF SELF-CONTROL

The four behavioral component aspects of self-control are: (1) self-assessment, (2) self-recording, (3) self-determination, and (4) self-administration. Bandura and Perloff (1967) offered a description of these components.

1. Self-assessment: The students examine their behavior and decide whether they wish to perform a specific behavior or class of behaviors.

Self-control is dependent upon the establishment of a goal that is within the realistic expectancies of the students' capabilities. Students' derived objectives, written contracts, target behaviors, criteria levels, and social interactions to be achieved all establish their expectancies for self and therefore are fundamental to teaching self-control. The experience of learning self-control is meaningless unless teachers also learn what students expect of themselves.

2. Self-recording: The students develop a system to record objectively the frequency of their performance for a given behavior or task and the degree to which they are successful in meeting their criteria as they stated them and as they were agreed upon.

In teaching students to internalize their control for completing or approaching a task, an external criterion or gauge must be established. The task then is to assist the students in ascertaining the effort required to finish or approximate completion of the task or behavior. The purpose in self-recording is to increase the students' awareness of self-directed responsibility. That means the degree of success (or failure) also must be internalized. Therefore, monitoring activities form one aspect of teaching them to look internally, as opposed to externally, for a description of success and failure. Success and failure are only relative and frequently are behavior controlling constructs until the students have the opportunity to determine the degree of accomplishment.

Several self-recording procedures may be used. A single line graph of time on task and achievement to date in relationship to goals set is quite sufficient (Exhibit 8-1).

3. Self-determination of success: The students determine from their self-recording the degree of success, adjusting objectives, strategies, and tactics in nature and amount to arrive at a new approach or a new task, and/or to a change in situation.

Behavioral contingencies and cognitive reflections may be built into the self-control program. Each day, or each week, students may receive rewards or lose privileges, depending on their capability of achieving a self-determined approximated level of success. The contingencies may be established by the students in relation with the teacher but must reflect reinforcement that they value highly. One of the reinforcers most highly valued by disruptive preadolescent and early adolescent youths is the opportunity to share the struggle for decision making with an interested adult. It may be true that self-control is learned in the ear of the teacher.

In short, the students' level of success and performance capability may change with age. They should be active participants in the contingency-setting process, obtaining feedback on that process as needed from the teacher, who in many social situations provided by the classroom may offer corrective feedback as a reward, as a coach would do for an athlete learning a motor skill.

4. Self-administration of reinforcement: This and corrective feedback constitute the types of reinforcers (which may or may not be self-determined), that promote performance adjustments in teaching appropriate responses to a given task in a given setting.

What does the research say? Various studies have examined one or more, but not all four, of these components. For example, the self-monitoring procedures of Thomas, Abrams, and Johnson (1971) incorporated both self-recording and self-assessment.

While there is a considerable body of literature dealing with the components of behavioral self-control in special treatment environments, only a few studies have been conducted in actual classrooms. Lovitt and Curtiss (1969) did find that a 12-year-old boy demonstrated higher rates of responding to academic tasks when he arranged his own contingencies. The contingency manager (the boy), not the reinforcement magnitude, accounted for this subject's gain in performance. Glynn (1970) found that self-determined reinforcement contingencies were effective in terms of improving academic performance with ninth-grade girls. Glynn raised the question as to the effectiveness of behavioral self-control procedures with younger

Exhibit 8-1 Student Behavior Check (Self-Recording)

Name_____

Date_____

Class Period_____

Directions:

If you find yourself not paying attention to your work put a check (✔) on the line provided. One line is equal to one minute. Give yourself one check (✔) for every minute you find yourself not paying attention.

(Period)

_____   _____   _____   _____   _____   _____   _____
_____   _____   _____   _____   _____   _____   _____
_____   _____   _____   _____   _____   _____   _____
_____   _____   _____   _____   _____   _____   _____
_____   _____   _____   _____   _____   _____   _____
_____   _____   _____   _____   _____   _____   _____
_____   _____   _____   _____   _____   _____   _____
_____   _____   _____   _____   _____   _____   _____
_____   _____   _____   _____   _____   _____   _____
_____   _____   _____   _____   _____   _____   _____
_____   _____   _____   _____   _____   _____   _____
_____   _____   _____   _____   _____   _____   _____
_____   _____   _____   _____   _____   _____   _____
_____   _____   _____   _____   _____   _____   _____
_____   _____   _____   _____   _____   _____   _____
_____   _____   _____   _____   _____   _____   _____
_____   _____   _____   _____   _____   _____   _____
_____   _____   _____   _____   _____   _____   _____
_____   _____   _____   _____   _____   _____   _____
_____   _____   _____   _____   _____   _____   _____
_____   _____   _____   _____   _____   _____   _____
_____   _____   _____   _____   _____   _____   _____

Total Checks _____   I was on task _____ minutes
Total Blanks _____   I was off task _____ minutes

Source: Prepared by Maribeth Montgomery-Kasik.

children, in this case with second graders. Broden, Hall, and Mitts (1971) used self-recording procedures in the classroom to increase on-task behavior with an eighth-grade girl and to decrease talk-outs with an eighth-grade boy. They found that self-recording procedures were most effective if used in conjunction with established reinforcers such as teacher praise and tokens.

Glynn, Thomas, and Shee (1973) investigated a means of training very young children in the use of behavioral self-control (self-assessment, self-recording, self-determination of contingencies, and self-administration of reinforcement were incorporated). The introduction of the self-control programs followed an externally administered token reinforcement program that made possible examination of the behavior maintenance capacity of the self-control process when using self-administered reinforcers. Other studies conducted out of the classroom have suggested that the direct introduction of behavioral self-control could be as effective as that of externally administered reinforcement (Bandura & Perloff, 1967). However, it must be reemphasized that most of these studies were conducted in laboratory settings, not in classrooms.

Self-control strategies are examined next in the behavioral management literature that tends to study the four stated components separately. The first is self-assessment.

Self-Assessment

Self-assessment requires students to confront the question of their willingness or readiness to initiate work on the internalization of direction. Self-direction is not easy to learn in today's society, with all its external controls. It is doubly difficult for children who may be overly controlled by adults. Adults seemingly assume that students must be thus protected, which can be interpreted to mean overly controlled, overly indulged, and overly coerced. Then suddenly, at some point in early adolescence, youths are forced to declare independence from adults to make them fully aware of the role of teenagers' self in society. It is only then that these young people are permitted to assess their goals and start to decide their lifelong course of action. There is no mystical point in the maturation process where individuals assume an evaluative role in determining a behavioral, academic, social, vocational, or life style course of action.

It is difficult for educators to determine precisely how far students can go in the process of constructing a self-management plan for a skill or a behavior to be learned. The teacher must estimate the students' degree of internal control and how to sequentially order and systematically present realistic objectives for their consideration. The task of initiating self-assessment is not easy—preadolescent children reject it as too difficult, adolescents as too easy. The premise remains, however, that self-control begins by requiring students to assess their own competencies, set their behavioral objectives, specify a plan with contingencies, and establish an evaluation or feedback system to record the results of the plan.

Translated to the classroom, students should be aware of their current skill levels, have some idea of what they need to progress, set realistic self-imposed objectives, and provide prearranged schedules of reinforcers as steps in the behavioral sequence are accomplished.

Traditionally, that is a far cry from what actually is practiced in the classroom. Teachers generally arrange the program and control administration of the contingencies. Preadolescents rarely are allowed to arrange their own educational environment, and as adolescents, if they are not totally self-directed, they are immature.

Lovitt and Curtiss (1969) analyzed the effects of self-imposed vs. teacher-imposed contingencies on academic learning tasks. They contrasted the specification of contingencies by the students with those of the teacher, with changes in academic response rate in math, reading, spelling, and writing as the tasks to be measured.

The data indicated that self-imposed contingencies, as opposed to teacher-directed ones, increased academic response rates. This was attributed to the manipulation of the contingency by the manager, in this case the student, not to the contingency system concept itself or to the magnitude of the reinforcement. Although adults' manipulation of reinforcers might alter the response rate for some students, the Lovitt and Curtiss data indicated that only student control of contingencies, not the process of explaining or not explaining them, produced favorable results.

The effect of manipulation by the contingency manager seems well substantiated: at least two experiments demonstrated that during periods of self-specified contingencies, students responded at higher rates of academic learning than when teacher-specified contingencies were administered. Contrary to popular opinion, when the teacher increased the reinforcement ratios, the student response rate decreased; it tripled when the students were in control of the contingencies.

Lovitt and Curtiss grouped response units from reading, math, and spelling into a single measure. It could have been that students were capable of specifying their goals and contingencies more clearly in some academic areas than in others. In this investigation of the effects of choice as an independent variable, students were given a number of daily lessons in math, reading, and a subject of their choice. The results revealed that their rates of responding were greater during periods of choice than during times of no choice. It appeared that, for the students in this study, being allowed to choose (even between two academic tasks) became a critical variable.

The educational implications are that as self-managing skills develop, students become more aware of the instructional environment, increasing their academic performance as they feel more control over it. Self-management no doubt involves behaviors other than those specified in studies such as that of Lovitt and Curtiss. The real question may be the degree to which educators are committed to promoting students' freedom to choose and arrange their own tasks and learning environment.

At this point, not all educators are willing to accept the concept that students' self-control begins by permitting them to set their own instructional goals. For many educators, it surely is easier to assign the task, explain it, and offer the contingency, thus providing an externally established criteria. There is strong evidence to suggest that students generally feel, "theirs not to reason why, theirs but to do and die" (Alfred Lord Tennyson), and that belief is counterproductive to internalizing self-control.

Self-Recording

Selecting a target behavior and having the student attempt to achieve it constitutes the focus of those interested in systematic behavioral modification principles. The principle of self-recording is quite simple: a behavior that is given immediate attention often increases in strength and occurrence, while decreasing the amount of attention on it tends to reduce its strength. The point here is that a teacher may give too much attention to an unwanted or undesirable behavior inadvertently.

Thomas, Becker, and Armstrong (1968) successfully used this technique to study behavior in the classroom by having teachers attend only to students displaying nondisruptive conduct. In a similar study, Hall, Panyan, Rabon, and Broden (1968) used teacher attention, feedback, praise, and other available reinforcers to control disruptive classroom behaviors by focusing solely on positive responses by the students.

It is almost a truism that disruptive students generally receive the lion's share of teacher/principal attention. Those needing undue amounts of adult attention as a result of rejection do not really care whether it is negative or positive; what they seek is the human interaction. Therefore, it is possible, if not probable, that educators inadvertently have reinforced disruptive behavior by showering such students with reactive attention.

Is peer recognition more effective than adult demands in teaching self-control? Peer recognition must be the absolute reinforcer in terms of value strength. The effectiveness of peer control on establishing and controlling rewards was demonstrated by increased arithmetic and spelling scores in a study by Evans and Oswalt (1967). Barrish, Saunders, and Wolf (1969) used a loss of classroom privileges to reduce out-of-seat and talking-out behaviors in a fourth-grade class. Hall, Panyan, Rabon, and Broden (1968) showed that teacher attention, a study game, and loss of between-period breaks all were effective in increasing an entire class's on-task study behaviors.

Self-Determination

McKenzie, Clark, Wolf, Kothers, and Benson (1968) used a token system backed by privileges and allowances to increase academic performance in a special education classroom. Broden, Hall, Dunlap, and Clark (1970) increased study behavior in a junior high special education class by using a point system in which tokens were redeemable for privileges available in the class and school. They demonstrated that while praise was effective, it was more so when coupled with points issued contingent upon the demonstration of acceptable behaviors with other junior high students.

None of the earlier studies dealt directly with the problem of what to do with students in a room where the teacher could not work directly with them most of the time, such as in the secondary classroom where teachers lecture to large classes, followed by independent study and, it is hoped, the timely completion of assignments in an acceptable manner. Self-monitoring by adolescents in the absence of direct teacher supervision has been shown to be effective in reducing noticeable facial tics (Thomas, Abrams, & Johnson, 1971); increasing classroom on-task study while reducing irrelevant talking-out behaviors (Broden, Hall, & Mitts, 1971); and, of all things, reducing smoking (McFall, 1970).

There also is the question of how long, or how well, a behavior can be maintained once it has been achieved. There is evidence (Broden, Hall, Dunlap, & Clark, 1970) that response maintenance for changes in instructional programs increases as students continue to reinforce their own performances. In fact, when external reinforcement has been withdrawn completely, it may even increase academic related skills on such difficult tasks as concept identification.

Several critical reviews of behavior modification have suggested that self-evaluation or self-reinforcement procedures should be incorporated into token reinforcement programs (Kazdin & Bootzin, 1972; O'Leary & Drabman, 1971) in special education classes where the students are severely disruptive. It is not generally assumed that behaviorally disordered youths can evaluate their own behavior and administer reinforcers. However, results from scattered studies and teacher observations indicate that such students behaved extremely well during self-evaluation periods, which lasted for seven days. A longer period is needed before self-evaluation as a process could be recommended as a standard classroom procedure for the behaviorally disordered. The accepted belief in the profession is that these youths will greatly overevaluate their behavior in order to receive awards.

Data to the contrary were obtained by Kaufman and O'Leary (1972). The behaviorally disordered adolescents in a psychiatric hospital school in their study were placed on token or loss of (denied) reinforcement while attending two remedial classes. One was a class where rewards were given, the other a cost (loss of reward) class. After the students had been in a token program and had exhibited very low rates of disruptive behavior for 25 days, they were instructed to evaluate their own behavior; that is, they were to evaluate how well they felt they had adhered to classroom rules. In an earlier token reinforcement period, the teacher had given students ratings exchangeable for prizes; in the self-evaluation phase, the young people rated themselves publicly and received prizes commensurate with those scores.

The level of disruptive behavior remained at the previous low levels for the remainder of the program, six days in one class (reward), seven in the other (cost/reward/cost). The teachers were monitored daily to ensure that there were no significant differences in their behavior in the reward and cost classes or in the different phases of the study. Teachers were observed for 30 minutes during each class meeting on a 20-second/observe/10-second record basis. The 11 categories of teacher behavior were:

1. Reprimand to class: verbal comment indicating disapproval directed to the class as a whole or to a group of students.
2. Praise to class: verbal comment indicating approval or commendation directed to the class as a whole or to a group of students.
3. Loud reprimand to individual: verbal comment indicating disapproval to an individual, clearly audible to the other members of the class.
4. Soft reprimand to individual: verbal comment indicating disapproval to a student that was not heard, or heard with difficulty, by other members of the class.
5. Loud praise to individual: verbal comment indicating approval or commendation delivered to a student in a manner clearly audible to the other members of the class.
6. Soft praise to individual: verbal comment indicating approval or commendation delivered to a student that is not heard, or is heard with difficulty, by other members of the class.
7. Educational attention, close: teacher interaction with student, primarily educational in nature, while within three feet of the individual (excludes praise and reprimand), e.g., teacher answering a question or correcting a paper when standing next to the youth.
8. Educational attention, far: teacher interaction with student, primarily educational in nature, while farther than three feet away (excludes praise and reprimand), e.g., while standing at front of room teacher tells individual to open book to page 1.
9. Negative facial attention: frowning, grimacing, or eyeing down a student when behavior is not accompanied by verbal reprimand.
10. Touching student: touching or restraining individual.
11. Redirecting attention: diverting student from disruptive or inappropriate behavior but making no comment about that conduct.

Considering the initial high levels of disruptive behavior, the maintenance of their good conduct for as long as seven days was an excellent improvement.

A follow-up study by Santogrossi, O'Leary, Romanczyk, and Kaufman (1973) at the same school attempted to determine the effects of self-evaluation per se on disruptive behavior. An effort was made to determine the duration or maintenance of appropriate behavior following transfer of control for a token program from teacher to students. The extent to which student self-evaluation related to that of independent observers and teachers also was examined.

Each pupil was observed in random order for at least 15 minutes per class (the median was 20 minutes) using the behavior codes and the method described by O'Leary, Kaufman, Kass, and Drabman (1970). Observations were made on a 20-second observe/10-second record basis. The nine categories of disruptive behavior were:

1. Out-of-chair: student moves from chair when not permitted or requested by teacher, no part of the youth's body touching chair.
2. Modified out-of-chair: student moves from chair with some part of body still touching it (excluding sitting on feet).
3. Touching other's property: student comes into contact with another's property without permission to do so; includes grabbing, rearranging, destroying property of another, and touching desk of another.
4. Vocalization: includes any unpermitted audible behavior emanating from the mouth.
5. Playing: student uses hands to play with own or community property so that behavior is incompatible with learning.
6. Orienting: turning or orienting response is not rated unless student is seated and turn must be more than 90 degrees, using the desk as a reference point.
7. Noise: student creates any audible noise other than approved vocalization, without permission.
8. Aggression: student makes movement toward another person to come into contact with that individual (exclude brushing against another).
9. Time-off task: student does not do assigned work for entire 20-second interval; for example, does not write or read when assigned.

As many as nine categories of disruptive behavior could be recorded in any 20-second interval, but only one instance of any category in that interval was listed. The daily level of disruptive behavior was calculated by dividing the total number of categories recorded by the total number of intervals observed.

Kaufman and O'Leary (1972) had not found any significant correlations between the students' evaluations and teacher's ratings. To explain that phenomenon, Santogrossi et al. (1973) hypothesized that the absence of a statistically significant correlation could be the result of (1) low variability in both teacher rating and pupil evaluation and/or (2) the inability of students to make fine discriminations about their conduct when the levels of disruptive behavior were low.

Self-Administration

Are there reasons to suspect that the changed behavior will continue following student takeover of control of contingencies? A number of possibilities may be considered, among them:

- The students may have found it a privilege to administer their own token reinforcements and therefore may have remained well-behaved in order to maintain that privilege.
- They may have suspected that failure to maintain good behavior would lead to discontinuation of the procedure, so they might get low ratings from the teacher (or even no tokens) in the future.
- The previous token programs may have stimulated the initiation of reading behaviors that later became reinforced by the intrinsic satisfaction associated with increasing such skills.
- The students may have been reinforced adventitiously for their high self-evaluation and good behavior since their level of disruptive behavior was low and they gave themselves those high ratings to correspond with their good behavior.

Santogrossi et al. (1973) were not able to demonstrate that highly disruptive adolescent boys in the children's psychiatric hospital could evaluate their own behavior and apply contingencies appropriately. The study used SRA Reading Laboratory (Parker, 1964) instructional materials. Students began at their own reading levels and proceeded at their own pace. They scored and recorded their own progress.

The following five rules were in effect and posted at the front of the classroom throughout the study: (1) no talking, (2) face front of room, (3) raise hands to speak, (4) work hard, and (5) work continuously.

In review, data from the study revealed that self-evaluation alone was generally ineffective in reducing disruptive behavior. The abrupt drop in disruption that occurred with the introduction of the teacher-run token program was maintained for several days, a finding similar to that of Kaufman and O'Leary (1972). However, rates of disruptive behavior in the follow-up study returned to their previously high level after a short while. It should be noted that in the Kaufman and O'Leary study, the students had been in a token program in which the teacher evaluated their behavior for 25 days, whereas in the second study, they were in a token program for only nine days before being given responsibility for evaluating their own behavior and receiving prizes commensurate with their self-evaluations. In both studies, the students did not immediately resume their former levels of disruptive conduct.

In short, Santogrossi, O'Leary, Romanczyk, and Kaufman (1973) reported that self-evaluation of disruptive behavior in a classroom did not reduce that conduct effectively. After a teacher-administered token program had reduced the disruption, the students were given full responsibility for evaluating and determining their own consequences. Within four days, they began to behave disruptively while simultaneously evaluating their conduct as appropriate and rewarding themselves accordingly—the effects thus were only short-lived. The remaining question then is: if greater lead time were permitted, would self-evaluation work?

Wood and Flynn (1978) attempted to maintain accurate self-reporting and evaluation of behavior in six predelinquent youths. Appropriate room-cleaning behavior was included among contingencies to increase its importance where it met criterion levels. By utilizing self-evaluation to determine consequences in order to increase the desired behavior, this study extended beyond that of Fixsen, Phillips, and Wolf (1972), who had determined that accurate self-observation by itself did not improve room-cleaning behavior.

The goals of the Wood and Flynn study were to determine the effects of self-evaluation, as compared to an external token system, and to demonstrate a method of establishing accurate self-rating and management of appropriate behavior in predelinquent youths.

The subjects were six predelinquent male youths who had been placed by Juvenile Court in a Living and Learning Center, a residential rehabilitation program. Their ages averaged 13 years and 4 months, and ranged from 10 years and 11 months to 15 years and 4 months. At the time of the study, their length of stay at the center had averaged 13 months. The entire treatment program was based on a token economy. The youths earned points for engaging in appropriate social, academic, and self-care behaviors and lost points for inappropriate conduct (e.g., cursing, incomplete homework, inadequate personal hygiene). At daily and weekly intervals, they could use the points to purchase a variety of privileges such as snacks, television viewing, allowance, and permission to leave the center.

Under both external reinforcement contingencies and self-evaluation training, room-cleaning behavior increased to an appropriate level but dropped back rapidly to near baseline levels when consequences (tokens for room-cleaning) were not given. Self-evaluations were more effective, as attested by the fact that when they were terminated, the youths did not return to previous baseline levels over a period of 60 days.

It would appear from these results that teaching self-evaluation within a token system is more effective than an externally imposed token system alone. The component that seems to account for the difference is what Wood and Flynn termed self-evaluative behavior. Through the use of ''accuracy points,'' all youths in the self-evaluation group learned to truthfully report the actual cleanliness of their rooms above an 80 percent level of agreement with an independent observer. Members of the token group did not report the level of cleanliness of their rooms and were not visited by an observer. However, when they were required to take an active role in evaluating their own room-cleaning behavior, the conduct was maintained beyond the treatment conditions.

These findings suggest the need for changes in token economy systems (Kazdin & Bootzin, 1972) to include a self-evaluation component by arranging the contingencies to require students to evaluate self-behavior accurately and honestly. Maintenance of behavior after termination of reinforcement appears to increase when self-evaluation is used by agreement between teacher and students.

SUMMARY: BEHAVIORAL SELF-CONTROL

Workman and Hector (1978) reviewed behavioral self-control where self-assessment, self-recording, self-determination of reinforcement, and self-administration of reinforcement were the principal techniques involved. Their analysis supported the value of self-control techniques for increasing on-task behavior and academic performance. Many of the students in the studies reviewed were classified as behaviorally disordered. Most of the studies of students with severe behavioral disorders did not use academic skills as a dependent measure.

Rosenbaum and Drabman (1979) reviewed a goodly number of self-control studies, focusing on externally-controlled vs. self-controlled procedures. They concluded that self-control was as effective in most cases as external reinforcement. They felt strongly that self-control techniques offered many real advantages in longer-term maintenance of positive behaviors, a recurring theme in most self-control studies. Most of these studies also used as subjects students who displayed disturbances ranging from the chronic disruptive to the severely emotional.

Rosenbaum and Drabman examined behavioral self-control techniques in classrooms with many different populations of students, including those with behavioral disorders. Their conclusion was that there was one significant treatment technique—that of continued self (student) and teacher assessment of behavioral change through time. They said corrective feedback was critical to behavioral change.

The literature reviews of behavioral self-control observed no critical factors related to age, service delivery model, dependent variables, or academic or social conduct. They also failed to clarify the relationship between daily teaching activities in public school settings and any one of the behavioral self-control techniques. What do exist are experimental, laboratory-based procedures that may have application in the regular or special (resource) classroom.

Behavioral self-control, by definition, is in operation where students exercise control over their learning environment by the administration and/or management of any one of seven potential techniques (Lovitt, 1973):

1. Skill Selected: a choice is made as to what skill to work on.
2. Time Scheduled: a decision is made as to when to work on a skill.
3. Stimulus Presented: material or instruction is offered to the student.
4. Stimulus Confirmed: students' responses are graded or evaluated.
5. Students Reinforced: youths select their own reinforcement.
6. Responses Recorded: correct or incorrect responses, actions, or behaviors are written down or evaluated.
7. Evaluation: students' relationships with their total programs are evaluated.

COGNITIVE SELF-CONTROL

Behavioral self-control is but one type of intervention in teaching self-control management to students. Its advantages are that it is simple, straightforward, mechanical—which means it can be used by a technician. Its outstanding aspect is that it provides students with the capability of internalizing self-control as a process if adequate and continuous feedback is provided.

The Psychoeducational Curriculum Approach

One contrasting method is the psychoeducational curriculum approach of teaching self-control as a cognitive function associated with the regular or special education curriculum (Fagen, Long, & Stevens, 1975). Fagen et al. are sensitive to the public school curriculum and have developed a self-control intervention that ties into it. Fagen and Long (1979) defined self-control as the ability to flexibly and realistically direct and regulate personal action or behavior so as to cope effectively with a given situation. Their definition included the following points:

- The locus for control is in the person.
- Capacity implies degree or amount of control that is variable within and across individuals.
- Flexibility means that behavior may or may not be expressed (i.e., freedom to choose between alternatives, including that of action vs. inaction).
- Self-control involves realism in that predispositions to action are aroused by stimuli that have observable substance and influence.

- Self-direction and regulation refer to volitional adjustments in focus and intensity of response to external pressures or inner impulses.
- Effective coping with a given situation means "an adjustment or change which increases self-esteem, prospects for more successful striving toward constructive goals, or understanding and helpfulness between self and others."

Their curriculum begins with classroom observation and analysis of disruptive behavior and requires that eight learner characteristics be identified:

1. Selection: the ability to perceive incoming information accurately
2. Storage: the ability to retain the information received
3. Sequencing and Ordering: the ability to relate actions on the basis of a planned order
4. Anticipation of Consequences: the ability to relate actions to expected outcomes
5. Appreciation of Feelings: the ability to identify and constructively use affective experience
6. Management of Frustration: the ability to cope with external obstacles that produce stress
7. Inhibition and Delay: the ability to postpone or restrain action tendencies
8. Relaxation: the ability to reduce internal tension.

Each of the learner characteristics represents a basic dimension of self-control. For example, storage pertains to memory processes, traditionally regarded as a cognitive ability, but memory may be disrupted by anxiety or emotional stress, even to the point of amnesia.

This cognitive self-control curriculum offers an alternative to behavioral self-control as it attempts to balance the interaction between cognitive thought and affective feelings. As stated earlier by Fagen, Long, and Stevens (1975):

> The basic function of a psychoeducational curriculum is to provide for planned-learning situations which stimulate two major personal developments: constructive expression of affective experience, and integration of facts and feelings. Such a curriculum must include clear statements of teacher goals (which can be translated into learner objectives), specific learning activities, and a variety of teaching strategies for building interest and self-esteem. (p. 56)

Teacher-learning experiences are rigidly structured in this approach. Students learn to use words, instead of physical force or aggression, to express feelings. They are taught to replace negative and blaming reactions with positive coping techniques.

Curriculum activities also are tightly structured when sequencing and ordering skills are taught as the planning and organizing of any academic or social lesson into discrete steps. Each specific step requires a rule to be associated with a lesson that is oriented and programmed as the next step to other academic and social rule-learning phases.

The self-control curriculum consists of eight areas that correspond to the eight learner characteristics or cognitive skills listed above that are assumed to be necessary for all academic and social learning. Each curriculum area must be introduced and explained in terms of its importance to the specific task to be learned. Exhibit 8-2 summarizes the eight areas and the specific cognitive traits or mental processes assumed to be important to each one.

Exhibit 8-2 Self-Control Curriculum Areas and Units

Area	Unit
Selection	1. Focusing and Concentrating 2. Mastering Figure-Ground Discrimination 3. Mastering Distractions and Interference 4. Processing Complex Patterns
Storage	1. Visual Memory 2. Auditory Memory
Sequencing and Ordering	1. Time Orientation 2. Auditory and Visual Sequencing 3. Sequential Planning
Anticipation of Consequences	1. Developing Alternatives 2. Evaluating Consequences
Appreciation of Feelings	1. Identifying and Accepting Feelings 2. Developing Positive Feelings 3. Managing Feelings 4. Reinterpreting Feeling Events
Management of Frustration	1. Accepting Feelings of Frustration 2. Building Coping Resources 3. Tolerating Frustration
Inhibition and Delay	1. Controlling Actions 2. Developing Partial Goals
Relaxation	1. Body Relaxation 2. Thought Relaxation 3. Movement Relaxation

Source: Reprinted from *Teaching Children Self-Control* by S.A. Fagen, N.J. Long, and D.J. Stevens as published by the Charles E. Merrill Publishing Co., Inc., 1975, and reprinted in *Specialized Education in Today's Secondary Schools* by David A. Sabatino and A.J. Mauser with permission of Allyn & Bacon, Inc., © 1978, p. 153.

Cognitive Self-Guidance Treatment

A second cognitive treatment program was developed by Meichenbaum and Goodman (1971). They hypothesized that self-control required the learning of several skills, two of which were: (1) problem solving and (2) means-end causality relationships. They also speculated that secondary skills, such as the acceptance of delays in gratification as opposed to the need for immediate reward, and reflectivity as opposed to impulsivity, also were important cognitive functions related to learning self-control.

This treatment method develops overt and usable verbal labels for feelings, reactions, and responses, which many times are unknown to or repressed by the students. In short, students learn to label, describe with words, and interpret with language (cognitively) the feelings and emotions that result in observable impulsive and unruly behavioral outbreaks.

Once the language for a feeling is learned, the approach requires students to define a problem area, something they want to work on, then develop a verbal reasoning strategy for self-correcting and self-reinforcing themselves through the problem as it occurs, acknowledging or denying that a solution has been achieved.

The adult's role in the treatment relationship is to provide a model. A problem area is discussed, the verbal identifiers are provided for feelings or responses, and the adult talks through the feeling. The student then practices the procedure, whispering the verbalization of feelings and response to the adult. The student then practices on simulated strawmen and real situations, discussing the outcome with the supervisor. The ultimate goal is to obtain a desired, not undesired, response to a real problem in the absence of the teacher. This type of self-instructional, self-regulatory, cognitive verbalization is said to work equally effectively on both academic and social learning problems (Reese, 1978).

The teaching aspect of this program is complex and is more therapeutic than the behavioral self-control method or of the Fagen and Long cognitive psychoeducational approach. The students' training in this process requires identification of an appropriate target behavior. They then develop overt verbal skills on an evaluation procedure, thus charting their own success or failure. Once again, research indicates that self-recording alone can produce a desirable change in behavior (Reese, 1978).

Varni and Henker (1979) studied the Meichenbaum and Goodman (1971) procedure of verbalization to elicit self-control. They reported it was effective in increasing academic performance while decreasing hyperactivity. The three male subjects were described as aggressive, excessively disruptive, destructive, and easily distracted. Comparison of pretest and posttest results of impulsivity revealed a significant improvement on the posttest scores while systematic observations made during classroom activities showed a dramatic decrease in hyperactive behavior on the tasks for which the verbalization procedure had been developed to provide a coping response.

The three subjects also were provided with instruction in monitoring and reinforcement procedures that, with verbalization training, were directed to reading and math. The results were most significant in reduction of hyperactive behavior when self-control verbalization procedures were included with monitoring and reinforcement. Transference of the effectiveness of the training procedure from clinical to classroom settings also was assessed systematically. The results revealed that self-control verbalization procedures did not improve classroom performance without adult supervision. It should be noted that the treatment sessions for this study were very few in number, as is true of many clinical analyses. If the verbalization training had been taught in the classroom, significant results might have been obtained.

Camp, Blom, Herbert, and van Doorninci (1977) studied the effectiveness of verbalized self-control as an intervention for reducing aggression in students of middle school age. Their training procedure utilized the Meichenbaum and Goodman approach but also contained a highly structured modeling and alternative solution problem-solving component. The data revealed that task performance on an impulse control test, word recognition test from the Wide Range Achievement Test (WRAT), and problem-solving subtest from the Wechsler Intelligence Scale for Children (WISC) improved following training, but aggressive behavior did not.

Bender (1976) studied modification of impulsivity in students. He compared self-control verbalization to tutor verbalization for reducing errors and creating latency of response (not immediate) on a simple matching task. Bender found that a self-control verbalization procedure, such as Meichenbaum and Goodman's, was more effective than tutor verbalization where the instructor stated the strategy for solving the problem and the subject merely responded yes or no. This study also reported that when students were instructed to use specific verbal control procedures, rather than just receive general task instructions, their time to completion of the work was greatly improved.

These results indicated that the Meichenbaum and Goodman procedure was effective for reducing impulsivity but that the behavioral change learned was specific to a particular verbalized task procedure and did not transfer to other tasks or behaviors.

A verbal self-control procedure investigated by Glenwick and Barocas (1979) also sought to increase impulse control in students. This training procedure was directed at increasing self-regulation and self-instruction to generate more reflective thinking in problem solving and thereby to reduce impulsivity through cognitive control. The procedure used the Meichenbaum and Goodman technique and was directed at increasing the students' feeling of control over their situation.

The major improvement shown by the group receiving treatment was on academic achievement tasks, in particular reading. Only slight gains were found in cognitive and intellectual abilities, except for impulse control. No significant behavior changes were noted, indicating that verbalization self-control training did not improve overt types of behavioral responses. Students still made impulsive errors in judgment in social learning behaviors. It did seem that academic tasks such as reading and math were more amenable to verbalized self-control instruction. Therefore, one possible conclusion is that the Meichenbaum and Goodman procedure is more effective on direct academic achievement learning than it is in correcting disruptive behaviors.

Kendall and Zupan in 1981 studied the effectiveness of a self-guidance, self-control procedure, comparing group and individual instruction. They also used the Meichenbaum and Goodman procedure but added a response cost contingency and reward system taken from behavioral self-control. The work was done with groups and with individual students and was designed to reduce hyperactivity. The investigators found that both treatment conditions led to improvement in impulse control and social role-taking performance as well as in teacher ratings of hyperactivity. Both group and individual instruction were generalized from training settings to the classroom.

This study indicated that self-control procedures could be used effectively in both group and individual instruction. It also showed that verbalization and behaviorism could be combined into a training program that was neither a pure Meichenbaum and Goodman approach nor a pure operant procedure. The positive results of this technique pointed to the utility of operant procedures combined with the verbal self-control structure procedure to effect change in a disruptive behavior such as hyperactivity. It thus is possible that students could find that the combination of thinking about a problem and seeing themselves work through it using behavioral controlling structures did work well. The author in fact has seen teachers work the two distinct laboratory procedures together to great advantage in the classroom. Verbal control of one's world creates cognitive control; sometimes feedback through contingency management and an initial structured organization of reinforcers can be most helpful.

SUMMARY: COGNITIVE SELF-CONTROL

This section has reviewed two cognitive self-control procedures, one developed by Fagen, Long, and Stevens (1975), the other by Meichenbaum and Goodman (1971). The former requires the teacher to apply direct teaching structures to eight cognitive processes—a psychoeducational approach to curriculum; in other words, educational curriculum directed at modifying basic psychological processes. This approach assumes that cognitive traits can be isolated and do respond to educational training. If that assumption is valid, the approach is most useful because it can be built into almost any curriculum. Otherwise, it is much more difficult to understand in relation to the behaviorally based ones described in the first section of the chapter.

Indeed, this is a more complex approach than the verbalization self-control advanced by Meichenbaum and Goodman. Their program is based on students' acquiring developmental control over thoughts and feelings by using speech. It draws heavily on the theoretical construct of social learning theory and the internalization of locus of control (see Chapter 7). Their procedure hypothesized that training in self-regulation and self-instruction would generate more reflection in problem solving and thereby result in improved cognitive, intellectual, and academic skills.

The training procedure employed the Meichenbaum and Goodman self-guidance technique, with instruction aimed at transferring locus of control of behavior from the instructor to the student. The technique gradually fades overt verbal guidance to covert self-guidance in a five-step sequence. No significant behavior changes were found, suggesting verbalization self-control did not improve reflective behavior as assumed. However, it seems that academic tasks such as reading and math did respond favorably to self-guidance instruction.

It would seem from this study that the Meichenbaum and Goodman procedure is more effective with direct academic tasks than with specific behavior changes. Further analysis of the effectiveness of a self-guidance, self-control procedure by Kendall and Zupan (1981) compared group with individual instruction. Their program was not a pure Meichenbaum and Goodman approach because it also included operant procedures. The effectiveness of such a training technique points to the utility of operant procedures combined with the Meichenbaum and Goodman procedure to effect change in a disruptive behavior such as hyperactivity.

This study's results indicated that the Meichenbaum and Goodman procedure was effective for reducing impulsivity. Unfortunately, that change did not generalize to posttesting on impulse measures. This would indicate that behavior change was specific to the training task and did not carry over to new situations.

Results of studies examining the effectiveness of a self-verbalized approach to self-control training indicate that procedures such as the Meichenbaum and Goodman program may be more effective in reducing qualitative task errors related to task approach. This procedure seemed to facilitate greater pains in academic performance, particularly in reading and math achievement (Glenwick & Barocas, 1979; Kendall & Zupan, 1981). Birkimer and Brown (1979) corroborated the Kendall and Zupan finding that procedures incorporating an operant self-control approach were more effective in reducing disruptive classroom behavior. When attempting to improve academic performance while reducing disruptive behaviors, it may be necessary to take a combined approach. A self-verbalized instruction program aimed at improved test scores that also includes a contingency and self-monitoring element may create a classroom with fewer disruptions, so it is more conducive to learning.

REFERENCES

Bandura, A., & Perloff, B. Relative efficacy of self-monitored and externally imposed reinforcement systems. *Journal of Personality and Social Psychology*, 1967, 7, 111-116.

Barrish, H., Saunders, M., & Wolf, M. Good behavior game: Effects of individual contingencies for group consequences on disruptive behavior in a classroom. *Journal of Applied Behavior Analysis*, 1969, 2, 119-124.

Bender, N.N. Self-verbalization versus tutor verbalization in modifying impulsivity. *Journal of Educational Psychology*, 1976, 68, 347-354.

Birkimer, J.C., & Brown, J.H. The effects of student self-control on the reduction of children's problem behavior. *Behavior Disorders*, 1979, 4(2), 131-136.

Broden, M., Hall, R.V., Dunlap, A., & Clark, R. Effects of teacher attention and a token reinforcement system in a junior high school special education class. *Exceptional Children*, 1970, 36(5), 341-349.

Broden, M., Hall, R.V., & Mitts, B. The effect of self-recording on the classroom behavior of two eighth-grade students. *Journal of Applied Behavior Analysis*, 1971, 4, 191-199.

Camp, B.W., Blom, C.E., Herbert, F., & van Doorninci, W.J. "Think aloud": A program for developing self-control in young aggressive boys. *Journal of Abnormal Child Psychology*, 1977, 86(2), 145-153.

Evans, G., & Oswalt, G. Acceleration of academic progress through the manipulation of peer influence. *Behavior Research and Therapy*, 1967, 5, 1-7.

Fagen, S.A., & Long, N.J. A psychoeducational curriculum approach to teaching self-control. *Behavior Disorders*, 1979, 4, 68-82.

Fagen, S.A., Long, N.J., & Stevens, D.J. *Teaching children self-control*. Columbus, Ohio: The Charles E. Merrill Publishing Co., Inc., 1975.

Fixsen, D.L., Phillips, E.L., & Wolf, M.M. Achievement place: The reliability of self-reporting and peer-reporting and their effects on behavior. *Journal of Applied Behavior Analysis*, 1972, 5, 19-30.

Glenwick, D.S., & Barocas, R. Training impulsive children in verbal self-control by use of natural change agents. *The Journal of Special Education*, 1979, 13(4), 387-397.

Glynn, E.L. Classroom applications of self-determined reinforcement. *Journal of Applied Behavior Analysis*, 1970, 3, 123-132.

Glynn, E., Thomas, J., & Shee, S. Behavioral self-control in on-task behavior in an elementary classroom. *Journal of Applied Behavior Analysis*, 1973, 6, 105-113.

Hall, R.V., Panyan, M., Rabon, D., & Broden, M. Teacher applied contingencies and appropriate classroom behavior. *Journal of Applied Behavior Analysis*, 1968, 1, 315-322.

Kaufman, K.F., & O'Leary, K.D. Reward, cost, and self-evaluation procedures for disruptive adolescents in a psychiatric hospital school. *Journal of Applied Behavior Analysis*, 1972, 5, 293-309.

Kazdin, A.E., & Bootzin, R.R. The token economy: An evaluative review. *Journal of Applied Behavior Analysis*, 1972, 5, 343-372.

Kendall, P.C., Zupan, B.A., & Braswell, L. Self-control in children: Further analysis of the self-control rating scale. *Behavior Therapy*, 1981, 12, 667-681.

Lovitt, T.C. Self-management projects with children with behavioral disabilities. *Journal of Learning Disabilities*, 1973, *6*(6), 15-28.

Lovitt, T.C., & Curtiss, K. Academic response rate as a function of teacher- and self-imposed contingencies. *Journal of Applied Behavior Analysis*, 1969, *2*, 49-53.

McFall, R.M. Effects of self-monitoring on normal smoking behavior. *Journal of Consulting and Clinical Psychology*, 1970, *35*, 135-142.

McKenzie, H., Clark, M., Wolf, M., Kothers, R., & Benson, C. Behavior modification of children with learning disabilities using grades as tokens and allowances as backup reinforcers. *Exceptional Children*, 1968, *34*(10), 745-753.

Meichenbaum, D., & Goodman, J. Training impulsive children to talk to themselves: A means of developing self-control. *Journal of Abnormal Psychology*, 1971, *77*, 115-126.

O'Leary, K.D., & Drabman, R.S. Token reinforcement programs in the classroom: A review. *Psychological Bulletin*, 1971, *75*, 379-398.

O'Leary, K.D., Kaufman, K.F., Kass, R.E., & Drabman, R.S. The effects of loud and soft reprimands on the behavior of disruptive students. *Exceptional Children*, 1970, *37*(2), 145-155.

Parker, D.H. *Teachers' handbook: SRA reading laboratory*. Chicago: Science Research Associates, 1964.

Reese, E.P. *Human operant behavior: Analysis and application*. Dubuque, Iowa: Wm. C. Brown Company Publishers, 1978.

McGuffey, W.H. *McGuffey's first [eclectic] reader*. Rev. ed. New York: American Book Company, 1896.

Rosenbaum, M.S., & Drabman, R.S. Self-control training in the classroom: A review and critique. *Journal of Applied Behavior Analysis*, 1979, *12*, 467-485.

Sabatino, D.A., & Mauser, A.J. *Specialized education in today's secondary schools*. Boston: Allyn & Bacon, Inc., 1978.

Santogrossi, D.A., O'Leary, K.D., Romanczyk, R.G., & Kaufman, K.F. Self-evaluation by adolescents in a psychiatric hospital school token program. *Journal of Applied Behavior Analysis*, 1973, *6*, 277-287.

Thomas, E.J., Abrams, K.S., & Johnson, J.B. Self-monitoring and reciprocal inhibition in the modification of multiple ties of Gilles de la Tourette's syndrome. *Journal of Behavior Therapy and Experimental Psychiatry*, 1971, *2*, 159-171.

Thomas, D., Becker, W., & Armstrong, M. Production and elimination of disruptive classroom behavior by systematically varying teacher's behavior. *Journal of Applied Behavior Analysis*, 1968, *1*, 35-45.

Varni, J.W., & Henker, B. A self-regulation approach to the treatment of three hyperactive boys. *Child Behavior Therapy*, 1979, *1*, 171-191.

Wood, R., & Flynn, J.M. A self-evaluation token system versus an external evaluation system alone in a residential setting with predelinquent youth. *Journal of Applied Behavior Analysis*, 1978, *11*, 503-512.

Workman, E.A., & Hector, M.A. Behavioral self-control in classroom settings: A review of the literature. *Journal of School Psychology*, 1978, *16*, 227-236.

Chapter 9

Substance Misuse: Drugs, Alcohol, and Tobacco[*]

Sheila Lane Davis and Suzanne Lanning-Ventura

INTRODUCTION

Students' use of drugs, alcohol, and tobacco put teachers into decision-making roles, where information can avoid misunderstandings and more importantly lead to appropriate programming with administrators, parents, and the adolescents. Teachers are in the unique position of observing the students more in a day than parents do. Teachers aware of the nature of substance usage and users may be better able to cope, educate, present, or at least recognize what to suspect.

This chapter takes the position that the assistance of both teachers and the parents is required in helping control or reduce drug abuse, and particularly in eliminating concomitant problems associated with the need for money, peer recognition, or behavioral escape.

A word of caution concerning the use of graphics in this chapter. The charts are designed to assist in understanding the implications of the drugs most commonly used by and available to students. They are not intended to be comprehensive.

While some substance abuse may produce minor side effects and problems, other uses can lead to serious situations that can be alleviated only through medical or psychological help. In those sensitive areas of concern, teachers may wish to augment the information here with additional readings such as those listed in Appendix C.

As young people near the age of early adulthood they encounter many confusing situations in which they must make decisions and choices. Often the decision not to decide, or to escape, or possibly to reject, society becomes the solution. Adolescents who cannot reduce anxieties using normal defense mechanisms

---

[*]Unless cited otherwise, all information on types and effects of drugs in this chapter is derived from the *Sixth Annual Report to the U.S. Congress from the Secretary of Health, Education, and Welfare*, 1976.

attempt to escape in an effort to relieve the pressures of conflict or develop coping abilities for easing or eliminating the problems. These escapes are manifested as running away, suicide, aggressive behavior toward society, or withdrawal. One form of psychological and physical withdrawal is through alcohol and drug use.

Compounding these pressures that youths face are the vast numbers of broadcast commercials and print advertisements promoting the use of drugs to relieve pain, tension, and anxiety, or to help individuals sleep or stay awake. With such models, it is little wonder today's youths see drugs as a solution. Advertisements portray alcohol drinkers not only as attractive but also as rich, successful, powerful, and exciting. Unfortunately, the message never shows the drinkers as foolishly or dangerously drunk. Cigarette smokers similarly are depicted as youthful, happy, and distinguished.

Young people cannot avoid these messages. They thus come to see drugs as widely accepted and even encouraged by the great adult society. As a result, learning how to deal with drugs has become a part of growing up in society. Experimenting with cigarettes, alcohol, and drugs such as marijuana has become part of the rites of passage into adult life for today's young people.

Traditionally, the jurisdiction for providing help or preventing these problems has been outside the schools. However, all educators have a responsibility to help troubled youths. The schools offer an excellent means for instigating preventive programs and helping adolescents search for alternatives in solving problems rather than seeking refuge in drugs and alcohol. To provide such programs, educators need accurate information about abusive substances and the extent of the problem in order to identify situations and the resources that will be needed to help.

HISTORICAL SIGNIFICANCE

Dependence on narcotic drugs was recognized as potentially dangerous to youths as long ago as 1912, a factor that led to passage of the Harrison Act of 1914 prohibiting the sale and possession of opiate drugs and cocaine. This act marked the beginning of a long-term government campaign against certain forms of drug abuse. Its aim was primarily at the underworld and did not affect the mainstream of society directly. Before that act, drug use and dependence had been conceived of primarily as an adult excess, in the same category as alcohol, tobacco, or sexual indulgence. The first public concern about youngsters, involving marijuana smoking in New Orleans in 1926, led ultimately to the Marijuana Tax Act of 1937. In the years immediately after World War II, public concern arose over a wave of heroin addiction and delinquency among poor youths in large cities such as New York (NIDA, 1980).

In the 1960s the problem became even more serious as middle-class adolescents took up illicit drugs as a part of the emerging youth culture. That decade saw a 38 percent increase in drug use in the population aged 18 to 24.

THE SCENE IN THE 1980s

Drug abuse among youths may not be the most prevalent social problem but the issue has not gone away, and in fact may be more serious than it was in the 1960s. According to a nationwide survey by the National Institute on Drug Abuse (NIDA) (Fishburne, Abelson, & Cisin, 1980) completed in 1977, a sample population of 18,436 high school students showed that the percent of illicit drug use (primarily marijuana) had risen from 55 percent to 62 percent in the preceding three years, with 56 percent reporting they had used marijuana at least once. Marijuana use among those 12 to 17 years old rose 5.7 percent between 1976 and 1977; 33 percent had used other illicit drugs, 93 percent had consumed alcohol, and 76 percent reported smoking cigarettes.

In California alone 32,000 juveniles were arrested for drug use in 1976 and up to 100,000 for "demonstrating dysfunctional behavior related to drug use and abuse." A staff report also estimated that across the country 200,000 to 300,000 youths in grades nine through twelve had experimented with amphetamines and barbiturates, half a million used marijuana weekly or more often, and more than 40,000 had tried heroin *(Better Schools, Better People,* 1979).

These awesome figures attest how widespread drug use and abuse are among young people. Students themselves corroborated the seriousness of drug use and abuse, calling it the most prevalent problem facing youths today (Smith & Fogg, 1978).

Where does the responsibility for ameliorating this problem lie? Parents, educators, and the community in general all should be aware and concerned. However, they first must become aware of what constitutes abuse, the personalities most prone to it, how to identify a problem, available treatment programs and preventive measures, and other information and referral sources. This chapter is designed to present information that will be helpful in identifying and treating abuses. For purposes of this chapter, alcohol, although discussed somewhat separately, is considered a drug and its consumption is viewed as a form of drug abuse.

USE AND ABUSE

The point at which drug use becomes abuse is a matter of degree, varying from one drug and one individual to another. That difference is determined by several factors, such as body weight, amount consumed, length of time used, and previous experience with the substance. However, drug abuse can be defined simply as drugs that are taken or administered under circumstances and at dosages that significantly increase their hazard potential. Addiction, or drug dependence, is defined as a "compulsion to take an immediate dose of an addictive drug when a previous dose wears off, presumably to avoid physical and psychological withdrawal symptoms" (Malcolm, 1976).

The following section summarizes the 1979 National Survey (Rittenhouse, 1979), the sixth in a series of nationwide research studies sponsored by the National Institute on Drug Abuse. These surveys provided extensive data on the use of a broad spectrum of legal and illegal substances and covered one major population group: youths. The primary focus was on the illicit drugs being used by large numbers of young persons: marijuana, cocaine, and hallucinogens. It provided prevalence estimates and trend data across the last two decades, including selected results from a more complex analysis.

The national survey involved more than 7,000 respondents aged 12 and older randomly selected from household populations across the United States. While some of the data presented here are based on analysis carried out for the purposes of this chapter, many of the basic findings are drawn from the more comprehensive report of prevalence estimates generated by the survey (Fishburne, Abelson, & Cisin, 1980); much of the interpretive discussion is based on an NIDA monograph (Rittenhouse, 1979).

Two measures of drug use frequency are reported on, lifetime and current. Lifetime frequency refers to the total number of times a person has used the drug in a lifetime, current frequency to the number of days in which the individual used the drug during the month (30 days) prior to response.

The lifetime frequency of marijuana use is presented in Table 9-1. The data in that table present the total number of times marijuana/hashish was used from the respondent's first experience with this drug up to response date. (Hashish is a more

---

Table 9-1 Lifetime Frequency of Marijuana/Hashish Use, 1979

Number of Times Used In Life	% of Youths in Poll Using
1 or 2 times	8
3 to 99 times	15
100 or more times	8
(Total percent ever used)	31

Source: Reprinted from *Teenage Smoking: Immediate and Long-term Patterns* by E. Green, Chilton Research Services, Washington, D.C. 1981.

Table 9-2 Usage by Type of Drug

Drug/Drug Class	Youths*
Marijuana/Hashish	31%
(95% confidence interval)	(29% to 33%)
Cocaine	5%
(95% confidence interval)	(4% to 7%)
Hallucinogens	7%
(95% confidence interval)	(6% to 9%)
Heroin	1%
(95% confidence interval)	(† to 1%)

* Youths are aged 12 to 17 years

† Less than one-half of one percent

Source: Sixth Annual Report to the U.S. Congress from the Secretary of Health, Education, and Welfare, 1976.

---

potent derivative of marijuana. Both are discussed in detail later in this chapter.) Only about 25 percent of the youths who had tried marijuana reported using it on just one or two occasions; a similar number said they had used it 100 or more times. Table 9-2 lists usage by type of drug.

THE USERS

Studies analyzing those involved with illicit substances have isolated certain personality types that are most associated with abusive behaviors. Individuals with low self-esteem and poor self-confidence most often are found in potential danger for drug use/abuse. Personality traits that may lead to potential problems are loneliness, anxiety, tension, self-doubt, poor self-concept, feelings of inadequacy, poor problem-solving strategies, and lack of self-identity. Such people have difficulty coping with everyday stress, are easily frustrated, and may have an improper sense of values. They may be social isolates or have difficulty fitting in (Pizza & Besnick, 1980).

These individuals may seek the effects of drugs as an escape, to enhance feelings of ''belonging,'' to help create a sense of confidence and adequacy, or to seek peer acceptance and approval. Many treatment programs are aimed at enhancing self-concept and improving self-confidence.

DRUGS AND OTHER ABUSIVE SUBSTANCES

To be able to adequately identify and/or intervene in actual or potential drug problems involving their students, all educators, but particularly teachers, must be aware of the types of drugs most commonly used, symptoms and characteristics associated with each type, the possible dangers of overdose, and side effects to look for. Teachers who have been educated in such factors can more effectively approach and apply treatment; they also can in turn educate their students to promote their awareness regarding the hazards, which in itself may be an effective preventive measure.

A drug is defined as any chemical that modifies the function of living tissues, resulting in physiological or behavioral changes. Continued use of drugs may result in a psychological or physical dependence. The more often they are consumed the more likely an individual will develop a tolerance to that substance. This involves the development of body or tissue resistance to the effects of a drug so that larger doses are required to reproduce the original effect. When a tolerance develops slowly and the drug also produces a physical dependence (e.g., heroin or alcohol), the increased dose requirement accelerates and intensifies the dependence as well as the monetary cost. The person then is "hooked" or addicted to the drug. (See Appendix B for a list of street terms involving drug use.)

Next are discussed the following categories of drugs and their possible effects and dangers: narcotics, stimulants, depressants, hallucinogens, cannabis (marijuana/hashish), and inhalants. Each substance type is discussed separately and each section ends with a summary of additional information that may be useful to teachers.

NARCOTICS

The term narcotic originally referred to a variety of substances that induced an altered state of consciousness. Narcotics now mean opiates. Opium is converted into a morphine base from which other substances such as heroin and codeine are synthesized. Narcotics, the most effective analgesics known, are useful in medical practice to relieve intense pain. They also are used as cough suppressants and to relieve diarrhea.

OPIATES

A federal law, the Harrison Narcotics Act of 1914, sought to limit the availability and regulate the distribution of opiates. Before that time, most opiates could be purchased without prescription. The law later was interpreted to mean that doctors could not supply addicts with narcotics for the purpose of maintaining their dependence. Congress since then has voted more than 50 amendments and additions to the Harrison bill in efforts to discourage the use of narcotics by increasing the criminal penalties for their possession or use.

Opium generally is believed to have been discovered in the Mediterranean area between 4000 and 2000 B.C. Greek doctors had found medical uses for crude opium by 400 B.C. However, where its medical value has been known, social problems from misuse also have occurred. In this country, the discovery of morphine and the invention of the hypodermic syringe were of great use in treating wounded soldiers who were in pain during the Civil War, but its liberal use led to a whole male generation of morphine addicts.

Opiates have a marked sedative, relaxing, and pain-killing effect. They are derived from opium, and dried juice of the unripe seedpod of the opium poppy (papaver somniferum). This group of drugs includes opium, morphine, heroin, codein and papaverine. The opiates are chemically related to such synthetic and semisynthetic narcotics as methadone (used as a treatment for heroin dependence), meperidine (Demerol), and Oxycodone (Percodan).

The opiate-like drugs act as depressants on the central nervous system. They also cause lethargy, drowsiness, and general confusion. Some other side effects include constipation, flushing of the skin, depression of the respiratory system, and constriction of the pupils of the eyes. Malnutrition also may occur as many addicts do not eat properly. Since the drugs often are taken intravenously, hepatitis or other diseases may develop from the use of unsterilized needles. Of course, there is always the possibility of overdose.

Continued use of opiates may lead to both physical and psychological dependence. When an addict discontinues the drug without aid of medication, a process called "cold turkey," painful withdrawal symptoms occur. This probably is one of the primary reasons most addicts hesitate to end their habit. A person may physically withdraw from use of opiates such as heroin within ten days to two weeks; however, a psychological dependence may linger and prevent "kicking the habit."

Heroin

Heroin is the most popular opiate abused by narcotics addicts. It usually is mixed with water, quinine, or milk sugar liquid and injected into the circulatory system (mainlining). It can be inhaled or taken orally, but mainlining produces a more potent, desired effect for the abuser.

Heroin is severely addictive. It produces a drowsy, floating euphoria and a trancelike stupor. Once addicted, the user always has the prospect of a deadly overdose.

A street user (junkie) does not take pure heroin. Such a dosage would be likely to result in death. The usual concentration is less than 5 percent. Heroin addiction is one of the most expensive habits and can cost an addict $100 a day or more. Because of that expense, a correlation is found between crime rate and heroin use: as the rate of heroin use increases, the crime rate also rises. Addicts usually cannot support their habit financially and tend to resort to crime to acquire the finances. They steal to get a ''fix.'' The cure rate for heroin addiction is very low, with most addicts experiencing a relapse after undergoing treatment and rehabilitation.

Codeine

Codeine is another opiate that is abused but usually is in the form of cough syrups. Even though it is less potent than heroin or morphine, it can produce withdrawal symptoms.

Meperidine or Demerol

Meperidine or Demerol is a synthetic narcotic that has medical use but is a proved addicting drug with street value. Addiction does not develop as rapidly as with morphine or heroin. The drug is used in hospitals for relief of pain and is a common prescription for postoperative surgery.

Darvon

Darvon is another synthetic drug that is used for relief of pain. There is some controversy as to its effectiveness as a painkiller. Some medical personnel claim to find aspirin practically as effective, but others argue this is not true. Some drug abusers find Darvon a satisfactory euphoria-producing agent.

Methadone

Methadone is a synthetic narcotic that has medical value and is in demand as a drug of abuse. For many heroin addicts, methadone has been most effective in eliminating the craving for that drug. Even though a heroin addict may switch to methadone addiction, the controlled dosage does not produce euphoria, and the person can become a productive member of society. Because it is an addictive drug, methadone has found its way to the illicit market. Large doses can produce desired ''highs'' in some people.

There are other substances that could be listed in the narcotics category. However, the ones described here are the ones abused most commonly by youths today.

Narcotics: Legal Implications

Conviction for possession of heroin, morphine, or methadone or other synthetic narcotics is punishable by a fine of up to $5,000 or imprisonment up to one year, or both. The penalty for manufacture or delivery of these substances is a fine of not more than $25,000 and imprisonment of up to 25 years, or both. Illegal possession of codeine or products containing codeine is a misdemeanor that can lead to a fine of up to $250, up to one year's imprisonment, or both. However, manufacture or delivery of any codeine product is punishable by a fine of up to $5,000 or imprisonment of up to one year, or both (NIDA, 1980).

The Comprehensive Drug Abuse Prevention and Control Act of 1970 (P.L. 91-513) provides the following penalties for narcotics: possession without a valid prescription, up to one year imprisonment or a fine of up to $5,000, or both, for a first conviction and double those amounts for a second; manufacture or distribution of most opiates is punishable by up to 15 years' imprisonment or a fine of up to $25,000, or both, for a first offense (double for the second offense).

STIMULANTS

Stimulants are substances that excite the central nervous system. Stimulants were first used by early man for religious and cultural reasons. With the advent of modern pharmaceutical methods, the number of stimulants has proliferated, as have the reasons for using them.

Some common stimulants are cocaine, amphetamines, dextroamphetamines, and methamphetamines. The stimulant caffeine found in coffee, tea, cola, etc., is the most widely used stimulant in the United States. These beverages are socially acceptable, but there may be questions as to whether or not they are abused.

Cocaine

Cocaine is one of the most dangerously abused stimulants. It is a derivative of the coca plant found in certain South American countries. Cocaine is a white, odorless powder with a bitter taste. It is a local anesthetic with short-term effects. It must be sniffed or injected every 5 to 15 minutes to maintain its effect. It also can be smoked. It does not lead to physical dependency but, although uncommon, a lethal dose is possible. Chronic use may result in loss of appetite, malnutrition, paranoia, and hallucinations. As the effects of cocaine wear off, a period of depression may follow. The effects sought from its use are a ''rush'' or lightheadedness, euphoria, energy, and a general state of happiness. The drug often is used as an aphrodisiac.

Amphetamines

These drugs provide euphoria and hallucinations. Like LSD (see Hallucinogens, infra), they frequently bring psychosis to the surface and lead to violence. The chronic user is withdrawn and prone to outbursts of rage and may become addicted.

On the street, amphetamines are referred to as "speed" or "uppers," "pep pills" or "Bennies." The brand names for amphetamines often prescribed are Benzadrine, Biphetamine, Desoxyn, and Dexedrine.

Amphetamines were first produced in 1887 but were not used medically until 1927. The drug was marketed as the Benzedrine Inhaler (for treatment of asthma) in 1932. During World War II, most armies used amphetamine tablets to counteract fatigue and increase alertness. Amphetamines now are prescribed for obesity, mild depression, narcolepsy (chronic sleepiness), and, in some cases, hyperkinesis (a childhood disorder characterized by short attention span and overactivity). They are commonly abused by students who self-administer them (NIDA, 1980).

Amphetamines: Symptoms and Effects

General effects of amphetamines include increased heart beat rate, blood pressure, and breathing rate. Low doses temporarily decrease appetite; they also seem to increase energy and aid learning, perhaps by maintaining attention span and by keeping the users awake. Memory is not improved, nor does learning occur at a faster rate. Some adolescents react to low doses with palpitations, sleeplessness, and anxiety but for most persons, small amounts can be used beneficially for medical purposes.

Higher doses exaggerate these effects and users may become talkative, restless, or excited. They may feel especially self-confident or powerful; ideas come and go quickly and may be confused. These users also may experience illusions and/or hallucinations. Some become irritable, anxious, and suspicious or panicky.

Injection of amphetamine into the veins, especially in large doses, speeds up and intensifies the effects. Self-injection with unsterile equipment may cause infection or hepatitis, which requires medical care. Injections of self-prepared solutions can cause lung, heart and blood vessel diseases that can result in death. While injection of pure amphetamine might lead to such infections, their usual cause is contaminants. Since overdoses rarely result in death, it is the severe deterioration of mental and physical health that may have led to one use of the phrase, "speed kills."

Tolerance—the need to take increasingly large amounts to get the same high—builds up at a rate that depends on the dose and the frequency of use. Some persons take high doses every few hours for an extended period of time or "run."

They may stay awake 72 hours or more and not eat anything during that time. Runs usually are followed by long sleeps, or "crashes," which in turn are followed by depression and hunger. Some authorities consider the depression an abstinence syndrome caused by physical dependence on amphetamine.

Hazards of high doses of amphetamine include risk of vascular damage or heart failure from an increase in blood pressure (which is sudden when amphetamine is injected). Other common effects are dry mouth, fever, sweating, insomnia, blurred vision, dizziness, and diarrhea. Continued high doses with an associated loss of appetite may lead to malnutrition (loss of weight, skin trouble, ulcers) and a physically worn-down condition that invites infection.

How each youth is affected and for what length of time depends on the user, the amount, and the particular type of amphetamine taken. Prescribed amounts usually are effective for three to four hours. Small doses cause no problem for most users but when regular use is discontinued, a period of depression, roughly equivalent in intensity and duration to the period of stimulation, follows (NIDA, 1980).

Amphetamines: Legal Implications

Illicit manufacture or delivery of amphetamines is a felony punishable by a fine of not more than $15,000 or imprisonment of up to five years, or both. Illegal possession of small amounts is a misdemeanor, carrying a fine of up to $250 or up to one year imprisonment, or both (NIDA, 1980).

Caffeine

Caffeine is a drug that may be classified as a stimulant. A drug in this case is defined as "any compound, synthetic or naturally occurring, that causes a psychological action on a living organism" (Benowicz, 1977). Caffeine fits this definition and is one of the most widely consumed drugs in society. A natural plant substance found in coffee beans, cocoa beans, tea, and kola nuts, caffeine is consumed for many reasons by a wide variety of people (some of whom would never consider using "drugs"). Some over-the-counter pain relievers and stimulants also contain various amounts of the substance (Benowicz, 1977). Exhibit 9-1 lists an array of caffeine ingestions and the amount of caffeine in each.

Caffeine: Symptoms and Effects

Most authorities agree that 200 mg (about two cups of coffee) is the amount that begins to cause a wide range of effects on the body (Exhibit 9-1). Some youths notice these effects in dosages as low as 50 mg. The following systems can be affected: central nervous, cardiovascular, gastrointestinal, and respiratory.

Exhibit 9-1 How Much Caffeine? Compare for Yourself

Source	Oz.	Caffeine (MGS)
Coffee		
Brewed	5	110-150
Instant	5	66
Decaffeinated	5	3
Tea		
Black or Green Leaf	5	70
Herbal	5	Negligible
Cola		
Beverage	12	40-72
Chocolate		
Cocoa	5	42-50
Milk Chocolate	1	33
Medications		
Anacin, Midol, Empirin,		
Coricidin D, Others	1 tablet	32-50
Excedrin	1 tablet	66
No-Doz	1 tablet	100
Dexatrim	1 capsule	200
Prolamine	1 capsule	140

Source: Reprinted from *Psychopharmacology in the Practice of Medicine* by Murray E. Jarvik with permission of Appleton-Century-Crofts, Inc., © 1977.

Caffeine stimulates the central nervous system in 30 to 60 minutes of being taken and its effects may last several hours. It can reduce or mask fatigue, improve the ability to think faster and more clearly, and sharpen senses. Caffeine also causes an increase in both heart and pulse rate.

It can affect the gastrointestinal system by causing nausea, diarrhea, vomiting, and occasionally even peptic ulcers. These effects probably are caused by the irritating oils in coffee or by an increase in gastric secretions.

According to the *Consumer's Union Report: Licit and Illicit Drugs* (Brecher, 1972), physical dependence on coffee (caffeine) may occur when five or more cups are consumed a day over an extended period of time. Psychological dependence, according to the report, may occur at a lower dosage. However, the exact amount that can cause dependence varies from person to person.

When heavy caffeine users abstain, they experience jitters, nervousness, irritability, and headaches known as the ''caffeine headache,'' 12 to 18 hours after drinking their last cup of coffee. Heavy coffee drinkers report an inability to work effectively and feelings of restlessness when they give up their morning coffee. Diarrhea also is a common complaint after heavy coffee intake, although tea may be constipating because of its tannic acid content. A dosage of one gram of caffeine (7 to 10 cups of coffee a day) can produce insomnia, restlessness, and excitement, which may progress to mild delirium, sensory disturbances such as ringing in the ears or seeing flashing lights, tense or tremulous muscles, convulsions, and even hallucinations (Grenden, 1974).

DEPRESSANTS

Barbiturates

Barbiturates are synthetic chemicals that depress the central nervous system as they act upon the cerebral centers. The substance is a synthesis of barbituric acid from urea and melonic acid, the oldest form of the hypnotic (sleep-inducing) drugs. A street name for them is "downers." Barbiturates are potentially dangerous sedatives. If they are taken in large quantities, the initial dreamy state may lead to mood changes that can easily erupt into violence. The major effect is depression of the brain's functioning. When taken in large doses, barbiturates upset the rhythm of respiration by depressing brain centers responsible for its maintenance.

Barbiturates are odorless and tasteless white powders that come in capsule and tablet form of different colors and sizes, liquid form for injections or oral dosages, and in suppository form, but oral use is the most common form (*Listen,* 1981).

Barbiturates: Symptoms and Effects

Some examples of barbiturates found on the market and streets are Amytal, Butisol, Nembutal, Phenobarbital, Seconal, and Tuinal. Some common street names for these drugs are "barbs," "reds," "yellow jackets," "downers," etc. Tranquilizers and methaqualone, although depressants, are not considered barbiturates because they differ both chemically and pharmacologically.

Barbiturates are used medically for such conditions as high blood pressure, peptic ulcer, and spastic colitis. They also are prescribed to relieve insomnia, anxiety, and tension. When injected improperly, the user may take on the intoxicated appearance of a drunk. When taking "downers" in severe cases, disorientation, aggressive behavior, paranoid delusions, and hallucinations may develop. In some cases, barbiturates and amphetamines are abused simultaneously to offset the resulting effects of each drug. A youth may take a "downer" (barbiturate) to induce sleep and an "upper" (amphetamine) to counteract the barbiturate "hangover" (NIDA, 1980).

Barbiturates, when properly prescribed and taken, can relieve anxiety and tension; if taken improperly or in large doses, they may produce drowsiness or sleep. Their effects change when consumed with certain other drugs. When a moderate dose is taken in conjunction with a moderate amount of alcohol, the drugs' potential action on each other and the resulting effects may be greater than the sum of two separate dosages. This process can result in an unintentional overdose and can easily prove fatal.

Barbiturates are addictive and withdrawal pains often are so terrifying that they lead to suicide. Withdrawal symptoms may vary among individuals, with the severity of the symptoms depending on the dosage and duration of use, but should always be supervised by a physician. Typically, during detoxification (withdrawal) the youth may feel restless or weak and suffer from abdominal cramps, nausea, and vomiting. These symptoms peak around the third day and convulsions may occur. This point is critical, as the convulsions may result in death. Readministration of the drug by a physician may be necessary at this point to prevent fatality. Death also may result from respiratory failure. Hallucinations or delirium may develop between the fourth and seventh days, with symptoms diminishing around the eighth day. Tolerance to repeated use may develop over time, but a tolerance for the amount necessary for a lethal dose develops only to a certain point. Psychological dependence also occurs with persistent usage.

Barbiturates: Legal Implications

Illegal possession of barbiturates is punishable in some states by a fine of $250 or up to one year's imprisonment, or both, and is considered a misdemeanor. Sale or manufacture may be met by a fine of not more than $15,000 or imprisonment of up to five years, or both. Penalties may vary among the states (NIDA, 1980).

Under federal law (P.L. 92-255, 1972), illegal manufacture or distribution of barbiturates is punishable by up to five years' imprisonment and/or up to a $15,000 fine if there are no prior convictions. Illegal possession with no prior convictions is punishable by up to one year of imprisonment and/or up to a $5,000 fine. The court also can place the offender on probation which, if satisfactorily completed, will remove the conviction from the record.

Tranquilizers

Tranquilizers are a complex group of depressant drugs that vary in their actions, effects, hazards, and medical uses. All have been developed since the 1940s, when it was hoped that they would replace other depressants (i.e., barbiturates) that had various undesirable side effects. Research has since revealed that tranquilizers also have undesirable side effects, can be habituating, and have a potential for abuse. Nevertheless, they have had a broad impact on medicine, particularly in psychiatry, and have been widely promoted by manufacturers as an important means of coping with stress. Their widespread use has led to a widespread medical and public debate over their availability and effectiveness (NIDA, 1980).

Tranquilizers can be divided into two groups: antipsychotic and antianxiety.

Antipsychotics

Tranquilizers are used most commonly to treat major psychiatric problems such as psychosis. There are about a dozen antipsychotic tranquilizers in use, including chlorpromazine (Thorazine), and trifluroperazine (Stelazine). Some are used to calm agitated psychotic adolescents, while others help to make severely withdrawn youths more accessible to therapy. Other clinical uses for antipsychotics include: prevention of drug-induced nausea in surgery, prevention of radiation sickness, and relief of chronic itching of the skin. They rarely are used nonmedically.

They are preferred over barbiturates because, in moderate doses, they calm without inducing sleep. They also do not cause physical dependence, a state in which the body adapts to the presence of a drug so that when its use is discontinued, withdrawal sickness occurs. Antipsychotic tranquilizers do, however, potentiate (intensify) the actions of other depressants such as opiates, barbiturates, and alcohol.

Antipsychotic Tranquilizers: Symptoms and Effects

The actions of antipsychotic tranquilizers on the central nervous system are not well understood, but it is believed they probably act on many portions of the brain. A dose of 25 to 50 milligrams will cause a person to become drowsy within an hour and remain that way for about five hours. Higher doses cause stupor and lack of coordination. Blood pressure tends to fall while heart rate may increase.

Antianxiety Tranquilizers

Antianxiety drugs such as Valium, Librium, Serax, and Miltown (or Equanil) are widely prescribed, sometimes unnecessarily, as daytime sedatives to reduce anxiety and tension associated with neurotic disorders, stressful situations, character disorders, and psychosomatic disorders. They are centrally acting, skeletal muscle relaxants and produce the desired calming effects without excessive sedative properties. They pose more of a misuse or abuse problem than do the antipsychotic tranquilizers because they are so widely prescribed and because they can produce habituation (craving the intoxication) and physical dependence when taken repeatedly over time, especially at high dosage.

Moderate doses provide muscle relaxation and antianxiety and sedative effects without impairing mental and physical functioning. They do not cause sleep but often are used to relax people so they can fall asleep. Higher doses can cause incoordination and drowsiness. Acute and chronic intoxication with these tranquilizers produces symptoms similar to alcohol intoxication—sluggishness, impaired thinking, emotional instability, exaggerated personality traits, slurred speech, and staggering gait.

Withdrawal from antianxiety tranquilizer dependence is characterized by twitching, insomnia, and major convulsions. Because these drugs are excreted slowly from the body, this reaction may take a few days to develop and a week or more to abate. Withdrawal can be dangerous and should be supervised by a physician.

Tranquilizers: Legal Implications

Unlawful manufacture, distribution, or possession with intent to manufacture or deliver is punishable by a fine of up to $1,000 and/or imprisonment up to three years. These laws are applied to minors at the discretion of the court (NIDA, 1980).

Under federal law, illegal manufacture or distribution, or intent to do either, can be punished by up to five years' imprisonment and/or up to $15,000 fine for a first offense. After that offense, the penalties double and, with two or more offenses, up to 25 years' imprisonment may result. Possession or obtaining tranquilizers by fraud involve jail terms and/or fines (NIDA, 1980).

Methaqualone (Sopors or Quaaludes)

The chemical name for Sopors or Quaaludes is methaqualone. Methaqualone is a central nervous system depressant—a nonbarbiturate sedative hypnotic. Several companies manufacture and distribute methaqualone for oral use in this country. Methaqualone is not indicated for women who are pregnant or may become so or for children under 14; caution should be taken when driving or using dangerous machinery because of its sedative effects. Care should be taken in using methaqualone with any other sedatives, analgesics, psychotropic drugs, or alcohol because of possible addictive effects. It should not be used continuously for periods exceeding three months. It is metabolized primarily in the liver and excreted through the kidneys.

Methaqualone originally was marketed as a medical alternative to barbiturates. This was thought particularly useful because methaqualone seemingly did not have the side effects associated with barbiturates such as hangover and addiction potential.

Methaqualone: Symptoms and Effects

Methaqualone when taken in larger doses for purposes other than to induce sleep produces extreme muscular relaxation. The user usually feels content and totally passive and finds it necessary to fight the urge to fall asleep. There is a loss of all motivation, motor coordination somewhat resembles a drunken state, and the pain threshold is lowered. Some street users have described the sensation produced as "peaceful," "calm," or "drunk."

Adverse physiological effects to Methaqualone include headache, hangover, menstrual disturbance, tongue changes, dryness of the mouth, depersonalization, dizziness, and numbness of the extremities.

HALLUCINOGENS

The term hallucinogen, when applied to any drug, refers to a substance whose principal effect is producing radical changes in the mental state, involving distortions of reality and hallucinations—the perception of phenomena that have no objective reality. Those drugs also have been labelled illusionogenic, psychedelic, and mind-expanding. Included in this group are drugs such as LSD, MDA, mescaline, psilocybin, phenocyclidine (PCP), PMA, TMA, DMT, STP (DDM), and morning glory seeds. The term also can be applied to natural substances such as jimson weed, nutmeg, and a variety of mushrooms. Although some other drugs, such as alcohol and cannabis, produce a hallucinogenic effect when taken in high dosages, they are not classified as hallucinogens since that is not their principal effect.

When a youth injects a form of hallucinogen, a synthesia or crossing of the senses occurs, creating the hallucinatory effect. This often is termed a "trip," such as visualizing a sound or hearing a color such as red or blue. There is no way to predict the type of "trip" or experience an individual may have, and therein lies the greatest danger of this type of drug. A given trip may be described as a positive or negative experience.

Hallucinogens: Symptoms and Effects

Some types of hallucinogens most frequently seen in the drug culture are discussed next.

LSD

LSD (lysergic acid diethylamide) is an odorless, colorless, tasteless chemical discovered by Dr. Albert Hofmann in 1938. It is one of the most potent mood-altering chemicals known. Its doses are measured in micrograms (millionths of a gram) and usually are taken in tablet or capsule form. Its effects last eight to twelve hours, although a higher dosage or mixing it with other drugs can prolong the effects. There is no known fatal dose.

During the 1950s and early 1960s, LSD experimentation was conducted legally by psychiatrists, other physicians, and mental health professionals for experimental therapy. It was used as a treatment for alcoholism, with mixed results. LSD psychotherapy for terminal cancer patients was another line of experimentation. Mind exploration, personal growth, and spiritual self-discovery are some of the purposes in using the drug.

Increased publicity about its unpredictable and sometimes dramatic effects brought about more experimentation, especially among youths. Some common motivations for adolescents' experimenting with or using LSD are: risk-taking, escape, relief from anxiety, enjoyment, group acceptance, or, as before, for personal growth.

LSD: Symptoms and Effects

Generally speaking, 30 to 90 minutes after an oral dose the effects felt are euphoria, clumsiness, giddiness, and occasionally a fluttery stomach. Illusions of geometric shapes and patterns, ''electric'' colors, and distorted shapes are experienced. The mind may become flooded with thoughts of profound insight and feelings of bliss.

Tolerance, the need to take larger and larger doses to produce the same effect, develops quickly with continuous use over three to five days. Once tolerance is achieved, the user no longer experiences the effects of the drug, but when use is discontinued for four or five days the individual regains sensitivity to it. A user tolerant to LSD also will be tolerant to hallucinogens of similar chemical structure such as mescaline and psilocybin. This phenomenon is known as cross-tolerance (NIDA, 1980).

LSD does not cause physical dependence—no withdrawal symptoms are experienced when regular use is discontinued. Occasionally, there are cases of habituation or psychological dependence in which a user experiences a craving for the intoxication. Whether this is the result of the person's persisting emotional problems or the drug itself has not been established.

Flashbacks are a potential hazard that, although rare, are more likely to occur among frequent users than those who seldom take the drug. In flashbacks, certain parts of the original drug experience recur spontaneously without the need for taking the drug again. They may occur at any time or place, in crisis or stress, or may be initiated by the use of other drugs such as marijuana or antihistamines. Their cause is not fully understood. Generally, the longer the time since ingestion of the drug, the less likely are the chances of a flashback. It is the fear of a flashback that can turn such experiences into a problem. A flashback should be handled with the same precautions taken in the care of a person under the influence of LSD (NIDA, 1980).

The effects of the pharmaceutical quality LSD and the street product generally available are quite different. Street LSD rarely is of dependable quality or purity. Many of the reactions attributed to LSD are not solely so; the additives, impurities, and other drugs sold as LSD may cause unexpected reactions. PCP, an animal tranquilizer, sometimes is sold as LSD and produces effects quite different from those of pure LSD.

LSD: Legal Implications

Under federal law, the penalty for possession of LSD is a fine to be determined by the court and/or up to one year in jail; sale is punishable by a fine and up to five years in jail.

Progressive states rich in social services, such as Wisconsin, punish LSD possession by a fine of up to $250, a maximum of one year in the county jail, or both. If it is a first offense, a person may be placed on probation by the court for one year. If this is completed satisfactorily, the record of the conviction is removed, leaving only a record of arrest. Possession of LSD with intent to sell, or actual sale, is punishable by a fine of up to $15,000, five years in prison, or both (NIDA, 1980).

PCP

PCP, "angel dust," and phenocyclidine all are names for a common street drug. It is a white, water-soluble crystaline powder that is used orally, smoked, injected, or sniffed. It can be found on the streets in tablets, capsules, powders, or sprinkled on marijuana. PCP is a depressant although it is sold and used as a hallucinogen. It often is found to be the active chemical in street drugs represented as THC (the active chemical in marijuana) and is easily manufactured illicitly. Dosage levels and effects vary and are difficult to control.

PCP was used for a period during the 1950s as an anesthetic and analgesic marketed under the trade name Sernyl. But certain side effects (especially after surgery) such as agitation, irritability, extreme excitement, visual disturbance, and delirium sometimes occurred, often lasting for a number of hours. PCP also was investigated as a possible agent in the treatment and understanding of mental disorders.

Because of the nature and frequency of the occurrence of adverse reactions of PCP, its use with humans was discontinued. The risk of adverse effects still is considered great enough to outweigh any usefulness in the treatment of humans. However, it has gained widespread acceptance as an anesthetic agent for certain animals and is marketed (for veterinary use only) under the trade name Sernylan.

It remains popular with street drug manufacturers and dealers despite its unpredictable, adverse reputation because it is quite inexpensive and profitable to make from chemicals that are fairly easy to obtain. "Angel dust" sprayed or sprinkled on leaves of some sort, usually mint, oregano, parsley, or marijuana, is a common street form of PCP. These leaves then are rolled into a "joint" (cigarette form) and smoked. Some common terms for these cigarettes are "crystal joints," "superweed," "angel hair," "CJ," and "KJ " (*Better Schools, Better People*, 1979).

PCP: Symptoms and Effects

Continued use of PCP and some other hallucinogens may cause adverse physical and psychological effects. The physiological effects caused by a less than anesthetic dosage (3 to 10 mg.) usually are: increased heart rate, elevated blood pressure, blockage of pain, flushing, sweating, increased deep reflexes, imperfect articulation of speech because of muscular uncoordination, visual disturbances (double or tunnel vision), dizziness, mild sedation, rapid involuntary eyeball movement, and constricted pupils. Other effects noted, although not as frequently, include drooling, nausea, and vomiting.

At 10.5 mg., drowsiness, abdominal cramps, bloody vomiting, and diarrhea have been recorded but these adverse reactions almost always are caused by a missynthesized batch. When larger doses are taken, major convulsions and coma can occur.

If toxic levels are reached, death can be caused by any number of reactions (or combinations thereof): status epilepticus (a series of rapidly repeated epileptic convulsions without any periods of consciousness between them), cardiac or respiratory arrest, or a hypertensive crisis from a rupture of a cerebral blood vessel. This overdosage potential clearly distinguishes PCP from other hallucinogens such as LSD, MDA, peyote, and psilocybin (NIDA, 1980).

Even in small doses, PCP's psychological effects can be very unpredictable. Adolescents' subjective reports vary but they indicate sensations different from other drugs. These generally are believed to be caused by the impairment of the user's ability to integrate incoming sensory stimuli. They have been compared to the effects of prolonged sensory deprivation that can cause users to lose their reality-testing ability and ego boundaries and can result in intellectual and emotional disorganization. Memory, perception, concentration, and judgment often are disturbed with regular usage of PCP.

A psychological danger with PCP is the risk of behavioral toxicity—that is, death by falls, fires, and other accidents. Evidence suggests that PCP users, especially chronic ingesters, are more likely to die from accidental means than any other group of recreational drug users.

When taken in large chronic doses, PCP can cause permanent brain and nervous system damage, long-lasting anxiety and depression (more than a year in some cases), suicidal tendencies, and psychosis. In California, a number of homicides allegedly have been committed by chronic heavy users while under the influence of the PCP.

PCP: Legal Implications

Federal penalties for illegal possession of PCP are up to one year's imprisonment and/or a fine of up to $5,000 for a first offense and up to two years and/or a fine of up to $10,000 for subsequent convictions. Illicit manufacture, distribution, or possession with intent to distribute can lead to up to 15 years' imprisonment and/or up to $25,000 fine for a first conviction, up to 30 years' imprisonment and/or up to $50,000 fine for subsequent convictions (NIDA, 1980).

Other Hallucinogens

Other types of hallucinogens on the streets that often are purchased by adolescents are mescaline, psilocybin, dimethosyphenylisophopylamine (STP or DOM), DMT, and THC. These are not as common among youths because some of them are difficult to obtain.

Mescaline is another hallucinogenic drug obtained from the peyote cactus plant. Physical dependence is unlikely with mescaline, but psychological dependence may develop.

Psilocybin is derived from the psilocybe mushroom. Reactions to it are similar to those of LSD and mescaline. As with mescaline, it is not easily accessible on the street.

STP is another illegal psychedelic drug. Youths report that the "serenity," "tranquility," and "peace" it produces are even stronger and more potent than LSD.

DMT, dimethyltryptamine, is another hallucinogenic drug of adolescent abuse. It takes effect faster than LSD but does not last as long. This drug may produce a psychological but not a physical dependency for adolescents.

THC or tetrahydrocannabinol generally is associated with marijuana but does warrant at least brief mention with the other hallucinogens. Fortunately, THC is rarely seen in the drug culture.

MARIJUANA

Marijuana (cannabis) is one of the least understood of all natural drugs although it has been known for nearly 5,000 years. Very early in history, the Chinese used it to relieve pain during surgery and the people of India used it as a medicine. In many countries, marijuana is used in religious ceremonies ("Pot Legalized," 1978).

Marijuana is the common name for the hemp plant. Historically, hemp fibers have been used for making textiles and rope, the seeds pressed into oil, and the leaves and flowers smoked for the intoxicating effects of their resin. Marijuana is an adaptable plant that grows well in most temperate climates, although the quality of the fiber and its drug potency vary.

The chemical in marijuana with the greatest mood-altering effects is delta - 9 - tetrahydrocannabinol (THC). The leaves and flowers also contain many related chemicals. Marijuana is used as dried leaves and flower parts, with or without seeds and stems. It ranges in color from greenish-brown to gold or dark brown, and may contain from none to 5 percent THC. Removing the strong-smelling resin in the leaves produces hashish, which is pressed into cakes or slabs. It usually is more potent than marijuana, having up to 12 percent THC. Hash oil, a highly refined form of marijuana, may contain up to 50 percent THC. Pure THC is not available outside of laboratories because it is expensive to produce and loses its potency when exposed to air.

Marijuana: Symptoms and Effects

As with smoking tobacco, marijuana gives off carbon monoxide that is linked to early fetal death (miscarriage), decreased fetal weight, and increased death rate after birth. Because of this and other effects not yet determined, marijuana should not be used during pregnancy. Marijuana may have far greater adverse effects on children, the elderly, those with chronic conditions (especially heart, lung and liver disease, diabetes, and epilepsy), pregnant women, persons with marginal fertility, and those who suffer from anxiety, depression, and psychosis.

Because children and teens are going through rapid physical, emotional, and psychological changes, their use (and especially heavy use) of marijuana can affect their maturation adversely. Regular use in the preteen or teen years can begin a lifelong pattern that can be difficult to change later, so necessary intellectual, survival, and emotional coping skills may not be learned. In addition, disruptions in youths' hormone balance may be extreme. Finally, there is a greater likelihood of automobile or motorcycle accidents when marijuana is combined with driving inexperience.

The effects from smoking marijuana vary from user to user. They depend largely upon the user's mood and expectations and the setting in which the drug is used. Marijuana can have some of the effects of hallucinogens, stimulants, and depressants and therefore is categorized into a classification of its own. The dosage and potency of the marijuana used also influence the overall effect.

For most youths, low to moderate doses of marijuana produce a feeling of well-being and relaxation, sometimes exhilaration, altered perception of time and distance, impaired short-term memory, and poor physical coordination. This often is manifested when working on less familiar, more complex mental tasks such as school assignments or when learning a new job. The "high" from one joint (marijuana cigarette) usually lasts two to three hours. Some first-time users report almost no effects at all. Because marijuana impairs reaction time, judgment, and perception of distance and time (even at low doses), it can be dangerous to drive a car or operate machinery while under its influence.

Some adverse reactions range from mild anxiety to panic or paranoia—in some cases, an acute psychosis. Other effects can include delusions, hallucinations, or illusions. These reactions can happen to anyone, but they are most likely seen in users who are anxious, depressed, or under stress, or who were borderline schizophrenics before using marijuana.

Because marijuana produces 50 percent more tar than tobacco smoke, there is an increased risk of lung damage and cancer when smoking it unfiltered. Smoking tobacco in addition to marijuana increases this risk. Sore throats and bronchitis are associated with long-term heavy marijuana smokers.

Persons with known heart conditions or high blood pressure are advised against using marijuana. During intoxication, marijuana increases heart rate and decreases blood circulation to the heart.

Marijuana: Legal Implications

The penalties and enforcement measures for simple possession of marijuana vary from state to state and from locality to locality.

Most states have penalties ranging from fairly mild to severe for possession, manufacture, sale, or possession with intent to deliver. Eleven states have decriminalized possession of marijuana—that is, the criminal penalties for possession have been replaced with fines such as those for civil offenses like parking violations. These states consider possession a misdemeanor rather than a felony; instead of being sent to jail, individuals apprehended with one ounce or less in their possession might be fined $100. Decriminalization laws do not reduce or eliminate all penalties for possession, sale, or distribution. Legalization is the term for the elimination of those penalties, and no states have legalized marijuana (NIDA, 1980).

INHALANTS

Inhalants are chemicals—usually gases or volatile liquids—that cause intoxication when they are sniffed in sufficient quantities. Common products such as paint thinner, model cement, and lighter fluid contain solvents that cause an intoxication resembling that of alcohol but that also are unpredictable and have many undesirable side effects. Aerosol propellant gases from an array of products have been inhaled for their mood-altering properties, sometimes with disastrous results.

Inhalants: Symptoms and Effects

Of all the volatile solvents, glue has been the most widely used, studied, and publicized. The effects of its main ingredient (toluene) resemble those of most of the other inhalants. Direct, voluntary inhalation of model cement (and most other solvents) is characterized by a brief period of stimulation with giddiness, euphoria, and muscle tremors, followed by a longer, dreamlike stupor.

Solvents are central nervous system depressants. Like other depressants (alcohol, barbiturates), they lower heart and breathing rate and impair judgment and muscle coordination. The intensity of these symptoms depends on the experience and personality of the user, the dose, the specific solvent inhaled, and the surroundings. Solvent intoxication tends to be short, from a few minutes to a couple of hours, and mild.

Tolerance does occur with regular use, which constitutes one danger of solvent inhalation. Cases of anemia, liver damage, and bone marrow deterioration are infrequent but are related to chronic solvent misuse. Craving for the intoxication may develop, but true physical dependence with withdrawal symptoms does not take place.

Petroleum-based solvents such as paint thinner, lighter fluid, and gasoline generally have similar but more extreme effects. Some of their components are known to be quite toxic (poisonous) and can cause tissue or nervous system damage. Additives to solvents may be as toxic as, or more than, the solvents themselves and may accumulate in the fat tissues until they reach dangerous concentrations. Lead in gasoline is especially toxic and is eliminated from the body very slowly.

Aerosols

Aerosol propellant gases such as fluorocarbons (Freon) and polyvinyl sometimes are inhaled for the effects they produce. They, too, are central nervous system depressants, with effects similar to those of the solvents. However, the hazards differ somewhat.

Products such as spray paint or vegetable oil sprays may become mixed with the propellant when the user attempts to inhale them. Some products are harmless while others are deadly to inhale: metals in paint may accumulate in the body, vegetable oil can coat the lungs and cause pneumonia. Glass chillers and gases under pressure are extremely cold when released from their container and may freeze the larynx or lungs. The U.S. Food and Drug Administration has attempted to place warnings on nonessential aerosol sprays or ban them altogether.

Anesthetics

Anesthetics such as ether, chloroform, and nitrous oxide occasionally are misused for their intoxicating effects. Ether is a volatile liquid (it evaporates at room temperature) that when taken by mouth produces an intoxication similar to that of alcohol. During the nineteenth century and as recently as World War II, ether often was used as an alcohol substitute.

Nitrous oxide (laughing gas) is another anesthetic, also sometimes used as an aerosol propellant, that is inhaled for its intoxicating effects. The user may feel giddy or exhilarated for about five minutes. Occasionally hallucinations occur. Excessive large doses may cause nausea, vomiting, or unconsciousness, in part because of a lack of oxygen; if the user does not get enough oxygen, death can occur.

Chloroform is capable of producing an alcohol-like intoxication but has never been very popular, in part because of its strong odor. It is known to be more frequently fatal than other anesthetics and alcohol.

Two other substances, butyl nitrite (poppers) and amyl nitrite, deserve mention as inhalants. These chemicals are stimulants rather than depressants. They are used therapeutically to ease high blood pressure by dilating the blood vessels but have recently seen an upsurge as under-the-counter products. They cause rapid but brief stimulation and may be dangerous to people with low blood pressure, glaucoma, or anemia.

Most youths who try inhalants do so only a few times or discontinue when they find something more "desirable" such as alcohol or other drugs. Users of inhalants tend to be young—between the the ages of 10 and 15—possibly because of easy accessibility and low cost. Excepting amyl nitrite, as of this writing there are no federal controls on any of the aforementioned substances.

ALCOHOL ABUSE

Alcohol (Fishburne, Abelson, & Cisin, 1980) is the most commonly abused drug in the United States, Canada, and Europe. In the United States alone, there are more than 9 million alcoholics out of about 110 million drinkers of all types.

Alcohol abuse continues to have serious and negative effects on the nation's adolescents. A popular myth is that kids don't drink any more, they now are into other drugs, such as marijuana. Alcohol used to be regarded as solely an adult drug problem. That, too, is a myth. The generation gap has been greatly exaggerated. Youths' favorite drug is the same as their parents' favorite: alcohol. A 1977 survey on youth alcohol consumption found that most American adolescents had had at least some experience with alcoholic beverages—80 percent at least one drink, 74 percent two or three drinks, and more than half of all adolescents drink at least once a month (NIAAA, 1981).

Reports of teenage drinking and driving show that incidence is increasing at an alarming rate. Some 8,000 youths are killed and nearly 40,000 are involved in serious accidents each year that are alcohol-related (NIAAA, 1981).

What is alcohol? It is the major active ingredient in wine, beer, and distilled liquor. It is a natural substance formed by the reaction of fermenting sugar with yeast spores. The intoxicating substance in alcoholic beverages is ethyl alcohol, which is a colorless, inflammable liquid that acts as a drug. It can produce feelings of well-being, sedation, intoxication, or unconsciousness, depending on the amount and manner in which it is consumed. Technically, alcohol can be classified as a food because it contains calories, but it has no nutritional value (NIAAA, 1981).

Alcohol: Symptoms and Effects

Alcohol is a drug that depresses the central nervous system as a general anesthetic, slowing down the activity of the brain and spinal cord. Alcohol enters the bloodstream rapidly (no digestion is required) and circulates to all parts of the body within a few minutes (Exhibit 9-2). Absorption can be slowed by food in the stomach. The body burns alcohol at a rate of half an ounce an hour. Ninety percent of the ethyl alcohol (ethanol) is broken down by the liver and the remaining 10 percent is eliminated through the lungs and kidneys (NIAAA, 1981). Alcohol is the only drug that causes visible damage to the brain. Chronic use can destroy the

Exhibit 9-2 Blood Alcohol Concentration (BAC) Chart

Quantity Consumed in 1 Hour		BAC	Effects
1 drink	½ oz ethanol*	.025	Minimal influence, pleasant feeling
2 drinks	1 oz ethanol	.05	Relaxation, released inhibitions, possible sedation or euphoria
4 drinks	2 oz ethanol	.10	Visible signs of intoxication; slow reactions; impaired coordination, perception, and driving; legal intoxication limit in most states
8 drinks	4 oz ethanol	.20	Confusion, slurred speech, difficulty staying awake, staggering, mood swings
12 drinks	6 oz ethanol	.30	Stupor, barely conscious
16 drinks	8 oz ethanol	.40	Coma
24 drinks	12 oz ethanol	.60	Possible death from alcohol overdose, respiratory failure, or accidental choking

Note: 1 drink = 1 12-ounce can of beer
        1 4-ounce glass of wine
        1 1-ounce shot of distilled liquor

* Ethanol (ethyl alcohol) is the intoxicating substance in alcohol.

personality and often is physically as well as psychologically addictive. Withdrawal from alcohol use can be as severe as from barbiturates (*Listen*, 1981).

Alcohol works on youths' bodies by being absorbed into the blood stream, 20 percent immediately through the stomach walls and the other 80 percent almost as fast after being processed quickly through the gastrointestinal tract. After it is consumed, alcohol eventually can be found in all tissues, organs, and secretions of the youths' bodies. The alcohol immediately acts on the brain's central control areas to slow down or depress its activity (*Listen*, 1981).

Although basically a sedative, alcohol seems to act temporarily as a stimulant for many youths after they first start drinking. This is because alcohol's initial effects are on the parts of the brain that affect learned behavior patterns such as self-control. After a drink or two, this learned behavior may be altered, making the students lose their inhibitions and talk more freely; on the other hand, they may feel aggressive or displeased.

Higher blood alcohol levels depress the youths' brain activity to the point that memory, as well as muscle coordination and balance, may be impaired temporarily. Still larger alcohol intake within a relatively short period of time depresses deeper parts of the brain, severely affecting judgment and dulling the senses of the youths.

What is drunkenness? Alcohol's effects on the body depend on many variables—the individual, the amount drunk, and the manner (speed) in which it is consumed. In addition, not everyone who drinks alcohol is considered an abuser or alcoholic. It is all a matter of degree.

Factors influencing how alcohol takes effect on the students' brain and body are:

1. how fast the youth ingests the drink
2. whether the stomach is empty or full
3. what type of drink is consumed
4. the youth's body weight
5. the youth's mood or expectations.

A person is considered legally intoxicated in most states if the blood alcohol content (BAC) is 0.10 percent or above. This means that one part of every thousand of the person's blood is pure alcohol. Such a situation normally would result when a person weighing about 160 pounds has had four drinks within one hour after eating. The drunkenness stage is reached with fewer drinks if body weight is less than 160 pounds or with more drinks if the person is heavier. In a few states, the legally drunk level is 0.15 percent. In any case, it is illegal to drive a car after the BAC level specified is reached (Addiction Research Foundation, 1979).

Drunkenness is characterized by a temporary and progressive loss of control over physical and mental powers because of excessive alcohol intake. Symptoms of drunkenness can vary but generally include the following:

1. impaired vision
2. distorted depth perception
3. thick speech
4. delayed motor reactions
5. poor motor coordination.

Problem-solving ability is impaired and mood becomes unpredictable, memory is impaired, and judgment may become distorted (Addiction Research Foundation, 1979).

Many myths surround home "remedies" claiming to alleviate drunkenness: cold showers, fresh air, black coffee, and exercise. However, these have no effect on blood alcohol content so they cannot produce soberness. The effect of alcohol must simply run its course. It takes about an hour and a half for the body to eliminate the alcohol content for each drink consumed. A hangover may be the end result. A hangover is the body's reaction to excessive drinking. Associated miseries such as nausea, gastritis, anxiety, and headaches vary among individuals. Doctors usually prescribe aspirin, rest, and solid food for relief of hangovers. There is no scientific evidence to support curative claims for coffee, raw eggs, oysters, chili peppers, steak sauce, vitamins, or other home remedies (Addiction Research Foundation, 1979).

Alcoholism

Not everyone who drinks is an alcoholic. As mentioned earlier, alcoholism is a matter of degree. When is alcohol drinking considered a problem? What designates an alcoholic from a normal drinker?

A "person who is powerless to stop drinking and whose drinking seriously alters his moral living pattern" is defined as an alcoholic (National Council on Alcoholism, 1977). Alcoholism is a progressive illness that cannot be caught or cured overnight. While it is difficult to define exactly when a person becomes an alcoholic, there are warning signs of which everyone should be aware:

- family or social problems caused by drinking
- job or financial difficulties relating to drinking
- loss of a consistent ability to control drinking
- "blackouts" or the inability to remember what happened while drinking
- distressing physical and/or psychological reactions if you try to stop drinking
- a need to drink increasing amounts of alcohol to get the desired effect
- marked changes in behavior or personality when drinking
- getting drunk frequently

- injuring yourself—or someone else—while intoxicated
- breaking the law while intoxicated
- starting the day with a drink (Johnson Institute, 1972).

Any one or more of these symptoms may indicate a drinking problem. Immediate action should be taken if such indications are found. It must be remembered that every time individuals take a drink, they die a little.

Why Do Youths Drink?

The first drink may have been taken out of curiosity, but continual consumption becomes ''the thing to do'' when copying parents and other significant individuals. Most adolescents are introduced to alcohol in their own homes (Maddox, 1970). Peer pressure has a tremendous effect on older youths' drinking behavior. Alcohol consumption is condoned by parents who prefer that over use of other drugs such as marijuana or pills.

Drinking alcohol is socially acceptable and becomes a symbol of maturity for some teenagers. Alcohol is readily available and relatively inexpensive. Since the drinking age has been reduced to 18 years in many states (some already are restoring it to 21), alcohol is easy to obtain, even by those who have no access to illicit drugs.

A negative reason why youths turn to alcohol is that they want to ''tune out'' or anesthetize the mind in order to block out unwanted feelings or thoughts. This behavior could be a manifestation of an escape avoidance from or avoidance of family, school, or social problems. Alcohol sometimes can be substituted for close relationships or as a ''cure'' for fears when courage or self-confidence is lacking. In such cases, it is used to block out feelings of loneliness, inadequacy, or self-doubt. In short, youths may drink alone, drink to get along, or use alcohol as medicine for troubles. The point to remember is that drinking never solves anything; it often makes matters worse. As people drink, they may develop a sense of guilt that can lead to more drinking and eventually to dependence on alcohol and to alcoholism.

Research conducted in Tennessee over a ten-year period reported youths' personality traits, attitudes, and characteristics that were predictive of potential alcohol abusers. The traits consisted of the following:

1. aspiration/performance discrepancy
2. unsupportive home environment
3. health problems
4. self-confidence

5. relationship between early health problems, motor skills development, and self-concepts
6. absence of a good male model in the home.

This study found that youths identified with alcohol abuse showed greater discrepancies between aspiration and performance level than those not involved. The abusers had greater aspirations but their performance levels fell short of their goals. They tended to desire more support and encouragement from peers and adults but in actuality received less at home than the nonalcoholic group. The abusers also had poorer health, poorer self-concept (self-forecasting more failure in school and sports), and poorer motor skills that resulted in low self-confidence. They also showed less communication with parents, and in their families, fewer fathers were the dominating force in the household (Bond, 1977).

Based on the results of this study and what is known about alcohol and youths, programs that are designed to enhance self-concept and improve peer-parent/progeny relationships and communication are warranted as rehabilitative and preventive measures for alcohol and drug use. What's more, alcohol abuse and alcoholism will continue to be the No. 1 problem with youths and adults until the nation begins to recognize that alcohol is a drug and alcoholism is a treatable illness, not a moral weakness.

TOBACCO

Despite the fact that the Surgeon General has determined that cigarette smoking is hazardous to health, the public continues to smoke at an increasing rate. Smoking has dangerous effects on even young, healthy people. The earlier individuals begin to smoke, the greater the risk to their health in future years. Smoking may even shorten the life span. Thirty years of intensive research have determined cigarettes to be so harmful that it is now illegal to sell them to persons under the age of 18 (AMA, 1981).

According to the American Heart Association (1981), each year cigarette smoking contributes to the deaths of about 325,000 persons in the United States. There are more than 54 million smokers in the nation and of those, more than 3 million are teenagers (AMA, 1981), and for the first time, more girls than boys are smoking (Table 9-3). Smoking is a difficult habit to break but, as more adults are quitting, more adolescents continue to start smoking.

Effects of Smoking

Tobacco contains nicotine, which acts on the heart, blood vessels, digestive tract, kidneys, and nervous system. It also contains minute amounts of tars and

Table 9-3 Teenage Smoking Behavior

Age and Smoking Behavior (1974)	Boys		Girls	
	N in 1974	N in 1979	N in 1974	N in 1979
12-14				
Never smoked or experimented only	496	246	496	257
Current regular smoker	23	8	27	14
Ex-smoker	28	14	26	10
Totals	547	268	549	281
15-16				
Never smoked or experimented only	253	132	256	118
Current regular smoker	66	27	73	27
Ex-smoker	45	18	33	15
Totals	364	177	362	160
17-18				
Never smoked or experimented only	208	102	230	105
Current regular smoker	113	47	96	29
Ex-smoker	44	15	42	11
Totals	365	164	368	145
Grand totals	1,276	609	1,279	586

other substances that may produce cancer as well as irritants that chiefly affect the bronchial tubes. Small amounts of carbon monoxide and arsenic also are present in tobacco smoke.

Cigarette smoking not only is the major cause of lung cancer, it also contributes to circulatory impairment, heart disease, chronic bronchitis, and pulmonary emphysema. Each day in the United States, 250 persons die from heart attacks, 100 from lung cancer who are smokers, while 150 die from other cigarette-related diseases (AMA, 1981). Even moderate smokers run the risk of coronary and lung diseases. However, it does help to stop, according to the American Heart Association (1981) because the death rate from coronary artery disease decreases among those who give up smoking and, after a period of years, approaches that of persons who never have smoked. In individuals who stop smoking, some abnormal changes in body tissue may revert toward normal.

Why Do Youths Smoke?

Around the ages of 12 to 14, young people usually begin to face peer pressures to smoke as they move away from their families and closer to their friends. At that time, they also are likely to rebel against adult authority and are willing to take more risks. Knowing this may help parents and teachers understand some of the reasons why adolescents start to smoke.

Teenagers themselves confirm that peer pressure often is the major reason they start smoking—those who smoke are more likely to have friends who smoke. The family also is a major influence. In families where the parents or older siblings serve as models for smoking, there is a greater chance that the younger members will acquire the habit. Youths also are influenced by advertisements that depict smokers as young and attractive people doing interesting and exciting things.

Statistics on Teenage Smoking

A 1974-1979 survey of immediate and long-term patterns of teenage smoking categorized the youths into four groups (Green, 1979):

1. those who were regular smokers
2. those who were smokers in 1974 but had quit by 1979
3. those who were nonsmokers in 1974 but were in 1979
4. those who were nonsmokers throughout the study.

The sample population included 2,553 teenagers interviewed in 1974, and 1,194 (46.8 percent) who were interviewed again in 1979. Their ages ranged from 12 to 18. The statistics are shown in Table 9-3 supra.

SUBSTANCE TREATMENT PROGRAMS

The greatest expense of drug, tobacco, and alcohol abuse is the cost of treatment. Millions of dollars are spent each year for hospitalization, residential centers, individual and group therapy, counseling, detoxification centers, behavior management programs, and community awareness projects. Most of these are treatment and rehabilitation programs directed to abuse after the problem has grown to a considerable extent.

The old phrase "an ounce of prevention is worth a pound of cure" may be apropos for the direction of drug programs. Prevention efforts can decrease time and monetary expense by nipping the problem in the bud. Prevention is most suitable in the field of education. Teachers, familiar with their students and concerned about their welfare, can instigate valuable training and preventive measures before a problem gets out of hand. They also are in position to observe their students frequently enough to detect behavior changes that may be caused by drug misuse (see Exhibit 9-3 for teacher checklist) and to provide guidance and models for appropriate behavior.

Exhibit 9-3 Teacher Checklist for Drug Abuse Identification

	No Change	Mild Change	Moderate Change	Severe Change
1. Change in usual daily patterns of behavior				
2. Change in attendance				
3. Change in discipline				
4. Change in work habits				
5. Change in performance				
6. Decline in physical appearance and dress				
7. Change in speech and language				
8. Signs of emerging opposite personality (i.e., a friendly person becomes depressed or hostile; a withdrawn or shy person becomes outgoing or boisterous)				
9. Rejection of old friend and secrecy about new friends				
10. Emergence of stealing behaviors				

Note: Not all of these changes occur as a result of drug use. It is necessary to exercise caution when interpreting any observation. It also is beneficial to be familiar with the student.

The rest of this chapter describes treatment programs developed for youths for preventive or rehabilitative treatment of abuse of drugs, alcohol, and tobacco. (Appendix C lists additional reading materials on substance abuse and treatment strategies and programs.) Many of the programs used for drug treatment also include alcohol abuse. Some of those discussed here can cover both.

Nonschool-Based Programs

The following treatment program procedures usually are conducted outside the school. They are administered by professionals trained in drug treatment and rehabilitation. Specific methods may vary from program to program, depending upon individual goals and philosophies. They are noted here to provide teachers with additional helpful information.

Withdrawal and Detoxification Centers

The center is defined by law as "a social rehabilitation facility established for the purpose of facilitating access into care and rehabilitation by detoxifying and evaluating the person and providing entrance into the continuum of care" (Mayer, 1979). This is a process whereby the physical and psychological need for a drug is gradually eliminated under medical supervision. Alternative detoxification methods include methadone maintenance and antagonistic drug procedures.

Methadone maintenance is the daily administration of methadone under medical supervision as a substitute for heroin and other opiate-type drugs. Methadone partially or completely suppresses the addiction or preoccupation with taking morphine-type drugs. This drug is addicting and has found its way into the illegal market. Although the addiction is only shifted from one drug to another, methadone addicts present more socially acceptable behaviors (Dohner, 1972).

Antagonistic drugs are still in experimental stages for treatment of narcotic addiction. They block the effects of narcotics, thus eliminating the need to continue use of the drug. An example of an antagonistic drug is cyclazocine (Dohner, 1972).

Psychiatric Evaluation and Therapy

These programs are based on psychotherapy and are conducted by trained psychologists or psychiatrists. They generally are initiated after detoxification to alleviate the remaining psychological dependence after physical withdrawal. The person may be seen individually or in groups. An additional option is a therapeutic community.

School-Based Programs

As discussed earlier, the most striking information in the research is that low self-esteem, poor interpersonal skills, and a general lack of social and personal competence provide a possible causal link to alcohol and drug abuse (Bloom, 1976). As a result of this research, increasing support for preventive programs dealing with the social and psychological factors underlying abuse has developed. This philosophy regards drug abuse as a symptom of a more basic problem.

Schools provide an excellent atmosphere for programs for coping with abuse. Not only can such programs help decrease or prevent abuse, they also may prevent many other dysfunctional behaviors, such as violence, delinquency, and vandalism.

Strategies

School-based prevention strategies that have been employed effectively as primary methods are discussed next.

Self-Esteem Building

This concept is based on the assumption that the school can be an important factor in building self-esteem, in addition to influences from the family. Specific techniques or formulas for esteem building may have to be implemented on an individual basis, depending on the age of the student and the type of problem. Specific classroom activities are only one aspect of building self-esteem; school and classroom climate are equally important, as well as activities outside the building.

Communication Training

This activity is closely linked to self-esteem, involving the development of effective communication skills. It emphasizes the importance of listening and communicating within the group. It also is helpful in promoting similar listening and communication skills between students and parents.

Values Clarification

This is a process of students' understanding, articulating, expressing, and acting on their values. They must be assisted in understanding the reasons for their choices, decisions, and actions.

Decision Making and Problem Solving

Effective decision making is just as critical to any prevention program as are self-esteem and values clarification. Activities to improve decision-making or problem-solving abilities consist of providing and structuring practice for various decision-making dilemmas that youths might encounter. Role-playing activities are one source. Guidance and peer modeling are critical elements, as are suggestions and rehearsal activities for selecting and understanding alternative solutions to a problem. A number of curriculum packages and manuals on decision-making techniques are available.

Peer Tutoring and Peer Counseling

Fellow students can be a powerful source for developing self-esteem and cognitive skills. A peer tutoring or counseling program involves students' working together to help each other. Such work situations may help relieve some of the pressures youths feel in regular academic settings. The program helps improve self-concept and confidence in both student and tutor. Careful preparation and training are necessary for a strong tutoring or counseling program.

Alternatives to Drugs

This is a broad strategy involving many different activities, primarily to circumvent boredom or aimlessness. Some programs do so by offering part-time employment opportunities or activities in community recreation centers. The school itself can provide opportunities in extracurricular activities such as sports, theater, music, etc. The range is virtually limitless. Alternative programs must be presented in conjunction with other strategies.

ALCOHOL TREATMENT PROGRAMS

In addition to programs outlined above, many other alcohol prevention and rehabilitation efforts exist for teenagers. These involve both school-based and nonschool-based treatment.

Nonschool-Based Programs

As in any substance abuse program, treatment should begin in the home. Parents and siblings need to take a hard look at the actions, attitudes, and values they model for impressionable youths and at the support they provide. Many community-based programs are available to teenagers and parents that can create improved communication and awareness of the seriousness of alcohol abuse.

Alcoholics Anonymous offers membership to young people. The service provides counseling, support, and information to concerned parents and youths. Various community groups offer workshops and seminars to promote local awareness and concern. Some religious organizations, mental health services, and other advocates offer communitywide services to assist families in dealing with the problems that arise when a member is an alcohol abuser.

School-Based Programs

The school is a potential resource for the treatment of youthful alcohol abusers. In addition to activities and programs discussed earlier, demonstration programs may be developed to devise innovative ways of delivering alcohol abuse treatment services and to assess their effectiveness in the secondary school. These can include assessment of changes in the students' school performance and in other aspects of their functioning and of the program's impact on school personnel and on other school programming.

TOBACCO ABUSE TREATMENT PROGRAMS

School and community agencies are promoting programs to deter adolescents from smoking. Most schools are required to teach the dangers of smoking. Health agencies such as the American Heart Association help educate young people by providing schools with teaching guides and materials on the hazards of smoking. However, the problem cannot be solved in the schools alone. Adolescence is the age when many students begin to experiment with cigarettes and are vulnerable to peer pressures. Schools can teach students to resist peer pressure and to stand firm on their own personal values.

Teachers are in position to provide students with valuable information on the effects of smoking on the body. Films, pamphlets, books, and posters are available through the library, health department, American Heart Association, and other agencies. School officials can help by instituting codes that prohibit cigarette smoking on the grounds. Cigarette machines can be banned in schools.

In addition to preventive measures, behavior management programs are available to help smokers kick the nicotine habit. Treatment procedures include stimulus saturation (excessive smoking is encouraged with the rationale that cigarette use soon will lose its reinforcing quality); aversion therapy or shock treatments; alternative reinforcement, extinction, or punishment therapy; and contingency management (see also Reese, 1978).

Success rates for behavior management programs vary since they depend greatly on the individual, the motivation to quit, and willpower. However, it must be kept in mind that there is no general cure for smoking. Many techniques may be tried before the most effective one is found. Discovering what will be effective is up to the discretion of the teacher. It may help to obtain information from family, other teachers familiar with the student, professionals trained in drug treatment, or other sources in the community.

SUMMARY

Despite the rapid growth of adolescent abuse of alcohol, drugs, and tobacco, there still are far too few answers as to how to cope with these enormous problems. Only a few adolescents seem willing to profit by help that may be available. Awareness of the problem, though by no means a solution, has the important virtue of attacking abuse as such—that is, the use of any destructive drug. Even if society discovered the key to developing adolescents' awareness, what would stimulate in all of them the desire to end or avoid abuse?

This is not merely a medical or psychological problem but one for society as a whole. The impulse to misuse drugs is an urge to escape reality that affects vast numbers of teenagers. What will make escape into drugs unnecessary and unacceptable to the many who seek it and cling to it? No one irrefutable theory explains the connection between society's way of life and the increasing presence of drug abuse, and answers will not be found easily.

This chapter may assist teachers in developing appropriate programming with administrators, parents, and the students, may lead to better understanding of their students' behavior, and may help efforts to work with them in accepting the world in which they live.

REFERENCES

Addiction Research Foundation, Toronto, 1979.

American Heart Association, 1981.

Benowicz, R.J. *Nonprescription drugs and their side effects.* New York: Grosset & Dunlap, Inc., 1977.

Better schools, better people: Now schools can help to prevent drug and alcohol abuse. Sacramento, Calif.: California State Department of Education, 1979. (ERIC Document Reproduction Service No. ED 188 047)

Bloom, B.I. *Primary prevention opportunities and problems.* Paper presented at ADAMHA Annual Conference of State and Territorial Alcohol and Drug Abuse, and Mental Health Authorities, U.S. Alcohol, Drug Abuse, and Mental Health Administration, Denver, 1976.

Bond, R.A. *Early predictors of alcohol abuse: A study of the relationships between intent, values, and personality variables from the 1960 TALENT data BOSE and alcohol abuse in later life.* Palo Alto, Calif.: American Institute for Research in the Behavioral Sciences, 1977. (ERIC Document Reproduction Service No. ED 195 900)

Brecher, E.M., & Editors of *Consumer Reports. The consumer's union report: Licit & illicit drugs.* Mt. Vernon, N.Y.: Author, 1972.

Cumulated index medicus. National Library of Medicine. Bethesda, Md.: U.S. Department of Health and Human Services, Public Health Service. National Institutes of Health, National Library of Medicine.

Department of Health, Education, and Welfare, Publication No. [ADM] 80-23. Washington, D.C.: U.S. Government Printing Office, 1980.

Department of Health, Education, and Welfare, U.S. Public Health Service, Publication No. [ADM] 78-568. Washington, D.C.: U.S. Government Printing Office, 1978.

Department of Health and Human Services, Publication No. [ADM] 81-312. Washington, D.C.: U.S. Government Printing Office, 1981.

Diagnosis and emergency treatment. Albany, N.Y.: New York State Department of Health.

Dohner, V.A. Alternatives to drugs. *Addiction,* Fall 1972, *3*(1), 30.

Drug Enforcement Administration. *Fact sheets.* Washington, D.C.: U.S. Department of Justice, 1975.

Drug Information Center and the Wisconsin Clearinghouse for Alcohol and Other Drug Information, National Institute on Drug Administration. Milwaukee: Wisconsin Department of Health and Social Services, 1977-1978.

Fishburne, P.M., Abelson, H.I., & Cisin, I.H. *National survey on drug abuse: Main findings, 1979.* National Institute on Drug Administration, Washington, D.C.: U.S. Government Printing Office, 1980.

Greden, J.F. Anxiety or caffeinism: A diagnostic dilemma. *American Journal of Psychiatry*, October 1974, *131*(2).

Green, E. *Teenage smoking: Immediate and long-term patterns*. Washington, D.C.: Chilton Research Services, 1979.

Institute for Chemical Survival. *Listen, 25*(10). (Supplement). Phoenix, Ariz.: Author, 1981.

Israelstam, S., and Lambert, S. (Eds.) *Alcohol, Drugs, and Traffic Safety*. Proceedings of the Sixth International Conference on Alcohol, Drugs, and Traffic Safety. Toronto, 1974.

Maddox, George, L. (Ed.) *The domesticated drug: Drinking among collegians*. New Haven, Conn.: College and University Press, 1970.

Malcolm, A. The amotivational syndrome: An appraisal. *Addiction,* February 1976, *23,* 28-49.

Mayer, S.E. *Client impact study on six detoxification centers (subacute receiving centers)*. Minneapolis: Rainbow Research, Inc., 1979. (ERIC Document Reproduction Service No. ED 198 021)

National Council on Alcoholism. *Alcoholism: A treatable disease*. The Johnson Institute, Washington, D.C.: Author, 1972.

National Council on Alcoholism. *Early bird warning signals of alcoholism*. Detroit: Author, 1973.

National Institute on Alcohol Abuse and Alcoholism. *Alcoholism.* Department of Health, Education, and Welfare, Alcohol, Drug Abuse, and Mental Health Administration, Washington, D.C.: U.S. Government Printing Office.

National Institute on Drug Abuse. *Community and legal responses to drug paraphernalia*. Department of HEW, Division of Resource Development Service Research Branch, Washington, D.C.: U.S. Government Printing Office, 1980.

Pizza, J., & Besnick, S. *The school team approach: Preventing alcohol and drug abuse by creating positive environment for learning and growth*. Washington, D.C.: U.S. Department of Education, 1980. (ERIC Document Reproduction Service No. ED 195 926)

Pot legalized for medicine. *U.S. Journal of Drug and Alcohol Dependence,* November 1978.

Reese, E.P. *Human operant behavior: Analysis and application*. Dubuque, Iowa: Wm. C. Brown Company Publishers, 1978.

Rittenhouse, J.D. (Ed.). *Consequences of alcohol and marijuana use*. (Department of Health, Education, and Welfare, Publication No. [ADM] 80-920.) Washington, D.C.: U.S. Government Printing Office, 1979.

Sixth Annual Report to the U.S. Congress from the Secretary of Health, Education, and Welfare. Washington, D.C.: Department of HEW, 1976.

Smith, G.M., & Fogg, C.P. Psychological predictors of early, late use, and nonuse of marijuana among teenage students. In D.B. Kandel (Ed.), *Longitudinal research on drug use: Empirical findings and methodological issues*. Washington, D.C.: Hemisphere Publishing Corporation, 1978.

Glossary of Terms

Alcohol: a drug that depresses the central nervous system as a general anesthetic, slowing the activity of the brain and spinal cord.

Alcoholic: a person who is powerless to stop drinking and whose drinking seriously alters the normal living pattern.

Alcoholism: a physical compulsion coupled with a mental obsession to drink.

Drug: any chemical that modifies the function of living tissues, resulting in physiologic or behavior change.

Drug Abuse: the taking or administering of drugs under circumstances and at doses that significantly increase their hazard potential, whether or not used therapeutically, legally, or as prescribed by a physician.

Drug Tolerance: the development of body or tissue resistance to the effects of a drug so that larger doses are required to reproduce the original effect.

Drug Use: the partaking of a drug with minimal hazard, whether or not used therapeutically, legally, or as prescribed by a physician.

Physical Dependence: the effect on the body tissues of the continued presence of a drug (even in the absence of psychologic dependence), revealed by disturbing or life-threatening withdrawal symptoms that develop when the drug is discontinued.

Psychologic Dependence: a tendency or craving for the repeated or compulsive use (not necessarily abuse) of an agent because its effects are deemed pleasurable or satisfying, e.g., drugs or food.

Toxic Psychosis: the result of continuing use of stimulant drugs (but it may occur after a single dose). The syndrome is characterized by vivid hallucinations, both visual and auditory, and by extreme paranoia; may develop 36 to 48 hours after administration and usually clears up within a week after cessation of the drug. The person may require hospitalization.

Street Use of Drug Terms

"Angel dust:" PCP, a hallucinogen; when sprinkled in joints of mint, parsley, oregano, or marijuana, it is termed "angel hair," "CJ" or "crystal juice," "KJ," or "superweed."

"Barbs:" Barbiturates, depressants; also called "reds," "yellow jackets."

"Coke:" Cocaine, a nonaddictive stimulant drug, usually "snorted" into the nose.

"Cop:" To obtain drugs; also, "score."

"Crash:" Come down off a high; prolonged sleep after high doses of amphetamines (or other drugs).

"Drop:" To swallow drugs; also, "eat."

Drug effects: Usually the initial or more intense feelings such as a "buzz," "flash," or "rush."

"Fix:" A heroin dose, also any injected drug dosage.

"Get hooked:" Become addicted to drugs.

"Go cold turkey:" Withdraw abruptly from drugs.

"Hash:" Hashish, a stronger form of marijuana.

"Highs:" Peak effects of taking any drug.

"Joint:" A marijuana, hash, or PCP cigarette.

"Junkie:" A drug addict.

"Line:" A line (or dose) of cocaine.

"Kick the habit:" Withdraw from drugs.

LSD: A mind-bending hallucinogen (lysergic acid diethylamide) that produces euphoria and visions of odd shapes or colors; also called "acid;" to take LSD is to "drop acid."

"Mainlining:" Injection of drugs directly into the circulatory system, such as with a mixture of heroin and water, quinine, or milk sugar; also, "run," "shoot," "skin pop" (subcutaneous or muscular).

PCP: See angel dust.

Poppers: Butyl nitrate depressants that are inhaled.

Quaaludes: Methaqualone, a nonbarbiturate sedative depressant, also called "sopors" or " 'ludes.''

"Run:" Frequent high doses (every few hours) of amphetamines for an extended period of time; also, to inject drugs.

"Rush:" An immediate high or lightheadedness resulting from a drug, particularly cocaine.

"Sniff:" To take drugs, primarily through the nose, especially cocaine; also, "snort," "toot."

"Speed:" Pep pills or "bennies," any of various amphetamines, especially Methedrine; also called "uppers."

"Stoned:" To get high on drugs; also: "Jonesed" (heroin), "in the O-zone," "ripped," "speeding," "strung out," "tripping," "wired," "wrecked," "zonked out."

Street user: A junkie.

Materials on Substance Misuse

BOOKS

Alpert, R., & Cohen, S. *LSD*. New York: New American Library, 1967.

Brenner, J.H., Coles, R., & Meagher, D. *Drugs and youth: Medical, psychiatric and legal facts*. New York: Liveright, 1970.

Burroughs, W., Jr. *Speed*. New York: Olympia Press, 1970.

Cohen, S. *The beyond within: The LSD story*. New York: Atheneum, 1967.

Fort, J. *The pleasure seekers: The drug crisis, youth and society*. Indianapolis: The Bobbs-Merrill Co., Inc., 1969.

Geller, A., & Boas, M. *The drug beat*. New York: Cowles Book Company, 1969.

Graham, J.D.P. (Ed.). *Cannabis and health*. New York: Academic Press, 1976.

Kaplan, J. *Marijuana—The new prohibition*. Cleveland: World Publishing Company, 1970.

Lindesmith, A.R. *The addict and the law*. New York: Vintage Books, 1967.

Lindesmith, A.R. *Addiction & opiates*. Chicago: Aldine Publishing Company, 1968.

Lingeman, R.R. *Drugs from A to Z*. New York: McGraw-Hill Book Company, 1969.

Rosenthal, M., & Mothner, I. *Drugs, parents, and children: The three-way connection*. Boston: Houghton Mifflin Company, 1972.

Scott, J.M. *The white poppy: A history of opium*. London: William Heinemann Medical Books, 1969.

Smith, D.E. (Ed.). *The new social drug: Cultural, medical and legal perspectives on marijuana*. Englewood Cliffs, N.J.: Prentice-Hall, Inc., 1970.

Spock, B. *Raising children in a difficult time: A philosophy of parental leadership and high ideals*. New York: W.W. Norton & Company, Inc., 1974.

Ullmann, L., & Krasner, L. *Case studies in behavior modification*. New York: Holt, Rinehart & Winston, Inc., 1965.

ARTICLES AND REPORTS

Alcohol and marijuana: Spreading menace among teenagers. *U.S. News & World Report*. November 24, 1975.

Bland, H.B. Problems related to teaching about drugs. *Journal of School Health*, February 1969, *39*(2).

Bureau of Narcotics and Dangerous Drugs. *Guidelines for drug abuse prevention education*. Washington, D.C.: U.S. Government Printing Office, 1970.

California State Department of Education. *A study of more effective education relative to narcotics, other harmful drugs, and hallucinogenic substances*. Sacramento, Calif.: Author, 1970.

Cohen, A.Y. Psychedelic drugs and the student: Educational strategies. *The Journal of College Student Personnel*, March 1969.

Dangers of combined marijuana-alcohol use by teenagers. *The Journal of the Addiction Research Foundation, 6*(2), 1977.

De Silva, R. The young American and the flight toward drugs. *The Washington Post*, July 3, 1977.

Drug Abuse: Escape to nowhere. Philadelphia: Smith, Kline and French Laboratories, 1968.

High school students and drugs. Columbus, Ohio: Institute for Development of Educational Activities, Inc., 1970.

Hochbaum, G.M. How can we teach adolescents about smoking, drinking and drug abuse? *Journal of Health, Physical Education, and Recreation*, October 1968.

Jones, G. America's youth: Angry . . . bored . . . or just confused? *U.S. News & World Report*, July 19, 1977, pp. 18-20.

Keutzer, C.S. Behavior modification of smoking: The experimental investigation of diverse techniques. *Behavior Research and Therapy*, 1968, *6*, 137-157.

Kitzinger, A., & Hill, P.J. *Drug abuse, A source book and guide for teachers*. Sacramento, Calif.: California State Department of Education, 1967.

Powell, J., & Azrin, N.H. The effects of shock as a punisher for cigarette smoking. *Journal of Applied Behavior Analysis*, 1968, *1*, 63-71.

Resnick, J.H. The control of smoking behavior by stimulus satiation. *Behavior Research and Therapy*, 1968, *6*, 113-114.

Rigert, J., & Shellum, B. Marijuana high: Teenagers often pay a high price. *Minneapolis Tribune*, July 20, 1977. (a)

Rigert, J., & Shellum, B. Doubts growing about marijuana's safety. *Minneapolis Tribune,* July 27, 1977. (b)

Ryback, R.S., Teenage alcoholism, medicine, and the law. *The New England Journal of Medicine,* October 1975, *293,* 719-720.

Street drug analysis and drug use trends, 1969-1975. *The Pharm Chem Newsletter,* 1977, *6*(4), 1-2.

Ungerleider, J.T., & Bowen, H.L. Drug abuse and the schools. *American Journal of Psychiatry,* June 1969, *125*(12).

Wilde, G.J. Behavior therapy for addicted cigarette smokers: A preliminary investigation. *Behavior Research and Therapy,* 1964, *2,* 107-109.

Yankelovich, Skelly, and White, Inc. *Raising children in a changing society.* Minneapolis: General Mills American Family Report, 1976-77, p. 92.

What To Do in Case of Overdose

1. Clear the room if possible but always keep a friend or familiar face near the subject.
2. Inquire among subject's friends to help determine the possible nature of drug taken.
3. If drug is unknown, treat symptoms only. It is safer to undertreat than overtreat. Often all that is needed is reassurance.
4. Make subject comfortable, lay the person flat, loosen clothes, keep individual warm.
5. If conscious:
    - call for physician immediately
    - treat for shock (warmth, rest, fluids)
    - if drowsy, walk subject around (may give coffee or juice for stimulation)
    - if overdose suspected, induce vomiting with lukewarm salt water (only if conscious)
6. If unconscious:
    - call physician immediately
    - maintain clear airway (clear mouth and throat, pull tongue forward, turn head to side with chin extended up and out)
    - look for any signs of difficult breathing (gasping, choking, skin pallor)
    - check for pulse
    - if breathing stops, apply mouth-to-mouth resuscitation
    - if resuscitation fails, apply external cardiac massage (CPR)
7. If convulsion occurs, wedge something (cloth, shirt, etc.) between subject's teeth to prevent injury. (Don't panic, convulsions usually are brief)

Source: Reprinted from *Diagnosis and Emergency Treatment* with permission of the New York State Department of Health.

Resource Materials

Pearlie M. Qualls

INTRODUCTION

Middle and secondary education teachers have important roles to play in identifying specific social development materials needed to assist students in coping with the demands of the school environment. This is especially true with students who are chronic classroom disrupters, socially maladjusted, behavior disordered, or emotionally disturbed. Even more important are the social interaction skills and techniques that middle and secondary students must master to function in the mainstream, adjust to the work world, and actualize their fullest potential both academically and socially.

Discipline and classroom management constitute one of the most difficult areas in which to purchase commercially prepared materials or media kits to supplement the curriculum because few materials are available. Teachers tend to rely on the systems and materials they have practiced using and feel at ease administering. There are many high-quality commercially prepared supplemental materials for instruction in the subject matter and content areas.

Since the passing of P.L. 94-142, The Education for all Handicapped Children Act of 1975, there has been an increasing need to provide instructional materials, training films, reference books, and other aids to both regular and special education teachers. This need was created by the legal mandate of providing the most appropriate instruction for handicapped students.

The purpose of this Appendix is to:

1. provide regular teachers at the middle and secondary levels with an overview of selective instructional materials, resources, and professional information concerning discipline and classroom management, and

2. provide special teachers at the same levels with the same overview to enable them to provide both direct and indirect services to disruptive handicapped students in the classroom.

The information here is not all-inclusive but, for both regular and special middle and secondary teachers, does list a broad range of instructional materials, training films, curriculum resources, reference books, behavioral analysis checklists, and other guides in effective classroom management.

INSTRUCTIONAL MATERIALS

ATTITUDES

TITLE/PUBLISHER	INTEREST LEVEL	INSTRUCTIONAL LEVEL	INSTRUCTIONAL AREAS	MATERIAL USAGE	COST
Developing Self Respect School Specialty Supply, Inc.	Grades 7-12	3.0-5.0	Self concept	Cassettes workbook	$69.00
Going Places With Your Personality. (set of 10 high interest-low voc. readers) FE 3495	Grades 7-12	2.5-3.5	Positive interpersonal habits	Textbooks	$17.75
Me And Others Set includes 2 color filmstrips, 3 cassettes, work-books and teacher's guide. Educational Design	Grades 4-12	3.5-8.0	Self explora-tion and developing attitudes	Multimedia kit	$129.00 $3.00 each
Personality: Roles You Play Set includes 2 filmstrips, 2 tapes Sunburst Communi-cations	Grades 7-12	4.5-6.5	Role playing, self-concept	Multimedia kit	$69.00
Rules and Rights: Juveniles Have Rights Too (Workbook, 12 units) Fearson Publishing	Grades 7-12	N/A	Positive atti-tudes toward law. Students rights and responsibilities	Workbook	N/A

INSTRUCTIONAL MATERIALS (cont.)

TITLE/PUBLISHER	INTEREST LEVEL	INSTRUCTIONAL LEVEL	INSTRUCTIONAL AREAS	MATERIAL USAGE	COST
The Ungame #UG 1200 School Specialty Supply, Inc.	Grades 7-12	4.0-5.0	Self concept	Game board	$9.95
BEHAVIOR AND BEHAVIOR MANAGEMENT					
IEP 2 Resource Kit; kit contains teacher cards. One card is developed for each task. Each card contains instrucational objectives, instructional activities, and classroom management folders. EBSCO Curriculum Materials	Grades 7-12	7.0-12.0	Behavioral/ attitudinal competencies	Kit with profile sheets	$11.00 kit
It's Positively Fun Love Publishing Co. (Contracting)	Grades 4-12	4.0-6.0	Managing learning environment	Spirit masters, Book	$6.95 $4.95
Positive Classroom Performance Love Publishing Co.	Grades 4-12	3.0-6.0	Behavior modification techniques	Workbook	$3.95

Instructional Materials (cont.)

TITLE/PUBLISHER	INTEREST LEVEL	INSTRUCTIONAL LEVEL	INSTRUCTIONAL AREAS	MATERIAL USAGE	COST
		CAREER EDUCATION			
Beyond High School, What--Multimedia kit BU 237 St. Paul Book and Stationery	Grades 9-12	4.0-5.0	Career decision making	Multimedia kit	$69,000
Job Attitudes Creative Visuals (Kit includes the company and the community, the role of the supervisor, developing good attitudes, and the importance of attitudes)	Grades 7-12	N/A	Developing appropriate attitudes	Multimedia (filmstrips and tapes)	$281.25 total kit

Instructional Materials (cont.)

TITLE/PUBLISHER	INTEREST LEVEL	INSTRUCTIONAL LEVEL	INSTRUCTIONAL AREAS	MATERIAL USAGE	COST
People Working Today (Series of 6 titles) Teacher's manual for each title included free) -Alex on the Grill -Bob the Super Clerk -Janet the Hospital Helper -Jester the Bellhop -Johnny at the Circuits - Julie at the Pumps -Kerry Drives a Van -Larry the Logger -Laura Cares for Pets -Tony the Custodian Janus Book Publishers	Grades 7-12	2.0	Career educa- tion, work rela- tions, and respect authority	Textbooks	$16.50 per set $1.85 per book
Skills For Living And Working BC 96 St. Paul Book and Stationery	Grades 7-12	4.0-5.0	Careers in terms of communications	Media Kit	$79.00

Instructional Materials (cont.)

TITLE/PUBLISHER	INTEREST LEVEL	INSTRUCTIONAL LEVEL	INSTRUCTIONAL AREAS	MATERIAL USAGE	COST
		CITIZENSHIP SKILL			
A Good Citizen at Home Poster Class Set 10 books, 8 posters and guide, Mayfex Assoc. Inc.	Grades 8-12	4.0-6.0	Citizenship and interpersonal social skills	Text, guide, posters, workbooks	$53.75
A Good Citizen at Home Poster Set (8 posters) -individual workbook -individual guide Mayfex Assoc. Inc.	Grades 8-12	4.0-6.0	Citizenship and interpersonal social skills	workbooks	$11.45 $3.95 ea. $3.95 ea.
A Good Citizen at Home Class Set 10 books and guide, Mayfex Assoc. Inc.	Grades 8-12	4.0-6.0	Citizenship and interpersonal social skills	workbooks	$39.50
Good Neighbors: Class Set--10 books & guide Good Neighbors poster class set (10 books, 8 posters & guide) Good Neighbor Poster set (8 posters) Individual workbook Individual guide Mayfex Assoc., Inc.	Grades 8-12	N/A	Social skills and inter- personal skills	Posters, books, workbooks, and guide	$39.50 $53.75 $11.45 ea. $3.95 ea. $3.95 ea.

Instructional Materials (cont.)

TITLE/PUBLISHER	INTEREST LEVEL	INSTRUCTIONAL LEVEL	INSTRUCTIONAL AREAS	MATERIAL USAGE	COST
Personal Law Kit SW 6070 St. Paul Book & Stationary	Grades 8-12	4.5-6.0	Legal Literacy	Multimedia Kit	$94.00
The Young American Series 1. In Your Family 2. In Your Community 3. In Your State 4. In Your Country 5. Know your Rights Fearon Publishers	Grades 5-12	N/A	Survival skills and social skills	Workbook	$.90 ea.
You, The Police, and Justice, Scholastic Book Services, (Anthology, Log books, posters)	Grades 9-12	4.0-6.0	Law and People	Kit	$99.50
COMMUNICATION SKILLS					
Bodytalk, (Cards, teacher's guide) Psychology Today	Grades 6-12	6.0-12.0	Non-verbal communication	Simulation game	N/A

Instructional Materials (cont.)

TITLE/PUBLISHER	INTEREST LEVEL	INSTRUCTIONAL LEVEL	INSTRUCTIONAL AREAS	MATERIAL USAGE	COST
Communication: Person To Person - Anthology - Logbook - Poster Set - Sound/Filmstrip - Teacher Guide Scholastic Book Services	Grades 7-12	N/A	Interpersonal communication	Multimedia and work-book	$1.85 .30 $4.75 $21.00 $4.00
Me & Others, Media Program EG 330 St. Paul Book & Stationery	Grades 7-12	4.0-5.0	Feelings and needs, open communication problem solving, another person's expectation	Multimedia Kit	$119.00
Person to Person Interaction Kit ZL 59 St. Paul Book & Stationery	Grades 7-12	3.0-4.0	Interpersonal Communication skills	Kit with workbook	$12.95
Relating-Set includes 2 filmstrips, 2 tapes Sunburst Communications	Grades 7-12	N/A	Human interaction	Multimedia	$69.00

Instructional Materials (cont.)

TITLE/PUBLISHER	INTEREST LEVEL	INSTRUCTIONAL LEVEL	INSTRUCTIONAL AREAS	MATERIAL USAGE	COST
Roll-A-Role Game UG 1215 St. Paul Book & Stationery	Grades 7-12	4.0-5.0	Communication in real life situations	Game board	$9.95
Tell It Like It Is: The Un-Game; Pennant Educational Materials (Game board, pawns, die deck of special cards- one for adolescents and adults, one for children)	Grades 4-adult	N/A	Communication problems	Game board	$8.50
The Ungame UG 1260 St. Paul Book & Stationery	Grades 7-12	4.0-5.0	Students learn to communicate feelings	Game board	$9.95
Value Clarification: A Handbook of Practical Strategies for Teachers and Students Hart Publishing	Grades 1-12	N/A	Communications, value clarification	Workbook	$3.95

Instructional Materials (cont.)

TITLE/PUBLISHER	INTEREST LEVEL	INSTRUCTIONAL LEVEL	INSTRUCTIONAL AREAS	MATERIAL USAGE	COST
CONSUMER EDUCATION					
The Tuned-In Consumer: BG51 A complete consumer education program St. Paul Book & Stationery	Grades 8-12	4.5-6.5	Consumer Education	Workbook Kit	$350.00
COPING SKILLS					
Putting Yourself In My Place (2 filmstrips, 2 cassettes, and teacher's guide) Guidance Associates	Grades 6-12	6.0-12.0	Adolescence peer group pressure and coping skills	Multimedia Kit	N/A
Your Emotions: The Coping Process Sunburst Communications	Grades 7-12	N/A	Coping skills	Multimedia Kit	$69.00

Instructional Materials (cont.)

TITLE/PUBLISHER	INTEREST LEVEL	INSTRUCTIONAL LEVEL	INSTRUCTIONAL AREAS	MATERIAL USAGE	COST
DECISION MAKING SKILLS					
Deciding – Class Set BP 9151X St. Paul Book & Stationery	Grades 8-12	4.0-5.0	How to of Decision Making	Kit	$18.00
Deciding for Myself: A Values-Clarification Series Clarifying My Values Set A My Everyday Choices Set B Where Do I Stand? Set C T. Paulson-Winston Press	Grades 6-Adult	N/A	Practice in values clarification	Kit	$2.52 per set $3.96 Leader Guide
Decisions & Outcomes BP 9153X St. Paul Book & Stationery	Grades 8-12	4.0-5.0	Application of decision making strategies		$18.00

Instructional Materials (cont.)

TITLE/PUBLISHER	INTEREST LEVEL	INSTRUCTIONAL LEVEL	INSTRUCTIONAL AREAS	MATERIAL USAGE	COST
If You Don't Know Where You're Going, You'll Probably End Up Some- where Else AG 248 St. Paul Book & Stationery	Grades 8-12	5.5-6.5	Planning for the future	Consumables	$7.25
Life Goals (3 film- strips, 3 cassettes, and teachers guide) Human Relations Media	Grades 6-12	6.0-12.0	Decision making goals, personal values and taking risks	Multimedia Kit	N/A
Life Goals: Setting Priorities Kit BU 619 St. Paul Book & Stationery	Grades 9-12	4.0-5.0	Realistic goal setting and weighing risks involved in decision	Multimedia Kit	$99.00
Life Styles Auction Game ZL 69 St. Paul Book & Stationery	Grades 8-12	3.5-4.5	Values, life opportunity informed decis- ions	Game	$19.95
Priority Simulation ZL 72 St. Paul Book & Stationery	Grades 9-12	4.5-5.5	Group decision making	Game	$16.95

Instructional Materials (cont.)

TITLE/PUBLISHER	INTEREST LEVEL	INSTRUCTIONAL LEVEL	INSTRUCTIONAL AREAS	MATERIAL USAGE	COST
FAMILY LIVING SKILLS					
Realities of Family Life. Includes: 18 cassette/filmstrips, 40 duplicating masters and teacher guide School Specialty Supply, Inc.	Grades 9-12	4.5-5.5	Survival skills & self concept	Multimedia program	$405.00
Realities of Family Life Media Program BG 601 St. Paul Book & Stationery	Grades 9-12	4.5-5.5	Sensitization to realities challenges, etc. of family life	Media program	$405.00
LEISURE TIME SKILLS					
Recreation & Leisure Time Time Edmark Associates	Grades 5-12	N/A	Developing Leisure Time	Multimedia workbook, consumables	$94.95

Instructional Materials (cont.)

TITLE/PUBLISHER	INTEREST LEVEL	INSTRUCTIONAL LEVEL	INSTRUCTIONAL AREAS	MATERIAL USAGE	COST
		PRE-VOCATIONAL SKILLS			
Getting A Job Fearon Publishing	Grades 9-12	3.6	Survival, careers, Social interaction	Textbook	$2.01
How To Become A Safe Worker 20 books and guide Mafex Associates, Inc.	Gades 7-12	N/A	Pre-vocational	Textbooks	$4.95 Guide $79.00 Book & Guide
I Like Me Class Set 10 books and guide	Grades 7-12	N/A	Pre-vocational & social inter-action	Workbooks	$41.00 set $3.95 indivi-dual book $3.95 guide

Instructional Materials (cont.)

TITLE/PUBLISHER	INTEREST LEVEL	INSTRUCTIONAL LEVEL	INSTRUCTIONAL AREAS	MATERIAL USAGE	COST
Job Attitudes, (kit includes 15 filmstrips & cassettes). Opportunities for Learning, Inc.	Grades 7-12	4.0-5.0	Pre-vocational	Multimedia kit	$281.50
Job Seeking Skills (series of 6 titles) Teacher's manual included free (extra book set of 8 titles)	Grades 7-12		Pre-vocational skills and career education	Book & workbook	$24.00 (set) $18.40 (extra books)
-Don't get Fired!		2.5			$2.95
-Get Hired		2.5			$2.95
-My Job Application File		2.5			$2.25
-Janus Job Interview Guide		2.5			$3.25
-Janus Job Interview Kit		2.5			$32.50
-Janus Job Planner Janus Book Publishers		2.8			$2.95

Instructional Materials (cont.)

TITLE/PUBLISHER	INTEREST LEVEL	INSTRUCTIONAL LEVEL	INSTRUCTIONAL AREAS	MATERIAL USAGE	COST
Pre-Vocational Kit. The kit includes: All in a day's work, It happened on the job, The world of careers, and Pathways to careers, Globe Book Company	Grades 4-12	N/A	Pre-vocational	Textbooks	$4.68 ea.
SELF CONCEPT					
Building Self-Respect, Multimedia Kit BU 234 St. Paul Book & Stationery	Grades 7-12	3.0-5.0	Self-respect self-awareness responsibility for one's behavior	Multimedia Kit	$69.00
Developing Self Respect School Specialty Supply, Inc.	Grades 7-12	3.0-5.0	Self-respect	Workbook & textbook	$69.00
Discover Your Hidden Talents Library Sounds Service International, Inc.	Grades 7-12	N/A	Self-concept	Media Kit	$23.50

Instructional Materials (cont.)

TITLE/PUBLISHER	INTEREST LEVEL	INSTRUCTIONAL LEVEL	INSTRUCTIONAL AREAS	MATERIAL USAGE	COST
Going Places With Your Personality Fearon Publishers	Grades 4-12	N/A	Self-concept	Booklet	$1.77
Happy To Be Me #CN 300 Opportunities for Learning, Inc.	Grades 4-7	N/A	Self-concept	Book workbook	$34.50
How Do I See Myself? Sunburst Communications	Grades 7-12	N/A	Self-concept	Multimedia Kit	$69.00
How To Like Yourself: Kit includes: filmstrips, and 2 tapes Sunburst Communications	Grades 7-12	N/A	Personality and mental health	Multimedia kit	$69.00
Interpersonal Life Skills #SC 222 School Specialty Supply, Inc.	Grades 7-12	4.0-5.0	Self-concept, self-appraisal perception skills	Multimedia program	$425.00

Instructional Materials (cont.)

TITLE/PUBLISHER	INTEREST LEVEL	INSTRUCTIONAL LEVEL	INSTRUCTIONAL AREAS	MATERIAL USAGE	COST
Interpersonal Life Skills Multimedia Program St. Paul Book/Life Skills; St. Paul Book & Stationery	Grades 7-12	4.5-5.5	Self-concept, self-appraisal skills, receptive & expressive communication, perceptive communication skills, synchronizing skills, relation-building skills	Multimedia	$425.00
Let's Improve Our Attitudes #CV 37181 Opportunities for Learning, Inc.	Grades 7-12	N/A	Self-concept	Kit, books and work-book	$159.25
Me & Others #ED 330 Opportunities for Learning, Inc.	Grades 4-12	N/A	Self-concept	Media kit	$119.00
Me & Others School Specialty Supply, Inc.	Grades 7-12	4.0-5.0	Self-concept and working with others	Text & workbook	$69.00

Instructional Materials (cont.)

TITLE/PUBLISHER	INTEREST LEVEL	INSTRUCTIONAL LEVEL	INSTRUCTIONAL AREAS	MATERIAL USAGE	COST
Learning Work Related Skills Opportunities for Learning, Inc.	Grades 7-12	4.0-5.0	Pre-vocational	Multimedia kit	$119.95
Occupations 1 Occupations 2 New Readers Press Division of Laubach Literacy International	Grades 7-12	4.0-5.0	Pre-vocational	Workbooks	$ 1.85 1.85
On The Job, (Kit includes cassettes, book and guides) Opportunities for Learning, Inc.	Grades 7-12	4.0-5.0	Pre-vocational	Multimedia kit	$249.00

Instructional Materials (cont.)

TITLE/PUBLISHER	INTEREST LEVEL	INSTRUCTIONAL LEVEL	INSTRUCTIONAL AREAS	MATERIAL USAGE	COST
Taking Charge of Your Life, #AG 286 School Specialty Supply, Inc.	Grades 7-12	3.0-4.0	self-concept and social interaction	Text & workbook	$69.00
The Gentle Art of Saying No: Principles of Assertiveness Set includes 3 film-strips, 3 tapes Sunburst Communications	Grades 7-12	N/A	Assertiveness training and self-concept	Multimedia kit	$99.00
The Ungame-Tell It Like It is! #AV 1 Opportunities for Learning, Inc.	Grades 4-12	N/A	Self-concept	Game board	$10.50
Understanding Your Feelings #LF 694 (4 color filmstrips, 4 cassettes, and guide) Opportunities for Learning, Inc.	Grades 4-7	N/A	Self-concept	Multimedia kit	$66.00

Instructional Materials (cont.)

TITLE/PUBLISHER	INTEREST LEVEL	INSTRUCTIONAL LEVEL	INSTRUCTIONAL AREAS	MATERIAL USAGE	COST
Understanding Yourself Steek-Vaughn Company Publishers	Grades 6-9	4.0-6.0	Self-concept	Text and workbook	$2.10
You And The Group Set includes 2 filmstrips, and 2 tapes Sunburst Communications	Grades 7-12	N/A	Group interaction and self concept	Multimedia kit	$69.00
Developing Self Respect School Speciality Supply, Inc.	Grades 7-12	3.0-5.0	Self-respect and self-concept	Text & workbook	$69.00
		SELF RESPECT			
How Do I See Myself? BU 260 St. Paul Stationery and Supplies	Grades 7-12	1.0-3.0	Self-images self-perceptions	Multimedia kit	$69.00
How To Like Yourself- Set includes 2 filmstrips,2 tapes Sunburst Communications	Grades 7-9	N/A	Personality and mental health	Multimedia kit	$69.00
Developing Self Respect Set includes 2 filmstrips,2 tapes Sunburst Communications	Grades 7-12	4.5-6.5	Self-respect	Multimedia kit	$69.00

Instructional Materials (cont.)

TITLE/PUBLISHER	INTEREST LEVEL	INSTRUCTIONAL LEVEL	INSTRUCTIONAL AREAS	MATERIAL USAGE	COST
		SOCIAL SKILLS			
How We Grow: The set covers, physical growth, mental growth, emotional growth, and social growth #VEY 000, 4 filmstrips, 4 cassettes, #VEX, 4 filmstrips, 4 records BFA Educational Media	Grades 6-9	N/A	Social skills	Multimedia and workbook	$94.00 $94.00
Learning To Be Together, Keeping People Apart, People are People Pulling #VFN 000, 4 filmstrips, 4 cassettes, #VFM 000, 4 filmstrips, 4 records BFA Educational Media	Grades 9-12	N/A	Social skills and social interaction	Multimedia kit and workbooks	$77.00 (both sets)
New Vision: Survival Skills. Set includes 8 filmstrips, workbook and 1 manual Creative Visuals	Grades 7-12	N/A	Social skills and survival skills	Multimedia workbook	$153.00
Read On! Write On! Books (Series of 2 titles) The Big Hassle, The Put-Down Pro Teachers manual for each title free Janus Book Publishers	Grades 6-12	2.5 2.5	Social skills	Book and work-books	$5.70 (set) $2.85 ea. $2.85 ea.

Instructional Materials (cont.)

TITLE/PUBLISHER	INTEREST LEVEL	INSTRUCTIONAL LEVEL	INSTRUCTIONAL AREAS	MATERIAL USAGE	COST
Skills for Living and Working (Consumables) BC 86 St. Paul Book & Stationery	Grades 7-12	4.0-5.0	Personal and interpersonal skills-employ cooperation, social relations	Textbook and workbook	$79.00
Taking Responsibility: Being Who You Are, Making Your Life Beyond Roles, A Family #VFR 000, 4 filmstrips, #VFP 000 4 filmstrips, 4 cassettes, 4 records BFA Educational Media	Grades 9-12	N/A	Survival skills, social skills, and social interaction	Multimedia kit and workbook	$77.00 (both sets)
The Ungame #UB 1200 School Speciality Supply, Inc.	Grades 7-12	4.0-5.0	Social skills and self-respect	Game board	$9.95
What It Takes- Developing Skills for Contemporary Living Fearon Publishers	Grades 7-12	N/A	Social living skills	Book and workbook	$2.01

Instructional Materials (cont.)

TITLE/PUBLISHER	INTEREST LEVEL	INSTRUCTIONAL LEVEL	INSTRUCTIONAL AREAS	MATERIAL USAGE	COST
You And Your World Fearon Publishers	Grades 5-12	3.0-4.0	Social skills, interpersonal skills, and survival skills	Workbook	$1.65 ea
SOCIAL INTERACTION SKILLS					
Discovery Kit Scholastic Book Services	Grades 7-10	N/A	Social interaction	Multimedia	$169.00
Drugs: Facts for Decisions New Readers Press 32 page booklet	Grades 7-12	5.6	Social interaction	Consumables and workbook	$125.00
Relating: The Art of Human Interaction. Kit includes: 2 filmstrips and 2 tapes Sunburst Communications	Grades 7-12	N/A	Human and social interaction	Multimedia	$69.00

Instructional Materials (cont.)

TITLE/PUBLISHER	INTEREST LEVEL	INSTRUCTIONAL LEVEL	INSTRUCTIONAL AREAS	MATERIAL USAGE	COST
The Turner-Livingston Communication Series Follett Publishers (The series include: The Television You Watch, The Phone Calls You Make, The Newspapers You Read, The Movies You See, The Letters You Write and The Language You Speak.)	Grades 7-12	N/A	Social inter-action	workbooks (consumables)	$1.71 ea.
SURVIVAL SKILLS					
Becoming Independent: Living Skills System Edmark Associates	Grades 9-12	N/A	Personal management, social develop-ment, house-hold management, practical academ-ic skills, home activities, com-munity activities, job readiness and work skills	Kit	$225.00

Instructional Materials (cont.)

TITLE/PUBLISHER	INTEREST LEVEL	INSTRUCTIONAL LEVEL	INSTRUCTIONAL AREAS	MATERIAL USAGE	COST
Getting Around-Activity Set, Activity Book In 308-Class Set St. Paul Book and Stationery	Grades 7-12	2.5-3.5	Using critical information. Using maps	workbook	$28.50
L.A.B.E.L./Learning Activities, Basic Education Lag, PP74. St. Paul Book and Stationery	Grades 7-12	2.0-5.0	Independent learning/ coping skills	Kit	$995.00
Making It on Your Own Mafex Associates	Grades 9-adult	N/A	Basic Survival	Textbook Transparencies	$58.95 for 10 books $25.00 for 10 books
Signs: Building A Survival Vocabulary Program St. Paul Book and Stationery	Grades 7-12	1.5-3.5	Functional vocabulary and using critical information	Workbook	$7.25
Survival Guide LC7 St. Paul Book and Stationery	Grades 7-12	3.0-5.0	Basic Life Skills	Workbook	$14.95

Instructional Materials (cont.)

TITLE/PUBLISHER	INTEREST LEVEL	INSTRUCTIONAL LEVEL	INSTRUCTIONAL AREAS	MATERIAL USAGE	COST
Survival Guides (series of 2 Title) Teacher's manual included free	Grades 7-12		Survival skills	Book & workbook	$16.50 (set)
-Finding a Good Used car		2.5			$2.85 ea
-Getting Around Cities and Towns		2.0			$2.85 ea
-Reading and Following Directions		2.6			$2.85 ea
-Reading a Newspaper		2.6			$2.85 ea
-Reading Schedules		2.5			$2.85 ea
-Using the Want Ads		2.5			$2.85 ea
Janus Book Publishers					
The Amazing Adventures of Harvey Crumbaker. Complete Skills For Living Library Specific units that may be purchased separately LC21,LC22,LC23,LC24 St. Paul Book and Stationery	Grades 7-12	4.5-5.5	Living on your own forms and following directions, coping as a consumer on the job, everyday communication	kit	$75.00 $19.95ea.

Instructional Materials (cont.)

TITLE/PUBLISHER	INTEREST LEVEL	INSTRUCTIONAL LEVEL	INSTRUCTIONAL AREAS	MATERIAL USAGE	COST
		VALUES			
Deciding For Myself: Values Clarifications Series WT 44, WT 45, Deciding for Myself Books St. Paul Book and Stationery	Grades 7-12	3.0-4.0	Values	Booklets set of 40 different titles	$21.95 $15.95
Developing As A Person (Duplicating Transparency Book) MRL 171 TD St. Paul Book and Stationery	Grades 7-12	4.0-5.0	Students develop strategies for clarifying values and making judgements	Consumables, duplicating books and transparencies	$8.95
Values Learning Lab XR 6032 St. Paul Book and Stationery	Grades 7-12	2.0-3.0	Identification of values	Kit	$29.95

Instructional Materials (cont.)

TITLE/PUBLISHER	INTEREST LEVEL	INSTRUCTIONAL LEVEL	INSTRUCTIONAL AREAS	MATERIAL USAGE	COST
		VOCATIONAL SKILLS			
Out of Work New Readers Press	Grades 12-post Secondary	6.8	Job training job finding for those out of work	Booklets	$1.50
Jerry Works In A Service Station Fearon Publishing	Grades 9-12	4.0-6.0	Vocational skills	Text,work-book	$1.20
The World Of Work New Readers Press	Grades 9-12	6.4	Want ads, job interviewing social inter-action	Textbook	$1.50

Instructional Materials (cont.)

TITLE/PUBLISHER	INTEREST LEVEL	INSTRUCTIONAL LEVEL	INSTRUCTIONAL AREAS	MATERIAL USAGE	COST
Overcoming Inferiority Set inclues 2 filmstrips, 2 tapes Sunburst Communications	Grades 7-12	4.5-6.5	self-concept	Multimedia kit	$69.00
Person to Person #ZL 59 Opportunities for Learning, Inc.	Grades 7-12	3.0-4.0	self-concept	Textbook	$12.95
Role-A-Role #AV 1215 Opportunities for Learning, Inc.	Grades 7-12	4.0-5.0	self-concept	Game board	$10.50
Shyness-Set includes 2 filmstrips and 2 tapes Sunburst Communications	Grades 7-12	N/A	Shyness and self-concept	Multimedia	$69.00
Taking Charge of Your Life, Involvement Kit AG 287 St. Paul Book & Stationery	Grades 8-12	3.0-4.0	self-concept self-confidence	Kit	$12.50

Supplemental Forms

Form 1 Assessing the Classroom Climate

Behavior Observation Form

PERSONAL IDENTIFYING DATA

Name _____ Date of Birth _____ Grade _____ School _____

Subject _____ Date/Day _____ Time _____

PHYSICAL DESIGN OF CLASSROOM

Description of Classroom:

___ Traditional
___ Specialty
___ Learning Centers
___ Others (Please specify) _____

Description of Classroom Activities:

___ Small group (How many) _____
___ Large group (How many) _____

Activity _____

Skills needed _____

What, if any, architectural barriers are in the classroom? _____

How might the above affect behavior? _____

PRESENTATION OF SUBJECT MATTER

___ Auditory   ___ Visual
___ Lecture   ___ Textbook/Papers
___ Media   ___ Chalkboard
___ Other (Please specify) _____

PERFORMANCE OF SUBJECT MATTER

___ Seatwork   ___ Individual
___ Boardwork   ___ Small group
___ Notetaking   ___ Large group
___ Other (Please specify) _____

(teacher completing the form)

Source: Developed by Pearlie M. Qualls, Learning Disabilities Supervisor, Milwaukee Public Schools, 1982.

Form 2 Checklist for Student Behavior

Behavior Observation Checklist[*]

Name _____   Teacher _____

Date _____   Subject _____

The student:	F	O	N
Acts without forethought			
Temper tantrums			
Aggressive			
Assertive			
Self-directed (motivation)			
Clings to others (esp. adults)			
Oversensitive			
Insensitive			
Excessive variation of mood			
Easily frustrated			
Hyperactive			
Facial tics or grimace			
Withdrawn			
Poor relationship with peers and/or adults			
Difficulty returning to class after interruptions			
Daydreams			
Is functionining within the classroom enviornment			
Sits at desk			
Raises hand			
Enters room appropriately			
Responds to bell by being in the classroom and attending to the teacher			
Appropriate interaction with peers within the classroom			
Able to deal with criticism appropriately			
Reacts to peer provocation appropriately			
a. verbal			
b. physical			
Reacts appropriately to teacher directives			

F= Frequently
O= Occasionally
N= Never

* May be used with Form 1 or independently.

Form 2 continued

	F	O	N
Able to deal with teacher expectations for the classroom			
Treats materials with proper care			
Puts materials away			
Able to work in small group (less than 10)			
Able to work in large group (More than 10)			
Able to work individually			
Leaves room appropriately			
a. when directed			
b. at end of class			
Displays appropriate behavior outside the classroom			
a. during recess			
b. during lunch			
c. during phy. ed.			
d. during music, art, etc.			
Able to deal with grades received			
MOTOR			
Poor posture			
Limited size and distance judgement			
Awkward walking movement			
General poor coordination			
Problems with using chalk, pencils, scissors, etc.			
Handwriting difficult to read			
Directs eyes towards teacher directed activity			
Able to copy from board, books, etc.			
Body in space			
Spatial sequencing			

F= Frequently
O= Occasionally
N= Never

Form 2 continued

LANGUAGE	F	O	N
Non-verbal			
Underdeveloped vocabulary			
Poor use of grammar			
Communicates on a concrete level			
Limited participation in group discussions			
COGNITIVE			
Comprehension			
Oral directions			
Reasoning ability			
Organization of time, materials, & self (tasks)			
Asks appropriate questions			
Responds appropriately to questions			
Remembers assignments			
Writes down assignments as given			
Able to volunteer information appropriately			
PERCEPTION AND MEMORY			
Able to attend to class activity			
Listens to discussions			
Writes or prints clearly			
Does assignments neatly			
Poor memory			
Limited attention span			
Distractable			
Inability to shift tasks			
Difficulty in discriminating symbols			
Low frustration tolerance			
Distracted by objects or movements			

F= Frequently
O= Ocasionally
N= Never

Form 2 continued

OTHER	F	O	N
Participates appropriately in classroom discussions			
Able to ask for help when needed			
Starts task within reasonable time limit			
Completes task on time			
Completes assignments as given			
Is responsible for work missed			
Able to take tests			
Hands in completed work			

F= Frequently
O= Occasionally
N= Never

Source: Developed by Pearlie M. Qualls, Learning Disabilities Supervisor, Milwaukee Public Schools, 1982.

Form 3 Parent Conferences

Recordkeeping Form

Date of Conf.	Reason(s)	Issues Discussed	Follow-up/ Intervention Strategies	Comments

Source: Developed by Pearlie M. Qualls, Learning Disabilities Supervisor, Milwaukee Public Schools, 1982.

Form 4 Evaluation of Student Behavior

Behavior Analysis

Name _____   Subject _____

Period of the day _____   Grade _____

1. Describe the unde sirable behavior:

   _____

   _____

2. Estimate how often the undesirable behavior occurs:

   A. Once a day _____
   B. 2-5 times a day _____
   C. 6-10 times a day _____
   D. More than 10 times
      a day _____

3. Describe the behavior you would like to take the place of the undesirable behavior:

   _____

   _____

4. Estimate how often the desired behavior occurs:

   A. Once a day _____
   B. 2-5 times a day _____
   C. 6-10 times a day _____
   D. More than 10 times a day _____

5. Describe what happen s after the undesired behavior occurs:

   A. The teacher _____
   B. The peers _____
   C. Significant others _____

Form 4 continued

6. Describe what happens before the undesired behavior occurs:

   A. The teacher _____

   B. The Peers _____

   C. The curriculum _____

   D. The classroom environment _____
   _____

7. Describe what happens after the undesired behavior occurs:

   A. The teacher _____

   B. The peers _____

   C. Significant others _____
   _____

8. What is the effect of the undesired behavior on the student's work: (Please check appropriately)

	A	F	S	N
A. Does not begin				
B. Does not participate				
C. Does not complete				
D. Does not turn in				
E. Destroys work				
F. Other (Please specify)				

   (A= Always   F= Frequently   S= Sometimes   N= Never)

   _____
   Teacher completing the form

   _____
   Date

Source: Developed by Pearlie M. Qualls, Learning Disabilities Supervisor, Milwaukee Public Schools, 1982.

Form 5 Anecdotal Record(s)

Recordkeeping Form: Student Conduct

STUDENT _____

SCHOOL YEAR _____

TEACHER _____

SUBJECT _____

Date	Time	Circumstances surrounding behavior	Description of behavior observed	Intervention strategies	Comments

Source: Developed by Pearlie M. Qualls, Learning Disabilities Supervisor, Milwaukee Public Schools, 1982.

Form 6 Student Classroom Assignments

**Recordkeeping Form: Program Schedule
for Secondary Students—Grades 9-12**

Student _____

Grade _____

Program Schedule

Hour	Subject	Room

For Secondary Students (Grades 9-12)

Check the appropriate boxes

☐ OJT (On the Job Training) Program

☐ Work Study Program

☐ OJE (On the Job Experience) Program

☐ Vocational Training/Exploration Program

☐ Other (Please specify)

☐ Sheltered Workshop

☐ Career Education Program

☐ O.E. (Office Education) Program

☐ D.E. (Distributive Education) Program

Source: Developed by Pearlie M. Qualls, Learning Disabilities Supervisor, Milwaukee Public Schools, 1982.

Index

A

Alcohol. *See* Substance abuse
Alternative Discipline and Suspension
  Program, 177-181
Antischool phobia, 151-152
Assertiveness training. *See* Personal
  development
Atlanta Program (of discipline),
  169-172
Attention-seeking, 14-15, 112-113
Authority issues. *See* Teachers

B

Behavior modification. *See* Social
  reinforcement
Behavior problems
  antischool phobia, 151-152
  attention-seeking, 14-15, 112-113
  chronic disobedience, 113-118
    crying, whining, 117
    interruptions, 116
    putting objects in mouth,
      117-119
    refusal to listen, 115
    temper tantrums, 115
    swearing, 117
    unwillingness to accept
      assignments, 115
  disruption of class, 14-15, 51-52,
    118-121
  distractibility, 121-123
  encopresis, 124
  enuresis, 125
  fears, 126
  hostile physical aggression;
    destructiveness, 140-148
  hyperactivity, 127-129
  hypoactivity, 129-130
  impulsiveness (cognitive), 132-133
  impulsivity, 130-132
  inattentiveness, 134
  inflexibility, 134-135
  instability, 135-136
  interpersonal behavior deficits,
    152-153
  lying, 136-137
  negativism toward self, 137
  overcompetitiveness, 138-139
  overview, 2-3, 86-89
  perseveration, 140
  psychosomatic complaints, 150-151
  self-concept, 149-150
  sexual deviations; interpersonal
    behavior deficits, 152-153
  shyness, nonassertiveness, 153-155
  social immaturity, 155-156
  social passivity, extreme, 139
  social withdrawal, 158-159
  tattling, 137

truancy, 156
verbal aggression, 157
Body cues (chart), 41

C

Chronic disobedience, 113-118
Class climate, 47-55
  assessment (chart), 362
  attention to feelings, 52-53
  closeness control, 54
  dealing with the present, 54-55
  hurdle help, 54
  knowledge of individual students,
    49-50
  maintaining communication, 52
  response to feelings, 54
  teacher interest, 154
Classroom control issues, 40-42,
  45-46
Classroom "jails", 6-7
Classroom management. See also
  Discipline; Social reinforcement
  body cues and their meanings
    (chart), 41
  class climate, 47-55
  control of school factors, 73-77
  environmental management, 79-82
  lectures as causal factor, 77-79
  managing student behavior, 55-59
  perspective on teaching, 30-31
  power and authority issues, 42-47
  trust and respect issues, 42-47
  when to manage, 55-59
Classrooms
  environmental management, 79-82
    physical arrangement (chart), 80,
      81
    informal classrooms, 81-82
    traditional classrooms, 79-80
Cognitive self-control. See
  Self-control
Corporal punishment
  alternatives to, 14-15
  behavioral disordered youth, 13-15

control and learning, 15-20
due process in public schools, 11-12
  Goss case, 11-12
  in-school suspension, 19-20
    timeout, 19-20
  litigational issues, 7-14
  protective rights, 9-14
    Ingraham case, 7, 9-10, 12, 13
  reasonable punishment, 12-14
  Zirkel Quick-Quiz Update on the
    Law Concerning Student
    Conduct, 23-24
Crime among children, 2
Court cases regarding discipline, 6-13
Curriculum development, social goals
  in, 207-209
Curriculum resource materials,
  211-215, 331-361

D

Decision making. See Personal
  development
Deep Springs College Program, 18-19
Detention. See Suspension
Deinstitutionalization. See Suspension
Discipline. See also Classroom
  management; Suspension
  Atlanta program, the, 169-172
    school climate survey (chart),
      171-172
  contingency management, 188-192
    D/D slip (chart), 190
    student behavior checklist
      (chart), 189
  court cases, 6-13
  current disciplinary problems,
    review of, 5-7
  Deep Springs College program,
    18-19
  Erie's New Direction Center,
    185-186
  LEAST approach to discipline, the,
    164-165
  overview, 1-3

positive discipline, 65-68
Positive Peer Culture, Group
  Guided Interaction program,
  186-188
Saturday school, the, 165-169
  attendance regulations, 167
  feedback and cost evaluation,
    167
  final student evaluation (chart),
    169
  parent evaluation (chart), 168
  physical facilities, 166
  staffing, 167
  suspension option form (chart),
    166
  teacher evaluation (chart), 170
  weekly student evaluation
    (chart), 168
steps to good discipline, 33-34
traditional disciplinary practices, 4
traditional principles of
  punishment, 4
Utah Statewide Program, 181-185
Vineland North program to
  reduce vandalism, 172-174
  analysis of the in-school
    suspension (detention) system
    (chart), 175
  detention proposal (chart), 173
Disruptive behavior, 14-15, 51-52,
  118-121
Distractibility, 121-123
Drugs. *See* Substance abuse
Due process in public schools, 11-12

E

Emotionality and learning disabilities.
  See Learning disabilities
Encopresis, 124
Enuresis, 125
Erie's New Direction Center, 185-186
Expulsion. *See* Suspension

F

Fearful behavior, 126
Forms, supplemental, 362-371

G

Group counseling process, 222-227
  benefits from, 223
  goals, 226
  know the students, 225
  leader's role, 223-225
  managing the group, 225
  purposes, 223
  types of groups in counseling
    (chart), 224

H

Hostile physical aggression;
  destructiveness, 140-148
Human relations skills. *See* Social
  development
Hyperactivity, 127-129
Hypoactivity, 129-130

I

Impulsiveness (cognitive), 132-133
Impulsivity, 130-132
Inattentiveness, 134
Inflexible behavior, 134-135
Instability, 135-136
Interpersonal behavior deficits;
  sexual deviations, 152-153
Instructional materials, 211-215,
  331-361
Isolation. *See* Suspension

J

"Jails." *See* Classroom "jails"

L

Learning disabilities. *See also* Social
development
achievement motivation in practice,
253
behavioral characteristics, 250-251,
254-256
inappropriate response to social
cues, 251-252
learned helplessness, 253-254
locus of control, 252
relationships with significant
others, 251
LEAST approach to discipline.
164-165
Lying, 136-137

M

Managing student behavior, 55-59
alteration of instructional methods,
58
checklist (chart), 363-366
emphasizing natural consequences,
56
evaluation of student behavior
(chart), 368-369
focus on specific behavior, 50-51
intervention signals, 57
parent conferences (chart), 367
planned ignoring of behavior, 56
preventive approach, 38-40
removal of temptations, 57
routine structure, 58
rule reminders, 58-59
student conduct record (chart), 370
student program schedule record
(chart), 371
removing disrupters, 51-52
teacher interest, 54
when to manage, 55-59

N

Negativism toward self, 137

O

Off-Campus Learning Center
(OCLC), 192-196
Overcompetitiveness, 138-139

P

Perseveration, 140
Personal development. *See also*
Self-control; Social development
assertiveness training, 243-247
assertive record (chart), 248
developing strong self-
assertiveness, 245
exercise (chart), 244
personal attributes list (chart),
244
picturing a new self, 247-249
positive beliefs, 243
reversing negative self-statements,
245
charts, 246
decision-making process, 44-45,
232-235
decision-making model, 235-236
decision-making wheel (chart), 234
personal decisions and feelings,
236-238
self-concept, 231-232, 238-243
self-realization, 232-236
Positive Peer Culture, Group Guided
Interaction Program, 186-188
Power issues. *See* Teachers
Psychosomatic complaints, 150-151
Punishment. *See* Corporal
punishment

R

Resource materials, 211-215, 331-361
Respect issues. *See* Teachers

S

Saturday School, 165-169
Self-concept
   student, 149-150, 238-243
      published materials, 256-257
   teacher, 30, 32-33
Self-control. *See also* Personal
   development
   basic concepts of, 260-263
   cognitive self-control, 272-279
      cognitive self-guidance treatment,
         275-277
      psychoeducational curriculum
         approach, 272-274
      self-control curriculum areas
         and units (charts), 274
   self-administration, 261, 269-271
   self-assessment, 260, 263-265
   self-determination, 261, 266-269
   self-recording, 260-261, 265
      student behavior check (chart),
         262
Self-realization, 232-236
Sexual deviations; interpersonal
   behavior deficits, 152-153
Shyness, nonassertiveness, 153-155
Smoking. *See* Tobacco
Social Development. *See also*
   Learning disabilities; Personal
   development
   avoiding failure and learned
      helplessness, 227-228
   curriculum resource materials,
      331-361
   eliciting social discussion and
      growth, 215-222
   group counseling process, 222-227
   objectives, activities, and materials
      209-211
      supplemental materials, 211-215
   observing social development,
      201-202
      care of self (chart), 205
      clothes and grooming (chart),
         205

      general sensitivity to setting
         (chart), 203
      social skill development related
         to work (chart), 203
      socially related vocational
         development... (chart), 204
   personal-social objectives, 202-207
   social goals in curriculum
      development, 207-209
Social immaturity, 15, 155-156
Social passivity, extreme, 139
Social withdrawal, 158-159
Social Reinforcement, 59-79. *See also*
   Classroom management
   behavior modification, 63-64
   behavioral contract, 71-73
      chart, 75
   clear teacher checklist (chart),
      66-67
   contingency management, 69
   control of school factors, 73-77
   counterconditioning, 62-63
   extinction, 68-69
   ideas for reinforcing activities
      (chart), 160-161
   modeling, 61-62
   negative practice, 69-70
   pairing, 70
   parent involvement, 64
   performance contract (chart), 74
   positive discipline, 65-68
   positive reinforcement, 63
   punishment, 70
   shaping, 60-61
   student ideas, 64-65
   systematic suspension contract
      (chart), 72
   timeout and systematic exclusion,
      71
   weekly academic contract (chart),
      76
Substance Abuse
   alcohol, 305-310
      alcoholism, 308-309
      blood alcohol concentration
         (chart), 306

treatment programs, 316
why youths drink, 309-310
bibliography, 325-327
current situation, 283
definition of, 283-284
depressants, 293-297
  barbiturates, 293-294
  methaqualone (sopors or
    quaaludes), 296-297
  tranquilizers, 294-296
glossary of terms, 321-324
hallucinogens, 297-301
  LSD, 297-299
  PCP, 299-301
historical significance, 282-283
inhalants, 303-305
  aerosols, 304
  anesthetics, 304
marijuana, 301-303
marijuana/hashish use (chart), 284
narcotics, 286
  legal implications, 289
  opiates, 286-289
    codeine, 288
    demerol, 288
    heroin, 287-288
    meperidine, 288
    methadone, 288
overdose, emergency care, 329
personality of users, 285
stimulants, 289-293
  amphetamines, 290-291
  caffeine, 291-293
    how much caffeine (chart), 292
  cocaine, 289
street use of drug terms, 323-324
tobacco, 310-312
  statistics, 312
  teenage smoking behavior
    (chart), 311
  treatment programs, 317
  why youths smoke, 311-312
treatment programs, 312-317
  nonschool-based programs,
    313-314
    alcohol programs, 316

school-based programs, 314-316
    alcohol programs, 316
  teacher checklist for drug abuse
    identification (chart), 313
  tobacco abuse treatment
    programs, 317
Supplemental forms, 362-371
Suspension. See also Discipline,
  85-107
  acting-out students, 86-89
  alternative forms, 93, 177-181
    Alternative Discipline and
      Suspension Program, 177-181
    ADSP referra criteria (chart),
      179
    Off-Campus Learning Center
      (OCLC), 192-196
    Philadelphia story, the, 196-197
    Saturday school, the 165-169
      attendance regulations, 167
      feedback and cost evaluation,
        167
      final student evaluation
        (chart), 169
      parent evaluation (chart), 168
      physical facilities, 166
      staffing, 167
      suspension option form
        (chart), 166
      teacher evaluation (chart), 170
      weekly student evaluation
        (chart), 168
  deinstitutionalization and status
    offenders, 176-177
  detention, 89
    administration detention
      assignment card (chart), 95
    referral notice to parents (chart),
      94
  expulsion, 98-99
  in-school suspension, 19-20, 93-98
    in-school suspension assignment
      sheet (chart), 97
  isolation, 99-106
  legal procedures in Illinois, 90-91
  rates, 92

reasons for, 91-92
systematic suspension contract
(chart), 72
timeout, 19-20, 71, 99-106
public school settings, 105-106
sequence of steps toward formal
timeout, 101-105

T

Tattling, 137
Teachers
accountability, 34-42
authority and power issues, 42-47
clear teacher checklist (chart),
66-67
respect for, 42-47
responses to student behavior,
35-42, 49-50
self-concept, role of, 30, 32-33
self-evaluation, 35
checklist for (chart), 36

training in classroom management,
30-31
trust and respect issues, 42-47
Timeout. *See* Suspension
Tobacco. *See* Substance abuse
Truancy, 156
Trust and respect issues. *See* Teachers

U

Utah Statewide Program, 181-185

V

Vandalism
Vineland North program to reduce
vandalism, 172-174
prevention, 20-21
Verbal aggression, 157
Vineland North program to reduce
vandalism, 172-174
Violence
prevention, 20-21